£25

W4H

# GEORGE BUCHANAN
# TRAGEDIES

*FOR FRANCE AND TRICIA*

# GEORGE BUCHANAN TRAGEDIES

edited by

P. Sharratt and P. G. Walsh

1983

SCOTTISH ACADEMIC PRESS

Published by
Scottish Academic Press Ltd,
33 Montgomery Street
Edinburgh EH7 5JX

ISBN 7073 0263 3

© 1983 Scottish Academic Press Ltd

All rights reserved. No part of this publication may be reproduced, stored in a retrieval system, or transmitted, in any form, or by any means, electronic, mechanical, photocopying, recording or otherwise, without the prior permission of the Scottish Academic Press Ltd, 33 Montgomery Street, Edinburgh EH7 5JX

Typeset and printed in Northern Ireland at The Universities Press (Belfast) Ltd.

CONTENTS

| | |
|---|---|
| Foreword | v |
| Introduction | 1 |
| *Jephtha* (text and translation) | 21 |
| *The Baptist* (text and translation) | 95 |
| *Medea* (text only) | 165 |
| *Alcestis* (text only) | 209 |
| Notes to the plays | 245 |
| Bibliography | 332 |
| Conspectus Metrorum | 334 |
| Indices | 338 |

# ACKNOWLEDGEMENTS

The publication of this volume has been assisted by grants from the Marc Fitch Foundation and the Carnegie Trust for the Universities of Scotland.

This volume forms the first of a projected modern edition of selected works of George Buchanan to mark the 4th centenary of his death. A full bibliography is also to be published.

# FOREWORD

Some preliminary explanation of the nature of our collaboration and of the shape of this volume is perhaps desirable.

The Introduction is the work of P.S. The text has been set up by P.G.W., who is responsible also for the translations of the biblical plays. The annotations are the fruit of our individual and joint reflections.

Some purists will doubtless be critical of the modernisation of spelling and punctuation, for these are not as Buchanan committed them to paper. But our aim has been to meet the needs of a wider readership than the small band of sixteenth-century specialists. We hope that many students accustomed to the conventions of spelling and punctuation encountered in Classical texts will enjoy these plays, and our aim is to ease their labour, just as Ruddiman did for his eighteenth-century readers.

Our original intention was to provide a systematic apparatus of variant readings from the early editions, but we soon became convinced that this labour would bear meagre results. There is no evidence of subsequent revision of the plays after publication, such as is observable in *The Psalm Paraphrases;* once committed to print, the dramas remained unchanged. We have been content to record the variant readings of the earliest edition of each play and of Ruddiman when these differ from our text. No manuscript evidence has survived.

An English translation has been provided for the two biblical plays, but we have not thought such help desirable for the two translations of Euripides. The Greek has been translated by Buchanan quite literally, so that the general sense can be obtained by consulting available renderings of Euripides. Translation of translations seemed otiose.

The essential difference between the biblical plays and the translations has dictated also the difference in annotation. The notes on *Jephtha* and *The Baptist* deal with the treatment of themes, the relation to the sixteenth-century background, the range of sources and of literary texture, and so on. But we have

## FOREWORD

assumed that students who scrutinise the Latin versions of Euripides will be concerned primarily with their merit as translations; they will above all wish to be informed of the Greek text translated by Buchanan where it differs from the standard editions of today. For this reason the annotation of *Medea* and *Alcestis* is more technical and jejune than is that of the biblical dramas.

The timely publication of Professor I. D. McFarlane's competent and comprehensive study of Buchanan (London 1981) has enabled us to exclude all but the barest biographical information. There are good summaries and discussions of the plays both in McFarlane's book and in R. Lebègue's *La Tragédie religieuse en France* (Paris 1929), which we should like to recommend to our readers.

We wish to express our gratitude to Mrs. Jennifer Peat, whose success in typing our chaotic manuscripts seems a minor miracle.

*University of Edinburgh*     P.S.

*University of Glasgow*     P.G.W.

# INTRODUCTION

George Buchanan (1506–1582) is as much a man of the French Renaissance as he is of the Scottish Renaissance, since his formative years were spent in Paris (1520–2, and about 1525–35), since he taught in Bordeaux (1539–43), and then after five years teaching in Coimbra, he returned to Paris for eight years before finally settling in Scotland. He was a close friend and professional associate of French humanists and poets during these vital years in the development of French culture; he was shaped by France, and he in his turn helped to shape French scholarship, French poetry and above all French drama. We shall therefore consider him here with reference to French, rather than to Scottish or English literature. What will emerge, however, is his place in the literature of Europe.

In recent years the French theatre of the sixteenth century, and the elaborate body of dramatic theory which supports it, have begun to receive the attention they deserve, but which many earlier critics and historians of literature had denied them. It is no longer possible to consider French sixteenth-century drama as a precocious, but unsuccessful, attempt to write like Corneille, Racine or Molière. While it is true that even the most accomplished of the French Renaissance dramatists, men like Jodelle and Garnier, do not equal the range and depth of some of their successors, and that their plays are rarely performed today, we are able to appreciate them on their own terms. We are able to surmount the difficulties inherent in this kind of drama (the lack of suspense, for example, and sometimes even the lack of action of any sort, and above all the insistence on a rhetoric which is becoming more and more alien to us) and to delight in the richness of the poetry, the psychological perceptiveness, the presentation of the moral conflict, and the unfolding of the plot.

When we turn from vernacular drama to plays written in Latin, the universal language in which Buchanan chose to write, we find that the same difficulties are present and intensified, and that further problems arise. Even at the height of the humanist

INTRODUCTION

movement Latin was the language of an intellectual elite, and the
number of adults capable of following the performance of a play
in Latin was relatively small. The Latin play was usually a
scholastic exercise, written for, and performed by, children as
part of the programme of rhetoric, of training in public speaking,
and as a practical illustration of moral philosophy. We might
expect that no exciting literary masterpiece could emerge from
such unpromising circumstances; yet when the college was the
*Schola Aquitanica,* or collège de Guyenne in Bordeaux, and the
young theatrically-minded teachers were Marc-Antoine Muret
and George Buchanan, and among the pupils who took part was
Michel de Montaigne, then we are likely to see the art at its most
excellent. Buchanan's plays, as we shall see, go far beyond the
needs of a school-play; his own literary genius and his profound
and sensitive religious and political concern ensured that his plays
were both suitable for acting by the pupils in his charge and, after
revision, were able to stand the test of time.

There is still some uncertainty about the exact date of composition of the plays, even though we are relatively well informed
about the years the Scotsman spent teaching in Paris and
Bordeaux.[1] There is not much to be learned from the dates of
publication: *Medea* was the first of the four to be published,
appearing in Paris in 1544 at the press of Michel Vascosan;
*Jephthes* does not appear until ten years later, (Paris, G. Morel,
1554) and *Alcestis* two years after that (Paris, Vascosan, 1556);
lastly, the *Baptistes* had to wait until 1577 when Thomas Vautrollier published it in London. In spite of this protracted publication, however, over more than thirty years, the plays were all
probably completed in Bordeaux at more or less the same time,
though it is likely that Buchanan had already worked on the
*Medea,* at least, in Paris.[2] Some of the confusion about the date
of composition and the order in which the plays were written
comes from apparently conflicting statements of Buchanan himself. The first of these comes from the *Vita ab ipso scripta* when
the author comes to discuss the time he spent in Bordeaux:

> Ibi in scholis, quae tum sumptu publico erigebantur, triennium
> docuit: quo tempore scripsit quattuor tragoedias, quae postea per
> occasiones fuerunt evulgatae. Sed quae prima omnium fuerat con-
> scripta (cui nomen est *Baptista*) ultima fuit edita; ac deinde *Medea*

INTRODUCTION

Euripidis. Eas enim ut consuetudini scholae satisfaceret, quae per annos singulos singulas poscebat fabulas, conscripserat: ut earum actione iuventutem ab allegoriis, quibus tum Gallia vehementer se oblectabat, ad imitationem veterum qua posset retraheret. Id cum ei prope ultra spem successisset, reliquas *Jephthen* et *Alcestin* paulo diligentius, tanquam lucem et hominum conspectum laturas, elaboravit.[3]

Now if this were the only information available, we should conclude that all four plays were written at Bordeaux between 1540 and 1543, that *Baptistes* was the first, then *Medea,* then *Jephthes* and *Alcestis*. There is, however, another source of information which is not at first easy to reconcile with the passage from the autobiography. It comes from a letter of 1579 to Daniel Rogers:

Quatuor Tragoediae meae sunt editae, e quibus duae sunt e Graeco translatae. Medeam non in hoc scripseram, ut ederetur, sed cum Graecis literis absque magistro darem operam, ut verba singula inter scribendum diligentius expenderem: amicis importune flagitantibus edidi, cum Latinas literas Burdegalae docerem, ac fabulam singulis annis pueris agendam dare cogerer. In ea cum multa negligentius elapsa essent, post aliquot annos retractavi eam, et quaedam in ea vulnera ita sanavi, ut adhuc cicatrices alicubi appareant. Tres reliquas majore cum labore ibidem effudi.[4]

This letter states clearly that *Medea* was written when he was learning Greek, that is presumably in Paris in the late 1520s or early 1530s, and at any rate long before he taught in Bordeaux. This suggests the *Medea* was composed before *Baptistes*. It is, of course, just possible that *Baptistes,* too, was begun long before in Paris, and if this was so, then the order given in the autobiography could still be the correct one. The preface to the play says of it 'meus quamquam abortivus, tamen primus est foetus' and it would make much better sense if this meant that it was his first work and not just his first play; there is, moreover, great attractiveness in the idea that the *Baptistes* could be earlier than 1540. Yet the autobiography clearly states that they were all written in Bordeaux. There is a simple way of reconciling the apparent contradiction: Buchanan translated *Medea* at the time he was learning Greek (this was a common practice in the Parisian schools at the time and other examples have survived; it is also

3

INTRODUCTION

how Erasmus composed his *Hecuba*). When he came to Bordeaux and found he had to put on an annual play, he did not at first put on *Medea,* which was no doubt still in a very rudimentary form, but decided to write a completely new tragedy of his own on the subject of John the Baptist. In this sense (even if he had not already written a version of this play in Paris) it could be said to be the first play he had written. In the following year he revised *Medea,* and then wrote the two others. After his careful reworking of *Medea,* and his realisation that there were many faults and imperfections in it, it is not surprising that he worked more carefully on *Jephthes* and *Alcestis.*

So much for the order of composition The dating is more difficult. We know from the published version of *Medea* that the play was performed in Bordeaux in 1543. This is the only direct reference to the performance of an individual play, and it raises certain problems. Since it seems likely that Buchanan left Bordeaux in this year, when were the others performed? From his own testimony it seems that he was there only for three years not four, so at least one of the plays must have been performed after his departure. I wish to suggest the following hypothesis: in 1542 he wrote and produced *Baptistes,* and in 1543 revised and presented *Medea;* during these same years he wrote the other two, but there was no time to produce them before he left. He had given them to the public, as he says, but this does not mean they were produced in his time at the collège de Guyenne.

In his recent study on Montaigne's early years, Roger Trinquet examines the question in the light of Montaigne's own statement about his part in these performances. Montaigne's account comes in the essay on education, *De l'Institution des Enfants* (I, 26):

> Mettray-je en compte cette faculté de mon enfance: une asseurance de visage, et soupplesse de voix et de geste, à m'appliquer aux rolles que j'entreprenois? Car, avant l'aage,
> Alter ab undecimo tum me vix ceperat annus,
> j'ai soustenu les premiers personnages és tragedies latines de Bucanan, de Guerente et de Muret, qui se representerent en nostre college de Guienne avec dignité.

Trinquet argues that since Montaigne was already twelve years old in 1545, at a time when Buchanan was no longer at the college, then he must have returned there in 1545 and gone back to teaching temporarily.[5] But Montaigne is showing off with the

## INTRODUCTION

quotation from Virgil, *Eclogues* 8.39; he says 'avant l'aage' when he became twelve he had played the leading roles, that is *before* 1545. In the absence of conclusive evidence we should be wary of making the few facts bear more weight than they warrant. We do not know whether all the plays were performed, and if they were, whether this was during Buchanan's stay in Bordeaux, nor do we know if each play was produced only once. It is not certain that the plays were put on in the order in which they were written, and we cannot tell from Montaigne's statement whether he acted in more than one play by Buchanan.

It is also interesting to surmise why Buchanan published the plays when he did. The *Medea* was published at the insistence of his friends, in a volume which contained two other translations of Euripides by Erasmus. Buchanan had already written several other works such as the *Fratres fraterrimi* (1535) and the *Franciscanus* (1538) but they were not published until 1566. *Medea* was in no way controversial and was unlikely to meet with disapproval. The prefatory letter to Prince John of Luxembourg mentions the difficulty of the task, and implicitly therefore the glory which would accrue to the translator. It may be assumed that at the time of going to press Buchanan's translation of *Alcestis* had not yet been written, or at least not completed, because it would otherwise almost certainly have been included in the volume. The delay in publishing *Alcestis* and *Jephthes* may be explained by the circumstances of Buchanan's life, his trial and imprisonment, his travels and other activities. They were eventually published at a time when there was a greatly increased interest in the theatre especially among his Parisian friends, and when Euripides was attracting the attention of scholars and teachers. *Baptistes* was a more controversial play, and Buchanan was not satisfied with the original hastily written version. It was finally published (and in England since he no longer had the same contact with France) as a warning to the young James the Sixth, and as a more general contribution to the contemporary discussion about kingship and tyranny.

If we wish to understand the place which Buchanan occupies in the history of drama, both in Latin and French, it is as well to start, as he himself did, with the translations of Euripides from Greek into Latin. Buchanan's translations are important because they are, for the most part, competent and accurate versions of

INTRODUCTION

the Greek dramatist, and because they are not without poetic merit in their own right. They are also important for the training they provided for the playwright in the style and techniques of Greek tragedy. Here we see in practice what the men of the Renaissance saw as the first step on the road to original composition: translation of the ancients, either from Greek into the more familiar Latin, or from Latin into the vernacular, which must ultimately give way to imitation, either in very rare cases in Greek, more usually in Latin, or increasingly frequently in the vernacular. All of this must take place before there could be original creative composition, according to the usual Renaissance theories. Indeed, the critical concept of originality in the post-Romantic sense was not known at the time.[6]

Buchanan's translations helped to make Euripides more familiar to his contemporaries. The *editio princeps* of the Greek is the Aldine edition of 1503; Buchanan could also have made use of the Hervagian Basel edition of 1537, republished in 1544 and 1551.[7] It is possible that he used this more recent edition, but as it is identical with the Aldine, it has no authority in its own right; in any case, if the *Medea* was blocked out earlier, it was certainly done from the Aldine. In our annotations we have referred to that edition, since it is more readily available now as it was in the Renaissance.

Euripides had already attracted the notice of translators. There are at least two unpublished verse translations into Latin preserved in the Bibliothèque nationale in Paris: the first of these (Ms latin 7884) dates from after 1507; it was written in Bologna by François Tissard and contains the *Medea*, the *Hippolytus* and the *Alcestis*. There is no reason to suppose that Buchanan had access to this beautiful calligraphic copy with illuminated title-pages dedicated to François de Valois. The other manuscript (Ms. Grec 2816) contains the text and translation of the *Medea* up to 1.763; the manuscript is unfinished, not defective. There is no mention of the translator or of the date, but it is most probably Parisian and seems to have been written around 1530. Once more there is nothing to associate this text with Buchanan, but it does provide another example of the early interest in Euripides and translation of him into Latin.

The most celebrated of the translators of Euripides before Buchanan was Erasmus, whose *Hecuba* and *Iphigenia at Aulis* first appeared in 1506 (Paris, J. Bade) and were often republished

(18 editions by 1540).[8] Buchanan certainly knew these versions. Mention should also be made of an edition of Erasmus's translation of the *Hecuba,* with the commentaries of Archibald Hay, a compatriot of Buchanan's, which was published in Paris in 1543 by Guillaume Bossozel. (There is a copy in the Bibliothèque Mazarine, Paris.) It is known also that Euripides was used as a class-room text in France, and the method seems to have been to ask each student to prepare a literal translation of the text partly at the teacher's dictation. There are extant at least two copies of Vascosan's Greek text of the *Hecuba* of 1552, to which has been added in manuscript a complete Latin translation: one of these is in the Bibliothèque nationale (Rés. Yb 825) and the other in the Pius XII Memorial Library of St. Louis University. The latter has been described at some length by Fr. Walter J. Ong.[9] The author is Nicolas de Nancel, pupil, secretary and biographer of Peter Ramus, both of whom were known to Buchanan. Apart from this class-room interest in turning Euripides into Latin, there were several vernacular versions. Just as the first printed editions of Euripides were Italian, so the earliest translations into the vernacular were into Italian. These need not concern us here.[10] Among the French versions we may note: *Troades* (Amyot? 1542? not published), *Hecuba* (Bochetel, 1544), *Iphigenia in Tauris* (Amyot? 1545–7? not published), *Iphigenia in Aulide* (Sebillet, 1549). There were one or two more translations in the following years, but it is significant that from about 1570 onwards, for one hundred and fifty years, no more French translations of the Greek tragedians were published. Seneca had ousted Euripides and his compatriots.[11]

In order to give Buchanan his correct place in the history of drama we must see him in relation to plays written in both Latin and French, and also in relation to the gradual emergence of Renaissance drama out of medieval Mystery and Miracle plays. These latter gradually disappeared as the sixteenth century progressed, partly because they did not correspond to the new approach to learning and religion, and partly because of their suppression by the Parlement of Paris in 1548 and by that of Bordeaux in 1556. But their popularity in the earlier part of the century points to a lively and continuing interest in the theatre, as well as a liking for plays which had a sacred subject. Another sort of play, the allegorical morality play, continued to be successful, both on a popular and an intellectual level; it is this which is the forerunner of the satirical play attacking the established church. Raymond Lebègue has shown that there are some elements here which come indirectly from classical Latin tragedy: 'Pièce peu étendue, action unique et limitée, sujet historique (ou légendaire), personnages peu nombreux et d'un rang élevé, événements graves ou même sanglants, ton généralement sérieux et même pathétique, enseignement moral. En outre, certaines moralités allégoriques comportent un événement funeste et sanglant, placé au dénouement ou un peu avant'.[12] I have quoted this comment at length in order to show that the progression from medieval to Renaissance drama is a gradual one. As Gustave Lanson showed in 1904, theoretical writing in France on the subject of tragedy is ultra-conservative until at least the middle of the sixteenth century, being based on Horace, Donatus and Diomedes: this can be observed in the notes to the many editions of Terence which appeared during these years; and even as late as 1567, six years after the publication of Scaliger's *Poetices Libri Septem* which for the first time in France spelled out the Aristotelian theory of tragedy, Henri Estienne thought it worth republishing the well-worn *De Tragoedia et Comedia* of Donatus in his edition of Erasmus's and Buchanan's translations of Euripides, presumably as a sort of critical justification of the plays. But in doing so Estienne appears to be taking no notice of the new departures in the writing of plays, both in French and Latin, in the very same humanist milieu he inhabited.

The first plays to appear in Latin at the beginning of the sixteenth century were medieval rather than humanist in conception. Two of these have survived, a *Comedia sancti Nicolai* (c. 1510) and a *Dialogus Passionis Jesu Christi* (published 1541); they are medieval, yet, as Lebègue states, we can detect in them the first glimmerings of the new humanist outlook. Much more important are the plays of the Italian Quintianus Stoa, whose *Theoandrothanatos*, published in 1508 and 1515, and *Theocrisis* (1515) contain a mixture of medieval and Renaissance elements; here we see a pronounced Senecan influence and an attempt to write Christian drama in an archaic Latin style. Among the authors of college plays in France one name stands out, that of Nicolas Barthélemy of Loches (b. 1478) who in 1526 was at the Collège de Marmontiers and in 1532 at the Collège du Cardinal Lemoine; his *Christus Xylonicus* appeared in 1529 and in 1531.

INTRODUCTION

He wrote a Passion Play, entitled also 'Tragedia', and Lebègue points out that the author has no idea of the nature of classical tragedy, being more familiar with Plautus and Terence (as so many people were at the time, and for a long time to come) than with the Greeks. It does not seem that these early Latin plays directly influenced later humanist writers like Buchanan, but they do indicate the interest in Latin drama in the preceding generation. Italian drama (both in Latin and in Italian) developed rather earlier than French drama, and the first plays were known to Frenchmen, both to those, like Baïf, Marot and Rabelais, who went to Italy and saw plays acted in Italian, and to those who read the plays either in Italian or Latin which were available in France. There is little evidence, however, of direct influence of Italian drama on French. Mention should also be made of *Acolastus* of Gnaphaeus (Guill. de Volder), and *Joseph* of Cornelius Crocus, first published in Antwerp in 1536, which had at least ten French editions between 1537 and 1546.

The writing of plays in Latin was very much in fashion at the time Buchanan was studying and starting his teaching career in Paris. In this sense he was not an innovator; his principal originality lies in the fact that he turned away from Plautus and Terence as models, not just to Seneca, but more importantly to Euripides. His subjects are still religious ones; his colleague, Marc-Antoine Muret, gave evidence of a different kind of originality when he wrote his *Julius Caesar,* since he chose a classical historical subject rather than one from the Bible or from classical mythology. Muret's play seems to have been written about 1544 and was published, with some commendatory verses by Buchanan, in early 1553.

Having seen, however briefly, how Buchanan fits into the history of writing tragedies in Latin, we must now consider his place in the overall history of the French theatre, by looking at the earliest tragedies to be written in French. It might seem that the honour of writing the first French tragedy must go to Théodore de Bèze for his *Abraham Sacrifiant* of 1550, the subject of which is clearly very close to that of *Jephthes*. It is not strictly a tragedy, however, since it has a happy ending, and Bèze himself says in his prologue that it has something of both tragedy and comedy. Etienne Jodelle, therefore, is usually considered to have written the first tragedy in French, since his *Cleopatre captive* was performed in February 1553 though not published until 1574.

INTRODUCTION

(It may be noted in passing that his comedy *Eugène* was performed a few months earlier in September, 1552.) The following years saw the composition of other plays by Jodelle, and the establishment of humanist classical drama as a recognised and important literary genre. Among the first plays were Jacques Grévin's *Jules César* of 1561 and La Péruse's Senecan *Médée*. With Robert Garnier, author of seven important plays, from *Porcie* (written 1564–5, published 1568) to *Les Juifves* (1583), and Jean de La Taille, whose four tragedies were written before 1562 and published ten years later, French classical tragedy, often exploiting biblical subjects, became firmly established. Buchanan is evidently a key figure in this development, and there is a real sense in which we can say that he was the first person to write classical tragedies in France. He did not write in French, and so Jodelle has received greater acclaim; it would of course have been almost unthinkable that he should write his plays in French, not just because he was a foreigner, and at a time when the French language was in a state of turmoil, but because he belonged to the international academic milieu which thought and felt spontaneously in Latin. His writing in Latin was not so much a manifesto as the most natural and direct way of communicating which he knew. Yet because his plays were known, either in the memories of his pupils, or in manuscript, or in the printed texts, or in one of the many translations which were made of the *Jephthes* and the *Baptistes,* his indirect influence on French literature has been very great indeed.[13]

Buchanan's two original plays were clearly directed against hypocrisy and idolatry in religious people, and also against tyranny. But the question has often been raised, whether *Baptistes* was also a *pièce à clé*.[14] Hume Brown thought that John the Baptist was to be identified with Berquin, who was burnt at the stake in 1529; he also found counterparts for the other main characters; for example Herod was François Ier.[15] There is some sense in this, since François did waver in his sympathies to the reformers, and since, after the Affaire des Placards of 1534, he was for a time less favourable to them. It is possible that when Buchanan wrote the play he had Berquin in mind, and this might even be an indication that the play was written before Buchanan's time in Bordeaux; but the identification is not really satisfactory. It is true that Buchanan's original audience would readily have associated King Herod with François for the simple reason that he was the only king they knew and had been reigning for a quarter of a century, but they would have been most unlikely to see François as a tyrant. Moreover, Hume Brown's identification of the other characters in the play (Herodias with the King's mother, Malchus with the Archbishop of Bordeaux) is too precise and abstruse to be convincing. Finally, the Berquin affair can have meant very little to the young pupil of 1540 or 1543, and nothing to the general public of 1577. There have been other identifications, for example that proposed by La Ville de Mirmont, which made John into Patrick Hamilton and Herod into James the Fifth, to which one may answer that this was too remote from Buchanan's audience;[16] that of D. MacMillan which equated John with Luther, and Herod with either François or James,[17] to which one may reply that there is no direct historical incident to which the play could refer, and that Buchanan's John bears little resemblance to Luther, except that they are both reformers of a religion which had become corrupt.

There is one more identification which must be discussed in some detail, that of John with Thomas More and Herod with Henry the Eighth. There is clear justification for this since Buchanan makes it himself in his First Defence before the Inquisition, though the text must be approached with caution because of the privileged and prejudiced circumstances of his trial. Buchanan has been talking of his religious differences with the Church of England, and concludes: 'Itaque cum primum potui ut illinc evasi, meam sententiam de Anglis explicavi in ea tragoedia quae est de Io. Baptista, in qua quantum materiae similitudo patiebatur, mortem et accusationem Thomae Mori repraesentavi, et speciem tyrannidis illius temporis ob oculos posui'.[18] It must be remembered that Buchanan is writing to save his skin, and that he is intentionally vague in the phrase 'quantum materiae similitudo patiebatur'; Raymond Lebègue felt that there was nevertheless some truth in the statement, since Buchanan must necessarily have disapproved of Henry's tyrannical treatment of More, but he was unable to find in the play any traits positively linking John with More or Herod with Henry, and stressed that in any case the play was full of anticatholic and antipapal allusions. Since the publication in 1907 of the documents from the Lisbon Inquisition, it has generally been accepted, though with some reservations, that the career of

INTRODUCTION

Thomas More has influenced *Baptistes*.

The clearest and fullest statement of the question is to be found in Aitken; I am not convinced, however, that More's death would have had as much impact in Bordeaux in the early 1540s as Aitken suggested. It was far removed in time and place from the concerns of Buchanan's students, and the event was too recent for it to have become a myth or symbol. Nor is John sufficiently like More for the parallel to be clear. Buchanan may have told his charges about Henry and More, perhaps as a cautionary tale about what might happen in France, but there is nothing to suggest that he did so, and in any case this would not explain how the general public, parents, friends and outsiders would have been able to understand. D.F.S. Thompson has commented 'With such intentions the play could of course be produced only on the Continent, and preferably at Bordeaux rather than at Paris',[19] but this seems to be almost conclusive proof that these were not the intentions. It would have been easy to make the identification clear.

The greatest obstacle to overcome is to decide why Buchanan chose this precise subject for this particular audience. There is danger of indulging in a circular argument, of using the play to establish what Buchanan's religious position was at the time (assuming for the moment that we know at what time it was written) and of using what we know about his religious attitudes, then and later, to determine what he meant in the play. Professor McFarlane discusses this whole question lucidly and adds some further illuminating remarks. He suggests that Buchanan might have been thinking of John Fisher, who to Henry's obvious annoyance had told the king in 1529 that his own death would be like that of the Baptist's, in that it was in the cause of marriage. McFarlane also points to another possible allusion, an oblique reference (only in the later revised version, of course,) to Mary Queen of Scots, after the murder of her husband and her remarriage. This allusion, depending on a transference of role from King to Queen, may well be intended. He continues 'the combination of sexual transgression and feminine influence on policy can be seen to refer obliquely to Mary Queen of Scots as well. Herod is blamed for heading the counsel of false courtiers and the Queen, instead of paying attention to the spokesman of the people, John the Baptist, who has the further merit of respecting the ancient laws and customs of his country'.[20] Perhaps this was

INTRODUCTION

in Buchanan's mind, but it must be emphasised that this cannot have been the intention of the original version, and it is rather too indirect to have much real dramatic force.

In spite of the partial validity of some of the identifications proposed, the final resolution of the problem must be sought elsewhere. Buchanan was not writing a political tract, nor a religious manifesto, but a work of the imagination. Any identification can be only partial, and the play is far greater and of more lasting significance than any set of exact identifications would allow. Lebègue refers also to a seventeenth-century identification of John with William Prynne and of Herod with Charles the First. The curious thing is that the parallel is by no means ridiculous, and underlines the value of the play. Might we not go further and suggest that the play is about religious or political persecution in any century? If the *Baptistes* is about James the Fifth, about François and about Henry, it is about tyranny and religious oppression, and the precise facts about the martyred religious heroes are secondary. We must credit Buchanan with greater subtlety and a finer sensibility than a rigorous equation of the characters with historical people would allow. His was a mind in turmoil, and his play is a dramatisation of the problems of conscience caused by the conflict of the new religion with the old. The *Baptistes* can be seen as an allegory with universal application. Buchanan uses the moving story of the Baptist, and not that of More or anyone else, to comment on the indulgence in physical violence by tyrants for personal or political ends, on martyrdom for fidelity to religious principles and on the opposition between pure and corrupt religion. Since he thought it was worth publishing as late as 1577 we can be sure he thought it had a wide application, that it was not too far out of sympathy with his own religious and political views at that date, and that it was a dramatic counterpart to his forthcoming treatise *De iure regni apud Scotos*.

When we turn to *Jephthes* we see that although it was written more or less at the same time as *Baptistes* it is more mature and more humanist in conception. The subject of the play seems to have been chosen because, like John the Baptist, Jephtha himself is the centre of a moving story. Even though there is not much possibility of constructing dramatic action round this story, it does contain a fundamental conflict which is capable of develop-

INTRODUCTION

ment. This play may be considered not so much as a *pièce à clé* but rather as a *pièce à thèse*, since the question of vows was topical; both Catholic and Protestant writers were concerned with establishing their validity and lawfulness.

Once more we have Buchanan's own words (though of doubtful sincerity) in the First Defence:

> De votis scripto in tragoedia de voto Jephthe meam sententiam ostendi cuius disputationis haec summa est: vota quae licite fiunt omnia servanda, ac multi etiam sciunt Conimbricae me orationem Barpt. Latomi super hac re contra Bucerum et legere libenter solitum, et semper laudare.[21]

This statement has sometimes been taken to mean much more than it actually says, and it is made to look as though Buchanan himself claims that he has been influenced by the controversy between Latomus and Bucer in the writing of his play. The main printed items in this controversy have been well documented, and three of these were letters in which the Catholic theologian and the reformer debated this problem along with many others. In one of them, dated July 12th 1543 (*Responsio Bartholomaei Latomi ad epistolam quandam Martini Bucceri de dispensatione Eucharistiae, et inuocatione diuorum, item de coelibatu sacerdotum: in qua interim Ecclesiae et sanctorum patrum auctoritas acerrime defenditur,* Paris, C. Wechel, 1544) Latomus gives the strict traditional view, based on the Law of the Old Testament, that vows must be fulfilled; but in this book there is very little else on the subject of vows. In his reply, dated 20th March 1544, Bucer argues that it all depends whether or not the vow is an acceptable one, cf. *Responsio altera et solida Martini Buceri* in *Scripta duo adversaria D. Bartholomaei Latomi LL. Doctoris et Martini Buceri* (Strasbourg, Wendel Rihel). Once more there is very little directly on the subject of vows, though there is something in the section *De coelibatu Sacerdotum* (p. 93 sqq.) and in *Praeceptum Dei de Voto* (p. 85). Finally, there is a short comment in the section *De coelibatu sacerdotum* in Latomus's reply: *Bartholomaei Latomi adversus Martinum Buccerum, de controversiis quibusdam ad religionem pertinentibus, altera plenaque Defensio,* published by Melchior Novesian in 1545; part of this is quoted in Aitken, p. 66, showing that Latomus claims that although God will not approve of the accomplishment of a rash vow, yet still it must be fulfilled. The controversy continues, but, as Lebègue has already noted, there is not much else on the subject of vows.

All in all the Bucer-Latomus controversy is disappointing as a source of Buchanan's interest in the topic. Lebègue suggested that Buchanan may have revised his play in 1544 or 1545 after reading the exchange of letters.[22] Roger Trinquet, as we have seen, proposes that Buchanan may have returned to teach in Bordeaux in 1545 and written the play then, in which case there would be no need for a revision: 'Les qualités de la pièce et l'excellence de sa composition ne se prêtent guère à l'idée d'un replâtrage ultérieur. Nous croyons donc plutôt que cette pièce—esquissée peut-être antérieurement—a été conçue et jouée un peu plus tard qu'on ne l'estime généralement'.[23] It seems to me that this ingenious explanation is not necessary. Buchanan does not claim to have read Latomus at Bordeaux but at Coimbra, and he is quite vague about what he thinks of the finer points of the debate. Moreover, as Lebègue noted, the view Buchanan proposed in 1550 is not the same as Latomus's view, since Latomus did not restrict himself to lawful vows: 'Ce passage qui me paraît volontairement ambigu, est un exemple de l'attitude à demi sincère que Buchanan eut devant ses juges'.[24]

I wish to suggest that Buchanan was not in fact influenced by this controversy when he wrote the play, since most of the relevant material was published too late. It is true, however, that his play was topical. This is brought out well by a recently discovered work in French, *Demonstrance des abuz de l'eglise, des constitutions humaines, de l'Eglise de Christ et de l'Antechrist, des voeux des Moines, et si en les rompant on offense Dieu*, [Geneva, J. Girard] 1545. This pamphlet against monastic vows purports to have been written 'De Paris, en Sorbonne, ces Calendes Grecques'.[25] Though it is useful to keep in mind such contributions to the intellectual climate of the day, I do not wish to suggest that Buchanan is here entering into theological controversy. In any case the exchange between Latomus and Bucer was not primarily about vows, as can be seen from the title of the first work of Latomus to which I refer.

Furthermore, although vows and especially monastic vows and priestly vows of celibacy, were topical in the early and mid 1540s, this was part of a continuing debate which had seen a revival of interest in the early part of the century, and again after the infiltration of Lutheran ideas into France in the 'twenties, but which had its roots in scriptural and canonical commentaries of the Middle Ages. Lebègue has listed some of the medieval writings on the topic. He takes Hugh of St. Victor as a typical medieval voice: human sacrifices were forbidden by the Law and there is no doubt about whether God approved of Jephtha's vow, but what is most important is the symbolic interpretation, that Jephtha symbolises Christ and his daughter symbolises the Church.[26] Another medieval view, and much more central, is that of Aquinas:

> Other actions are good considered in themselves, and for this reason can be the matter of a vow, yet they may have an evil result, *in which case the vow may not be observed*. This happened in the case of Jephte, who, as related in *Judges,* made a vow to the Lord, saying: 'If you deliver the Ammonites into my power, whoever comes out of the door to meet me when I return in triumph shall belong to the Lord. I shall offer him up as a holocaust'. This vow could have an evil result, were he to meet some animal that should not be sacrificed, such as an ass or a human being, as indeed happened. Hence Jerome says, 'In vowing, he was foolish because he did not use discretion, and in keeping the vow he was impious'. Yet the Scripture says that the Spirit of the Lord came upon him, because his faith and devotion which moved him to make the vow were from the Holy Spirit. For this reason, because of the victory he won and because he *probably repented of his evil deed* (which however prefigured something good) he is placed in the catalogue of the saints.' (cf. *Hebrews* II. 32).[27]

It is possible that Buchanan knew Aquinas, and this medieval tradition which castigated Jephtha as mistaken while admiring the strength of his piety. The tragic flaw in Jephtha's character which makes the play such a compelling one is already present in the discussion of Aquinas, and Buchanan saw its potentialities for intellectual drama rather than for reform-propaganda. It seems to me that Buchanan stands aside from the contemporary discussion of vows and also from contemporary views about the true importance of the story of Jephtha. It should be remembered that much if not most Catholic scriptural exegesis in the French milieux Buchanan frequented was of an allegorical nature. A good example among many is a book by Joannes Arboreus, published in Paris in 1540 by Simon de Colines, entitled *Primus tomus Theosophiae,* the preface of which bears the inscription 'ex sacro Sorbonicae domus musaeo', thus showing its orthodoxy. The

INTRODUCTION

sixth chapter, 'Jephte deliquit suam offerendo filiam in holocaustam, nec eius votum probatur', comments on his rashness and includes a casuistic discussion about whether God inspired the vow or not; following St. Ambrose it talks of the 'miserabilis necessitas' of fulfilling the vow. The commentary goes on to list various 'anagogical' interpretations, such as that Jephtha stands for Christ and his daughter for the Church, as we have already seen in Hugh of St. Victor. Other interpretations are those of Godfrey Tilmann who, in his *Allegoriae simul et Tropologiae in locos utriusque Testamenti* (1551) sees both Jephtha's daughter and John the Baptist as monastic figures, and of Claude d'Espence whose *Collectaneorum de continentia libri sex* (1566) which mentions John the Baptist in the context of Jephtha and sees Jephtha's daughter as a sort of nun. There is another way in which the story of Jephtha, like that of Abraham and Isaac, was used by contemporary writers, to illustrate the power parents rightly have over their children: this may be observed in a book by Charles de Bovelles, *De voto, libero arbitrio, ac de differentia orationis* (Paris, 1529, lxi v°), and also in Claude d'Espence's *De continentia*. This topic was of general interest at the time, as can be seen from Rabelais's discussion of it in the *Tiers Livre* (1546). It will readily be seen how far Buchanan is from either the allegorical or the legalistic approach to the story of Jephtha, but it is worth seeing how it was used by his contemporaries.

In conclusion on the subject of vows it is necessary to note that it has sometimes been argued that since Buchanan attacks the clergy and the monks, and in particular various Catholic practices, such as the use of statues, and since, on occasion, such as in the First Defence, he says that priests should be allowed to marry or they should observe their vows, then he must be against vows. Yet the matter is not so simple. *Jephthes* cannot simply be an attack on vows: the presentation of a rash and stupid vow scarcely implies that all vows are absurd and indeed rather implies the opposite; and if all vows are absurd, then *Jephthes* will be considerably less gripping and the conflict will disappear altogether.[28]

*Jephthes* raises also the question of sacrifice. This subject too was topical because of discussions about the Eucharist, and Buchanan seems to have been particularly interested in it. He tells us himself in the First Defence that he had taken part in discussions on the sacrifice of the mass, but without saying what exactly his opinion was, though he does say he had had doubts about the Eucharist (Aitken p. 20). Jephtha's sacrifice of his daughter can be seen as a parallel of God's sacrifice of his Son and can therefore be indirectly linked with the sacrifice of the mass. It is worth noting that there had been a controversy on the sacrifice of the mass in 1534, the year of the Affaire des Placards which was also very much concerned with this topic, between Bucer and Ceneau, the Bishop of Avranches, of which the main items were as follows: (i) *Axioma catholicum seu institutio christiana qua asseritur et probatur praesentia corporis Christi in Eucharistia adversus Bucerum, Berengarianae Haeresis instauratorem;* (ii) *Defensio adversus axioma catholicum, id est criminationem R.P. Roberti Episcopi Abrincensis;* and (iii) *Appendix ad Coenam Dominicam* by Ceneau. All the reformers had much to say about the sacrifice of the mass. There is no need to go further into the matter here; I mention it merely to show something of its contemporary relevance. There can be no doubt that Buchanan's contemporaries would associate the discussion of sacrifice in the *Jephthes* with the theological debate.

Buchanan draws on another source which treats of a sacrifice, the *Iphigenia* of Euripides, which had been translated by Erasmus, and which Buchanan would surely have translated himself if Erasmus had not forestalled him. The human sacrifice in this play does not depend on a vow, but fulfilled a condition which was necessary in order that Artemis should be appeased, and the Greeks allowed to leave Aulis. In this case the victim of the sacrifice had already been designated by Calchas, so nothing is left to chance as in Buchanan's play. Buchanan took very seriously the myth which Euripides presents in this play; he made the parallel with Jephtha's daughter, and thought it worth reviving it and offering, as it were, the combined version to his audience in the early 'forties and his reading public in the mid 'fifties. *Jephthes* is a good example of the way a Renaissance writer was able to combine the threads of classical and Christian culture. The combination of the biblical narrative with one borrowed from Euripides shows how the author is able to fuse his two principal literary and cultural sources.

Both *Jephthes* and *Baptistes* are dramatic representations of conflict and both describe extreme, clearly-defined cases of conscience. Each of these plays has been seen on occasion as a vehicle for religious propaganda, but it seems unlikely that this was how

Buchanan intended them to be read. I have argued elsewhere,[29] from an analysis of Buchanan's use of Euripides, Lucretius and Seneca in *Jephthes* that there is a strong element of irony in this play. The same degree of irony does not appear in *Baptistes*, yet there is a certain detachment in that play too. In neither play is Buchanan partisan or polemical; he is committed, certainly, but to toleration and the suppression of superstition, aggression and tyranny.

## Notes to the Introduction

1. For biographical information see McFarlane, I.D., *Buchanan*, London, Duckworth, 1981.
2. For a discussion of the dating of the plays see McFarlane, op. cit., pp. 93–4, 118–120, 193–4, and 379.
3. See Aitken, James M., *The Trial of George Buchanan before the Lisbon Inquisition*, London, 1939, pp. xviii–xx.
4. Letter dated Edinburgh, 9th November, 1579, in *Opera omnia*, 1725, II 755.
5. Trinquet, Roger, *La Jeunesse de Montaigne*, Paris, Nizet, pp. 457–70; cf. McFarlane, op. cit., pp. 93–4 and 194.
6. See Gastor, Grahame, *Pléiade Poetics*, Cambridge, 1964.
7. See Delcourt, M., *Etude sur les traductions grecques et latines en France depuis la Renaissance*, Brussels, 1925.
8. Erasmus's translations of Euripides may be readily consulted in the modern edition by Jan Hendrik Waszink, North-Holland Publishing Company, Amsterdam, 1969.
9. Ong, W.J., 'A Ramist translation of Euripides', in *Manuscripta*, St. Louis, 8, 1964, 18–28.
10. See Pertusi, Agostino, 'La scoperta di Euripide nel Primo Umanesimo', in *Italia Medioevale e Umanistica*, II, (1960), 101–152 and 'Il ritorno alle fonti del teatro greco classico: Euripide nell'umanesimo e nel rinascimento', in *Byzantion*, 33, 1963, 391–426.
11. Cf. Delcourt, op. cit.
12. Lebègue, Raymond, *La Tragédie religieuse en France*, Paris, 1929, p. 106. The reader is referred to this book for an excellent full account of Buchanan's plays.
13. For an account of the translations of Buchanan's plays see McFarlane, op. cit., pp. 201–2 and 390–1; on French sixteenth-century drama, reference may be made to McFarlane, I.D., *A Literary History of France*, London, 1974, pp. 424–457.

14. See especially, Lebègue, op. cit., pp. 210–15, Aitken, op. cit., pp. 128–35 and McFarlane, *George Buchanan,* pp. 379–92.
15. Hume Brown, P., *George Buchanan, Humanist and Reformer: a Biography,* Edinburgh, 1890, pp. 121–5.
16. La Ville de Mirmont, H. de, 'Les tragédies religieuses de Buchanan', in St. Andrews *Memorial,* ed. D.A. Millar, 1906
17. MacMillan, D., *George Buchanan,* Edinburgh, 1906, p. 85.
18. See Aitken, op. cit., p. 24.
19. Thompson, D.F.S., 'George Buchanan: the Humanist in the Sixteenth-century world', in *Phoenix,* 4, 1950, p. 81.
20. McFarlane, op. cit., p. 387.
21. See Aitken, op. cit., p. 12.
22. Lebègue, op. cit., p. 233.
23. Trinquet, loc. cit.
24. Lebègue, op. cit., p. 231.
25. Recorded in Higman, Francis, *Censorship and the Sorbonne,* Geneva, Droz, 1979, p. 137.
26. Lebègue, op. cit., pp. 229–30.
27. Aquinas, *Summa Theologiae,* 2a 2ae 88.2 ad 2, Blackfriars translation by Kevin D. O'Rourke, O.P. This view may be partly shaped by Cicero, *Off.* 3.95f.; see *Baptistes* 1250n.
28. For further discussion of these questions see McFarlane, op. cit., pp. 193–7.
29. 'Euripides latinus: Buchanan's Use of his Sources', forthcoming in *Acts of the Fourth Neo-Latin Conference* (Bologna).

# IEPHTHES
## SIVE
## VOTUM
### TRAGOEDIA
AUCTORE
GEORGIO BUCHANANO SCOTO

## AD ILLUSTRISSIMUM VIRUM CAROLUM COSSAEUM, FRANCIAE MARESCALUM AC APUD TAURINOS REGIS FRANCORUM PRAEFECTUM, IN IEPHTHEN TRAGOEDIAM PRAEFATIO

Absurdam fortasse rem facere quibusdam videbor qui ad te, hominem ab ineunte aetate militaribus imbutum studiis et inter arma tubasque semper versatum, munusculum hoc litterarium mittam. sed ii fere hoc absurdum existimaturi sunt qui aut harum rerum inter se consensionem non satis animadvertunt, aut tuum ingenium parum habent perspectum. neque enim inter rei militaris et litterarum studium ea est quam plerique falso putant discordia, sed summa potius concordia et occulta quaedam naturae conspiratio. quamquam enim superioribus aliquot saeculis sive hominum inertia sive falsa quadam persuasione divisae fuerunt hae professiones, nunquam tamen perversa imperitorum opinio tantum potuit ut ipsae inter se veterem illam et naturalem, ut ita loquar, cognationem obliviscerentur. omnes enim omnium aetatum imperatores qui res praeclaras gesserunt aut ipsi doctissimi fuerunt aut viros doctrina illustres summo amore prosecuti sunt. neque profecto fieri potest ut magnus et excelsus animus, qui neglectis rebus caducis aeternitatis memoriam ante oculos habet propositam, non etiam memoriae et antiquitatis custodes litteras amet. neque alii fere sunt qui litteras oderunt et contemnunt quam qui, vita per ignaviam et flagitia turpiter acta, conscientiam posteritatis reformidant, ut non minus vere quam eleganter mihi cecinisse videatur Claudianus:
>    Gaudet enim virtus testes sibi iungere Musas;
>       carmen amat quisquis carmine digna gerit.

contra vero, qui omne suum studium in eo posuerunt ut perfectae virtutis imaginem sibi ad imitationem proponerent,
>       et quae natura negavit
>    visibus humanis, oculis ea pectoris

2 MARESCALUM *1554* MARESCALLUM *R*   7 ii *R* hi *1554*

haurirent, quanta eos laetitia affectum iri putemus si eius quam tantopere animo persequuntur vivum et spirans simulacrum (ut ita dicam) nacti fuerint? sed et praeter hanc mutuam virtutis admirationem et naturae quam dixi consensionem, accedit utilitatis etiam mutuae quaedam species. nam ut illustrium facinorum auctor non immerito eum suspicit, quem virtutis tradendae magistrum et illustrandae artificem esse videt, et velut parentem colit non eum a quo huius qua fruimur lucis brevem usuram acceperit, sed alteram illam longe diuturniorem vitam in posteritatis memoria collocatam speret; ita ille alter libenter amplectitur segetem et materiam suae gloriae sibi oblatam,
  qua se quoque possit
tollere humo, victorque virum volitare per ora.
uterque enim etsi opinione hominum imparem, pari tamen studio ex eodem fundo gloriae fructum petit. sed haec ad omnes communiter pertinent qui, ut ait Sallustius, praeclari facinoris aut artis bonae famam quaerunt. illa vero tua sunt propria, quod a primis usque adulescentiae spatiis ea fuisti in patriam caritate, in bello fortitudine, in pace temperantia et aequitate, ut omnibus qui litteras colunt tuarum virtutum exemplar edideris, quod posteritati ad imitationem proponere et possint et debeant; quod litteras, Philippi Cossaei fratris tui episcopi Constantiensis patrocinio orbatas, in diverso vitae instituto tamen fovendas ac tuendas susceperis; quod doctissimos homines semper tecum habeas, quibuscum etiam in medio saevissimi belli ardore 'Musisque Minervam temperes, et Geticum modereris Apolline Martem'; quod filium ita litteris instituendum in pueritia cures, ut hanc tam amplam laudis et gloriae hereditatem a parente acceptam non solum tueri sed etiam augere posset. me autem absentem, nec ulla alia re quam litterarum commendatione tibi cognitum, ita complexus es omnibus humanitatis et liberalitatis officiis ut si quis ingenii mei sit fructus, si qua vigiliarum velut fetura, ea merito ad te redire debeat. quod quidem adeo avide facit meus hic Iephthes, ut qui antea publicam lucem et coetus hominum reformidabat, te patrono fretus prodeat, et in spem nonnullam etiam publici favoris sese erigat. quid enim non illis sibi speret auspiciis, quibus disciplinam militarem ad antiquae severitatis exemplum videt emendatam, et vetustam belli gloriam Galliae restitu-

tam? cum bellica fortitudine legum et iustitiae cultum, cum summa omnium rerum licentia summam omnium rerum non modo tuam sed etiam tuorum omnium continentiam videt coniunctam? his ego causis impulsus, hanc meam lucubra- tiunculam sub tuo potissimum nomine in manus exire volui. tu vero (ut spero) hoc meum sive tuorum in me officiorum testimonium, sive meae erga te benevolentiae significationem—quae tua est humanitas, et in litteras amor—boni consules. vale.
   Lutetiae Parisiorum, quinto Kal. Aug. MDLIIII.

### ARGUMENTUM EX LIBRO IUDICUM SUMPTUM

Iephthes Galaddi filius patre defuncto a fratribus domo pulsus est, quod negarent aequum esse ut nothus cum legitimis filiis in hereditate paterna dividenda aequaretur. is cum ob inopiam collecta manu latrocinio viveret, ac fortitudinis magnum specimen dedisset, primum a cognatis, deinde a reliquis Hebraeis dux factus est adversus Ammonitas, qui viginti prope annorum gravissima servitute eos presserant. profecturus igitur in expeditionem, vovit se, si victor reverteretur, qui primus domo sua egrederetur eum deo sacrificaturum. prima revertenti occurrit unica filia; eam deo immolat.

ARGUMENTUM 10 eum *R* eum se *1554*
*Argumentum alterum (Carolo Utenhovio F. auctore), quod in R apparet, ignorat 1554*

# IEPHTHES

## *PERSONAE*

Angelus prologus

Storge mater

Iphis filia

Chorus indigenarum puellarum

Iephthes imperator

Symmachus amicus

Sacerdos

Nuntius

# PROLOGUS

ANGELUS

*ANG.*   Magni Tonantis huc minister aliger
caelo relicto mittor Isaci ad lares
solumque promissum Isaci nepotibus,
solum regendis destinatum gentibus
si pacta sacri intaminata foederis                 5
servasset, arma sed modo quod Ammonia
expavit arto servitutis sub iugo,
tulitque quicquid triste crudele asperum
iratus audet victor aut victus timet.
vix docta tandem calamitatibus, deum              10
agnoscere patrum coepit, et nefarios
mentita cultus numinis ludibria
inspecta nosse, nota flocci pendere;
et sero quamvis ad patrem rediit suum.
humana sed mens, nescia modum ponere              15
rebus secundis, intumet successibus.
quo plura hominibus contulit bonitas dei,
occaecat animos altior securitas,
vanoque fastu turgidos superbia
stimulat inanis. qualis in dominum furit          20
equi ferocis contumax protervitas
imperia paulum si remissa sentiat,
ac vix, lupatis domitus et calcaribus
duris cruentus, redit ad officium et suo
obtemperat ero, sic populus hic pervicax          25
cervice dura, pronus in peius, flagrum
si conquievit paululum, novos deos
adsciscit et se dedit aliis ritibus,
ignota sacra sequitur. atque adeo parens
benignus animos turgidos licentia                 30

10 vix . . . deum *1554*: hac clade fracta gens rebellis vix deum *1597,
R*   16 rebus, secundis *interpunxerunt edd. omnes*

bello fameve pestilentive aëre
frangit, rebellem comprimens ferociam.
at rursus, animi ne cadat fiducia
serie malorum continenter obruta,
35 mittit prophetas, bellicos mittit duces,
qui servitutis liberatos asperae
vinclis reducant pristinisque ritibus
servire cogant, arma nunc Ammonia
ut excitavit in rebelles ac, dei
40 iussis relictis, impiis erroribus
se mancipantes; sed modum statuens suae
irae propitius liberatorem dedit,
non e potentum quempiam numero, gravem
turba clientum liberisve turgidum,
45 sed e paternis exsulantem sedibus
Iephthen suisque fratribus spretum, satum
genetrice vili, ne superba gens suis
adsignet armis quod manu gestum est dei,
ut sciat et Ammon hactenus se viribus
50 non floruisse propriis, sed vindicem
caelestis irae. porro ne Iephthes quoque
se metiatur exitu huius proelii
et intumescat insolens rebus bonis,
damno obruetur protinus domestico,
55 cedentque fracti contumaces spiritus.
etenim arma in hostes perfidus cum sumeret,
belli secundus si daretur exitus
quodcumque primum se obviam ferret sibi
promisit aris se daturum victimam.
60 heu, quanta moles imminet tibi mali,
miserande! quantis obruere luctibus!
ut te propinqui credulum spes gaudii
fallit! propago sola, quae patriam domum
tibi nata servat, prima patri se offeret
65 ut gratuletur prosperum armorum exitum,
magnoque solvet faenore ac iugulo luet
felicitatis misera praecox gaudium.
atque ecce mater tristis egreditur domo,
quam somniorum nocte tota terruit
70 tremendus horror, nataque parenti comes,
prae se ferentes mentis aegrimoniam

maerore vultus, gestibus, silentio.

           STORGE *mater*    IPHIS *filia*
*ST.* Eheu, recenti corda palpitant metu,
mens horret, haeret vox in ipsis faucibus,
nec ora verbis pervium praebent iter. 75
nocturna sic me visa miseram territant,
et dira turbant inquietam insomnia
gravibusque curis pectus urunt anxium.
at tu, nitentis summe dominator poli,
averte in hostes luctuosum et funebre 80
omen, mihique placidus et natae meae,
quae sola spes et familiae solacium
superest, senectae columen unicum meae.
*IPH.* Quin ominare, cara mater, laetius
vanaeque causas abice aegritudinis, 85
et ista mentis turbidae ludibria
secura sperne spretaque obliviscere.
*ST.* Utinam liceret, sed metus, veluti recens
quoties recordor, concutit formidine
mentem, atque imago somnii tristissimi 90
oberrat animo; pectus horrificat timor.
iam cuncta passim blanda straverat quies
mutumque nox induxerat silentium;
vidi luporum concito cursu gregem
rictu cruento spumeo rabido, unguibus 95
saevum recurvis, praecipite ferri impetu
imbellia in pecora vidua pastoribus.
tum pavidi ovilis fida custodia canis
lupos abegit, atque ad infirmum pecus,
trepidi timoris exanime adhuc memoria, 100
denuo reversus e sinu timidam meo
agnam revulsam dente laniavit truci.
    o sol, o vaga lumina lunae,
    pictaque tacito sidera mundo,
    et tu, nox mihi conscia curae, 105
    nigris referens somnia pinnis,
    si quid natae miserae impendet,
    si quem casum fata minantur,
    caput hoc prius in Tartara miserum
    detrudite, dum spes ambiguae 110

alternantibus angunt curis
incerta suae pectora cladis.
*IPH.*   Cur misere animum crucias, mater,
luctuque tuo cumulas luctum
115   publicum, et acres renovas curas?
omine laeto reducem potius
positis questibus excipe patrem,
qui, nisi vano mens augurio
credula nimium pectora fallit,
120   spoliis aderit clarus opimis
remque et laudem et decus aeternum
genti referens patriaeque suae.
*ST.*   Non hunc tenorem Parca mihi vitae dedit.
quod tempus unquam lacrimis caruit mihi,
125   ex quo parentis primum ab alvo prodii?
primum iuventa servitutem patriae
tristesque vidit hostici agminis minas,
pecorumque raptus, sterile sine cultu solum,
caedes cruores vastitatem incendia,
130   profana sacra mixta. non unquam mihi
secura vitae fluxit ulla portio.
ut trudit undas unda, fluctus fluctui
cedit sequenti, pellitur dies die,
semper premuntur praeterita novis malis;
135   dolor dolori, luctui est luctus comes.
fratrem patremque perculit belli furor;
confecta curis mater inter funera
cognata senuit; perduelles perfidos
armis maritus urget. his maius nefas
140   tamen veretur animus. *IPH.*   Immodicus timor
facile sinistris adhibet auguriis fidem.
*ST.*   Utinam secundis audiam rumoribus
virum reversum sospitemque exercitum
salva familia. *IPH.*   Veniet haud dubie parens
145   incolumis. idem bella qui suasit deus
salvum reducet laude cumulatum nova.

CHORUS

Iordanis, vitreo gurgite qui rigas
convalles virides, pascua dividens

135   luctui *1554, R:*   luctus *1597*

fecunda Isacidum flumine languido,
et nunquam posita frigoribus coma                150
formosum Solymae palmiferae nemus,
en unquam miserae candidus adferet
curarum vacuae Lucifer hunc diem
cum cernam patriam libera liberam
quae nunc servitii vincula barbari                155
infelix patitur? nobilis Isaci
sanguis degeneris fert domini iugum,
et quos nec Phariae rex tumidus plagae
urgens falciferis terruit axibus,
nec trux purpurei saevities freti                 160
undarum refluis obruit aestibus,
nec deserta Arabum vomeris inscia,
nec portenta hominum mole Cyclopia
fregerunt, timidi mancipium sumus
Ammonis. gravius flagitium est malo               165
sub turpi domino segne iugum pati.
at tu, summe parens, qui mare turbidum
componis, placidi qui maris aequora
Cauri nubiferis flatibus excitas,
et terrae stabilis dura tremoribus                170
fundamenta quatis, mobilis et poli
sistis praecipitem cum libuit fugam,
   cladibus tandem satiate nostris
   desine irarum, propiusque fessis
   gentis afflictae facilis bonusque          175
     consule rebus.
nostra si poenas meruit severas
culpa, si quondam tibi separatam
abicis sortem, vitiis iniquus
si pater nostris minus obsequentes                180
deseris natos, et inexpiata
ante dilecti populi querelas
   despicis ira,
nec tibi Syrus neque dirus Ammon
nec Phari rector tumidus minacis                  185
expetat poenas, neque sit profano
in tuis castris gladio potestas.
ignis armatus potius trisulci
tu, pater, dextram iaculis tremendis,

190     vindicis flammae face contumaces
    obruas urbes, Chaos aut patentis
    devoret terrae miseros colonos,
    aut superfusis adoperta tellus
        hauriat undis.
195     ne ferox hostis tumeat secundis
    insolens rebus, populusque muti
    stipitis cultor, tua qui nefando
    polluit ritu sacra; ne, quod ira
    saeviit in nos tua, vertat Ammon
200     in suas laudes, carie peresi
    ture dum placat simulacra trunci,
    teque vesano neget ore gentem
    semper addictam tibi se premente
        posse tueri.
205     a miser, quantos tibi risus iste
    mox dabit fletus! breve diluendum est
    gaudium longis lacrimis. citato
    advolat cursu levis hora; tempus
    (vana ni vatem species inani
210     spe fovet), tempus properat, vicissim
    cum gravis victor mala servitutis
    sentiet durae. neque enim cruorem
    usque sanctorum patiere inultum,
    nec tuas aras dabis exsecrandis
215     pollui sacris. utinam supremae
    terminus vitae mihi in hoc supersit,
    patrio donec tibi sacra ritu,
    dum tibi gratum memori canamus
        pectore carmen.

220     sed ecce celeri nuntius properat gradu.
    ni fallit animus, ⟨huc⟩ venit ab exercitu.
    agnosco, sic est. scire quid ferat iuvat.

                NUNTIUS   CHORUS   (IPHIS)

    *NUN.*   Salvete, veteris Abrahami filiae
    vereque sancti sancta progenies patris.
225     istaecne Iephthae est imperatoris domus,
    an me fefellit error ambiguum viae?

    221 huc venit *Walsh*: venit *metro repugnante 1554:* advenit *R*

CHO.   Et ista Iephthae domus et haec est filia.
sed quam reportas spem refer, si quid vacat.
NUM.   Nempe istud ipsum missus huc sum ut nuntiem.
fusis fugatis hostibus, victoria                           230
re laude parta, salvus est exercitus;
haec summa. CHO.   Paucis plurima ut complexus es!
audita primum an visa fers edissere.
NUN.   Visa acta vera certa, non rumoribus
collecta vanis, affero, ut qui proelii                     235
pars ipse fuerim. CHO.   Ut gesta res est expedi.
NUN.   Vobis libenter gaudium hoc impertior.
aurora primum luce cum rosea polum
perfudit, Ammon segnis impatiens morae
equis virisque bellicorum et curruum                       240
strepitu tremendo late inundarat solum.
iamque explicata legio peditum per suas
stabat cohortes ferro et aere splendida.
turmae curules ante curvis falcibus
ibant minaces; fuderant se in cornua                       245
equites utrimque. noster autem exercitus
campi patentis ultimos colles tenens,
non asper armis nec paratu bellico,
sed corda foetus numinis fiducia
iraeque iustae vindices animos gerens.                     250
ibi noster inter imperator agmina
praecone misso tentat absque sanguine
finire bellum iure et aequis legibus:
uterque populus ut vetusti finibus
contentus agri ab alteris iniuriam                         255
vimque abstineret, rapta dominis redderet,
pacemque bello et certa dubiis praeferat.
contra superbus militum hostis copiis
armisque fretus increpat ferociter
praeconem, acerbis et minis calumniam                      260
addit: duello se petere puro et pio
agros vetustos, unde quondam Ammonidas
expulerat armis vique proles Isaci
egressa terrae finibus Niloticae.
quos si tenere perstet atque iniuriam                      265

249 corda foetus *1554*:   corda, fretus *R*

bello tueri praeferat quam reddere
erepta per vim, vindices sibi deos
non defuturos aequa postulantibus;
sin parta per vim iure malit linquere
270  Solymaea gens, et sponte cedat finibus
quos limes Arnon et Iabocus terminant,
qua solitudo cogit agros ultima
Iordanis usque ad lente euntis flumina,
aequis paratos facere pacem legibus,
275  factamque gentis utriusque commodo
sancte tueri. haec praeco postquam rettulit,
renuntiare protinus Iephthes iubet:
nec se parentes nec suos Ammonio
populo dedisse fraude vel vi damna, nec
280  quos repetat agros nunc fuisse finium
Ammonis unquam, saeculis quos iam tribus
propago Iacobi absque controversia
tenuit. 'nec ulla facta mentio interim est
de iure dubio, vel ioco vel serio;
285  nisi forte, Chamos quae deus tenuit tuus,
tibi iure cedent, noster autem quos deus
possedit agros, deseret. non deseret,
sed ut ante bello victor agros hostibus
ademit, idem iustus arbiter modo
290  huius secundos exitus pugnae dabit
etiam secundum ius et aequum.' ut rettulit
haec praeco, rauci clangor aeris aethera
pulsat, virorum clamor, armorum fragor,
fremitus equorum, curruum stridor boat;
295  caelum remugit; fracta tellus axibus
gemit; recussum duplicant montes sonum.
virtute et astu quisque pro se nititur;
ferit, feritur; pellitur, pellit; cruor
permutat amnes; nocte sub densa polum
300  pulverea nubes occulit. numero ferox
instabat Ammon, numinis fiducia
et causa nostris aequat animos iustior.
dum neutra cedit, urget acies utraque,
ecce inter umbras pulveris, cadentium

271 Jabocus *R* (cf. Vulg. ap. *Iud.* 11.22, Jaboc): Jebocus *1554, 1597*

lamenta gemitusque inter atque hortantium 305
voces, refulsit nube diducta dies
et utrasque turmas redditus caelo fragor
implevit. humilis omnium mentes pavor
consternat, ense languido torpent manus,
gelidumque lentos frigus artus alligat. 310
ibi imperator voce noster maxima
alacrique vultu: 'te, parens rerum, ducem
tuumque sequimur angelum. deus, deus
inimica flammis sternit illis agmina,
totusque turmis fulget aether igneis.' 315
haec vox utrumque postea quam exercitum
pervasit, amens alter in fugam ruit,
pavido novatis instat alter viribus.
nec his sequendi finis aut illis fugae
fuit, tenebris donec atra nubilis 320
nobis quietem, illis latebras, nox dedit.
CHO.   Cur victor ergo non reducit copias?
NUN.   Mane, universi nondum habes belli exitum.
CHO.   Forsan refectis hostis instat viribus?
NUN.   Si quidem resument mortui vires novas; 325
namque omne robur perfidae gentis deus
uno coegit demetendum proelio.
ergo aut perempti corporum cumulis locum
in quo steterunt obtinent, aut lurida
fusi per agros strage pascunt vultures. 330
et ne resurgat denuo bellum novum
multos in annos, dux futuri providus
prospexit; etiam peperit et nepotibus
seris quietem. victor arma Ammonium
per omne nomen celeriter circumferens, 335
bis dena muris vertit oppida dirutis.
tectis perustis puberes dedit neci,
vastavit agros. debiles tantum senes,
pueri tenelli et feminae imbelles solum
vacuum pererrant, patriae et casum gemunt. 340

CHORUS

O aurei dux luminis
sol, qui recursu praepete

vices diurnas temperas,
et igne flammifer vago
345 partiris orbi tempora,
post lustra tandem quattuor
iubar beatum in liberos
fundis nepotes Isaci.
inauspicatos impetus
350 hostis superbi dextera
Iephthaea fregit, spiritus
Ammonis acres contudit,
et praedo praeda factus est.
nec tela Scythico profuit
355 pennata nervo spargere,
rapax nec axis impetus
minax recurvis falcibus,
nec vis equorum aut fortium
densae phalanges militum
360 premente texerunt deo.
iamiam discite perfidi,
iamiam agnoscite. non lapis,
non lignum deus est, neque
quod vel sculpserit artifex
365 caelo dextera ferreo,
vel plastes facili manu
finxit, vultum hominis luto
mentitus madido, deus
noster arduus aetheris
370 arces incolit igneas,
et rerum sator et salus,
maiestate sua potens,
nec cerni facilis neque
mortali docilis manu
375 certam ducere imaginem.
vecordem ille superbiam
regum frenat, et impia
vota et spes nimias malum
iustus ducit ad exitum.
380 ille innoxia pectora
saevis pressa doloribus
praesenti auxilio levat;
et de pulvere pauperem

et custodem olidi gregis
sceptra attollit ad aurea, 385
pastorum diademate
ornans tempora regio.
hunc unum dominum et deum
terrae daedala machina
sub quocumque iacet die 390
agnoscat, colat atque amet,
et quam sol oriens novis
subiectam radiis ferit,
et quam sub medio die
incendit propioribus 395
flammis, quique bibit Tagum
fulvo gurgite nobilem,
et qui perpetua nive
damnatas habitant plagas.
eia Hebraides, aureis 400
comptae colla monilibus,
perfusa ambrosiae coma
suave fragret odoribus.
eia Hebraides, Indicis
comptae tempora gemmulis, 405
terram multicoloribus
late spargite floribus.
cessant tinnula cymbala,
cessant nablia cum lyra
victori domino novum 410
carmen dicere? tibiae
cessat multiforae sonus?
quis terram pede libero
plaudit, mollibus et choris
festo laetus et otio 415
curas diluit asperas?
festas victima dux gregis
aras imbuat, Arabis
suaveolentia nubila
ignis halet odoribus. 420
et tu, progenies ducis,
magni spes generis, cape
cultus, filia, splendidos,
et patrem reducem piis

425  laeta amplectere brachiis.
    iamiam purpureos sinus,
    Iphi, assume, retortulum
    iam cirrum cohibe. ferit
    aures, en, fremitus virum;
430  ipse est, ipse parens adest.

          IEPHTHES

    Regnator orbis, unus et verus deus,
    solumque numen propitium pollens potens,
    idem severus ultor et clemens pater,
    tuis tremendus et severus hostibus,
435  tuis amicis lenis et salutifer,
    irae timendae sed tamen placabilis,
    amore fervens idem et inritabilis,
    nos servitutis iusta presserunt mala,
    meritasque poenas dedimus impii impiis,
440  qui, te relicto rege patrono deo,
    rerum parente fonteque perennis boni,
    ad saxa stultas muta fudimus preces
    et vana surdis vota lignis fecimus.
    pudet fateri; mentis aeternae capax
445  homo, rationis particeps, mentis inopes
    truncos adorat, tura vivus mortuo
    praebet suumque metuit artifex opus.
    ergo relicti qui reliquimus sumus.
    poenas subacti dedimus et fracti malis,
450  cum nunc Idume, nunc Palestinae manus,
    nunc dirus Ammon, nunc Syrus contaminat
    hereditatem gentis et sortem tuae.
    malo eruditi et hostium ludibrio
    tandem coacti vix reversi ad te sumus.
455  at tu, benignus atque misericors deus,
    iusti furoris frena compescis tui.
    iram remittis et odii oblivisceris,
    et abdicatos filios culpa sua
    restituis iterum misericordia tua.
460  defectionis ceu scelestae sit parum
    veniam dedisse sontibus, cumulas novis

    431 orbis, unus *R*: orbis unus, *1554*

etiam triumphis laudibus victoria.
exutus armis hostis arcu languidus
abiit remisso; bellici currus fugam
totis morantur sparsa campis funera,  465
volucresque pascit qui superbus vincula
Solymis parabat; contegit strages agros,
cruorque tumidas auget undas barbarus.
ergo, creator orbis et magne arbiter,
memores libenter mente grata gratias  470
agimus habemus, supplicesque victimis
tuas ad aras patrio litabimus
ritu, canentes te deum ac patrum patrem,
qui per rubentis gurgites tumidos freti
nostris dedisti tutum iter maioribus,  475
cum te iubente pigra moles aequoris
posuit procellas, mobilis stupuit liquor
cursu coacto, et vitreus crystallino
muro pependit pontus hinc et hinc, viam
praebere iussus. foederis memor tui,  480
placidus propitiusque accipe haec servi tui
exigua quamvis vota, grato pectore
tamen profecta debitaque nuper tibi.
quod primum ad aedes sospiti occurret meas,
tuas id aras imbuet grata hostia  485
suo cruore, tuis beneficiis licet
par nulla possit comparari victima.
at tu benigne memoris animi munera
interpretaris. ut fideliter tua
promissa solvis, vota sic reddi tibi  490
fideliter gaudes, potentiam exserens
erga rebelles, exserens clementiam
erga timentes. vis nec ulla est altera
cui terra caelum pareant et Tartara.

IPHIS IEPHTHES SYMMACHUS CHORUS

*IPH.* Prodeo. parentis reducis ut laeta ac lubens  495
conspicio vultus! o mihi secundum deum
genitor verende, sine frui amplexu tuo.
cur, genitor, a me torva vertis lumina?
*IEPH.* Me miserum. *IPH.* In hostes omen hoc vertat deus.

500   IEPH.   Utinam, sed in nos recidit. IPH. Heu, quid audio?
      IEPH.   Miserae parentem filiae miserrimum.
      IPH.   Hei mihi, tremesco. salvus est exercitus?
      IEPH.   Est salvus. IPH. Et tu victor? IEPH. Ita se res habet.
      IPH.   Nulloque corpus sauciatus vulnere?
505   IEPH.   Sic est. IPH. Quid ergo de profundo pectore
      secreta ducis ingemens suspiria?
      IEPH.   Id scire non est tibi opus in praesentia.
      IPH.   Hei mihi, quid in te misera peccavi, pater?
      IEPH.   Nihil, sed in te, misera, peccavit pater.
510   IPH.   In me profecto, quod sciam, erratum est nihil,
      nec si fuisset id tibi molestiam
      adferre debet. nam parentum iniurias
      aequo necesse est liberi ut animo ferant.
      IEPH.   Sapienter ac ut te decet, nata, loqueris.
515   quantoque tu sapientius loqueris, meum
      pectus recludis altiore vulnere.
      IPH. Quodcumque mentem, genitor, exercet tuam
      omitte. cunctis parta per te civibus
      tuo dolore gaudia haud contamines,
520   tuaque amicos sine frui praesentia.
      IEPH.   Nobis pariet absentiam haec praesentia.
      IPH.   Belli pericla forte rursum te vocant?
      IEPH.   Discrimen armis gravius imminet domi.
      IPH.   Bello periclum gravius esse domi potest?
525   IEPH.   Bello salutem repperi, perii domi.
      IPH.   Immo et familia salva per te et patria est.
      IEPH.   Est, gratiamque debeo hoc nomine deo.
      IPH.   Ac nomine isto semper utinam debeas!
      IEPH.   Sed vereor ista ut salva persistant diu.
530   IPH.   Quare secundae nunc, pater, cum maxime
      res sunt, precari votaque decet solvere,
      non, cum reflavit sortis aura mobilis,
      palpare numen precibus, in re prospera
      obliviosa sacra neglegentia
535   deserere. facilem quisquis incolumis deum
      sibi demereri studuit, ubi res ingruit
      adversa, nixus conscientiae bonae
      fructu rogare numen audet propitium
      iam sponte, vota nuncupat securius,
540   et certiore spe futura concipit.

*IEPH.* Iamdudum id ipsum facere mecum cogito.
*IPH.* Quid te moratur? *IEPH.* Haec relinque, filia,
curanda nobis. quod puellares decet
animos et annos, id tuae curae puta.
*IPH.* Non mihi alienum est quicquid ad patrem attinet. 545
*IEPH.* Fateor, sed interim ut domi recte omnia
sint provide, et morem patri tuo gere.
huc rursus ad nos post brevi revertere;
adesse oportet te sacrificio statim.
*IPH.* Fiet, revertor. heu misera, quidnam patri 550
mutavit animum pristinum erga liberos?
hoc nemo nuper fuerat indulgentior
nec liberorum quisquam amantior parens,
qui nunc severus taetricus tristis ferox
vultu minaci bellicum prae se ferens 555
adhuc tumultum. quicquid est, metuo nimis.
id adsequi unum nequeo, quod propter me ait
sese dolere, nullius quae conscia
culpae mihi sim qua parentem offenderim.
o feminarum sorte vulgus aspera 560
productum in auras, quas, licet culpa vacent,
rumor malignus dente rodit invido!
pro facto habetur quicquid ira finxerit
servi loquacis, quod maritus suspicax
commentus ipse est, malevola aut vicinia. 565
quid suspicetur genitor, in mea manu
non est. remedium id arbitror tutissimum,
intaminata conscientia frui.
*SYMM.* Probe locuta es, digna patre filia
victore, casta digna matre et patria. 570
humana quamvis finxerit malignitas
crimen, repostos perspicit sensus deus,
illoque vincit purus animus iudice.
speranda ab illo et expetenda praemia
vitae peractae. patris autem iniuria 575
aequi ac iniqui perferenda est liberis.
proinde patri morigera domum interim
revise. si quid fama divulgaverit,
hic aucupabor persequens vestigia
tui parentis, mox tibi indicavero. 580
*CHO.* Quin hoc, amice, pergis agere, Symmache?

SYMM.　Id diligenter fiet.　CHO.　At quantum potes
isto puellam libera trepidam metu.
hoc poscit abs te ius amicitiae vetus,
585　quae culta primis usque ab incunabulis
fidei tenore semper uno perstitit;
hoc poscit ipsa patria, quae Iephthae suam
debet salutem.　SYMM.　Quin tace, ac fidei meae
permitte.　CHO.　At illud callide ut fiat vide,
590　animique caecos penitus excutias sinus.
SYMM.　Ne metue, nec me poterit ille nec volet
celare sensus; apta novi tempora.

### CHORUS

I felix pede fausto.
et qui pectoris imo
595　cernit clausa recessu
idem testis et aequus
iudex, coepta secundet.
at te, pessime livor,
audax nectere fraudes,
600　et committere ficto
dulces crimine amicos,
et rumore maligno
sanctae foedera taedae
praeceps solvere, caros
605　qui gaudes sua patres
contra pignora caeco
linguae armare veneno,
idem testis et idem
secreti arbiter aequus
610　te clausum tenebrosi
antris abdat Averni,
unde has nec vaga sedes
unquam fama revisat.
o quantum ille laborum
615　tecum detrahet una!
quam mortalia diris
curis pectora solvet!

593　i felix *1597*　infelix *1554*

SYMMACHUS IEPHTHES CHORUS

*SYMM.* Quidnam repente, ductor armis inclite,
mutavit oris pristinum statum tui?
quae maestitudo laeta turbat gaudia? 620
metus recessit, perduelles perfidi
poenas luerunt, parta patriae quies.
cum gratuletur civitas victoriam
tibi, tuumque patria nomen laudibus
in astra tollat cantibus festis fremens, 625
qui publici auctor gaudii es, non publicae
felicitatis esse debes particeps?
*IEPH.* O grata sortis infimae securitas!
felice natum sidere illum existimo
procul tumultu qui remotus exigit 630
ignotus aevum tuta per silentia.
*SYMM.* At ego beatum potius illum duxero
cui vera virtus peperit aeternum decus,
quem de tenebris erutum popularibus
splendore, vulgo et separatum a deside, 635
gloria futuris merita saeclis consecrat.
at qui sopori deditus et ignaviae est
et vitam inertem pecudis instar transigit,
nil interesse opinor an sit mortuus
an morte vitam obscuriorem duxerit, 640
cum par utrumque supprimat silentium.
quapropter in te cuncta cum congesserit
quaecumque amicum numen homini dare potest,
laudes honores rem decus victoriam,
benignitatem agnosce gratus numinis 645
nec sordidis sententiis res splendidas
corrumpe, cum nil possit esse gratius
deo beneficii quam memor animus dati.
*IEPH.* Praeclara dictu res honor victoria
decus triumphus, parta bello gloria. 650
at quae videntur fronte prima suavia,
eadem intuere propius, et intelliges
condita fellis acri amaritudine.
fortuna nulli sic refulsit prospera
adversa ut illam lance non penset pari. 655
tristia secundis et secunda tristibus

ante 618 *SYMMACHUS IEPHTHES (CHORUS omisso) edd. omnes,
sed cf.* 746, 782

vicissitudo acerba sortis temperat.
putas beatum me, beatitudinem
fulgore inani metiens et plausibus
660   vulgi, miseriae quem premunt certissimae.
      SYMM.   Quin finge sortem benevolam ex sententia
tibi polliceri cuncta; quid superest adhuc
quod concupiscas? spretus, exsul patria,
domo repulsus, inque solitudinem
665   detrusus altam, pauperis dominus casae,
repente veluti somnio dives, tamen
felicitatis arbiter iniquus tuae
conquereris. altam ferre si sortem nequis,
pusillus animi es; sin nequis agnoscere
670   benignitatem numinis, dignissimus
rebus relictis pristinoque es tugurio.
per ferrum et ignes regna mortales petunt;
tibi nec petenti principatus contigit.
suo cruore plurimi victoriam
675   redimunt, suorum caede, damno publico;
quam tu incruento Marte, salvo exercitu
incolumis ipse rettulisti, patriae
auctor salutis, hostium terror, inopi
de sorte dives, liber e servo. modo
680   ignobilis, nunc clarus altum vertice
pulsas Olympum gloria; media modo
e plebe, populi principem locum tenes.
ad absolutam nil beatitudinem
deest parte ab omni praeter animum muneris
685   tanti capacem et prosperis rebus parem.
      IEPH.   Ut video, amice, publicus te error tenet.
at mentis oculis limpide si cerneres
quam magna magnis sint malis obnoxia,
tantopere quem nunc laude prosequeris statum
690   rerum mearum, diceres miserrimum.
      SYMM.   Non paene vitio semper id nostro evenit
et inquietae mentis inconstantia,
neutram ut feramus lance sortem aequabili?
tranquillitatem pauperis laudat casae
695   dives, nec alta classico silentia
turbata, somnos liberos insomniis,
curis vigilias; pauper aurum purpuram,

servos clientes, apparatus regios,
aedesque laxas fine nullo laudibus
tollit, beatos divites solos putat. 700
sed rem suopte expende utramque examine;
sors neutra pura est omnibus molestiis.
inopes egestas angit, opulentos metus;
diti est voluptas, pauperi securitas.
acerba laetis sors utrimque miscuit. 705
sed illa certe existimanda est optima
quae multa paucis laeta condit tristibus,
divina qualem tibi dedit clementia
cumulatam honore laude re victoria.
quam abnuere stulti est, perfidi haud agnoscere, 710
nescire modice ferre vix reor viri.
*IEPH.* Frustra mederi pharmacis vulgaribus
conare nostro vulneri. sanabilis
haec plaga non est, intimis vitalibus
insedit, alte in viva penetrans viscera. 715
eoque luctus est acerbior meus
quod culpa damnum, miseria errorem gravat.
*SYMM.* Quin apud amicum quicquid est edissere,
fidisque ne vereare credere auribus.
*IEPH.* Ecquid memoria te subit voti mei? 720
*SYMM.* Quod nempe salvo es pollicitus exercitu?
*IEPH.* Rem loqueris ipsam. quod utinam prudentior
voto fuissem nuncupando et cautior!
*SYMM.* Quis hic sit error comminisci non queo.
*IEPH.* Qui me meamque perditurus est domum. 725
*SYMM.* Oblata poterit perdere omnes victima?
*IEPH.* Quae sola generis supererat spes filia.
*SYMM.* Hanc immolabis? quae iubet necessitas?
*IEPH.* Quod prima nobis obvia redeuntibus.
*SYMM.* Quod tandem in hac re nata commisit scelus? 730
*IEPH.* Promissa certam vota postulant fidem.
*SYMM.* Hic scrupus animum scilicet premit tuum?
*IEPH.* Premit, nec avelli ante pectori meo
poterit, nefanda quam cruentus victima
miser ubi miseros perditus perdam meos, 735
illisque iustas ac mihi poenas luam.
at tu, corusci rex vibrator fulminis,
quem contremiscunt terra caelum Tartarus,

si quando iussis obsequens prompte tuis
740 gratum quod esset dixerimve aut fecerim,
audi precantem et vota dexter adiuva.
non nunc superbas postulo victorias
festosque plausus. redde rursum proelia;
crudelis in me victor Ammon inruat
745 et noxiam animam mille plagis exigat.
  CHO. Heu mutatio subitae sortis!
ut perpetua serie laetum
nil mortalibus usque relictum est!
IEPH. Aut tu trisulcis dividens caelum ignibus,
750 in me, scelestum parricidam et impium,
molire telum flammeo actum turbine;
iam nunc nocentem et, si supersit amplius
vitae, futurum noxium in dies magis,
detrude vivum sub profunda Tartara.
755 SYMM. Non transigenda temere res est tam gravis,
turbata caeco dum tumultu mens furit.
compone tete. cum quiescet impetus
et liber animus sana consilia audiet,
una cum amicis cuncta statues libere.
760 IEPH. Consilia dubiis remedium rebus ferunt.
qui consulit cum nullus auxilio est locus
addit miseriis sponte stultitiam suis.
SYMM. Remedia semper integra re suppetunt.
IEPH. Nempe medicinam cum modus patitur mali.
765 SYMM. Si sors initio res videtur ardua,
non est quod animum protinus despondeas;
quin consulendum censeo vel eo magis.
quod saepe visum est uni inexplicabile
expediit alius facile. si cedant bene
770 consulta prave, te sequetur gloria;
si male ceciderint, tu tamen culpa vacas.
auctore magno desipere paene sapere est.
quod si undequaque claudit omnes exitus
invicta vis aut fatum ineluctabile,
775 nec explicare consilia sese queunt,
idem probabunt, quicquid eveniet, quibus
usus fuisti in consulendo auctoribus;
sin ipse reliquis facinus insciis novum
perages, rogatus qui probaturus fuit

eventa primus arguet. quamquam sciat  780
remedia nulla, scisse vult credi tamen.
CHO.   Ne commonentem recta sperne, nam fere
temere patrati poenitentia est comes.

### CHORUS

Quamquam tristia, quamquam ingrata
referam et luctus luctibus addam,  785
stat sententia promere cuncta
ordine matri, miserae et natae.
aut consilio forte aut precibus
fatum avertere triste licebit.
subit interea communi hominum  790
sorti impendere lacrimas. primum
quid deplorem? miserum an patrem?
quem sic valida compede vinctum
consilii exsors detinet error,
ut sola putet impietate  795
se pietatem posse tueri.
miserae an doleam fata puellae?
quam vernantem primo aetatis
flore tenellae, spes ad opimas
eductam, non hostica bella  800
patria capta captam eripiunt,
non dira lues caelo immissa
perimet, patrio sed mactatu
victima diras imbuet aras,
et vice brutae pecudis iugulo  805
calidam sanguinis evomet undam,
artus ferro trunca tenellos,
quos nec violet barbarus hostis
nec montanae feritas ursae
crudo auderet carpere dente.  810
victore feret patre misella
quae nec victore hoste tulisset.
vos, hostilia passim campis
sparsa cadavera, si quis vita
venit exutos sensus ad artus,  815

801 *fort.* eripient?

gaudete, aspras cernite poenas
victorem de sese exigere.
haec nimirum est addita nostrae
vitae sors, ut tristia laetis
820  vicibus subeant, tenebrae ut soli,
ut veri aspera bruma tepenti.
nulla est adeo pura voluptas
quam non taetro felle dolores
vitient. levitas perfida sortis
825  vice saeva res hominum miscet.
sic ubi placidis sternitur undis
aequor tacito lene sereno,
nigram glomerans turbo procellam
tumidos longe cumulat fluctus.
830  hinc remeabilis impetus aestus,
illinc Cauri flabra protervi
per freta dubiam spumea puppim
rapiunt. nostrae haec facies vitae est
inter caedes furta tumultus,
835  et graviores morte timores
mortis; si quid laeti inluxit,
velut arentes inter stipulas
flammae evanida lux fugitivae
celeri velox avolat aura,
840  dein perpetuis nexa catenis
longi subeunt agmina luctus.

IEPHTHES   SACERDOS

IEPH.   O sol diurnae lucis auctor, o patres,
o quicquid hominum sceleris immune es, procul
averte vultus exsecrandis a sacris.
845  aut tu, cruorem virginalem innoxium
potura tellus, hisce patulos in specus
sinuque vasto me vora; dum non nocens
perire possim, quolibet me obrue loco.
vel ipsum adire non recuso Tartarum,
850  modo parricida Tartarum non incolam.
quid Tartarum aio? Tartarus mihi est domi.
quo me profusis maesta coniunx lacrimis

848  possim *scripsimus auctore W.S. Watt:* possum *edd.*

rogabit ore? nata quo intuebitur
moritura vultu? colla complectens preces
quas admovebit voce lamentabili? 855
*SAC.* Hic ultimorum consequi luctus solet
comes malorum, cum medentium manum
vulnus recusat, aut peractum cum scelus
remedia refugit. tu miser sis an secus,
tua repostum est in manu. integrum tibi est 860
natam sacrifices necne, sive, ut verius
dicam, integrum non est, nisi si quis miser
sponte esse cupiat. integrum quomodo tibi est
id perpetrare sacra quod vetat parens
natura, pietas cui reluctatur, deus 865
quod abominatur? primum amare liberos
natura nostris inseruit affectibus,
nec nostra tantum motus iste pectora
percellit; altum quicquid aequor permeat
celeri natatu, quicquid alis aëra 870
findit, quod utero cumque cunctorum parens
tellus creavit, sentit adfectus sacros.
nam patris hanc aeterna providentia
caelestis animis indidit mortalium
ad educandos utilem vim liberos, 875
et continendam publicam concordiam
orbis, recentemque subolis propaginem
semper novandam. quoque nomen artius
imprimeret istud mentibus, dici pater
et esse voluit; nec modo exemplo sui, 880
sed et ferarum et alitum atque piscium
patriae probavit caritatis vinculum.
nos, quibus, ut hominis serviamus nomini,
peculiaris debet esse humanitas,
longe a ferarum vincimur clementia. 885
nec scelere nostras inquinare dexteras
sat est; nefandum facinus adscribere iuvat
caelo. cruentis victimis confingimus
gaudere numen, quod nec Aegyptus dei
ignara patrat nec superstitionibus 890
Assyria falsis una deditissima.
quam caede puras nos manus est aequius
servare, puris e parentibus satos,

et pura caste sacra iussos numini
895 offerre! nostro non litatur victimis
deo cruentis bubulove sanguine,
polluta nullo corda sed contagio
et mens recocta veritate simplice
illi offerenda et casta conscientia.
900 IEPH.   Cur ergo leges victimas sacrae imperant?
SAC.   Non quod bidentis caede gaudeat deus
famemve caesi carnibus vituli expleat,
sed audientes esse nos monitis iubet.
IEPH.   Non nuncupata vota oportet reddere?
905 SAC.   Sed nuncupare iusta tantum lex iubet.
IEPH.   Istud fuisset rectius ab exordio
id polliceri quod probant ritus patrum.
nunc, re peracta, quod semel votum est deo
lex missa caelo nos iubet dependere.
910 SAC.   Mactare natos quae parentes lex iubet?
IEPH.   Quae vota iussit nuncupata reddere.
SAC.   Fasne est vovere quod nefas est reddere?
IEPH.   Quin immo summum est vota non solvere nefas.
SAC.   Quid si cremare iura vovisses patrum?
915 IEPH.   Nemo ista sanus vota nuncupaverit.
SAC.   Cur? nonne sacris quod repugnent legibus?
IEPH.   Sic est.   SAC.   Quid ergo qui trucidat liberos?
IEPH.   Non tam quid agitur interest quam cur agas.
SAC.   Parere iussis tibi videtur numinis?
920 IEPH.   Mactare natum iussit Abramum deus.
SAC.   Qui iussit, idem quoque vetuit occidere.
IEPH.   Cur ergo iussit?   SAC.   Ut probaretur fides
saeclis futuris.   IEPH.   Cur vetuit?   SAC.   Ostendere
vel hinc volebat victima oboedientiam
925 magis placere.   IEPH.   Nempe sacro numini
parere oportet?   SAC.   Scilicet.   IEPH.   Iubet deus
vovere?   SAC.   Sane.   IEPH.   Et vota solvi postulat?
SAC.   Sic est.   IEPH.   Morantes increpat, et a perfidis
poenas reposcit?   SAC.   Nihil habes hic quo tuum
930 possis tueri facinus. infandum scelus
qui perpetrare spondet, ultro adfectibus
stultis suisque paret ille insomniis.

916 repugnent *1554;*   repugnet *1597, R*

proinde voti quicquid illud est, deum
crudelitati desine adscribere tuae.
nec qui scelestos odit et nefarios 935
ritus sacratis exsecratur legibus,
scelere quod odit posse placari putes.
divina vox est una simplex veritas
sibique constans. quod semel iussit, ratum
fixumque perstat tramite immutabili, 940
nec ad sinistram dexteramve paullulum
deflectere licet. intueri unum hunc scopum
verum est, ab una lege consilia suae
vitae capessere, quando ceu facem deus
hanc esse iussit, quae per incertas vias 945
errore caeco regeret instabiles gradus.
ab hac lucerna cum procul te sentias
flexisse temere, nunc, priusquam longius
abducat error, in viam rursus redi.
si stulta vota credis infandis sacris 950
posse expiari, falleris. crudelitas
ista cumulabit, non scelus tollet tuum.
nec falsa species decipiat animum. deus
ut rite sacris gaudet oblatis, ita
nefanda vota respuit. nec abstulit 955
impune, quamvis concitus studio pio,
admovit ignem qui profanum altaribus.
igitur amica monita ne sperne, et deum
placare dum vis concitare desine,
non instituto qui coli gaudet tuo 960
sed sibi probatis lege ritu moribus.
IEPH.   Hos, qui videntur sapere saepe plurimum
vulgusque supra se imperitum venditant,
plerumque verae comperi prudentiae
minimum tenere. nemo neglegentius 965
ritus vetustos servat, et mysteria
facit minoris. vulgus indocile ac rude
voti tenax est, nescium fraudis; ratum
quod pollicetur numini semel putat,
ut nil sit aliud sapere iam me iudice 970
quam scire velum noxiae praetendere,

943 *fort*. tuae?

fucumque factis pessimis inducere.
quin potius illud cogitare erat aequius,
culpa carere quam videri innoxios
975 aut fraudulentae cautionis tegmine
velare mentis improbae versutias.
pietatis ergo quisquis aemulos volet
suos haberi liberos, ne litteris
hos erudire studeat aequo impensius.
980 nam litterarum quo quis est peritior,
huic est sacrorum cura neglegentior.
SAC.   At rursus audi, si vacat, vir optime,
quam caeca fallat credulum ignorantia.
errore vulgi qui tuetur se, nihil,
985 opinor, ideo peccat excusatius.
nec istud unquam moribus regnum malis
permittat ille maximus rerum parens,
ut recta plebis improbae consensio
in prava vertat, e bono ut faciat malum.
990 nec si tyrannis blandiens palpatio
peiora laudet, recta mutans nomina,
efficiet ut quae visa multitudini
honesta sunt honesta fiant protinus.
una est honesti forma simplex, quam neque
995 vel vis tyranni vel potentum auctoritas
adulterare poterit aut corrumpere.
nunc, quo quis est e plebe ferme indoctior,
auctoritatem adsumit arrogantius
diiudicandi in rebus obscurissimis,
1000 et pertinaci, quod fere ignorantiae est,
animo tuetur dogma susceptum semel.
nec interim aequo expendit examine, mala
an recta sint quae pertinaciter tenet,
sed cum inter omnes maxime caecutiat,
1005 caecus videntes caecitatis arguit.
ut cui perusta febre fervent viscera
amara cuncta credit, unumque autumat
se sapere cum desipiat unus maxime,
sic vos, tenebris pectus atris nubili,
1010 iis imperare quaeritis quibus aequum erat
parere. quorum oportuit sententiam
sequi, esse comites cogitis, et impingere

in saxa firmam sponte pellentes ratem.
religio vera est veraque pietas deum
non instituto colere quod commentus es 1015
tibi ipse, sacris victimas non quaslibet
mactare, sed quas missa legum caelitus
decreta poscunt et patrum mores probant.
*IEPH* Quodcumque gestum est mente sincera, deo
gratum est, bonique dona semper consulit 1020
quaecumque corde sunt profecta simplice;
nec numen aurum sed animum dantis probat.
*SAC.* Si recta vitiat mentis improbitas malae,
non ideo curva stultus animus corrigit.
nam quae vocatis recta simplicia proba 1025
sunt vanitatis plena dementissimae,
nisi esse possit forte quicquam vanius
quam ad veritatis lumen oculos claudere.
dein caecitatem lapsus in spontaneam
titulis honestis in scelere laudem petis, 1030
rerumque tollis omnium discrimina
dum iniqua iusta, foeda honesta mobilis
pendere vulgi statuis ex sententia.
quod si potestas tanta sit sententiis
stultorum ut aequa iniqua faciant protinus, 1035
ut sint profana sacra, ius iniuria,
cur non et illud arbitremur posse eos,
ignes in undas, undam in ignes vertere,
mutare lignis saxa, vitam mortuis
revocare? motus temporum sistant citos 1040
et sempiternas transferant rerum vices?
quod si arbitraris haec supra mortalium
vires et uni conditori obnoxia,
quas ille leges prodidit semel, puta
aeque perennes ac ratas, aut amplius, 1045
nec ullum in illas esse ius mortalibus.
nec qui supremus imminet mundo dies
edicta rumpet illius. caelum et solum
et aëra et aquas solvet ignis ultimus;
de lege vero quae data est divinitus 1050
non carpet apicem temporis longinquitas.
*IEPH.* Vos ista per me, si libet, sectamini,
quos iuvat haberi antistites prudentiae;

ego veritatem malo stultam et simplicem
1055 quam splendidam fuco impiam sapientiam.

CHORUS

O Isacidas matrona inter
rarum exemplum sortis amicae,
quam subito te fortuna atrox
exitio submersit, et illum
1060 prope tangentem sidera fastum
obruit, atrae et more procellae
luctu gaudia vertit acerbo!
heu, nunquam homini sat compertum
quid petat aut quid vitet in horas.
1065 quis tibi nuper non invidit,
dux fortissime? cui prope supra
votum acciderant prospera cuncta,
clari generis splendor, casti
thalami, suboles digna parente,
1070 partaque valida gloria dextra.
qui nunc subitae mole ruinae
obrutus ipsis es miserandus
hostibus, ac tua vota retractans
imples miseris astra querelis.
1075 nempe erroris nebula et taetris
ignorantia saepta tenebris
sic humanas sepelit mentes,
nec perspicuis animi quisquam
oculis radios cernere potis est
1080 veri simplicis, aut virtutis
nudae rectum insistere callem.
sed veluti sub luce maligna
per secretos nemorum anfractus
lubricus error mille viarum
1085 dubio occursu ludit euntes,
inter varios semita flexus
nulla placet neque displicet ulla;
sic iter homines praeterpropter
dubia incerti mente vagamur.
1090 hic venalem funere laurum
otii impatiens dum sibi quaerit,

luctu alieno dura per arma
redimit vanae murmura famae.
captatores alius captans
dulci steriles pignore lectos 1095
multa pensat plebe clientum,
atque intenta fraude vicissim
corvos ludere gaudet hiantes.
cunarum alter murmura blanda,
tenero et balbas ore querelas 1100
non mutaverit opibus Croesi,
aut quas divite lucidus unda
rutilas Hermus volvit arenas.
verum nemo tam sapienter
vitam instituit, consilium ut non 1105
damnet decies ipse suum una
   forsitan hora.
atque en, prodit squalida luctu
miseram comitans nata parentem.
quam dissimiles, pro dolor, illis 1110
quae conspicuae nuper cunctis
laetaeque novi laude triumphi
paene attigerant vertice Olympum!
nuper ad invidiam usque beatae,
nunc exemplum nobile sortis 1115
variae. sic deus humana rotat,
instar volucris pulveris acti
turbine celeri mobilis aurae,
aut hibernae more procellae
quae violenti flamine Cauri 1120
obruit altos grandine montes,
mox, ubi roseo fulsit ab ortu
fax perspicui pura diei,
late albentes fusa per agros
vix conspecto sole liquescit. 1125

### STORGE  IEPHTHES  IPHIS

*ST.* O spes inanes! festa nuptialia
tibi parabam, nata. lucem cernere
illam expetebam, sorte cum te prospera
auctam viderem liberis et coniuge

1130 claro beatam. te senectutis meae
fore pollicebar columen ac solacium.
de te augurabar falsa frustra insomnia.
nunc me, insolenti saeviens ludibrio,
sortis furentis impotens immanitas
1135 felicitatis de supremo culmine
deiecit, uno cuncta vertens impetu.
O ter beatos, liberis quos hosticus
orbavit ensis, pestilens aut aëris
lues, famesve, scelere quorum lacrimae
1140 carent, doloremque imputare aliis queunt!
at hic in uno scelere sescenta scelera
fortuna miscet; liberorum carnifex
parens, scelesta sacra ritu barbaro,
arae cruentae victimis nefariis.
1145 si sancta sancte sacra tantum numini
credis probari, tolle morem barbarum;
crudelitate sin propitius sit deus,
et me trucida victimam cum filia.
    IEPH. Acerbitatis plus satis complectitur
1150 sors nostra per se, nihil ut accedat mali.
quam ob rem omitte meque teque incendere
nil profuturis luctui conviciis.
nam saeva quamvis sit calamitas omnium,
sors nostra multo ceteris est saevior.
1155 coniuncta vestris innocentia est malis,
et labe sceleris miseria infelix caret.
ego nec scelestus esse queo ni sim miser,
nec calamitosus sceleris expers degere,
solusque cogor facere facinus et pati.
1160     ST. Nempe ipse tete sponte cogis et volens.
    IEPH. Utinam ista nostri vota sint arbitrii,
promissa nec sit abnegare nefarium.
    ST. Scelesta vota grata non sunt numini.
    IEPH. Fuisse grata testis est victoria.
1165     ST. Quid? polliceri quod tuum non est potes?
    IEPH. Mea nata non est? ST. Est, sed etiam ut sit mea.
commune pignus cum sit, uni cur patri
mactare, vitam mihi tueri non licet?
quod si liceret liberos addicere
1170 parentis alterius libidini, et impio

dirimere amoris vinculum divortio,
plus iure matri parte cederet sua,
matri, salutis quae sit auctor, quae patri
iam sponte natam perdituro subtrahit.
quid? nuptiales si pararentur faces 1175
virumque legeret filiae suae pater,
non hic parentis utriusque arbitrium
commune pariter liberis incumberet?
at haec societas impotens et arrogans
est coniugalis copulae consortium, 1180
servare matri non licere, perdere
licere patri, si modo quis perdidit
hanc quam trucidat, cuius astans funeri
immanitatis gloriatur ambitu.
qui claustra dum revellit animae, dum latus 1185
mucrone saevo reserat et vitalibus
haurit morantem sub profundis spiritum,
cupit videri, non eget solacio;
famam aucupatur liberorum e sanguine, et
compensat aura sanctimoniae scelus, 1190
seseque iactat laude parricidii.
tu si parentis exuisti in liberos
mentem, furenti percitus vecordia,
permitte saltem matris indulgentiae
amare, non amare quod summum est scelus, 1195
servare summum quod nefas est perdere,
quod prodidisse sponte parricidio
est gravius omni, quod trucidare propria
manu ferarum immanius truculentia est.
si dividendum pignus esset mutui 1200
amoris, aequa lege non divisimus
ut tu uti abuti morte vita filiae
possis, redundent ad genetricem modo
luctus dolores lacrimae suspiria.
o rupe dura durior, vel robore 1205
prognate crudo, cotibus vel asperis
inter ferarum lustra, nec generis tenens
nostri nec ulla sanguinis vestigia!
num flente nata, lacrimante coniuge,

1202  filiae *1597, R*   filii *1554*
1203  redundent *1597, R*   redundet *1554*

1210 maestis propinquis, liberorum carnifex
ullum doloris indicem gemitum dedit?
quin ad paternos, nata, procidis pedes?
oratione si quid aut lacrimis potes,
cor flecte durum, frange mentem ferream.
1215 IPH.  Miserere, genitor, te per hanc rogo manum
voti potentem, compotem victoriae,
per si quid unquam merita sum de te bene,
si quando parvis comprimens te brachiis
onus pependi dulce de collo tuo,
1220 per si quid ex me tibi voluptatis fuit;
depone mentem liberos erga trucem
et diritatis huius obliviscere.
aut si quid in te ex parte peccatum est mea,
profer. quod instat cumque levius perferam,
1225 si luere poenas iure me cognovero.
quid ora vertis? misera quod feci nefas
cur esse patri debeam exsecrabilis,
ut contueri non queat vultus meos?
IEPH.  Nil, nata, per te perpetratum est. hoc meum
1230 nefas, meum istud est scelus totum, meae
immerita poenas pendis imprudentiae.
ego teque meque, misera, perdidi miser
votis nefandis. quod utinam prudentior
verbis fuissem aut proelio infelicior,
1235 et morte honesta, tot virorum fortium
inter catervas caesus hostili manu,
praeoccupassem miseriae portum meae!
ingrata nunc me vita mihi superstitem
luctus reservat semper ut videam novos.
1240 tibi per nefanda sacra iuro quae deo
renuente vovi, per mali cumulum mei
et luctuosam memoriam cladis tuae,
si morte redimi mors vicaria queat,
vitam libenter, filia, tibi impenderem.
1245 ecquid beatus videor esse vos supra?
IPH.  Aeque atque nos aut amplius etiam miser.
ST.  Apud parentem quando levis auctoritas
est huius, unum coniugem coniunx rogo
atque id supremum: me mori pariter iube.
1250 mortem imputare, si me amas, potes mihi,

sin oderis, tibi. doloribus exime
me morte, teque libera molestiis.
*IEPH.* Patratur una caede sceleris plus satis.
*ST.* O sanctitas, o fas et innocentia!
peccare metuit immolator filiae. 1255
*IPH.* Omitte, mater, lacrimas, carissima,
omitte questus, iurgia et convicia.
et tu, pater, quae pectus anxium premit
depone curam, nec meam propter necem
ultro citroque verba commutaveris. 1260
quod non volentem dura te necessitas
istuc coegit, multa mihi faciunt fidem,
maestitia praesens, pristina indulgentia,
et nullius mens criminis mihi conscia
cur commereri debeam mortem a patre. 1265
quapropter istud quicquid est, necessitas
quod cogit, ultro non recuso perpeti,
et quam parenti patriaeque debeo
animam libenter reddo. et illud ultimum,
nil postulatura, genetrix, posthac, rogo, 1270
ne quid patri causa mea succenseas
neu sis molesta. mortuis si quis super
sensus sepultis est eorum quae gerunt
vivi, futurum crede manibus meis,
ut si quid aliud, id quidem gratissimum 1275
si vos beatos prospereque degere
sim certa vitam; nec parentes ad meos,
officia vitae mutua quibus debeo
reddere vicissim et educandi solvere
pretium, senectae infirmitatem sustinens, 1280
ex me redundet luctus atque acerbitas.
*ST.* Utinam, precari si pie et sancte id licet,
dominetur Ammon, pristinum ferat iugum
Iudaea! quamvis serva, certe viveres
aut morte saltem non nefanda occumberes. 1285
saevisset in nos levius insolentia
hostis furentis quam patris victoria;
novaque fati sed miserrima vice
servire votum est et calamitas vincere.
o semper in nos vel favens etiamnum atrox 1290
fortuna, quantis gaudii usuram brevem

luctus acerbi faenerasti lacrimis!
*IPH.*   Quin potius illi iusta supplicia luant.
nos, si necesse est, immerentes sanguine
1295   aras piemus, totque caedes hostium
pensemus una sponte gratique hostia.
*IEPH.*   Heu nata, nunc intellego demum miser
quam foeda saeva dira dissignaverim
qui prole tali temere meme orbaverim.
1300   sed ipse de me sponte poenas exigam.
te namque iniquum est dare meae dementiae
poenas, puellam innoxiam, superstite
auctore luctus. ipse stultitiae meae
supplicia pendam. nec mihi exprobrabitur
1305   ab invida vicinia, quod ultima
sub spatia vitae parricida filiae
mihi peperci, liberumque sanguine
vili redemi turpis auram gloriae.
at tu beata hac caritate in patriam
1310   patremque vive, cuius aetas dignior
superesse. quamque gratiam nequit parens,
persolvat ille, solus aequa qui potest
pro dignitate huic indoli rependere.
*IPH.*   Omitte, genitor, has moras innectere,
1315   meumque dictis mollibus frangere animum.
nec fas nec aequum te mea fungi vice.
me vota poscunt. itaque tibi animam libens
hanc reddo patri, reddo patriae meae.
nec ulla Iephthae me redarguet dies
1320   non stirpe dignam. tolle age, abduci iube.
devota morti et consecrata victima
proieci amorem lucis. omnis est mora
molesta. mater, iam vale, carissima,
et vos, penates patrii, in quibus dies
1325   laetos peregi, spes ad amplas molliter
educta, claris destinata nuptiis.
o fata, fata, et morte defuncti patres,
accipite placide destinatos patriae
manes saluti. tuque, lux novissima
1330   hodierna nostris haurienda oculis, vale.

1298  dissignaverim *potior forma* designaverim *edd. omnes*

## CHORUS

Laus feminei famaque sexus
et generosae gloria stirpis,
animi nimium virgo virilis,
licet iniuria tibi fatorum
utiliores abscidit annos, 1335
licet immanis feritas Parcae
teneri florem carpserit aevi,
quod tibi vitae fors detraxit
fama adiciet postuma laudi.
et qua primis Phoebus ab Indis 1340
rutilae tollit lumina flammae,
te posteritas sera loquetur.
te qui primi flumina Nili
bibit, et curru qui Sarmatico
solidum non timet ire per Istrum, 1345
  concinet olim
non formidine mortis inerti
pavidam, patriae donasse alacrem
natura tibi quos dedit annos.
nostris longum tu dolor et honor 1350
virginibus, tibi thalami expertes
maesto ululatu flebile carmen
per redeuntes recinent annos.
at vos, vestri dedecus aevi,
animam patriae reddere segnes, 1355
vos aeternis tenebrarum umbris
teget oblivio longa sepultos,
et generis pudor et telluris
pondus inutile, quos et praesens
spernit et altera nesciet aetas. 1360

### STORGE  NUNTIUS

*ST.* Heu misera! an omnis spes salutis occidit,
effare. *NUN.* Res ut inter adversas quidem,
non pessime agitur. *ST.* Si quid accidit boni,
ea blandientis sortis est crudelitas;
venena dulci melle taetra temperat. 1365
quapropter ede quicquid occultas mali.
usus dolendi longaque experientia
induxit animo callum; ut amplius mihi

nocere posset nil reliquit sors sibi.
1370 parata certa est sed misera securitas.
*NUN.* Ut gesta res est ergo paucis accipe.
cum staret aras ante tristes victima
iam destinata virgo, purpureum decus
per alba fudit ora virgineus pudor,
1375 coetus viriles intuerier insolens,
ut si quis Indum purpura violet ebur,
rosasve niveis misceat cum liliis.
sed se per ora cum pudore fuderat
perspicua certae iuncta vis fiduciae,
1380 interque flentes sola fletibus carens
vultu remisso constitit firma ac sui
secura fati. quas tenebat lacrimas
propinqua morti virgo, populus non tenet.
alium parentis beneficium recens movet,
1385 et servitutis patriae exemptum iugum,
et solitudo familiae clarissimae;
alius acerbam sortis ingemuit vicem,
longoque luctu breve redemptum gaudium,
raroque stabilem rebus in laetis fidem.
1390 florem iuventae deflet ille, et siderum
similes ocellos, aemulamque auro comam,
supraque sexum pectoris constantiam.
et forte solito gratiorem afflaverat
natura honorem, ceu supremo munere
1395 dignata funus nobilis viraginis.
ut iam ruentis aequor in Tartessium
Phoebi recedens esse gratior solet
splendor, rosaeque vere supremo halitus
colorque cupidos detinet oculos magis,
1400 sic virgo fati stans supremo in limine,
parata morti, nec recusans molliter
turpive torpens exitus formidine,
commorat omnes, versaque in se lumina
vulgi stupentis traxerat miraculo,
1405 et triste cunctis attulit silentium.
*ST.* Narrare porro perge facinoris modum,
neu parce matris auribus. nihil potes
adferre triste, ut tristiora non sibi
proponat animus. cuncta iam praecepta sunt.

## IEPHTHES

*NUN.* Animi virilis tum puella lumina 1410
ad clara tollens astra, concipit preces
ex ore casto, voce non fracta malis:
'Aeterne rerum genitor atque hominum parens,
tandem propitius gentis errori tuae
ignosce, et istam victimam lenis cape. 1415
quod si furoris exigis piaculum,
quaecumque nostra contumax superbia
supplicia meruit, te parentem deserens,
utinam luatur hoc cruore. saepius
utinam liceret sanguinem profundere et, 1420
hic si parentum et civium sita est salus,
in me furoris impetum ac irae tuae
per mille mortes saepius deflectere.
at tu, sacerdos, quid metuis?' etenim metu
gelido tremebat. 'Ades, et hanc luce exime 1425
animam; morantem solve corporis obicem.
populum parentem meque voto libera.'
ut haec locuta est, ille iamdudum parens
visus cruentus saeviorque tigride,
oculos amictu lacrimis madens tegit, 1430
seseque damnans votaque temeraria.
fletu sacerdos obrutus vix solvere
animae meatus potuit; et maesto diu
taciturna turba torpuit silentio.
ut vocis autem pervium patuit iter, 1435
non ille gemitus, esse nec qualis solet
fremitus doloris atque lamentatio,
sed contionis gratulantis murmure
confusa turba, teque praedicantium,
adversa sortis inter asprae vulnera 1440
et blandientis laeta dona, feminam
unam beatam maxime et miserrimam.
nam plaga quamvis alte ad ossa sederit,
magni doloris magnum habes solacium.
*ST.* Solamen ipso luctuosius malo 1445
quod leniendo exasperat malum vetus,
luctusque acerbi memoriam semper novans
reducta cogit vulnera recrudescere.
quo fortiore nata tulit animo necem,
hoc angit animum tristior meum dolor. 1450

# JEPHTHA

## PROLOGUE

*ANGEL.* I am the winged agent of the mighty Thunderer. Forsaking the heavens, I am dispatched here to the house of Isaac, to the land promised to Isaac's descendants. This land was appointed to govern the nations if it preserved unspotted the terms of the sacred treaty. But now lying beneath the constricting yoke of slavery it has come to tremble at the arms of Ammon, and to endure such grim, cruel, savage treatment as the angry victor presumes to inflict, or the conquered victim fears. But at last, barely schooled by disasters, this nation began to acknowledge the God of its fathers. Having falsely adopted wicked cults, it began to scrutinise and recognise such mockery to the deity, and having recognised it to despise it; however late it returned to its father.

Yet[15] the human mind cannot impose limits to success, but grows arrogant in good fortune. The more God's goodness bestows on men, the deeper the complacency which blinds their minds. Empty arrogance fires them swollen with superfluous pride. They resemble the obstinate temerity of an aggressive horse, which once it feels the control slightly relaxed rages against its master. Subdued by the curb and bloodied by the harsh spurs it sullenly resumes its duty and obeys its master. In the same way this headstrong people, stiff-necked and inclined to the worse, acquires new gods, devotes itself to other rites, and pursues unknown ceremonies if the whip rests silent for a little while.

Thereupon[29] the kindly father shatters their minds, inflated with self-indulgence, by means of war, hunger or wind of infection, and so crushes their insurgent aggression. But on the other hand, he does not wish their inner trust to fail and be perpetually overwhelmed by a train of hardships; so he sends prophets, he sends war-leaders to free them from the bonds of grim slavery and recall them, and to compel them to tend their ancient ritual.

So in the present case he roused the arms of Ammon against those who revolted against him, against those who abandoned God's commands and devoted themselves to wicked errors; yet he set a limit on his anger, and mercifully bestowed a deliverer. This is not some figure from the ranks of the powerful, a figure imposing with his crowd of dependants or arrogant with his offspring, but Jephtha, an exile from his father's house, despised by his brothers and sprung from a lowborn father. So this proud race may not attribute to their arms what God's hand has achieved; and Ammon may realise that he has not succeeded hitherto by his own strength, but as the avenging agent of divine anger.

Moreover,[51] so that Jephtha too may not assess himself by the outcome of this battle, and grow proud and arrogant with success, he will at once be overwhelmed with domestic loss, and his arrogant airs will be shattered and retreat. For when he took up arms against the faithless foe, he promised that if he were accorded a successful end to the war he would offer as victim on the altar the first object which confronted him. Poor man, what a mountain of ills overhangs you! With what massive griefs will you be overwhelmed! How you are beguiled, too trusting, by the expectation of attendant joy! Your only child, the daughter who for you keeps watch on her father's house, will be the first to meet her father to felicitate him on the successful issue of his arms; great will be the interest with which the poor child will discharge and with her throat's blood pay for the premature joy of that success.

But[68] see, the mother emerges doleful from the house. The quaking terror of her dreams has frightened her all night long. The daughter accompanies her mother; both exhibit sickness of heart with grieving faces, gestures and speechlessness.

STORGE (*mother*) IPHIS (*daughter*)

*ST*. Ah, how my heart throbs with new fear! My heart trembles, my voice cleaves to my very throat, my mouth offers no open passage for words; for the spectres of the night terrify me repeatedly in my wretchedness. Grim dreams trouble me in my restless state, and sear my troubled heart with oppressive cares. Do you, highest Lord of the shining heavens, divert this grievous and funereal omen upon our enemies, and be benign both to myself and to my daughter, the sole remaining hope and consolation of the household, the single stay of my old age.

*IPH*. Dear mother, rather let your prophecy be more joyful, and dismiss these causes of baseless distress. Be sunny; scorn these risible mockeries of a troubled mind, and once you have scorned them, forget them.

*ST*. I pray that I could, but whenever I recall that fear anew it makes my heart palpitate with panic, and the picture of that grimmest of dreams swims before my mind. Terror stupefies my breast. Soothing sleep had now laid all things everywhere to rest, and night had ushered speechless silence over all. I saw a pack of wolves rushing at full speed with bloody, foaming, savage jaws, and raging with bent claws, dash pell-mell for the peace-loving flocks bereft of shepherds. Next the dog, faithful guardian of the fearful fold, drove off the wolves; and then returning to the weakling flock which was still half-dead in recollection of that trembling fear, it tore the shrinking lamb from my arms and mangled it with merciless teeth.

O[103] sun, O roaming light of the moon, O dappled stars in the silent sky, and you, night, who share my cares and bring back black-winged dreams, should any doom overhang my poor daughter, should fate threaten any misfortune for her, first thrust this wretched person of mine into Hell whilst my expectations are uncertain and with intermittent cares trouble a heart as yet unsure of its misfortune.

*IPH*. Why, mother, do you torture your mind so wretchedly, and with your grief increase the people's grief, and renew sharp anxieties? Rather you must lay aside your complaints and welcome my returning father with joyful expectation. For unless my mind with empty anticipation beguiles an over-trusting heart, he will be here, glorious with rich spoils, bearing back to his family and his native land achievements, praise and eternal glory.

*ST*. Fate has not granted me this manner of life. What period has ever failed to bring me tears since I first came forth from my mother's womb? First my youth witnessed the slavery of my land, grim threats from the enemy column, the plunder of cattle, our land barren and uncultivated, slaughter and bloodshed and ravaging and fire, the intermingling of things sacred and profane. No days of my life have ever flowed on untroubled. As wave pushes on wave, as one billow gives way to the next, as day is driven out by day, so evils past are ever harried by new ones. Sorrow is companion to sorrow, grief to grief. The madness of war shattered my brother and my father; my mother grew old, wearied with troubles, amidst the deaths of her kinsmen. My husband is in arms, pressing hard on treacherous foes. Yet my heart fears some outrage greater than these.

*IPH*. Fear uncontrolled readily lends credence to unpropitious prophecies.

*ST*. I pray that I may hear that my husband has returned to applauding cries and that his army is safe, with no harm to his family.

*IPH*. My father will return safe beyond doubt. The God who advised him to make war will bring him home safe, adorned with new glory.

### CHORUS

O Jordan, watering green valleys with your glassy flood, cleaving the fertile pastures of the sons of Isaac with your sluggish stream; O grove of Jerusalem clad in palm-trees, so beautiful since you never shed your foliage through the cold; will the bright Light-bearer ever bring this day before our wretched eyes so that we are bereft of cares, when we shall be free and see our land free—our land which now endures unhappily the bonds of slavery beneath the barbarian? The decadent blood of noble Isaac bears the yoke of a master. That people which the arrogant king of Egypt's land, bearing down on us with scythe-bearing wheels, did not intimidate, the people which the harsh savagery of the Red Strait with its resurgent billows did not overwhelm, the people which the Arabs' desert lands, ignorant of the plough, and the monstrous structure of men with its Cyclopian mass did not destroy—we, this people, are become faint-hearted, and are the property of Ammon. To endure a slothful yoke under a paltry lord is a crime more heinous than a deed of wickedness.

But[167] now, highest father, you who calm the disordered sea and arouse the waters of the peaceful main with the cloud-bearing squalls of the north-west wind; who shake the unflinching foundations of the steady earth with quakings, and when it is your pleasure halt the headlong flight of the scudding sky; now at last, replete with our disasters, abandon your wrath. Draw nearer, and with ready kindness show regard for the weary fortunes of our troubled race.

If[177] our sinning has deserved harsh punishment, if you reject our chosen destiny once set apart for you, if you our father through displeasure at our vices abandon your children for neglecting your service, and with anger unappeased spurn the complaints of the people you earlier loved, let not the Syrian nor grim Ammon nor the arrogant ruler of threatening Egypt seek that punishment for you. Grant no power to the profane sword in your camp. We would rather, Father, that you arm your right hand with fearful darts of three-forked fire, and overwhelm our wanton cities with a torch of avenging flame; or let the chasm of Hell swallow the wretched cultivators of the gaping land, or the earth covered with submerging waters consume them.

Let[195] not our fierce foe wax proud and arrogant with success, a nation which worships the speechless trunk, and defiles your ritual with sacrilegious ceremonies. Let not Ammon divert to his own praise the savagery of your anger against us, while he appeases with incense the image of a trunk eaten with decay. Let him not claim with lunatic lips that you cannot protect from his oppression the nation perennially dedicated to you.

You[205] wretch, what tears this laughter of yours will presently bring you! Your short-lived joy must be dissolved by lengthy tears. The fleeting hour flies by at breakneck speed; the time wings on (unless vain appearances nurture the prophet with empty hope), the time wings on when the conqueror will in turn experience the ills of oppressive slavery. For you will not allow the blood of your holy ones always to be unavenged, nor will you permit your altars to be defiled by ritual meriting a curse. I pray that the final stage of my life may not be reached till we can conduct our ceremonies to you according to ancestral ritual, and till we can sing songs welcome to you with mindful heart.

But[220] look, a messenger hastens with swift step. If my mind does not deceive me, he comes here from the army. I recognise him; this is in fact the case. I am eager to know what news he brings.

### MESSENGER   CHORUS   (IPHIS)

*MESS.* Greetings, daughters of ancient Abraham, holy offspring of a truly holy father. Is this the house of the general Jephtha, or has some error misled me in my doubt about the route?

*CHO.* Yes, this is the house of Jephtha, and this his daughter. But tell us what hopeful news you bear back, if you have leisure.

*MESS.* I have in fact been sent here to report this very thing.

The enemy are routed and put to flight; victory, success, glory have been won. The army is safe. This is the gist.

*CHO*.  So many tidings compressed in so few words! Tell us first whether your words are of things heard or of things seen.

*MESS*.  I bring news of events witnessed and performed, true and definite, not gathered from empty rumours; for I myself took part in the battle.

*CHO*.  Explain how the battle was waged.

*MESS*.  This joy I gladly bestow on you. As soon as dawn flooded the sky with rosy light, Ammon bridled at sluggish delay, and had deluged the ground far and wide with horses, warriors and the fearful din of war-chariots, And now the brigade of infantry, gleaming with iron and bronze, fanned out and took its place amongst its cavalry-units. Squadrons of chariots with curved scythes on their wheels advanced menacingly in the van; the cavalry had poured out on to both wings.

But[246] our army held the hills at the edge of the open plain, not bristling with arms and war-equipment, but with hearts full of trust in God, and spirits eager to vent just anger. Thereupon our commander sent a herald between the lines, and tried without bloodshed to end the war legally and with these fair conditions: both peoples were to be satisfied with the boundaries of their former territory, and refrain from inflicting injury and violence on the other. They were to restore plunder to its owners, and put peace before war and certainty before uncertainty.

In[258] reply the arrogant enemy, relying on his military forces and arms, fiercely abused the herald and with bitter threats added this lie: he was seeking in holy and sacred war those ancient lands from which the descendants of Isaac, after they left the boundaries of the Nile territory, had once expelled the followers of Ammon by force of arms. If the Israelites persisted in retaining them, and preferred to defend injustice by war rather than restore what had been snatched by violence, the avenging gods would not fail the Ammonites as they demanded justice. But if the people of Jerusalem preferred justly to abandon what they had won by force, and voluntarily evacuated the territories bounded by the lines of the Arnon and the Jaboc, where the furthest desert encloses the lands as far as the streams of the sluggish-flowing Jordan, they were ready to make peace on equal terms, and to defend it piously when ratified to the advantage of both races.

When[276] the herald reported these conditions, Jephtha ordered him to bear back at once this message: neither he nor his ancestors had harmed the Ammonite people by deceit or force; and the lands which he now sought had never belonged to Ammon's territories, for Jacob's descendants had held them without dispute for the past three generations. "No mention has ever been made in the interval, jokingly or seriously, about uncertain rights, except perhaps that what your god Chamos held will pass to you by right, whereas our God will abandon the lands He possessed. He will not abandon them, but as previously He deprived his enemies of their lands as victor in war, so too now as just Judge He will bring a successful outcome to this battle, according to justice and right."

After[291] the herald related this message, the clanging of harsh-sounding bronze smote the air. The shouting of men, the din of arms, the whinnying of horses, the grating of chariots sounded forth. The sky bellowed in reply, the earth torn by wheels groaned, the mountains in echo redoubled the sound.

Each[297] warrior strove on his own account with strength and guile, striking and being struck, pushing and being pushed. Gore changed the face of rivers. A cloud of dust shrouded the sky in thick darkness. Ammon, confident in his numbers, advanced, but trust in God and the juster cause made our men's spirits equal.

As[303] neither line yielded and both pressed on, suddenly amidst the clouds of dust, amongst the anguished cries and groans of those brought low and the shouts of those spurring them on, the clouds parted, the light flashed out, and a crash emanating from heaven rang through the units of both armies. Abasing fear stupefied the minds of all; their hands grew sluggish and their swords lethargic. Icy cold froze their enervated limbs. Then our commander cried with voice high-raised and eager look: "Father of the world, we follow you as Leader, and your angel. It is God, yes God, who with those flames levels the enemy lines. The whole sky gleams with squadrons of fire."

After[316] these words penetrated both armies, the one rushed madly into flight, and the other pressed on the fearful enemy with renewed strength. The second did not cease pursuing nor the first fleeing until black night with its cloudy darkness offered rest to us and cover to the enemy.

CHO.  Why then does the victor not bring back his troops?

JEPHTHA

*MESS.* Stay, you have not yet heard the outcome of the whole battle.

*CHO.* Does the enemy perhaps press with strength renewed?

*MESS.* Only if the dead shall acquire new strength; for God has forced the entire flower of that treacherous race to be harvested in a single battle. So the slain enemy in piles of corpses hold the position at which they stood, or strewn over the fields in ghastly carnage they feed the vultures. And our leader, with thought for the future, has ensured that no new war will break out afresh for many years; he has won peace even for descendants late-born. In victory he has swiftly borne his arms through the whole of Ammon's nation, and upturned twice six towns after destroying their walls. He has burnt their houses, executed their youth, ravaged their lands. Only feeble elders, slight children, women unfit for war wander over the desolate soil and lament their land's calamity.

CHORUS

O sun, ushering in golden light, regulating with swift return the changes of day, distributing the seasons over the world with your flame and wandering fire, at last after four times five years you pour your blessed rays on the descendants of Isaac now free.

Jephtha's right hand has shattered the ill-starred attacks of the proud enemy, has crushed the eager spirits of Ammon; the plunderer has become the plunder. It did not avail him to scatter winged arrows from his Scythian bow-strings. The grasping onset of his wheels, threatening with their bent scythes, the power of his horses, the thick lines of his brave soldiers did not shield him from God's oppression.

Now[361] you must learn and acknowledge this, faithless men. A stone or log is not God; neither is the sculpture achieved by a creative hand with the iron chisel, nor what the modeller fashions with supple hand when he counterfeits a human face with damp clay.

Our[368] God dwells aloft in the fiery citadels of the upper air. He is both Creator and Saviour of the world, powerful in his majesty. He is not readily seen, nor amenable to depict a clear self-image by mortal hand. He curbs the mad arrogance of kings, and with justice steers unholy vows and excessive hopes to an evil outcome. He lightens with immediate help innocent hearts

## JEPHTHA

oppressed with savage griefs. He raises the poor man from the dust and the guardian of the rank flock to the golden sceptre, and adorns the brows of shepherds with a royal diadem.

The[388] adorned fabric of the earth, under whatever part of the sky it lies, must acknowledge, worship and love him alone as Lord and God; whether it is the land which the rising sun strikes with fresh rays as it lies below, or the land which the sun towards midday scorches with fire brought closer, or the land which drinks the Tagus, renowned for its yellow waters, or the peoples who dwell in regions condemned to perennial snow.

Come[400] now, Hebrew women, bedeck your necks with golden jewels, and let your perfumed hair smell sweet with the scent of ambrosia. Come now, Hebrew women, adorn your heads with the choice gems of India, and sprinkle the earth far and wide with flowers of diverse colours. Are the clashing cymbals silent, do the harp and lyre refrain from playing a new hymn to our victorious lord? Is the sound of the perforated pipe not heard? Who is there to beat the ground with feet unfettered, joyfully to dissolve harsh cares with refined dancing and festive holiday? Let the leader of the flock stain the festive altars as sacrificial victim, and the smoky fragrance of fire breathe forth with the aromas of Arabia.

Do[421] you, daughter, offspring of our leader, hope of his great line, put on fine raiment, and joyfully grasp your returning father in devoted embrace. Iphis, now put on bright robes, twist back and tie up your curly locks. Listen, the din of warriors strikes our ears; it is he, it is your father himself at hand.

### JEPHTHA

Ruler of the world, one true God, unique deity of mercy, power and strength, harsh avenger but kindly father, fearsome to your own and harsh to your foes, gentle bearer of salvation to your friends, figure of dreadful anger yet willing to be appeased, warm in love yet goaded to wrath, merited ills of slavery have oppressed us, and we have paid a deserved penalty to wicked men for our wickedness. For we abandoned you, our king, advocate and God, father of the world and source of enduring good; we poured out foolish prayers to dumb rocks, and made empty vows to deaf logs. The confession induces shame; man who can grasp eternal wisdom and has a share in reason worships trunks innocent of sense, offers incense, though a living being, to a dead object, and though himself the craftsman fears his own creation.

So[448] we were abandoned for abandoning you. We paid the price by being subdued and crushed by evils when now Idumaea, now the forces of Palestine, now grim Ammon, now the Syrian polluted the inheritance and destiny of your race. Schooled by our ills, impelled at last by the mockery of our enemies, we reluctantly returned to you.

But[455] you, a God so kind and merciful, restrain the bridle of your just rage. You soften your anger, forget your hatred, and by your mercy restore your sons who had resigned their position through their own fault. As though it were insufficient to have pardoned the guilty for their wicked secession, you enhance them further with fresh triumphs, glories and victory. The enemy has departed stripped of arms, enervated, with bowstrings slack; corpses scattered over the whole plain hinder the flight of his war-chariots, and he who arrogantly ordered chains for Jerusalem is the food for birds. Carnage cloaks the fields, and the barbarian's blood raises the swollen waters.

This[469] is why, creator and mighty judge of the world, we mindfully, gladly and gratefully give and maintain thanks to you, and in prayer we shall sacrifice at your altars with victims according to ancestral ritual. We shall sing of you, God and father of our fathers, who proffered a safe route to our forbears through the swollen waters of the Red Sea, for on your command the massive expanse of the sea became sluggish, and laid aside its storms. The speedy waters compressed their course in motionless gaping; the glassy sea was suspended on both sides in walls of crystal, for it was bidden to afford a path.

Mindful[480] of the compact made with you, be pleased to receive in kindly fashion this vow of your servant. Though insignificant, it stems from a grateful heart and is freshly owed to you. The first thing to encounter me on my safe return at my house will be your welcome victim and will steep your altar with its blood, even though no victim can be counted equal to your kindnesses. But you must with good will consider this as the gift of a mindful heart. You both redeem your promises faithfully and rejoice that vows are faithfully paid to you; you practise your power against those who war on you, but practise clemency towards those who fear you. There is no other strength which earth, sky and hell obey.

IPHIS   JEPHTHA   SYMMACHUS   CHORUS

*IPH.* I am come forth. How glad and happy I am to see the

## JEPHTHA

face of my sire back with us! Father whom I must revere second only to God, allow me to enjoy your embrace. Why, father, do you turn your frowning eyes from me?

*JEPH.* Wretched am I.

*IPH.* May God divert this omen on the enemy!

*JEPH.* That is my wish too, but it rebounds on me.

*IPH.* Alas, what is this I hear?

*JEPH.* The most wretched father of a wretched daughter.

*IPH.* Woe is me, I tremble. Is the army safe?

*JEPH.* It is.

*IPH.* And you are victorious?

*JEPH.* That is so.

*IPH.* And your body undamaged by any wound?

*JEPH.* True.

*IPH.* Why then do you groan and sigh secretly from the heart's depths?

*JEPH.* You need not know the answer at the present time.

*IPH.* Alas for me! What sin have I committed against you, father, in my wretchedness?

*JEPH.* None; your father has sinned against you, poor girl.

*IPH.* There is certainly no sin committed against me of which I am aware, and even if there were, this ought not to trouble you; for children must endure with equanimity wrongs inflicted by parents.

*JEPH.* My daughter, you speak prudently and appropriately, and the more prudently you speak, the deeper the wound with which you expose my heart.

*IPH.* Father, whatever troubles your mind, forget it. Do not taint with your grief in any way the joys won through you for all the citizens, and allow your friends to enjoy your presence here.

*JEPH.* This presence here will breed for us an absence.

*IPH.* Perhaps war-dangers summon you back?

*JEPH.* A hazard sterner than war overhangs the house.

*IPH.* Can there be at home a danger sterner than war?

*JEPH.* I found salvation in war; at home I am undone.

*IPH.* Not so; both your family and your land are safe through you.

*JEPH.* True, and I owe thanks to God on that count.

*IPH.* And may you always owe it on this count!

*JEPH.* Yet I fear that this safety may not continue long.

*IPH.* So, father, while our affairs are now most favourable it is right to pray and pay our vows. We should not coax the deity with prayers when the fickle breeze of fortune blows against us, and then abandon ceremonies in thoughtless negligence when we are prosperous. The man who when secure has shown eagerness to win God's ready favour, can rely when adversity looms on the reward of a good conscience; he dares to pray of his own accord to the kindly deity, he pronounces his vows with greater equanimity, and with more certain hope takes thought for the future.

*JEPH.* I have for long been planning inwardly to do this very thing.

*IPH.* What hinders you?

*JEPH.* My daughter, leave this for me to take care of. Consider as your task what befits the spirit and years of a girl.

*IPH.* All that affects my father is within my province.

*JEPH.* Agreed. But meanwhile ensure that all within the house is in place, and indulge your father's wishes. Come back to us here a little later; you must attend the sacrifice directly.

*IPH.* It shall be so; I shall return. Poor me, what has changed my father's disposition towards his offspring? Not long ago none was kinder or a greater lover of his children than he. But now he is harsh, tetchy, grim, aggressive, still announcing on threatening face the disturbances of war. Whatever the cause, I greatly fear it. The one thing I cannot understand is that he says his grief is on my account, yet I can think of no sin by which I have offended my father.

What[560] a harsh fate the breed of women experiences when brought forth into the world! Though free of blame, they are bitten by the envious tooth of malevolent gossip. The fictions invented by the anger of the talkative servant, the lies uttered by the suspicious husband himself, or by malicious neighbours, are regarded as fact. I cannot control the suspicions of my sire; the safest remedy, I think, is enjoyment of an unspotted conscience.

*SYMM.* Your words are honest, daughter worthy of your victorious father, worthy of your chaste mother and your land. Though men's malevolence has invented a charge, God sees our hidden thoughts, and in his judgment the unspotted mind prevails. From him we must anticipate and beg the rewards of life once completed. But children must bear the ill done by a father, just or unjust. So indulge your father, and meanwhile return into the house. If rumour spreads any news, I shall get tidings here as I follow your father's footsteps, and then I shall inform you.

*CHO.* Friend Symmachus, you should certainly proceed to do this.

*SYMM.* This shall be done with care.

*CHO.* Now as best you can free the apprehensive girl of this fear. The long-standing rights of friendship demand this of you. It has been cultivated from the cradle, and has always continued with the single course of loyalty. Our land itself which owes its safety to Jephtha demands this.

*SYMM.* No need to tell me; leave it to my trust.

*CHO.* See it is done astutely. Delve deep and shake out the hidden recesses of his mind.

*SYMM.* Fear not; he will neither be able nor wish to hide his thoughts from me. I know the appropriate moment to enquire.

### CHORUS

Go, make your way successfully with happy end, and may he who beholds the hidden things of the heart in their innermost recesses both as witness and just judge favour your plans.

As[598] for you, most wicked malice, so bold at devising deceits, and condemning dear friends on feigned charges, and with malevolent gossip proceeding headlong to loose the compact of the sacred marriage-torch, you rejoice to arm loving fathers with the blinding poison of the tongue against their dear children; so may that witness and just judge of our hidden lives enclose and secrete you in the caverns of murky hell, so that wandering gossip may never come back to this abode. How much toiling will he remove when he removes you! From what grim cares will he deliver mortal hearts!

### SYMMACHUS   JEPHTHA   CHORUS

*SYMM.* Leader famed in arms, whatever is it that has suddenly transformed your former looks? What sadness disturbs your happy joys? Fear has vanished, the treacherous foe has paid the penalty, peace has been won for our native land. Since the state felicitates you on your victory, and our land raises your name to the stars in praise, sounding loud with festive song, ought not you who are the cause of the public joy to partake in the public happiness?

*JEPH.* How pleasant is the tranquillity of the lowest condition! I account him born under a lucky star who lives his life unknown in secure silence, far removed from the din of affairs.

*SYMM.* Nay, I shall account as blessed rather him for whom true excellence has won eternal fame, whom deserved glory has rescued from the darkness of the masses, separated from the idle mob, and hallows for future generations. But if a man surrenders himself to sleep and sloth, and passes his life in idleness like cattle, I count it a matter of indifference whether he is dead or lives a life more shrouded than death, for a like silence oppresses both.

So[642] since a kindly deity has bestowed on you all that he can give to a man—praises, distinctions, achievement, glory, victory—be grateful, and acknowledge the kindness of the deity. Do not defile your glorious achievements with mean observations, for nothing can be more welcome to God than a spirit mindful of a kindness conferred.

*JEPH.* Achievement, distinction, victory, honour, triumph, glory won in war sound splendid on the tongue. But look closer at things which seem pleasant at first sight, and you will realise that they are spiced with the sharp bitterness of bile. On no man has prosperous fortune shone in such a manner that hostile fortune does not match it on the balanced scales. A harsh alternation of fate tempers sadness with success and success with sadness. You count me blessed, measuring blessedness by empty brightness and the plaudits of the mob, but the most palpable wretchedness oppresses me.

*SYMM.* Why, imagine that a kindly fate was promising you all you desired; what still remains for you to long for? You who were rejected, exiled from your land, driven from home, thrust into the depths of loneliness, the owner of a poor cottage, have suddenly become rich as though in a dream, and yet you judge your own happiness unfairly, and complain. If you cannot endure a high fortune, you are petty-spirited; but if you cannot acknowledge the kindness of God, you are most worthy of the position you have vacated, and of that hut which you dwelt in earlier.

Men[672] seek the kingship by fire and sword, but the chief position has accrued to you without your even seeking it. Most men win victory at the price of their blood, the slaughter of their followers, and loss to the state; but you have won it by war without blood, without damage to your army, and without harm to yourself. You are the cause of our land's salvation, you inspire terror in the enemy, you are rich after being impoverished, free after being enslaved. You were lately of low rank, and now glorious in fame you strike high Olympus with your head; you were lately from the heart of the common folk, and now hold the chief place among the people. You lack nothing for blessedness in any way except a spirit large enough for so great a task and equal to your prosperity.

*JEPH.* My friend, in my view a common misapprehension possesses you. But if you saw clearly with the eyes of the mind how high estate is subject to great evils, you would pronounce as most wretched the condition of my affairs which you now address so vehemently with praise.

*SYMM.* Does it not virtually always happen through our fault and the vacillation of a troubled mind that we bear neither fortune impartially? The rich man praises the peace of the poor cottage, the deep silence undisturbed by the war-trumpet, sleep free of insomnia and wakefulness free of troubles. The poor man praises interminably gold, purple raiment, slaves, dependants, regal furniture and massive houses; he thinks that the rich alone are blessed. But if you assess each of the two conditions by its own weight, neither is free from every trouble.

Poverty[703] distresses the poor, and fear the rich; the rich man gets pleasure, the poor tranquillity. In both cases fate mingles the bitter with the joyful. But certainly we must consider best the lot which seasons many joys with few sadnesses; this is the lot which God's kindness has given to you, for it is crowned with distinction, praise, achievement and victory. Rejection of it I consider the act of a fool, refusal to acknowledge it the act of a traitor, and the inability to bear it with moderation a subhuman trait.

*JEPH.* In vain do you try to heal my wound with common remedies. This blow cannot be healed. It has come to rest in my innermost vitals, pressing deep into my living entrails. And my grief is all the more bitter because sin intensifies the damage and wretchedness the fault.

*SYMM.* Do state whatever it is before your friend, and do not fear to entrust it to loyal ears.

*JEPH.* Does any recollection of my vow occur to you?

*SYMM.* You mean the vow which you promised if the army were safe?

*JEPH.* You broach the very matter. If only I had been wiser and more cautious in the terms of the vow!

*SYMM.* I cannot call to mind what this mistake is.

*JEPH.* One which will destroy myself and my house.

*SYMM.* Can the offering of a victim destroy everyone?

*JEPH.* That victim is my daughter, the sole surviving hope of my family.

*SYMM.* Will you sacrifice her? What need commands it?

*JEPH.* Because she was the first to meet us on our return.

*SYMM.* What crime, I ask, has your daughter committed in this matter?

*JEPH.* Promised vows demand unflinching observance.

*SYMM.* Clearly this scruple afflicts your mind.

*JEPH.* It does indeed, and it cannot be torn from my heart until I am bloodied by a sacrilegious victim, and I, a wretch undone, shall undo my wretched kin, and shall pay the penalty appointed both for them and for myself.

But[737] do you, O King, who brandish the flashing thunderbolt, at whom earth, sky and hell tremble, if ever in ready obedience to your commands I have said or done any pleasing thing, hear my prayer and favourably aid my vow. I do not now demand proud victories and joyous plaudits. Restore the battles; let cruel Ammon charge against me and be victorious, and with a thousand blows demand my guilty life...

*CHO.* Alas for the transformation of swift-moving fate! How true it is that no happiness ever survives in unbroken continuity for men!

*JEPH.* ...Or as you split the sky with three-forked lightning, direct against me, this wicked and unholy slayer of my kin, a missile driven by a whirlwind of flame. Thrust me alive down into the depths of hell, for I am already a wrong-doer now, and if my life continues further I shall become more guilty with each day.

*SYMM.* So serious a step is not to be taken rashly while the mind is uncontrolled, disturbed by blinding confusion. Pull yourself together. Once passion subsides and the mind is free to listen to sound advice, you must decide the whole matter in detached fashion in the company of friends.

*JEPH.* Advice brings a remedy for doubtful issues. The man who consults others when there is no occasion for help adds stupidity of his own accord to his miseries.

*SYMM.* Remedies are always available while the matter is undecided.

*JEPH.* But only when the nature of the evil permits of healing.

*SYMM.* If fortune initially seems hard, there is no need to fall at once into mental despondency. No, I think you must take counsel all the more because of it. Often when something seems insoluble to one person, another copes with it easily. If matters which elicit poor advice turn out well, the fame will accrue to you; if they fall out badly, you are still not to blame. An act of folly prompted by a person of weight is virtually an act of sense.

But[773] if an invincible power or unavoidable fate bars the way out on every side, and the course of action recommended cannot develop, the advisers whom you have employed for consultation will approve, whatever the result. But if you carry through a novel plan without informing the others, the man who if asked for advice will approve, will be the first to condemn the outcome. He may know no remedies, but he wishes to be regarded as knowledgeable.

*CHO.* Do not despise one who offers good advice, for repentance usually accompanies a deed rashly performed.

### CHORUS

Though I shall recount sad and unwelcome tidings, and add griefs to griefs, I hold fast to my decision to reveal all things in sequence to the mother and the wretched daughter. Perhaps it will be possible to turn aside grim fate by advice or by entreaties.

Meanwhile[790] I am disposed to weep over the general fortune of mankind. Which shall I bewail first? Should it be the wretched father? He is bound by strong chains and held fast by a fault bereft of counsel, so that he believes that he can maintain piety only by impiety.

Or[797] should I lament the fate of the wretched girl? In the spring of the first flower of her tender years, after being raised for splendid hopes, she is not seized and snatched away by enemy warfare after the capture of our land, nor will a grim contagion sent from heaven destroy her; but her father will slay her, and as victim she will stain the grim altar. Set in the place of brute cattle, she will pour from her throat a warm wave of blood, her young limbs cut down by the steel—the limbs which no barbaric foe is to assail, and which the savagery of a mountain bear would not dare to rend with merciless teeth.

Though[811] her father was victorious, the poor girl will endure from him what she would not have endured even if the enemy had been victorious. Ye corpses of the enemy scattered here and there over the plain, if any feeling accrues to limbs stripped of life, rejoice and observe that the victor is demanding harsh punishment from himself.

Assuredly[818] this lot of ours has been imposed upon our lives, that sadness encroaches on happy fortune as darkness on sunlight, as harsh winter on balmy spring. There is no pleasure so uncompounded that griefs do not mar it with their foul bile. The treacherous fickleness of fate confounds human affairs with savage change. In the same way when the sea is placid with silent calm and lies motionless with tranquil waves, a whirlwind gathers a black storm and raises swollen waves to a massive height. On the one side the force of the ebbing tide, on the other the blasts of the wanton north-west wind snatch an unstable craft through the foaming seas.

This[833] is an image of our life spent amidst slaughter, brigandage, disorder and fears of death more oppressive than death. If any joy dawns, it swiftly flies away on the hastening breeze like the vanishing light of a fleeting flame in dry straw. Then columns of enduring grief approach, joined in unbroken chains.

JEPHTHA    PRIEST

*JEPH.* O sun, creator of the light of day, O ancestors, O all you men who have no part in sin, turn your faces far from this accursed sacrifice. Or do you, earth which is to drink in the innocent blood of the maiden, suck me into your open caverns and devour me in your boundless womb. As long as I can die in innocence, bury me anywhere. I do not refuse to enter hell itself, so long as I do not dwell in hell as slayer of my kin.

But[851] why do I mention hell? My hell is in my home. With what countenance will my wife, ravaged with floods of tears, entreat me? With what looks will my daughter gaze on me now that she is doomed to die? What prayers will she utter in pitiable tones with arms around my neck?

*PRIEST.* This grief often attends as companion of extreme ills when a wound rejects the hand of healing agents, or when a crime committed eschews all remedies. It lies in your own hand whether you are wretched or otherwise. It is open to you to choose whether you sacrifice your daughter or not; or to speak more truthfully, it is not an open choice unless one wishes to be wretched voluntarily.

How[863] is it open to you to carry through what our sacred mother nature forbids, what our love of kin struggles against, and what God loathes? Nature has implanted in our emotions the love of children first and foremost, nor does this feeling strike our human breasts alone. All creatures that swiftly swim through the deep sea, all that cleave the air with wings, all that the earth, mother of all, has brought to life in her womb, have these sacred feelings.

For[873] the perennial providence of the heavenly Father has instilled into the minds of men this force useful for rearing children, for controlling the general harmony of the world, and for ever renewing a fresh line of offspring. And so that he might implant this title more intimately in our minds, he desired to be called and to be a father. But it was not only by his own example but also by the example of beasts and birds and fish that he demonstrated the bonds of a father's love.

But[883] we, who ought to have a unique humanity to show allegiance to the title of man, are vastly inferior to the wild beasts in kindness. It is not enough for us to pollute our hands with sinning; we delight in attributing the sacrilegious deed to heaven. We pretend that God takes joy in bloody victims, a ritual which neither Egypt which does not know God nor Assyria uniquely devoted to false superstitions perpetrates.

How[892] much better that we keep our hands unspotted with blood, since we are sprung from unspotted parents and have been bidden chastely to offer unspotted sacrifices to God! Our God is not offered gory victims or the blood of cattle; but hearts defiled by no pollution, a mind refined by ingenuous truth, and a chaste conscience are to be offered to him.

JEPH. Why then do our sacred laws enjoin victims?

PRIEST. Not because God rejoices in the slaughter of a sacrificial sheep, or satiates his hunger with the flesh of a slain steer; rather he bids us harken to his warnings.

JEPH. Should we not fulfil vows which have been uttered?

PRIEST. Yes, but the law bids us utter only vows that are just.

JEPH. It would have been better initially to promise what our fathers' customs approve; but now the thing is done, and the law descended from heaven bids us fulfil what has been once vowed to God.

PRIEST. What law bids parents slay their children?

JEPH. The law which bade fulfilment of vows proclaimed.
PRIEST. Is it right to vow what it is sacrilege to fulfil?
JEPH. Rather, the greatest sacrilege is not to carry out vows.
PRIEST. Supposing you had vowed to burn our fathers' laws?
JEPH. No man of sound mind would proclaim such vows.
PRIEST. Why? Surely because they are at odds with sacred laws?
JEPH. That is so.
PRIEST. What then of the man who slaughters his children?
JEPH. It is not so much what is done as why one does it.
PRIEST. Do you consider it right to obey the deity's commands?
JEPH. Yes, but God ordered Abraham to slay his son.
PRIEST. And having commanded this, he also forbade him kill.
JEPH. Why then did he command it?
PRIEST. That Abraham's faith might be demonstrated to future generations.
JEPH. Why then did he forbid it?
PRIEST. Even from this episode he wished to show that obedience pleases him more than a sacrificial victim.
JEPH. Surely we must obey the holy deity?
PRIEST. Obviously.
JEPH. Does God bid us make vows?
PRIEST. Yes indeed.
JEPH. And he demands that vows be implemented?
PRIEST. He does.
JEPH. He rebukes the tardy and demands punishment from the faithless?
PRIEST. You have no excuse here by which you can defend your deed. He who binds himself to carry out unspeakable crime obeys without compulsion his own dreams and foolish feelings. So[933] whatever that vow of yours, cease to associate God with your cruelty. Do not believe that he who hates and loathes criminal and wicked rites performed under consecrated laws can be placated by the sin which he abominates. God's voice is the single, simple, self-consistent truth. What he has once ordained continues fixed and implanted on its unchangeable course, and cannot diverge in the slightest degree to left or right. One must train one's eyes on this one, true mark, and from that one law

fashion the strategy of one's life, for God has ordained that this be, as it were, a torch to guide our unsteady steps over ways made uncertain through blind wandering.

Since[947] you feel that you have rashly diverged far from this lamp, return now to the path before your wandering leads you further astray. If you think that foolish vows can be expiated by unspeakable sacrifices, you are misled; this cruelty will increase rather than remove your crime. Do not let wrong appearances deceive your mind. God spurns wicked vows as much as he takes joy in sacrifices duly offered. The man who ignites unhallowed fire at altars does not withdraw it unpunished, however devoted the zeal with which he was stirred.

So[958] do not despise this friendly advice, and cease to anger God in your wish to placate him. He rejoices in being worshipped not according to your decree but by the law, rite and customs which he approves.

*JEPH.* I have often found that men who seem to be the wisest and who claim that common folk are less knowledgeable than themselves usually possess the least true wisdom. None is more careless in preserving ancient ritual; none disregards sacraments more. The untaught and ignorant crowd holds fast to vows, and has no truck with deceit; it regards as ratified what it has once promised to God.

Hence[970] in my judgment wisdom nowadays spells nothing other than knowing how to screen one's guilt and put a fair complexion on most wicked deeds. But on the contrary the juster attitude would be to be free of guilt rather than to appear innocent or to clothe the trickery of a wicked mind with the covering of deceitful circumspection.

Therefore[977] if in future a man wants his children to be regarded as keen to embrace piety, he should not be eager to school them in letters more intensively than is right; for the more learned a man is in letters, the more unenthusiastic his zeal for the sacred rites.

*PRIEST.* Now in your turn, noble sir, if you have leisure hear how blinding ignorance deceives the over-trusting. He who defends himself by error commonly held does not, in my view, sin more excusably thereby.

That[986] Father of creation so great would never entrust this kingdom to such wicked manners that the unanimity of a depraved populace turns right into wrong, transforms good into evil. If the wheedling that coaxes tyrants should praise the worse course by changing the terms of what is right, it will not at once make honourable what the crowd regards as honourable. There is one undiluted form of the honourable, which neither the power of the tyrant nor the authority of the powerful will be able to water down or defile.

As[997] things are, the more ignorant a man from the common folk usually is, the more haughtily he arrogates the authority of pronouncing judgment in matters most uncertain; and (what is usually the mark of ignorance) with obstinate spirit he defends a belief once adopted. Meanwhile he does not weigh with just scrutiny whether his fast-held tenets are evil or right; but although his lack of vision is the most pronounced of the whole populace, the blind man accuses those with sight of blindness.

People[1006] like you are like the man whose entrails are ablaze and roasting with fever; he thinks that everything is bitter, and believes that he alone is sane when he is totally delirious. Your hearts too are clouded in black darkness, and you seek to give orders to those whom you should obey. Those by whose opinion you should be guided you compel to be your associates, and to run aground on rocks the ship which they propel undamaged by their own efforts.

True[1014] religion, true piety is not to worship God by a practice which you have self-deceivingly established for yourself, and not to slaughter any victims whatsoever in sacrifice, but those which the decrees of laws sent from heaven demand, and which ancestral custom approves.

*JEPH.* Whatever is performed with a sincere mind is welcome to God, and he always puts to our credit the gifts which issue from a pure heart. It is not gold but the spirit of the giver which the deity approves.

*PRIEST.* If the wickedness of an evil mind mars what is right, it does not follow that a foolish spirit straightens what is bent. What people like you call right, pure and honest are acts full of the most lunatic stupidity—if there can chance to be anything more stupid than to close one's eyes to the light of truth.

Next,[1029] having fallen into wilful blindness you seek praise in your wrongdoing by use of honourable labels. You abolish distinctions of all kinds when you decide that what is just and unjust, mean and honourable depends on the opinion of the fickle mob.

But[1034] if there is such validity in the opinions of fools that they forthwith convert the unjust into the just, the profane into the sacred, injustice into right, why should we not believe that they can also turn fire into water, water into fire, that they can change rocks into beams, can bring life back to the dead? Can they halt the swift movements of the seasons, and reverse the perennial changes in creation?

If[1042] however you think that these matters lie beyond the powers of men and are subject to the Creator alone, you must believe that the laws once revealed by him are equally or even more enduring and fixed, and that men have no rights against them. Even the last day which overhangs the world will not destroy his commands. The final fire will make heaven and earth, air and waters dissolve, but length of time will not detract a tittle from the law bestowed by God.

JEPH. If such is your pleasure, these matters I leave you to pursue, who delight in being regarded as the high-priests of wisdom. But I prefer foolish and simple truth to impious wisdom gleaming with deceit.

### CHORUS

Matron who among the daughters of Isaac personified a unique exemplar of a kindly lot, in what sudden destruction has harsh fortune drowned you! It has buried low the pride which almost touched the stars, and like a black storm has turned joys to bitter grief.

Alas,[1063] man can never properly establish what he is to seek or what to avoid at each hour! Who did not lately envy you, bravest of leaders? Unlimited success almost beyond your prayers had befallen you—the glory of a famed race, a chaste marriage, a daughter worthy of her father, and fame won by a strong right hand.

But[1071] now buried by the debris of sudden destruction you are worthy of the pity even of your enemies. As you seek to withdraw your vow, you fill the stars with wretched complaints. Assuredly the mist of error, and ignorance shrouded in foul darkness so bury the minds of men that none can descry the rays of unvarnished truth with the clear eyes of the mind, nor tread upon the right path of virtue unadorned. It is like being in malevolent light, where through remote windings of woodland hazardous he slaughters the daughter at whose death he stands boasting in the ostentation of his monstrous behaviour.

As[1185] he wrenches off the bars to her life, as he opens her side with his fierce sword and drains the breath lingering in the depths of her entrails, he needs no consolation though he seeks to appear to need it. He anticipates glory from the blood of his children, he balances the crime with an air of virtuousness, and he plumes himself with the glory of parricide. If you are so pricked with raging madness that you have thrown off the spirit of a parent to his children, allow a mother's kindness at any rate to love what it is the greatest crime to fail to love, to preserve what it is the greatest sacrilege to destroy, what it is worse than any parricide to have willingly betrayed, what it is more monstrous than the savagery of beasts to slay with one's own hand.

If[1200] our pledge of mutual love should be divided, we have not divided her on equal terms; for you can exploit or misuse the life or death of our daughter, but the griefs, sorrows, tears, sighs pour over her mother alone. You are harder than hard rock, or sprung from unseasoned timber or from rough flint-stones amidst the haunts of wild beasts, retaining no traces of our race and blood!

Has[1209] this executioner of his children emitted any groan to reveal grief as his daughter weeps, his wife sheds tears, and his kin shows sadness? My daughter, why do you not prostrate yourself before your father's feet? If you can achieve anything by entreaty or tears, soften his hard heart and break down his mind of steel!

IPH. Have pity, father. I beg you by this hand of yours which attained its vow and gained victory, by whatever merits I have deserved of you, by whatever pleasure you gained from me when I gripped you with my tiny hands and hung, a sweet burden, from your neck—abandon your harsh purpose towards your offspring, and forget this grim threat.

Or[1223] if on my part any sin has been committed against you, reveal it. Whatever fate looms, I shall bear it more lightly if I know that I am deservedly paying the penalty. Why do you avert your face? What wickedness have I done in my wretchedness that I must be accursed in my father's eyes, so that he cannot bear to gaze upon my face?

JEPH. Daughter, you have committed no crime. This is my impious deed, mine the entire crime, mine the rashness for which all undeserving you pay the penalty. Poor wretch, I in my wretchedness have destroyed with my heinous vow both you and myself. Would that I had been more circumspect in my words or less successful in battle, so that slain by an enemy hand amidst bands of brave men so numerous I could have anticipated by an honourable death the harbour of my wretchedness!

As[1238] it is, a life unwelcome preserves me as survivor so that I may continually behold fresh griefs. I swear to you, my daughter, by that impious sacred promise which I vowed against God's wishes, by the sum of my evils, and by the grievous recollection of your calamity, I would gladly surrender my life for you if your death could be redeemed by the substitution of mine. Do I seem in any sense more blessed than you?

*IPH*. No, you seem equally as or even more wretched than we.

*ST*. Since the influence of the girl upon her father is so meagre, a spouse asks this one final favour of her spouse: bid me die with her. If you love me, you can ascribe the death to me; if you hate me, to yourself. By my death deliver me from my griefs and free yourself from a nuisance.

*JEPH*. More than enough evil is perpetrated by the one slaughter.

*ST*. What virtuousness, what sense of right, what innocence! The ritual slayer of his daughter is afraid to sin!

*IPH*. Dearest mother, cease to shed tears. Cease your complaints, reproaches and rebukes. And do you, father, lay aside the worry which assails your troubled heart, and do not bandy words between you because of my death. Many things persuade me that grim necessity has forced this course on you against your will; your present sadness, your past kindness, my awareness of no wrong through which I should deserve death of a father.

So[1266] whatever the fate which necessity impels, I readily consent to suffer, and I gladly offer my life which I owe to my father and my land. I ask you, mother, for this final favour, and will demand nothing hereafter—do not on my account be angry with my father, nor cause friction. If the buried dead retain any recollection of the activities of the living, you must believe that my shade will be happy with nothing so much as the certainty that your lives are blessed and successful, and that no grief and bitterness wells over from me upon my parents, to whom I should render in my turn life's duties which I owe them, and pay the price of my rearing by supporting the feebleness of their old age.

*ST*. If this prayer can be dutiful and pious, I pray that Ammon may be our lord, and that Judaea may endure her former yoke. Though enslaved, you would certainly preserve your life, or at any rate you would not perish by an impious death. The arrogance of a mad enemy would have raged less oppressively against us than the victory of your father. By a strange and most wretched whim of fate it is my prayer to be enslaved, and disaster to be the conqueror. O fortune ever harsh towards us even now when you support us, at the price of what grievous tears of bitter sorrow did you loan us the brief enjoyment of happiness!

*IPH*. No, let the enemy rather pay just punishment. Let me, if I must, though innocent, bring expiation to the altar with my blood, and with one victim readily and gladly compensate for the slaughter of so many foes.

*JEPH*. My daughter, now at last to my grief I realise how foul, savage, and grim was the purpose I contrived in rashly orphaning myself of such an offspring. But unbidden I shall exact punishment of myself; for it is unjust that you, an innocent girl, should pay the penalty for my madness whilst I, the cause of your grief, survive. A jealous neighbourhood shall not lay it at my door that I, the murderer of my daughter, spared myself in the late period of my life, and that I won the popularity of base fame with the blood of children which cost me little.

But[1309] you, so blessed in this affection of yours for your land and father, must live on, for your young years are more deserving of further life. Let him who as father cannot requite you offer the recompense which he alone in virtue of his rank can justly repay to this noble nature.

*IPH*. Father, cease to contrive these delays, and to weaken my purpose with soft words. It is neither lawful nor just that you should perform my role. The vow demands me; so I gladly offer this life of mine to you my father and to my land. No day will demonstrate that I am unworthy of Jephtha's stock.

Come,[1320] bear me off, bid me be led away. Since I am vowed to death, a victim consecrated, I have cast off my love of life. All delay is oppressive. Dearest mother, I bid you now farewell, and you, ancestral house, in which I spent happy days, raised with gentle upbringing for noble expectations, and prepared for a splendid marriage.

You[1327] fates, you fates and ancestors now dead, receive indulgently my shade offered for the salvation of my land. And you, light of this day, the last light which my eyes shall absorb, farewell!

CHORUS

Praise and glory of the female sex, splendour of your noble race, maiden with a spirit truly manly, though the injustice of the fates has deprived you of your more serviceable years, and though the monstrous savagery of Fortune has plucked the blossom of your youthful life, your renown after death will add to your glory that portion of life of which chance has deprived you.

Where[1340] Phoebus among the furthest Indians raises the light of his ruddy fire, generations late-born will tell of you. He who drinks the waters of the furthest Nile, and he who does not fear to ride over the ice-bound Danube in his Sarmatian chariot will at some distant time sing how you, deterred by no sluggish fear of death, readily offered for your native land the years which nature bestowed on you.

You[1350] will for long be the sorrow and glory of our maidens. Those who have no part in marriage will sing for you repeatedly as the years come round a song of weeping with mournful lament.

But[1354] as for you, the disgrace of your age, so reluctant to offer your lives for your country, long forgetfulness will conceal and bury you in eternal shades of darkness. You are the shame of your race and a useless burden on your land, despised by the present generation and doomed to be unknown to the age to come.

STORGE   MESSENGER

*ST.* Tell me in my sad wretchedness whether all hope of salvation is lost.

*MESS.* Considering your unhappy fortunes, the worst has not befallen.

*ST.* If any blessing has accrued, it manifests the cruelty of Fortune's caress; she flavours the bitter poison with sweet honey. So reveal to me whatever evil you are concealing. My experience of and long practice in grief have grafted hard skin on my mind; fortune has left herself nothing by which she could harm me further. In store for me is tranquillity secure but melancholy.

*MESS.* Hear, then, briefly how the matter went. As the maiden now stood, an imminent victim, before the grim altar, her virginal modesty spread a crimson blush over her white countenance, for she was unaccustomed to gazing upon bands of men. It was as if a man were staining Indian ivory with crimson, or intermingling roses with snowy lilies.

But[1378] joined with her blushes a palpable force of unwavering confidence had suffused her face. Whilst others wept, she alone was dry-eyed as she stood with features relaxed, constant and untroubled about her fate. The tears which the maiden close to death contained the people did not contain. One was moved by the recent blessing of her father, and the removal of the yoke of slavery from the land, together with the deprivation of that most renowned family; another lamented the bitter change of fortune, the brief happiness purchased at the cost of long grief, and in times of joy the confidence which rarely endures. A third bewailed the bloom of her youth, her dear eyes like stars, her hair which rivalled gold, and a steadfastness of heart transcending her sex.

It[1393] chanced that nature had breathed over her a beauty more pleasing than her wont, as if she regarded the death of the noble heroine as worthy of a final gift. Just as the departing brightness of Phoebus is often more attractive as he slips into the Tartessian waters, just as the fragrance and colour of the rose capture the eyes more at the close of spring, so the maiden had stirred all present as she stood at the furthest threshold of fate, prepared for death and not like a coward numb with craven fear rejecting her end. She diverted and drew the eyes of the crowd upon herself as they stood astonished at the marvel, and she caused a melancholy silence to fall on all.

*ST.* Proceed further to tell the manner of the deed, and spare not a mother's ears. You can report nothing so grim that my mind does not pose before itself a grimmer scene. I have already anticipated everything.

*MESS.* Then that girl of manly spirit raised her eyes to the bright stars, and uttered a prayer from chaste lips, her voice unbroken by her evil fortunes: "Eternal Begetter of the universe, Father of men, now finally show mercy and pardon to the sin of your race, and receive this victim with gentle heart. But if you demand expiation of our madness, whatever the punishment our stubborn arrogance has deserved in abandoning you our Father, may this blood atone for it. I wish that I could shed this blood more often, and if the salvation of my parents and fellow-citizens lies in me, I wish that I could turn the force of your fury and anger repeatedly on myself with a thousand deaths. But why, priest, do you tremble?" For he with cold fear was shivering. "Draw near, and remove this life of mine from the light of day; loose the hindering barrier of my body. Discharge from the vow the people, my father and myself."

As[1428] she spoke these words, her father who for long had appeared bloodthirsty and more savage than a tigress, was suffused with tears and covered his eyes with his garment, and condemned both himself and his rash vow. The priest, overwhelmed with weeping, could scarcely loose the passage of her breath, and the hushed crowd was for long numb in sorrowful silence.

But[1435] when a way lay open for their voices, there was none of the usual groaning nor the din of grief and wailing customary at such times. Instead there was a confused din, a buzz from the assembly felicitating you and praising you as a woman who, amidst the hostile wounds of a harsh fate and happy gifts of a pandering fortune, was unique in the heights of both blessedness and utter misery. For though the blow has entered deep to your innermost bones, you have a great consolation in your great grief.

*ST.* This consolation is more painful than the ill itself; with its soft touch it irritates the long-standing sore. It renews continually the recollection of bitter grief, and it forces the wound which had closed over to break open afresh. The braver the spirit with which my daughter bore her death, the sorer the anguish which gnaws my heart.

# BAPTISTES
## SIVE
## CALUMNIA
## TRAGOEDIA
### AUCTORE
### GEORGIO BUCHANANO SCOTO

# GEORGIUS BUCHANANUS IACOBO SEXTO SCOTORUM REGI
## S. P. D.

Cum omnes mei libelli, postquam tibi erudiendo sum appositus, ad te familiariter accedunt salutant confabulantur et in tuae clientelae umbra conquiescunt, tum hic meus BAPTISTES pluribus de causis tui nominis patrocinium audentius sibi poscere videtur; quod meus quamquam abortivus tamen primus est foetus, et adulescentes a vulgari fabularum scaenicarum consuetudine ad imitationem antiquitatis provocet, et ad pietatis studium, quod tum ubique fere exagitabatur, animos excitare pro virili contendat. illud autem peculiarius ad te videri potest spectare, quod tyrannorum cruciatus et, cum florere maxime videntur, miserias dilucide exponat. quod te nunc intellegere non conducibile modo sed etiam necessarium existimo, ut mature odisse incipias quod tibi semper est fugiendum. volo etiam hunc libellum apud posteros testem fore, si quid aliquando pravis consultoribus impulsus vel regni licentia rectam educationem superante secus committas, non praeceptoribus sed tibi, qui eis recte monentibus non sis obsecutus, id vitio vertendum esse. det dominus meliora, et, quod est apud tuum Sallustium, tibi bene facere ex consuetudine in naturam vertat. quod equidem cum multis et spero et opto. vale.

Sterlino, ad Kalend. Novembres. 1576.

# PERSONAE

Prologus

Malchus Pharisaeus

Gamaliel Pharisaeus

Ioannes Baptista

Chorus Iudaeorum

Herodes Rex

Herodias Regina

Reginae filia

Nuntius

# PROLOGUS

Veteres poetae fabulantur Protea
quendam fuisse, in omnes qui se verteret
formas nec ullis contineri vinculis
posset, liquentes nunc in undas dum fluit,
nunc flamma stridet, nunc ferus rugit leo, 5
viret arbor, horret ursus, anguis sibilat,
in cuncta rerum transiens miracula.
at ego profecto fabulam istam comperi
longe Sibyllae veriorem oraculis.
nam quotquot homines video, tot me Proteos 10
videre vultus credo qui sumant novos
seseque vertant in figuras quaslibet,
subiecta quorum maxime calumniis
fortuna semper scaenici est spectaculi.
nam si vetustam fabulam quis proferat, 15
turbant molesti, tussiunt et nauseant.
at si novam quis attulit, tum protinus
vetera requirunt comprobant laudant amant.
illiberali respuunt fastidio
nova et, priusquam noscere queant, exigunt, 20
recteque dicta interpretationibus
vitiant malignis, omnia in peius trahunt;
ipsique somno dediti ac ignaviae,
vacui laboris invident laboribus
aliorum, et omnem collocant operam suam 25
ut deprehendant quod queant reprehendere.
si quis sit error, antevortunt Lyncea
visu, notaque perlinunt censoria;
bene dicta surdis auribus praetervolant.
horum severa supercilia nihil moror 30
tristemque vultus taetrici arrogantiam.
at si quis adsit aestimator candidus
qui puriores promoventi litteras

2 in . . . verteret *1577:* qui se in omnes verteret *R*

studeat benignus et favore sublevet,
35  et (quando ab omni parte sincerum nihil
humana gignit mens) levibus erroribus
ignoscat, illi fabulam afferimus novam
aut potius historiam vetustam interpolem:
Baptista quondam ut, regia libidine
40  et invidorum subdolis calumniis
oppressus, indignam innocens subiit necem.
porro vocare fabulam veterem aut novam
per me licebit cuique pro arbitrio suo.
nam si vetusta est ante multa saecula
45  res gesta, veteres inter haec censebitur;
sin quod recenti memoria viget novum
existimemus, haec erit prorsus nova.
nam donec hominum genus erit, semper novae
fraudes novaeque suppetent calumniae,
50  livorque semper improbus premet probos;
vis iura vincet, fucus innocentiam.

MALCHUS  GAMALIEL *Rabini,*  CHORUS

*MAL.*   Misera senectus et supremi spiritus
propinqua meta fataque infelicia,
in hosne vitae longioris terminum
55  tribuistis usus, serviente ut patria
polluta templa cernerem nefarie,
profana sacra mixta? vidi impervii
arcana fani fracta, sacrum postibus
aurum revulsum. quicquid aut Gabinii
60  cupido rapere potuit aut Antonii
haurire luxus, periit, ac ludibrio
etiam Cleopatrae fuimus, infandum, gulae.
ac ne deesset parte ab ulla indignitas,
rex, Antipatri Semiarabis pronepos,
65  crudele sceptrum saevus Herodes gerit.
Iudaea Idumae servit, Arabarchae Sion,
Solyma profano, populus impio dei.
tot sortis inter saevientis vulnera,
in servitute quamlibet gravi, tamen
70  scintilla quaedam dignitatis pristinae
adhuc supererat, disciplinae et patriae

vel qualecumque specimen, ipsis hostibus
etiam verendum; coeperat victor ferox
et purpuratae non minima pars curiae
honore leges prosequi Iudaicas.  75
hac recreati spe caput vix tollere
fessi miseriis coeperamus, cum nefas
ortum repente est, unde nullius mali
metus imminebat. ecce Baptistes novus,
non e profanis editus parentibus  80
interque cultus educatus exteros,
sed gente noster, genere Levites, deo
primis dicatus usque ab incunabulis,
pontificis ipse natus, ipse pontifex
brevi futurus, ni cupitae gloriae  85
fructus acerbos rapere mallet quam suo
maturam honoris legere messem in tempore.
is ergo ruris devii solos colens
solus recessus, sanctitatis taetricae
vulgus fefellit imperitum imagine.  90
hirto capillo, terga opertus pellibus,
victu ferino, et id genus praestigiis
in se ora vertit omnium. plebs credere
vatem repente redditum mundo novum.
et iam sequacis ille vulgi exercitum  95
traduxit ad se, iam relictis urbibus
hunc populus unum suspicit, proceres colunt,
reges verentur. ille stolidae insania
plebis superbus, alter ut Moses nova
dat iura. lymphis expiare crimina,  100
adulterare ritibus leges novis
audet vetustas. ut furore facilius
vulgi fruatur, omnibus probris patres
lacerat, secundis plebis usus auribus.
quod si furentis insolenti audacia  105
latronis huius nemo se conatibus
opponat, illa celebris orbi sanctitas
brevi peribit, immo perit, immo periit.
*GAM.*   Professionem nil temere nostram decet
statuere; mites lenitas decet patres.  110
iuvenum temeritati dari venia potest;

102  furore *1577, R:*   favore *1609*

        at nulla nostram poterit excusatio
        velare culpam. paululum da irae locum;
        residat impetus et dolor deferveat.
115     *MAL.*   Et tu, Gamaliel, hic sacrilegus quae facit
        tua, ut videtur, approbas sententia.
        *GAM.*   O Malche Malche, nec probo aut damno prius
        quam quale quodque sit sciam. quod vatem ad hunc
        spectat, vir adeo, quantum ego audio, malus
120     non est nec odio sic premendus publico.
        *MAL.*   O sidera o caelum o solum! huic etiam viro
        non deest patronus, esse qui malum neget.
        *GAM.*   Qui vitia carpit, qui docet mores bonos,
        praeitque primus quam indicat aliis viam,
125     hunc esse mihi persuadeas malum virum?
        *MAL.*   Qui iura spernit, qui docet sectas novas
        novosque ritus, qui petit conviciis
        populi magistros, pontificibus detrahit,
        hunc esse mihi persuadeas bonum virum?
130     *GAM.*   Si in nos severi et taetrici aeque iudices
        essemus, aliis quam sumus saepe asperi,
        minus paterent publicis conviciis
        flagitia nostra. blandiamur quamlibet
        nobis, beati praedicemur, caelites
135     vulgo putemur integri casti pii;
        at nemo nostrum maximis vitiis vacat.
        *MAL.*   Ut haec, Gamaliel, vera sint, num cuilibet
        e plebe fas est praesuli male dicere?
        plebs audiat, plebs pareat, sit sobria,
140     iniecta frena non recuset. qui praeest,
        plebs si quid erret, eam reducat in viam.
        lex ipse sibi sit; si quid autem erraverit,
        est qui scelestum cernat et plectat deus.
        *GAM.*   Et tibi videtur aequa lex haec? *MAL.* Maxime.
145     *GAM.*   Quinam? *MAL.* Quia propria est plebis ignorantia
        error temeritas imperitia caecitas.
        *GAM.*   E plebe media saepe deprehenderis
        qui principum non cesserit prudentiae.
        *MAL.*   Quin ergo cathedra cedimus opilionibus?
150     *GAM.*   Opilio Moses, opilio David fuit.
        *MAL.*   Eos erudivit cuncta spiritus dei.
        151 eos *1577:*   hos R *dubitanter*

*GAM.* Hunc poterit idem qui erudiit illos deus.
*MAL.* Nobis relictis erudiet illum deus?
*GAM.* Non sceptra spectat, non parentum stemmata,
decusve formae aut regias opes deus, 155
polluta nullo corda sed contagio
crudelitatis, fraudis et libidinis;
hoc ille templo spiritus capitur sacer.
*MAL.* Equidem, Gamaliel, fatear ut verum, mihi
videre pridem sacrilegam hanc sectam tua 160
sententia probare. non possum amplius
celare tacitus cum tuis maioribus
indigna facias. qui tueri debeas
auctoritatem maxime unus omnium
nostram, repugnas maxime, idque in gratiam 165
iuvenis furentis. per deum, rogo, edoce
qua spe ista tentas? aut quid hinc captas lucri?
forte ille honores aut opes dabit tibi
qui dignitatem funditus nostri ordinis
evertit omnem, nosque ad inopiam vocat? 170
*GAM.* O Malche, vero procul aberras a scopo,
nostram tueri dignitatem si putes
nos posse fastu viribus superbia.
non haec parentes ratio nostros extulit.
*MAL.* Vetusta veteres, nostra nos magis decent; 175
suique vivat quisque more saeculi.
*GAM.* Quin potius omnes bona bonos semper decent.
*MAL.* Si quid paterni spiritus nobis foret . . .
*GAM.* Et nos paternis viveremus moribus.
*MAL.* . . . poenas luisset morte nebulo hic, non minis. 180
*GAM.* Aliena nostro ab ordine est crudelitas.
*MAL.* Quicquid deo praestatur, id sanctum et pium est.
*GAM.* Morti immerentes impia est pietas dare.
*MAL.* Hunc immerentem, cuncta qui evertit, vocas?
*GAM.* Si peccat ille, quin palam redarguis? 185
quin lumen ingenii exseris illic tui?
rudem peritus, doctus indoctum, senex
aggredere iuvenem. fors reduces in viam,
et tibi apud omnes comparabis gloriam.
*MAL.* Curanda non est ista plaga molliter, 190
sed fune, ferro et igne, vel si quid scias
quod fune, ferro et igne sit crudelius.

*GAM.*   Sit ille qualem dicis aut peior etiam
si vis, dare unum te tamen decet tibi,
ut ante moneas hominem amice et leniter,
ne malle quisquam praecipitare te putet
dubium salutis, dexteram quam tendere
iam pessum eunti. plurimum interest tua
ad famam ut omnes, invidi etiam, intelligant
servare te omnes velle, perdere neminem
nisi obstinata mente qui praeceps ruat.
unum oro saltem, te priusquam longius
abducat ira, cogita quid adsequi
hac obstinata pertinacia queas.
*MAL.*   Nempe illud, hostem ut opprimam, soler bonos,
dubiosque firmem, et impudentes terream,
legesque patris hoc cruore sanciam.
*GAM.*   Quin potius illud adsequere, ut omnibus
grassatus esse viribus tyrannidis
credare, sanctum donec opprimeres virum,
ratione quem non potueris convincere.
*MAL.*   Sit sanctus ille, sit gravis quantumlibet,
divinus illum spiritus non dirigit
quando instituta prisca patrum neglegit.
et quando apud vos nil reperio praesidi,
contra ruinam regium auxilium petam.
*CHO.*   Recte Gamaliel admonet me iudice,
et tu monenti obtempera. sed consili
recti hostis ira mentis aciem obnubilat,
auremque monitis obstruit salubribus.
*GAM.*   Ille abiit ira incensus et fastu tumens.
ego quod licebat sedulo pro viribus
monui furentem, spiritus nixus feros
lenire verbis mollibus; fidum dedi
consilium. at ille tantum abest ut gratiam
ingratus habeat, etiam ut oderit bene
de se merentem. vulgo ita modo vivitur,
nostrique coetus vitium id est vel maximum,
qui sanctitatis plebem imagine fallimus,
praecepta tuto liceat ut spernere dei.
contra instituta nostra si quid audeas,

198 tua *1577:*   tuam *R*
221 tumens *R*:   timens *1577*

conamur auro evertere adversarios,
tollere veneno subditisque testibus
opprimere. falsis regias rumoribus
implemus aures; quicquid animum offenderit, 235
rumore falso ulciscimur. et incendimus
animum furore turbidum et calumniis
armamus irae saevientis impetum.
nullius ille nunc memor modestiae
graditur ad aulam. comminiscetur novas 240
sectas oriri, sacra patrum deseri,
auctoritatem regiam ludibrio
patere, demum quicquid illi commodum est,
honesta sceleri nomina obtendens suo.
his si moveri senserit regem parum, 245
inveniet aliud saevius telum. in caput
iurata regis clamitabit agmina,
secreta fieri colloquia, nefarium
facinus parari, consilia clam concoqui,
coetus coire nocte, privatas opes 250
per factiones impias augescere.
haec ille finget aut atrociora, ut est
animi impotentis, barbaraeque iugiter
crudelitatis auctor. haec in regias
stillabit aures toxica ingenii sui. 255
hoc adeo cunctis paene semper regibus
commune vitium, facile delatoribus
praebere sese. quo quid est crudelius
fictum, facilius creditur. vanos metus
fingunt sibi ipsi; mobilis famae levem 260
sequuntur auram. qui fideliter monet,
timidus habetur, languidus torpens hebes.
virtutis olim vertimus iam nomina,
virtute nulla splendidi; sed splendidis
titulis superbi fallimus vulgus rude. 265
quod ad prophetam spectat hunc, modestius
se noster utinam gereret ordo et cautius!
si missus huc est ille consilio dei,
humana poterit nulla vis obsistere;
sin fraude tectum comminiscitur nefas, 270
sese ipse gladio subito confodiet suo.
interpretetur quisque pro ingenio ut libet;

si quis sequatur hic meam sententiam,
cruore puras servet innocuo manus
275 nec temere sancti prodigus sit sanguinis,
ne, quae statuimus in alios crudeliter
exempla, recidant postea in nostrum caput.
immanitatis non sat Herodes habet
ni facibus irae subditis accreverit
280 animi furentis impotens crudelitas?

CHORUS

Quanta mortales latebris opacis
nox tegit mentes! quibus in tenebris
degimus lapsu celeri fugacis
    tempora vitae!
285 occulit falsus pudor impudentem,
impium celat pietatis umbra,
turbidi vultu simulant quieta,
    vera dolosi.
qui fuit tristi gravitate vultus,
290 unicum vitae specimen modestae,
aestuat praeceps furiis et atrox
    fervet in iras.
qualis Aetnaeis vapor e caminis
saxa convolvit celeri rotatu,
295 qualis arentem coquit in favillam
    flamma Vesevum,
talis hunc caecus furor ultionis
cogit in vatem ruere innocentem,
ut truci nudam male veritatem
300     crimine vexet.
tu mali tanti genetrix, cupido
gloriae vano tumefacta fastu,
lausque fucati specie superne
    splendida honesti,
305 mentis ut regnum semel occupasti,
fascinas blandis animos venenis,
et relegata ratione turbas
    pectoris aulam.
te fugit verum pietas pudorque,

296 flamma Vesevum *1579, R*: flammave saevum *1577*

te fides, et quae melioris aevi 310
hospes infames vitiis reliquit
   ultima terras.
si quis o, frontis nebulis remotis,
artifex nudas daret intueri
pectoris curas, penitus revelans 315
abditae caecum penetrale mentis,
cerneres miris variata formis
monstra non magno stabulare in antro
plura quam terris ferat in remotis
Nilus et Ganges, Libyeque saevis 320
feta portentis, latebrisque nigris
   Caucasus horrens.
non ibi tigris rabies cruentae
deesset aut fulvae feritas leaenae,
non sitim nulla saturata strage 325
dira saevorum ingluvies luporum,
nec venenata basiliscus aura
pestifer, longumque ferens soporem
aspis, et caudae metuendus uncae
scorpius telo, lacrimisque fictis 330
personans seram crocodilus algam,
nec doli vulpis, Phariaeque fallax
   ludus hyaenae.
ficta crudeles pietas tyrannos,
impios mores stola fimbriata 335
celat. in panno tenui recondit
nuda se virtus, tuguri sub umbra
rustici; nec se titulis superbis
vendit, insanosque fori tumultus
ridet et plausus popularis aurae, 340
nec cliens magni foribus patroni
adsidet. vitae tacitos beatae
rure secreto sibi nota tantum
   exigit annos.

REGINA HERODES

*REG.* Tu lentus usque auctoritatem regiam 345
labare nondum sentis, in tuum caput

323 ibi *1577*: tibi *1615*

nondum parari caecus insidias vides.
nam concitator iste vulgi si alterum
supersit annum, vincla carcerem cruces
350   frustra mineris. iam suas circumspicit
vires superbus, prosequentum iam grege
obscurat aulae regiae satellites.
    *HER*.   A turba inermi quod times periculum?
    *REG*.   Secreta si conventicula fieri sinas,
355   a genere nullo non timendum existimes.
    *HER*.   At hic ruentem sponte populum ad se docet.
    *REG*.   Magis timenda est fusa late factio.
    *HER*.   Crimen refellit istud hominis sanctitas.
    *REG*.   Hoc tecta velo saepe flagitia latent.
360   *HER*.   A purpuratis vis timenda est satrapis.
    *REG*.   Et a severis fraus timenda hypocritis.
    *HER*.   Inops inermis, unda cui sedat sitim,
dat silva victum, terra gramineum torum,
quem cogitare poterit is sceptris dolum?
365   *REG*.   Vides amiculum, et cibum et potum vides,
at quod reclusum pectore gerit non vides.
    *HER*.   Condicio regum misera, si miseros timet.
    *REG*.   Si nil timendo praeda fit, miserrima.
    *HER*.   Quid ergo tutum iam supererit regibus?
370   *REG*.   Omnia, quieti si quod obstat auferant.
    *HER*.   Nempe hoc tyrannus interest regi bono;
hic servat hostes, hostis ille civium est.
    *REG*.   Utrumque durum est, et perire et perdere;
sed si eligendum est, praestat hostem perdere.
375   *HER*.   Cum non necesse est alterum, utrumque miserum est.
    *REG*.   Tanto in tumultu nihil agendum est aspere
cum concitatur mobilis vulgi furor,
leges religio auctoritasque principis
contempta plebi est infimae ludibrio?
380   cave lenitatis falsa species avocet
tibi mentem ab aequo. quae videtur lenitas
propius tuenti summa erit crudelitas.
dum parcis uni factioso et perdito,
is perditum omnes, in caput quos hic tuum
385   armare satagit. finge fieri, quod fore

349 carcerem *1577, R*:  carceres *1621*

108

tandem necesse est, concitari mobile
ad arma vulgus, cuncta passim lugubri
ardere bello, vasta linqui praedia,
urbes cremari, virgines per vim rapi,
manusque dubia conseri victoria; 390
cum frena legum ruperit licentia,
damnabis istam sero tum clementiam.
atque ecce coram pestis et mali caput.
hic censor ille est. hunc roga; plura audies,
ni fallor, ab eo, fama quam vulgaverit. 395
nec miror esse sceptra qui spernant tua,
quando ipse pravos lenitate provocas.
*HER.* Cum multa possis, facere viribus modum
regum bonorum est. *REG.* Itane? iam sceptris modum
hic faciet? huius regnum habendum arbitrio est? 400
si regis esset animus in te . . . *HER.* Quin abis?
mihi haec relinque. *REG.* Quin abeo, ne denuo
in os ut ante contumelias feram.
regina inulta quando cedit infimis,
quae spes fovebit aequitatis ceteros? 405

HERODES IOANNES CHORUS

*HER.* Iamne abiit? abiit. hoc agamus interim.
non est quod id te moveat aut novum putes,
si laesa mulier nobilis dives potens,
regina denique, gravius aequo irascitur.
vel ipse testis esse poteris optimus 410
quantum saluti faverim semper tuae.
namque universae plebis odium te petit
et ad luendas flagitat poenas reum;
dolentque proceres et sacerdotes fremunt.
atque adeo quid sit quod querelam publicam 415
incendat, edam breviter. omnes ordines
laceras maledicis contionibus palam,
vulgusque veterum decipis legum rude
letale spargens dogmatis virus novi,
et turbulentis vocibus regni statum 420
tranquillitatemque labefactas publicam;
parere prohibes milites duci suo,
parere populum Caesari, vulgo nova

dum regna spondes. liberos iugo extero
425  fore polliceris speque vana concitas,
gentem rebellem nec sinis quiescere,
et calamitatum ceu tulissemus parum,
Romana demens arma rursus provocas.
nec dubito quid sis ausus absens, cum palam
430  mihi impudicas exprobraris nuptias,
et odia populi nixus in me accendere,
fratremque mecum proelio committere
tentaris, in te quod erat. ac velut parum
scelerum patrasses, ausus omnia in omnium
435  pariter salutem, bella iam caelo paras
et sacra, quibus hoc hactenus regnum stetit,
abolere tentas. haec populus omnis fremit,
lentumque legum me queruntur vindicem
patriarum. at in te durius nihil tamen
440  a me profectum est, et modo quicquid favor
iudicis amici et benevoli poterit dare,
tribuetur a me liberaliter tibi.
neque enim tyrannum genuit avidum sanguinis
vestri pater me Assyrius aut Aegyptius,
445  et patria et altrix et parens eadem mihi
vobisque terra est. infima quoties perit
de plebe quisquam, corporis membrum mei
toties revelli existimo, meus cruor
mitti videtur. facilem et aequum iudicem
450  Herodem habebis; si refellere cetera
obiecta poteris, quicquid in me dixeris
olim meosque, gratiam facio tibi.
tu teste populo intelliges iniuriam
neglegere propriam, persequi me publicam.
455  utinam ipse reliqua diluas sic crimina,
severitatis ut mihi nullam tua
occasionem linquat innocentia!
CHO.   Hac perge carus esse; vives posteris
clarus. nec auro nec catervis militum
460  tam crede regna tuta quam quae caritas
et aequitate parta defendit fides.
IO.   Tenenda populi frena cui credit deus,
audire oportet multa, cuncta credere
necesse non est. quaestus invidia favor

timor dolorque saepe vera supprimunt. 465
e plebe si quis aut patrum inclementius
me credit in se prolocutum quidpiam,
vitam necesse est arguat prius suam
orationem quam meam culpet. mea
haec ratio semper fuit, uti reprehenderem 470
delicta publica publice. occulte nihil
facio doceove; non latebras aucupor
caecas, nec homines sed vitia redarguo.
cum me rogarent milites quonam modo
servire possent pariter et regi et deo, 475
pulsare vetui, rapere, vim facere, dolo
circumvenire improvidos; componere
cupidinem iussi ad modum stipendii.
nec spem novarum praedico rerum, nisi
quam vos prophetis ex vetustis creditis 480
mecum. nec unus interim e tot milibus,
auctore me qui principem contempserit,
profertur. ista, sive fama rettulit
seu finxit ira caeca dum praeceps furit
studio nocendi, nuda facile veritas 485
per se refellet. sacra quam pie colam
et instituta vetera, nullum certius
indicium opinor quam meorum criminum
praeclarus index quod palam non prodeat,
clam murmuret ubi facile fit fictis locus. 490
quod te negavi posse fratris coniugem
habere iure, id ipse tecum cogita,
utrum placere tibi sit aequius an deo.
atque utinam is animus omnibus itidem foret
quicumque regum sese amicitiae dicant, 495
ut vera malint proloqui ac salubria
quam blanda damno mox futura. quot malis
praeclusus aditus esset et molestiis!
ego si quid olim liberius ac verius
dixi, tu, ut aequum est aequitatis vindicem, 500
aequi bonique bonus et aequus consule;
tuaeque fines hos statue potentiae,
mensura legum quos tibi praescripserit.

475  possent *R*   possem *1577*

quod ius in alios hic habes, in te deus
aliosque reges omnium rex obtinet.
proinde quicquid de capite statues meo,
statuere id ipsum crede de tuo deum.
*HER.* Cum in astra venies, loquere tum caelestia;
terrena iura patere dum terram coles.
*IO.* Terrena vereor regna, pareo regibus;
aeterna patriam regna puto, regem colo.
*HER.* Res ipsa clamat regibus quam pareas,
parere regem qui tuis vis legibus.
*IO.* Si ferre leges mihi liceat, edicerem
parere populos regibus, reges deo.
*HER.* Sat litigatum est. rursus hunc abducite.
perplexa res est. donec cuncta certius
comperta pateant, stat nihil decernere.
*CHO.* Qui de tyranni oratione se autumat
perspicere mentis posse sensus abditos,
ne turbido se credere speculo sciat.
utinam secundet cuncta caelestis parens!
sed ominari metuit animus quae timet.
*HER.* Fortuna regum quam misera sit et anxia,
nec fando poterit explicare oratio
nec cogitando mentis acies adsequi.
nos esse vulgus liberos solos putat,
solos beatos, quos egestas obsidet,
formido cruciat, misera servitus premit.
quodcumque populus diligit cupit timet,
audet fateri libere; procul metu
fruitur modestis opibus. at nobis foris
persona honesta est induenda; cogimur
vultu benigno humaniter promittere,
palam profari iusta, ficto pectore
differre bilem, supprimere odia in suum
tempus, minari maxime cum maximae
causae timoris anxium pectus premunt.
spernit modestum principem plebs, asperum
odere. vulgo serviendum est mobili
et imperandum. nil meo arbitrio gero.
hunc si prophetam perdo, populum offendero;
si servo, regno consulo parum meo.
quid ergo agendum est? idne dubium est? imperi

habenda ratio est; ipse mihi sum proximus.　545
si ob sceptra populo serviendum est, stultius
quid esse poterit regna quam pessum dare,
placere vulgo dum studes? plebs gaudia
irasque temere sumit et temere abicit.
nunc stat cruore auctoritatem regiam　550
stabilire. vulgus facile post placabitur.
si serpere malum latius praesens sino,
remedia vincet. ausus est videlicet
mihi impudicas exprobrare nuptias
in os; id illi impune si permisero,　555
non stabit illic hominis impudentia.
iam sceptra leges ad suas flecti volet,
iam vincla captis induet, iam non regi
sed regere cupiet, iura regibus dabit,
confundet imis summa. gliscenti malo　560
statim medendum est; antequam crescat, recens
flamma opprimenda est. contumelias novas,
veterem ferendo, provocas, iniuriam.
populo secundo si expetere poenas queam,
populi faventis gratiam non neglegam;　565
si nequeo, regno cuncta stat postponere.
quid Malchus iste garriat de legibus,
quas curiosas quaestiones litibus
inexplicatis iactet, id nihil mea
referre credo, modo populus unam hanc sciat　570
legem tenendam, praeter ut leges mihi
licere quidvis esse legitimum putet.

## CHORUS

O spatiosi conditor orbis,
cuius trepidant omnia nutum,
caelum nitidis ignibus aptum,　575
tellus vario florida cultu,
tumidum refluis aestibus aequor,
nonne ad nostras pertulit aures
fama prioris conscia saecli
aevi splendida facta prioris?　580
cum tu validae robore dextrae
auro atque opibus regna superba

ipsa exstinxti a stirpe revellens,
illorum ut nos agro insereres,
585 agro haud ense aut iaculis nostris
aut consilio vique parato.
sed nos caeli favor omnipotens
per fera tutos agmina duxit.
non tu rex ille Isacidarum,
590 non tu gentis deus Hebraeae?
cuius ductu perfida castra
proculcavimus, hoste perempto.
non confisi robore nostro
sed duce et auspice te, praeclaras
595 saepe retulimus patriae palmas.
numquid penitus deseris, olim,
genitor, populum tibi dilectum?
numquid fabula linquimur hosti?
spreta est pietas, religio iacet,
600 fraus purpurea regnat in aula;
populus tamquam victima sanctus
dat pia saevae colla securi.
vates pereunt ense tyranni.
nostris gaudent luctibus hostes.
605 et pietatis sub praetextu
meriti poenas regna gubernant;
meritos regnum poena coercet.
exsurge, tuo populo fer opem,
exsurge, parens optime, et hosti
610 da te talem cernere qualem
te viderunt aequore patres
Rubro Pharios mergere currus;
qualem vatis fatidici olim
te puer oculis vidit apertis
615 dantem igniferis frena quadrigis
totis flammas spargere campis.
te caligine pulsa erroris
humanae qui lumina mentis
obruta caeca nube recondit,
620 et quae primo sole tepescit
tellus, et quae mergere ponto
cernit rutilae lumina flammae,
unum agnoscat cuncta potentem.

MALCHUS  IOANNES

*MAL.*   Sic se profecto res habent mortalium,
ut optionem si tibi obtulerit deus, 625
incertus erres quid recuses, quid velis.
opes honores rem tibi et tuis cupis?
quae perdiderunt saepe voti compotes.
hosti imprecaris vincla carcerem fugam?
quae saepe pariunt maximam illi gloriam 630
tibique damnum. quod adeo verum meo
didici periclo, exempla ne longe petam.
nam cum remotis montium degens iugis
Baptista vulgus fascinaret hic novus
plebisque secum credulae traheret gregem, 635
ego Pharisaeae dignitatis vindicem
me praestiti unum ceteris cunctantibus.
nec experiri cuncta desii prius
quam dura sontes vincla presserunt manus
hostemque carcer publicus compescuit; 640
aulamque totam criminum implevi. at nihil,
ut video, prosunt vincla carcer crimina.
sic plebis animos occupavit impiae
vis dira pestis, omniumque pectora
letale virus perbibere, ut illius 645
clades honorent, ingemant periculis.
quacumque pergo me exsecrantur, indicant
me digito, iniquo me intuentur lumine;
illi favetur sacrilego, qui sustulit
rerum universa et ordinum discrimina, 650
et excubatur ante clausum carcerem.
nihil miserius esse nobis arbitror
qui nos omissis rebus aliis commodo
populi dicamus. quisquis illi mancipat
se, collocatam gratiam sciat male, 655
ut qui maligno semper ingenio solet
favere pravis, optimates spernere.
quo conferam me? quid querar primum? quibus
potissimum irascar? cui opem primum feram?
pseudoprophetam populus impius colit; 660
mussant rabini, conivet rex, neglegunt
proceres. ruentes solus his umeris ego,

his fulcio umeris patrios ritus, manum
nullo admovente. publicam solus vicem
665   doleo. quid igitur? deseram munus? sacra
legesque prodam dignitatemque ordinis,
meque esse patiar hostibus ludibrio?
patiar profecto. nam quid aliud iam queam?
feramne solus, ferre quod cuncti abnuunt,
670   et me ruinae publicae obiciam? deus
sua tueatur. quando iam sic vivitur
ut quisque caveat sibi, ego mihi sum proximus.
si male gero rempublicam, in meum caput
ruina verget. qui favent nunc maxime
675   stanti, iacentem calcibus primi petent.
si bene geram rem, gratiam male collocem,
nihil parabo praeter invidiam mihi.
nunc Gamalielis sero consilium placet,
nisi forte sero nemo resipiscere potest.
680   malo ego requirant hic meam constantiam
quam re peracta temeritatem puniant.
quod cuique visum est sentiant. molestiis
ego me explicabo, et gratiam resarciam
hoc cum propheta; nec animi simplex homo
685   renuet, opinor. duriorem si mihi
se ostendet, omnes admovebo machinas
ne populus illum credat artibus meis
periisse. populum si reconciliavero,
non undequaque cesserit res pessime.
690   atque ipse, opinor, ipse nimirum est. vide
qui coetus illum sacrilegum sequitur comes!
in urbe media nos inanes interim
inter cathedras desidemus. at libet
audire primum quid magister hic ferat.
695   *IO.*   O magne rerum rector auctor arbiter,
te quicquid aër continet laxo sinu,
quaecumque tellus educat, quicquid suis
fretum sub undis nutrit, agnoscit deum,
sentit parentem, legibus semel datis
700   obsequitur ultro tramite immutabili.
iussu tuo ver pingit arva floribus,
fruges dat aestas, fundit autumnus merum,
hiems pruinis vestit albicantibus

montes; in aequor curva volvunt flumina
moles aquarum, mare reciprocat vices, 705
noctem Diana, Phoebus incendit diem
et inquieta lustrat orbem lampade.
nil denique usquam est sive caelo seu solo
quod non libenter pareat regi suo,
amet parentem et officiis quibus potest 710
in conditorem studia declaret sua.
at solus homo, quem ceteris longe magis
gaudere decuit et obsequi iussis dei,
contemptor unus inter omnes maxime est.
praecepta spernit, frena legum reicit, 715
in omne praeceps facinus it; libidine
metitur aequum, ponderat ius viribus.
MAL.   Principia recte sese habent tibi hactenus.
IO.   Nec tam per orbem devias miror vago
errore gentes quam populum qui se dei 720
hereditatem iactat, et conviciis
incessit alios impiosque clamitat,
cum nulla, qua sol cumque terras adspicit,
gens orbe toto vivat effrenatius.
MAL.   Sane locutus cuncta vere es hactenus. 725
IO.   Nec ista vulgi culpa tantum est mobilis.
levita longe veste fulgens candida,
legisque scriba turgidus scientia,
et vos verendi aetate matura senes—
obliquus error devio flexu abstrahit. 730
viduae orphanique causa vestra ad pulpita
succumbit, opprimitque dives pauperem;
iniqua iuxta et aequa sunt venalia.
MAL.   Disrumpor ira; tacitus haec ut audiam?
IO.   At vos, rabini, sanctitate ceteros 735
praestare qui simulatis et scientia,
et vos, sacerdotum sacrata dignitas
princepsque sacri pontifex collegii,
decimatis omne terra quod profert olus.
non vos anethum menta ruta et allium, 740
urtica non vos aut viride faenum fugit.
at si legendum, si docendum scilicet
responsa vatum et sanctioris orbita
monstranda vitae, vestra demum auctoritas

745 est muta, muti non latratis hic canes,
circumfrementes vestra non ovilia
lupos abigitis. quid lupos dixi? lupi
vos estis ipsi, vos gregem deglubitis,
vos lana vestit, lac sitim sedat, famem
750 caro. gregem non pascitis; vos pascitis.
    *MAL.* Facessat hinc in maximam malam crucem
concordia. egone patiar amplius meo
sic insolenter contumeliam ordini
fieri? deus me si ex Olympo mitteret
755 hac lege ut haec sint audienda, deseram
mandata potius ista quam dici audiam.
durare nequeo ulterius. heus tu, vir bone,
turbae magister unice, haec nempe est tua
doctrina? populum incallidum sic instruis?
760 *IO.* Si probus es, ad te haud attinent quae dicimus.
*MAL.* Ad te sacerdotem attinet traducere?
*IO.* Bene puto dici cum malis dictum est male.
*MAL.* Parere iuvenem convenit maioribus.
*IO.* Parere cunctos convenit magis deo.
765 *MAL.* Te iussit igitur ista proloqui deus?
*IO.* Iubet profari vera cunctos veritas.
*MAL.* Tacuisse vera saepe multis profuit.
*IO.* Cum scelere iuncta nil moramur commoda.
*MAL.* Scelus videtur, ni scelus dicas, tibi?
770 *IO.* Scelus videtur tot perire milia
spectare, possim cum reducere in viam.
*MAL.* Reducere? gregis nonne pastores sumus?
*IO.* Si res quidem eadem est pascere et deglubere.
*MAL.* Rerum tuarum sat age, nostra desere.
775 *IO.* Vicina cum res agitur, agitur et mea.
*MAL.* Quis tandem es, oro, auctoritate hac praeditus?
tune ille Christus patribus promissus es?
*IO.* Non sum. *MAL.* Propheta es ille? *IO.* Non sum. *MAL.* Es Helias
*IO.* Nec Helias sum. *MAL.* Si nihil es horum, neque
780 spes nostra Christus nec propheta nec Helias,
quinam auctor audes esse baptismi novi?
quem te esse tandem perferemus? indica.
*IO.* Vox sum in remotis montium clamans iugis:
'Viam parate, facite rectas semitas
785 veniente domino. cuius adventu cavae

in plana valles explicabunt se, solo
saxosa montes culmina aequabunt.' ego
in nomen eius abluo populos aquis,
cui detrahendis servus etiam socculis
indignus essem, nemo quem agnoscit, licet　　　790
versetur inter vos et usque obambulet.
*MAL.*　Quos iste laqueos nectit atque ambagibus
eludit! istam quam tibi sic vindicas
auctoritatem quo probas miraculo?
*IO.*　Possem ego vicissim te rogare etiam, tuam　　　795
auctoritatem quo probes miraculo.
*MAL.*　Ut contumax est! quamlibet celes, tamen
quid in furorem te rapiat omnes sciunt.
nostra profecto crescere invidia cupis,
rem comparare gloriamque incommodo　　　800
nostro, artibusque vis potens fieri malis.
nec decipis nos; ipse tete decipis.
nec primus ista es fallere aggressus via.
postremus utinam debitas poenas luas,
aut potius animum in melius admonitu meo　　　805
mutes, et, auctor ut fuisti errantibus,
mutatus auctor sis revertendi in viam.
vidi severam veste sanctimoniam
prae se ferentes ut facile facerent fidem
animi modesti et simplicis; post artibus　　　810
ubi his honores comparassent et opes,
nudare sensim ingenia, probitatem prius
bene simulatam propalam contemnere,
et frena veris moribus permittere.
quod si hac honorum tendis ad fastigia,　　　815
rerum imperitum fallit ignorantia.
non isto ad altam tramite itur gloriam.
ni me fefellit pessime non pessimus
magister usus et senecta usus parens,
famae reique consules melius tuae　　　820
si tuta potius adpetas quam splendida.
*IO.*　Si vera dico, recta facio, cur mihi
quisquam imperare debeat silentium?
sin falsa, doctus imperito id indica.

796　probes *1577, R*:　probas *1578*

825  MAL.  Horum pigebit, morte cum poenas lues.
    IO.   Istaec minare fata formidantibus.
    MAL.  Si vivo longum, faxo non laetabere
          hac contumacia. scies quid sit senes
          neglegere, scribas iurgiis proscindere,
830       dictis rabinos provocare procacibus.
          et quando amicos nos habere neglegis,
          quid possit odium forte cognosces senum.

CHORUS

          Ad furta qui se comparat
          nocturna vitat lumina;
835       odit facem sicarius
          sui furoris consciam.
          puer recusat pharmaca
          condita amaro absinthio;
          abhorret a salubribus
840       vulnus resectum emplasmatis.
          occulta cui mentis mala
          secreta rodunt pectora,
          huic est molesta veritas
          quae cor revelat turbidum.
845       at vos, severi hypocritae,
          quos fronte duros taetrica
          lucrum iuvat nefarium, ex
          errore vulgi creduli
          quantumlibet recondita
850       celaveritis crimina,
          quamvis tegatur sordida
          sentina mentis impiae,
          vos vestra conscientia
          secreta rodens arguit;
855       vos clausus intra viscera
          occultus exest carnifex,
          duro flagellans verbere.
          o ter beatum et amplius
          qui purus animi ad iudices
860       non fit reus domesticos,

857 duro *edd.* surdo R *dubitanter ex Juv.* 13.194

clauso nec in praecordiis
tortore semper vapulat!

MALCHUS CHORUS REGINA

*MAL.* In rege nulla certa spes est; publicam
suamque causam prodidit pravo ambitu.
populo placere dum studet, dum gratiae 865
venatur auram lenitatis imagine,
me plebis irae nixus est supponere,
suasque voluit vindicare iniurias
meo periclo; nempe Baptistae necem
ut si videret aegrius ferre populum, 870
populo paratus capite confestim meo
litare; populus si tulisset leviter
novae interemptum factionis principem,
quod se ultus esset maxima cum gloria
credi volebat, callide. sic exhibent 875
alterna reges civium de sanguine
spectacula sibi, et caede ludunt mutua.
quodcumque vulgus approbat sibi vindicant,
a se patratum praedicant. laudi suae
nostri laboris adrogant industriam. 880
popularis aura si favoris flexerit
secus ac putabant et petebant, transferunt
culpam in ministros, et cruore innoxio
animaque vili crimen avertunt suum.
superest doloris sola nostri particeps 885
regina, tigris orba ceu catulis furens,
Baptista thalami quod prioris foedera
polluta coram rege non probaverit
palamque vetitos lege damnarit toros
cum uxore fratris. flamma dum recens calet 890
irae aestuantis, turbidae menti faces
supponam alamque commodis sermonibus.
atque ecce sese in tempore offert commode.
*CHO.* Nunc flamma flammae, toxicum nunc toxico
accedit. instat ultimum periculum. 895
*MAL.* Regina, salve, splendidum gentis decus,

866/7 auram, lenitatis imagine/me plebis *interpunxerunt edd*.

et sola regni digna tanti culmine.
*REG.* Et tu, rabine Malche. sed quid tristis es?
*MAL.* Idem quod animum, ut arbitror, pungit tuum.
900 *REG.* Fortasse. sed tu quid sit ede apertius.
*MAL.* Ecquid animo aequo fers dignitatem tuam
sperni, per orbem sacrosanctam regii
auctoritatem nominis vilescere,
et sceptra vulgi subici ludibrio?
905 *REG.* Quid ergo faciam? quod remedium sit doce.
*MAL.* Iras et animis et tuis natalibus
thalamisque dignas corde tandem concipe.
*REG.* Iam dudum id actum est. rumpor ira, lacrimo
obiurgo clamo, sed nec ira et lacrimis
910 promoveo quicquam. verba venti dissipant.
*MAL.* Si auctoritate qua decet apud coniugem
esses, inultas sic tuas iniurias
tulisset aut, ut verius dicam, suas?
*REG.* Studia ipse populi, Malche, cernis. forsitan
915 hac rex putavit posse poena spiritus
acres retundi et mitigari audaciam.
*MAL.* Tu si feroces spiritus coercitos
putes latroni huic vinculis et carcere,
erras. ferarum saevit acrius furor
920 quas fracta fudit cavea quam quas deviis
silva alta semper educavit montibus.
quid liberatus non aget, cuius colit
nunc vincla populus? provocata accenditur,
non mitigatur ira. contumeliis
925 elatus animus ad furorem impellitur.
*REG.* Quin lenietur potius hoc beneficio,
quod qui perierat pertinacia sua
sit liberatus regia clementia.
*MAL.* Quod tu beneficium, ille putat iniuriam,
930 seseque vinctum quam solutum saepius
per te meminerit. *REG.* Asperum ingenium refers.
*MAL.* Id paene cunctis insitum est mortalibus;
quod bene patraris, gratia ilico perit,
quod male patraris, nullus obliviscitur.
935 odere cuncti propemodum beneficia

913 suas *R*   tuas *1577*
914 ipse *1577, R*:   ipsa *1628*

quorum memoriae iuncta sunt maleficia.
Baptista quoties memor erit meriti tui,
meminisse toties sceleris eum sui puta.
se scelere credet non solutum sed tuo
animo nocentem, liberum pravo ambitu; 940
poenam remissam, in tempus iram supprimi.
*REG.* Ingenia saeva mitigat benignitas.
*MAL.* Longo quod usu in peius usque induruit,
multo facilius fregeris quam flexeris.
*REG.* Quin ergo dubiam quid sit e re praemones? 945
*MAL.* Reddam expedita haec facile si credas mihi.
*REG.* Modo praemoneto; nulla erit per me mora.
*MAL.* Quaerendo agendo providendo, haud otio,
res magnae aguntur. *REG.* Si nihil promoveris
quaerendo agendo providendo, non magis 950
praestat quiesse quam negotium ut tibi
frustra facessas et aliis sis risui?
*MAL.* Quod saepe vis non perficit, vincit labor.
nec alta quercus icta subito sternitur,
nec vertit aries bellicus primo impetu 955
muros. frequenter quae putaris perfici
non posse, tempus expedit; quae non potest
plerumque ratio, expugnat importunitas.
proinde prensa. lacrimis misce preces
irasque monitis, blanda dicta iurgiis; 960
ambi maritum sedulo omnibus modis,
occasiones usquequaque amplectere.
si peragi aperte res nequit, tendas dolos.
quod spectat ad me, certa stat sententia
nisi re peracta neutiquam desistere. 965

CHORUS

Tandem livor et impiis
accensus furiis dolor
vires saevitiae suae
in vatem exseruit pium.
illinc saeva calumnia 970
dirae iuncta tyrannidi
pugnat fraude nefaria,
hinc innoxia veritas

nullo fulta satellite
975 spernit terrificas minas.
tot telis petitur caput
unum, tot pariter doli
intentant iuveni necem.
ille, ut tunsa furentibus
980 ilex dura aquilonibus
aut rupes remeabili
quam fluctu mare verberat,
nullo concutitur metu.
o numen venerabile
985 cunctis, candida Veritas,
quam nec bellica vis metu
nec fraus insidiis potest
firmo pellere de gradu,
sola non metuis graves
990 fortunae instabilis vices.
non obnoxia casibus
ullis, pectora robore
armas insuperabili;
et vitae dominam et necis
995 Parcarum indomitam manum
nobis esse vetas gravem.
sed cesso vatem convenire, nuntio
ut impleam aures omnium miserrimo?
atque eccum ante ipsas carceris stantem fores.
1000 propago sanctis sanctior parentibus,
et innocentiae una pristinae fides,
incolumitati, dum tempus sinit, tuae
consule. rabinus Malchus intentat dolos
occulte, inops regina consilii furit;
1005 blanditur aula, rex suam sententiam
dissimulat; alii vera mussant dicere.
iam tempus instat ultimi discriminis.

IOANNES CHORUS

*IO.* Quid est pericli? *CHO.* Mortis urget terminus.
*IO.* Haec summa nobis imminentis est mali?
1010 *CHO.* Quo nullum in hominem cadere possit amplius.

1003–4 dolos/occulte, inops *1577*: dolos:/occulte inops *R*

*IO.* Ut vis tyranni cesset ac dolus, feret
hanc sponte nobis temporis longinquitas
pravo timendam at innocenti optabilem.
*CHO.* At tu salutem neglegas tuam licet,
te ratio nostri tangat. istos spiritus 1015
paulum remitte, precibus animum regium
flecte. per amicos non inexorabilem
spero futurum. *IO.* Sedulo nonne hoc ago?
*CHO.* Utinam tibi istam praebeat mentem deus.
*IO.* Nihil precari est opus; is animus iam diu est. 1020
explere properat rex meo iram sanguine,
nec ego recuso. qui magis regem queam
placare quam cum volumus eadem et nolumus?
*CHO.* Bona verba. *IO.* Quid igitur mihi auctor es? duo
reges utrimque facere pugnantia iubent. 1025
caelestis alter, misericors clemens bonus;
terrenus alter, impotens ferox malus.
mortem minatur alter; alter me vetat
mortem timere, pollicetur praemium
vim non timenti. corpus alter perdere 1030
potest; at alter corpus una et spiritum
torquere flamma poterit inevitabili.
hi cum repugnent, consule utri paream.
*CHO.* Placare nunquam postea Herodem datur,
oblata si nunc praetereat occasio; 1035
dei sed ira semper est placabilis.
*IO.* Divina quanto saevit ira lentius,
hoc mota poenas exigit severius.
*CHO.* Sic fata spernis quae deus mortalibus
timenda voluit esse? neve corporis 1040
animique sanctum dirimeret consortium
oblata temere causa, vinclo mutuo
amoris animum corpori connexuit.
*IO.* Non sperno mortem, at morte momentanea
fugio perennem. quem deus lucis mihi 1045
concessit usum, reddo repetenti libens.
*CHO.* Itane relinquis orphanos parens tuos?
*IO.* Nunquam orphanus erit qui deum credit patrem.
*CHO.* Nil te propinqui, nil amicorum movent
lacrimae, impotenti quos tyranno deseris? 1050
*IO.* Non desero, sed potius ab eis deseror.

namque institutam ab initio mundi viam
in fata curro. nempe lege hac nascimur
quicumque lucis fruimur almae munere,
1055 condicio cunctos una cohibet; tendimus
in mortem, eo nos singuli ducunt dies.
mortem esse poenam voluit improbis deus,
bonisque portum, terminum longae viae,
ad longioris vitae initium ianuam
1060 quae nos perennis splendidam ad lucis domum
mittat renatos verius quam mortuos.
de carcere hic est exitus mortalibus
et ad carentem morte vitam transitus;
hac universus praeiit coetus patrum,
1065 cuncti sequentur. quis ubi liquit carceres
non cursor animo rapitur ad metam? freto
quis aestuoso nocte tenebrosa vagus
portu recuset se quieto condere?
quis exul errans per peregrini soli
1070 deserta tesca doleat in patriam cito
sese reverti? laetus ergo tramite
decurso ad ipsam stare metam me puto.
iam prope peractae liber e vitae freto
prospicio terram. de peregrino solo
1075 domum revertor, optimum primum patrem
visurus, illum nempe patrem qui solum
revinxit undis, induit caelum solo,
regitque certas mobilis caeli vices;
servator auctor rector unus omnium,
1080 cui cuncta vivunt viva iuxta ac mortua.
ut flamma sursum sponte volvit vortices,
undae deorsum perpeti lapsu ruunt,
propriumque pergunt ire cuncta ad fomitem,
iamdudum anhelat spiritus caelo editus
1085 rerum ad parentem lucis aeternae incolam,
quem contueri est vita, mors non cernere.
non, si pruinis obstet horrens Caucasus,
aër procellis, unda tempestatibus,
tractusque nimiis invius caloribus,
1090 eo ire pergam? non, tot ut videam duces
reges prophetas iudices pios, via
rumpenda vel si mille mortes obstruant?

ergo recluso corporis de carcere,
eo evolare spiritus liber cupit
quo cunctus ibit orbis serius ocius. 1095
nam longa vita nil, opinor, aliud est
quam lenta duro servitus in carcere.
o mors laboris una laxamen gravis,
o mors doloris portus et mali quies,
notumque paucis commodum mortalibus, 1100
formido pravis et bonis votum, tuo
sinu recepta naufragum hoc corpusculum,
et sempiternae duc quietis in domum
quo non sequetur vis dolus calumnia.
CHO.   o te beatum hac pectoris constantia, 1105
o nos misellos quos iners animi metus
felicitatis privat hoc consortio!
quando igitur ipse quod opus est facto tenes,
salve valeque sempiternum dicimus.
   quam discors hominum tramite dispari 1110
   versat lis animos! non metuit mori
   qui nil commeruit; qui meruit mori,
   si vanis leviter mors crepuit minis,
   exsanguis trepidat degeneri metu.
   quam mortem fugiunt naviter improbi 1115
   per flammas, per aquas, saxaque devia,
   tam mortis cupidi praecipitant boni
   inlustres animas dura per omnia.
   nempe ignota malis commoda mors habet,
   et fati comes est vita beatior. 1120
   nec toti morimur, sed melior rogos
   nostri pars avidos spernit, et aethera
   sublimis patrium scandit, et igneos
   inter caelicolas certa animas manet
   sedes innocuas; at male conscios 1125
   manes exagitant sulphureo in lacu
   crinitae colubris Eumenides nigris,
   et ieiuna avidi guttura Cerberi,
   et nunquam saturi copia Tantali.
   hinc formido malis, hinc bona spes bonis 1130
   et vitae fragilis prodiga pectora,

1115  naviter] gnaviter *R*   graviter *1577*

dum vitam properant infragilem sequi.
o Siren magicis illecebris potens,
et fallacis amans vita fugax boni!
1135 tu nobis teneris blanditiis mali
vicinum effugium claudis et obstruis
portum perpetuae pacis amabilem,
nullus terror ubi Martius increpat
nec rauco reboant classica murmure,
1140 nec pirata rapax aequora territat
nec latro tacitum trux nemus obsidet,
nec sceptri misera praedo cupidine
insanus populis exitium creat
nec, felix placido solus ut otio
1145 torpescat, tenues cladibus obruit,
nec viles animas qui miserabilis
vulgi pro titulis mutet inanibus;
sed tranquilla quies almaque faustitas
et simplex probitas omnia possidet,
1150 et ferri in tenebras indocilis dies
et vita alterius nescia funeris,
et luctus queruli nescia gaudia.
o dulce hospitium corporeae domus
et vitae nimium carcer amabilis,
1155 iam tandem magicis exue nexibus
mentem caeligenam, quam patriae suae
oblitam gremio amplecteris ebriam
Lethes somniferae deside toxico,
et laetam thalami degeneris iugo.
1160 o fallax lutei tegmen amiculi,
vanesce in cineres rursum abiens tuos,
ut rursus patrio reddita mens polo
puri se radiis luminis expleat;
et te pestiferis morte laboribus
1165 et mentem anxiferis solve molestiis.

REGINA

Pharisaeus igitur spem fefellit; rex pari
se vanitate pariter et me prodidit,
vulgi loquacis dum timet rumusculos.
formido misere, nata quid rerum gerat,

saltationis nuper in convivio 1170
cui rex frequenti praemium spoponderat
quodcumque peteret. illa Baptistae caput
in lance pepigit se petituram, et feret,
feret profecto, nisi parum notus mihi
sit regis animus. liber invidia necis 1175
in me odia populi vertet, ut reor, libens,
et ego peracta re libenter id feram.
odium ultionis gaudio, maculam lucro
pensabo. turpe est esse atrocem feminam,
turpe, nisi reges esse inultos turpius 1180
foret. sed ambo proferunt pedem domo
rex et puella. quo propior est spes, metus
hoc gravius urit. cuncta fortunet deus!

HERODES  PUELLA  REGINA

*HER.*  Deliberatum quid rogares iam tibi
satis videtur? *PUELL.*  Sic satis, si quidem satis 1185
promissa regum certa sint et regia.
*HER.*  Ne metue firma testibus coram fide
sancita. regni posce dimidium mei
vel si quid animo carius regno est tuo,
feres; volentem nulla vis averterit. 1190
*PUELL.*  Istud brevi iam quale sit videbimus.
*HER.* Iam posce, certum est. *PUELL.* Nil opus regno tuo
mihi est, quod aeque rege te meum reor
ac si ipsa teneam. rem facilem et aequam peto.
*HER.*  Non ego, sed ipsa ne feras tibi in mora es. 1195
*PUELL.*  Da in hac recisum lance Baptistae caput.
*HER.*  Quod verbum ab ore temere tibi, virgo, excidit?
*PUELL.*  Non temere. *HER.* Donum virgini indecens petis.
*PUELL.*  Non indecorum est facinus hostem perdere.
*HER.*  Hic igitur ira dignus hostis regia est? 1200
*PUELL.*  Is dignus ira est, scelere qui hanc meruit suo.
*HER.*  Quod nunc remedium plebis odio reperiam?
*PUELL.*  Parere populi est, imperare regium.
*HER.* Aequa imperare regium est. *PUELL.* Quod iniquum erat
prius, imperando facere rex aequum potest. 1205
*HER.*  At imperandi lex facit regi modum.
*PUELL.*  Si principi quod placuit est ius, iam modum

    non regibus lex, legibus sed rex facit.
    *HER.*   Pro rege fama me tyrannum perferet.
1210 *PUELL.*   At sceptra metuit.   *HER.*   Metuit, et garrit tamen.
    *PUELL.*   Compesce ferro.   *HER.*   Regna male servat metus.
    *PUELL.*   Et regna vertit facile scelerum impunitas.
    *HER.*   Securus est quem civium servat fides.
    *PUELL.*   Necesse reges est timeri, diligi
1215 necesse non est.   *HER.*   Odia crudelem premunt.
    *PUELL.*   In rege vulgo lenitas contemnitur.
    *REG.*   Haec tota, opinor, tendit huc oratio,
    promissa vana ut effluant. nondum mihi
    regum videre nosse quae sint munera.
1220 si honesta credis esse regi et turpia
    quae honesta vulgus credit esse et turpia,
    falleris. amici proximi, socer gener,
    fratres sorores, civis hostis pauperum
    sunt vincla, vana regibus vocabula.
1225 diadema quisquis induit capiti semel,
    vulgaris omnes ponat officii gradus.
    nil arbitretur turpe quod regi utile,
    nullum indecorum facinus esse existimet
    suae salutis quod facit causa. salus
1230 a rege populi pendet; igitur consulit
    populi saluti quisquis in regem est pius.
    tantine sanguis huius erit homunculi
    ut tu diebus sollicitus ac noctibus
    non conquiescas? deme nobis hunc metum,
1235 sceptris pudorem, vastitatem moenibus,
    armis rapinas, civicum bellum omnibus.
    statuere magno oportet exemplo et novo
    ut sacrosancta regna sint mortalibus.
    scelus patravit; scelere pessum eat suo.
1240 si nil patravit, coniugi pereat tuae.
    da coniugi hostem. coniugem si neglegis,
    promissa redde filiae rex et parens.
    *HER.*   Promissa certum est optima reddere fide.
    at illa, si me consulet, sapientius
1245 optabit.   *REG.*   At si consulet me, ne sua
    consilia mutet.   *HER.*   Itane? sicne oportuit

1245  sua *R*   tua *1577*

iurasse temere, sic puellae me meam
obstringere fidem, salutem regnum opes
vitam necemque feminae committere?
*REG.*   Promissa regum certa firmet veritas.        1250
*HER.*   Quando negare non licet, quod modo licet
admoneo rursum et oro ne quid sanguine
sexuque vestro et regio culmine parum
dignum patrare cogat iracundia.
*REG.*   Haec mitte; nostrae linque curae cetera.    1255
*HER.*   De vate si quid statueritis durius,
vestra illa culpa, vestrum erit periculum.
*REG.*   Iam vindicata dignitas est regia,
ne pateat ulli in posterum ludibrio.
iam faxo populus pervicax de regibus                 1260
loqui modeste vel malo discat suo.
et sive reges aequa iniquave imperent,
aequo ferenda populus animo omnia putet.

### CHORUS

Davidis regnum Solymaeque turres
et locupletis Solomonis arces,                       1265
unde tam dirus furor in prophetas,
sanguinis iusti sitis unde saeva?
quam decet normam pietatis esse,
unicum est vitae specimen scelestae.
furta vis caedes dolus et rapinae                    1270
sunt tuae tirocinium palaestrae.
non sacerdoti pietas nefandis
fraudibus suadet cohibere dextras.
cultor idoli populus reliquit
omnium rerum dominum et parentem.                    1275
pro deo lignum colitur lapisque;
his calent arae vitulis et agnis,
et suae dextrae simulacra adorat
artifex. vitam sine lege truncum
poscit, a muto eloquium precatur.                    1280
pauperi dives, dominus ministro
supplicat. ritus pereunt vetusti.
te prophetarum cruor innocentum

1268  quam *1577*   quem *R*

iudicis magni rapit ad tribunal;
1285 pauperes clamant, viduaeque caelum
    questibus implent.
ergo te iustae manet ultionis
poena non mendax, nisi fallor augur.
namque qui fastus premit insolentes,
1290 arbiter caeli, maris atque terrae,
spectat ex alto lacrimasque plebis
et preces tristes meminit, manuque
vindice infandi sceleris propinquas
exiget poenas. quibus intumescis
1295 insolens victor tibi vertet arces.
barbarus miles tua possidebit
praedia; externo domino refundet
vinitor fructus tuus. alta qua nunc
surgit in caelum Solomonis aedes,
1300 exterus messem faciet colonus.
ergo dum praebet tibi paenitendi
numinis favor spatium, relictis
turpiter vitae vitiis peractae,
exteri ritus simulacra pelle;
1305 et sitim fraterni avidam cruoris,
et famem argenti cohibe profanam.
sed nec exactae male paenitebit
te tuae vitae, neque sacra ab aede
exteri ritus simulacra pelles;
1310 nec sitim fraterni avidam cruoris
nec famem argenti fugies profanam.
ergo te pestis vitiosa carpet,
te fames bellum macies egestas
opprimet donec merito rependes
1315    sanguine poenas.

NUNTIUS  CHORUS

*NUN.*  Quis indicabit ubi reperiam gentium
comites prophetae, nuntium ut tristem feram?
*CHO.*  Nisi forte properas siste paulisper gradum,
eloquere paucis; scire quid feras iuvat.
1320 *NUN.*  At non iuvabit scisse scire quod cupis.

1299 Solomonis *R*   Solomontis *1577*

*CHO.* Ut ut se habent res, ne moram invide brevem.
*NUN.* Scisti puella ab rege quid petiverit?
*CHO.* In lance vatis sibi caput caesum dari.
*NUN.* In lance vatis abstulit caesum caput.
*CHO.* O facinus atrox! ille caelestis vigor         1325
decusque vultus morte tristi emarcuit,
et ora nuper plena sacro numine
clausit perenni dira vis silentio.
*NUN.* Quid fles? inanes mitte questus fundere.
*CHO.* Cum flenda videam et audiam, flendum negas? 1330
*NUN.* Si flenda mors est, mortuos illi fleant
quorum sepultae spes iacent cum corpore,
qui post soporis terminum brevissimi
reditura membra non putant et alteram
superesse vitam. mortuos miseri fleant              1335
miserosque tantum. neminem facere potest
fortuna miserum. similis insontem licet
sontemque maneat terminus vitae, tamen
male morietur nemo qui vixit bene.
de genere miseros exitus si iudices,                1340
miseros putabis tot patres sanctos, quibus
crux ensis unda flamma clausit spiritum.
nam veritatis qui satelles occidit
pro religione patriisque legibus,
ominibus illum prosequi bonis decet,                1345
votisque vitae poscere similem exitum.
*CHO.* Vere profecto es elocutus omnia.
at nos, opinio quos et errores trahunt,
dum fata fugimus, fata stulti incurrimus:
ignis pepercit, unda mergit; aëris                  1350
vis pestilentis aequori ereptum necat;
bello superstes tabidus morbo perit.
differre, non vitare fata dat deus,
et faeneramur mortis in dies moras
morbis periclis luctibus molestiis.                 1355
nec longa vita est aliud ac longi mali
catena, mortis nexa ad usque terminum
serie perenni. nec ligati hoc vinculo
servire miseri nos putamus; exitum
quam servitutem potius exhorrescimus.               1360

## THE BAPTIST

The ancient poets tell that there was a certain Proteus who transformed himself to every shape, and could be encompassed by no bonds as he now melted into liquid waters, now crackled as a flame, now roared as a fierce lion, sprouted as a tree, bridled as a bear, hissed as a snake, as he changed into every kind of remarkable object. I have certainly found this tale much truer than the oracles of the Sibyl. I believe that in all the men I see I behold as many Proteuses who assume new features and turn themselves into every possible shape; and the success of a stage-play always runs the gamut of their calumnies especially.

If[15] anyone produces an ancient plot, they make annoying interruptions, they cough and retch. But if anyone introduces a new one, they at once demand and approve and praise and love the old. They reject what is new with niggardly contempt, and drive it off-stage before they can make its acquaintance; they taint correct expressions by malicious interpretations. They criticise everything as inferior. They have abandoned themselves to sleep and sloth, and with no work to occupy them they are envious of the toils of others, and apply all their efforts to finding something to censure. Should there be an error, they excel Lynceus in sharpness of sight, and mark it with the censors' blot. Things happily expressed they flit by with deaf ears. The stern brows of these men and the pained arrogance of their crabbed countenances I disregard.

But if there be present any honest critic keen and well-disposed towards a writer whose standards are more exacting, to offer encouragement with his applause and to pardon minor errors (for nothing created by the human mind is in every respect untarnished), to him we bring a new play, or rather an old story refurbished, of how the Baptist of old was crushed by royal lust and the crafty calumnies of jealous people, and though innocent met an undeserved death. But so far as I am concerned, every man can call the play old or new according to his judgment; for if an event enacted many centuries ago is old, this will be reckoned among the old, but if we consider as new what is fresh from recent recollection, this will certainly be new. As long as the human race lasts, new deceits, new calumnies will always exist, and wicked spite will always oppress worthy men. Violence will prevail over right, deceit over innocence.

MALCHUS GAMALIEL *Rabbis* CHORUS

*MAL.* Wretched old age, and imminent finality of my last breath, and unhappy fate, have you committed the end of my extended life to this experience, that I should behold our land in slavery, our temples sacrilegiously polluted, things sacred and profane confounded? I have seen the hidden parts of our unapproachable shrine shattered, the sacred gold torn from the doorposts. All that the greed of Gabinius could grab or the extravagance of Antony could devour has gone, and we have been the butt too for Cleopatra's gluttony, an unspeakable fate. And so that no humiliation would be lacking on any side, savage king Herod, great-grandson of the half-Arab Antipater, wields his cruel sceptre. Judaea is the slave to Idumaea, Sion to an Arab ruler, Jerusalem to one profane, God's people to one unholy. Amidst so many wounds of raging fortune, in slavery however oppressive, some spark of ancient dignity still survived, some token however slight of our ancestral discipline, worthy of the respect even of our very enemies. The fierce victor and some considerable part of the empurpled senate had begun to accord honour to Jewish laws.

Renewed[76] by this hope, we had scarcely begun to raise our heads from the weariness of our wretched state when sudden sacrilege arose from a quarter where fear of no ill threatened. A new Baptist has appeared, not sprung from profane parents or raised amidst foreign cults, but one of us by race, a Levite by tribe, dedicated to God from his very cradle; the son of a priest and himself destined soon for the priesthood, had he not preferred to prise off the bitter fruits of grasping glory rather than to gather the harvest of distinction at the due time when ripe.

So[88] dwelling alone in the lonely crannies of the unfrequented countryside he has beguiled the simple folk with the appearance of stern sanctity. With his shaggy hair, his frame covered with skins, his diet of wild game and deceits of that kind, he has attracted the attention of all. The common folk believe that a new prophet has suddenly been bestowed on the world. And now he has drawn to himself an army of an attendant mob, now the people abandon their cities and look up to him alone; princes cultivate him, kings revere him. He is become arrogant through the frenzy of the stupid crowd. He issues new laws like a second Moses, he has the effrontery to purge sins with water, and to defile the old laws with new rites. So that he may more easily enjoy the frenzied support of the mob, he rends the elders with all kinds of rebuke, and has the benevolent ear of the common folk. But if, as he rages with haughty recklessness, no-one withstands the forays of this brigand, that integrity of ours, famed before the world, will soon die—or rather it is now dying or indeed has already died.

*GAM.* It befits our vocation to decide nothing rashly. Gentleness is appropriate to mild elders. Indulgence can be granted to the rashness of the young, but no excuse will be able to cloak the guilt which we incur. Grant some short respite to your anger; let your emotion subside, and your resentment lose its heat.

*MAL.* Gamaliel, it seems by your opinion that even you approve the deeds of this impious man.

*GAM.* Malchus, Malchus, I neither approve nor condemn before I know the nature of any case. So far as this prophet goes, what I hear suggests that he is not such a bad fellow, and should not be afflicted as you suggest with the hatred of the community.

*MAL.* Stars, sky and earth! Even this man is not without an advocate to say that he is not wicked.

*GAM.* Can you persuade me that the man who rebukes vices, teaches good manners, and walks first on the path which he enjoins on others is wicked?

*MAL.* Can you persuade me that the man who despises laws, promotes new sects and new rites, attacks with abuse the teachers of the people, and disparages the priests is good?

*GAM.* If we were equally harsh and stern in judgment of ourselves as we are often crabbed to others, our evil deeds would be less exposed to general censure. However much we may flatter ourselves, be proclaimed as blessed, be considered godlike, holy, chaste and dutiful by the common folk, none of us is free from the greatest vices.

*MAL.* Even assuming that this is true, Gamaliel, it is surely not right for any man of the commons to revile his superior? The common people should listen, obey, be sober, not reject the curbs imposed upon them. It is the task of the man in authority to lead the commoners, if they stray, back to the path. He must be his own law; if he sins, God is there to witness and to punish him for his crime.

*GAM.* And does this law seem just to you?

*MAL.* Indeed it does.

*GAM.* How, then?

*MAL.* Because it is the nature of common folk to be ignorant, wrong, rash, inexperienced, blind.

*GAM.* One can often find a man from the ranks of common folk who does not fall behind the wisdom of his leaders.

*MAL.* Why don't we then vacate our office in favour of rustics?

*GAM.* Moses was a rustic; so was David.

*MAL.* God's Spirit schooled them in all things.

*GAM.* The God who schooled them will be able to school this man.

*MAL.* What? Will God abandon us and school him?

*GAM.* God does not look to sceptres, ancestral genealogies, beauty of appearance or royal wealth, but to hearts stained with no infection of cruelty, deceit and lust. This is the temple in which that holy Spirit is enclosed.

*MAL.* To confess the truth, Gamaliel, you have long seemed to me to approve by your opinion this sacrilegious sect. I cannot hide this by my silence any further, since you act in a manner unworthy of your forbears. Though you more than anyone else ought to defend our authority, you oppose it most strenuously, and all to favour a lunatic youth. In God's name tell me, please, what hope lies behind this attempt of yours? What profit do you seek to gain from this? I suppose the man who seeks utterly to overthrow the entire dignity of our position and summons us to beggary will confer distinctions or wealth on you?

*GAM.* Malchus, you stray far from the mark of truth if you think that we can protect our dignity by pride, violence and arrogance. It was not this regimen which raised high our forbears.

*MAL.* The old ways were better for the ancients, our ways befit us. Each should live according to the character of his generation.

*GAM.* Not so; good ways always befit all good men.

*MAL.* If we had any of our fathers' spirit in us. . .

*GAM.* We too would live according to our fathers' ways.

*MAL.* . . .this villain would have paid the penalty by death, not threats.

*GAM.* Cruelty is foreign to our rank.

*MAL.* Whatever is offered to God is holy and pious.

*GAM.* It is an impious piety to consign the innocent to death.

*MAL.* Do you call him innocent when he overturns our whole world?

*GAM.* If he sins, why not refute him openly, why not reveal the light of your talent in that task? As a man of experience you must confront the novice, as a man of learning the ignorant, as an old man the youth. Perhaps you will bring him back to the path, and win glory for yourself before all.

*MAL.* This wound is not to be healed by gentle treatment, but by rope, sword and fire, or whatever you know to be more cruel than rope, sword and fire.

*GAM.* Granted that his nature is as you describe, or even worse if you will, it is none the less fitting that you allow yourself the sole indulgence of giving the man prior warning in a friendly and soft manner. In that way none can think that you prefer to cast down one whose salvation is in doubt rather than to extend your right hand to one already hell-bent on self-destruction. It is wholly in the interest of your good name that all men, even the envious, realise that you wish to save all men, and to destroy none save him who rushes headlong with obdurate mind. I make this one prayer at least—before your anger diverts you too far, ponder what result you may achieve by this unbending obstinacy.

*MAL.* The answer is surely that I can repress the enemy, console the good, strengthen the doubtful, deter the shameless, and fortify our ancestral laws by this bloodshed.

*GAM.* On the contrary, what you will achieve is to be thought an aggressor, using all the violence of tyranny until you could bring down the holy man whom you could not refute by reason.

*MAL.* However holy and however serious he may be, the divine Spirit does not guide him, since he neglects the ancient practices of our fathers. Since I find no support in those of your station, I shall seek royal help to ward off destruction.

*CHO.* In my judgment, Gamaliel's advice is right; obey his warning. But anger is the enemy of right counsel, and clouds the keen vision of the mind, and closes the ear to healthy advice.

*GAM.* Malchus has gone, fired with anger and swollen with pride. I have given him in his rage careful advice to the utmost of my powers and so far as was possible, striving to soothe his fierce spirits with soft words. I offered trusty counsel. But in his ingratitude he is so far from showing gratitude that he hates even one who deserves well of him.

This[227] is a common feature of life nowadays, and certainly the greatest fault of our circle, that in beguiling the ordinary folk with the appearance of holiness, we can with safety despise God's commands. Should someone dare any action against our practices, we try to overthrow such opponents by the use of gold, remove them with poison, and destroy them with counterfeit witnesses. The king's ears we fill with false tidings; we take vengeance on any offence caused to our own ears by spreading false rumour. We both inflame minds disturbed by madness, and feed the impact of savage anger with the weapon of calumnies.

Malchus[239] is now on his way to the palace without thought of any moderation. He will falsely claim that new sects are rising, that the rites of our fathers are being abandoned, that the king's authority is exposed to mockery, using in fact any argument appropriate for the king, and he will cover his wickedness with honourable pretexts. If he finds the king insufficiently roused by these charges, he will devise some other more savage weapon. He will keep crying that bands have been conspiring against the person of the king, that secret consultations are taking place, that a wicked crime is being hatched and designs secretly cooked up, that groups are gathering by night and increasing their private resources by means of wicked factions. These or tidings more dreadful he will counterfeit, as a spirit without control does, and he continually devises barbaric cruelty. These poisons of his own invention he will let drip into the king's ears.

This[256] indeed is always a common fault in almost all kings, that they readily make themselves available to informers. The more cruel a fiction, the more readily it is believed. Kings fabricate for themselves empty fears; they pay attention to the fickle breath of unsubstantial gossip. The adviser of integrity is accounted cowardly, effete, stupid, dull. We have long ago transformed the senses of virtue because we shine with no virtue; but in our arrogance we deceive the ignorant crowd with shining claims to it.

So[266] far as this prophet is concerned, if only our order would show a more moderate and careful attitude! If he was sent here by God's plan, no human force will be able to confront him; but if he is devising wickedness clothed in guile, he will on the instant pierce himself with his own sword. Each man can draw his conclusion as his mind dictates; but if any one were to follow my opinion on this matter, he would keep his hands clean of innocent blood, and not be rashly wasteful of that sacred blood. Otherwise the precedent which we cruelly set in attacking others may later rebound on our own heads. Is the monstrous behaviour of Herod not sufficient, without the uncontrolled cruelty of his savage mind blazing higher through anger's torches being thrust beneath it?

CHORUS

How deep a blackness shrouds the minds of men in their shadowy hiding-places! In what darkness do we pass the period of our lives which speed away in swift flight!

An assumed modesty cloaks the shameless; the cover of piety conceals the impious. On their faces men who are disturbed feign tranquillity, and deceivers feign truthfulness.

The person who shows stern seriousness of countenance, and is a model unparalleled for moderate life, seethes and is driven headlong by madness, and blazes fiercely into anger.

Just as the smoke from the furnaces of Etna makes the rocks bound along in swift rolling movement, just as the flame bakes Vesuvius into dry ashes, such is the blind madness for vengeance impelling this man to rush upon the innocent prophet, so that with his harsh charge he may foully confound the naked truth.

You[301] bring to birth such evil, O desire for glory swollen with empty pride, and you, praise accorded to honour with your veneer of gleaming outward show. When once you have seized the kingdom of the mind, you bewitch men's spirits with alluring poison, and by exiling reason you throw into confusion the temple of the heart.

Truth,[309] devotion, modesty flee from you; faith too, and that virtue which was the guest of a better age, and was last to abandon our notorious lands to their vices.

O,[313] if only some contriver could remove the clouds of man's countenance, and permit us to gaze on the naked cares of the heart, exposing the dark sanctum of the mind hidden deep within, then you would see dewlling in that tiny cavern monsters of varied and wondrous shapes, greater in number than those which Nile and Ganges breed in distant lands, and Africa teeming with savage prodigies, and the Caucasus bristling with dark lurking-places.

THE BAPTIST

The[323] madness of the bloodstained tigress would not be absent from there, nor the fierceness of the tawny lioness, nor the grim gluttony of savage wolves whose thirst is sated by no carnage, nor the baneful basilisk with its poisoned breath, nor the viper causing extended sleep, nor the scorpion so fearsome with the weapon of its jagged tail, nor the crocodile whose feigned weeping resounds through the dry seaweed, nor the wiles of the fox, nor the deceiving sport of the Egyptian hyena.

Feigned[334] devotion cloaks the cruelty of tyrants, the fringed robe wicked manners. Naked virtue hides herself in thin rags in the shade of a rustic hut. It does not sell itself under proud labels. It laughs at the lunatic din of the forum and the applause of the crowd's favour, and does not sit as a dependant at the doors of a great patron. Known to itself alone, it demands silent years of happy life in the sequestered countryside.

QUEEN HEROD

*QUEEN.* You are ever slow-witted. Not yet do you feel the royal authority slipping away, not yet in your blindness do you see the ambush being laid against your person. If this rabble-rouser should survive for a further year, in vain would you threaten him with bonds, prison and the cross. Already in his pride he vaunts his strength, and overshadows the clients of the royal court with his flock of followers.

*HEROD.* What danger do you fear from an unarmed crowd?

*QUEEN.* If you allow secret gatherings to take place, you must believe that there is no class whom you should not fear.

*HER.* But the people, whom he teaches, voluntarily rush to him.

*QUEEN.* A faction pouring in from far and wide is more to be feared.

*HEROD.* The holiness of the man refutes this charge.

*QUEEN.* Crimes often lurk hidden beneath such a cloak.

*HER.* Violence is to be feared from empurpled viceroys.

*QUEEN.* And deceit is to be feared from stern-faced hypocrites.

*HER.* He is without wealth or arms, river-water slakes his thirst, the woodland gives him food, the earth a grassy bed; what guile will such a man be able to devise against a sceptred king?

*QUEEN.* You see his clothing, you see his food and drink, but what he has hidden in his heart you do not see.

*HER.* The condition of kings is wretched if it fears the wretched.

*QUEEN.* It becomes most wretched if it is plundered through fearing nothing.

*HER.* In that case what safety will now remain for kings?

*QUEEN.* All will be safe if they silently remove what impedes them.

*HER.* Surely this is the difference between the tyrant and the good king, that the king keeps watch on enemies, whereas the tyrant is the enemy of the citizens.

*QUEEN.* Both dying and destroying are grim experiences, but if a choice must be made it is better to destroy the enemy.

*HER.* When one is unnecessary, both courses are wretched.

*QUEEN.* Must we do nothing harsh in this great commotion, when the madness of the fickle crowd is roused, and laws, religion, and the authority of the prince are scorned and mocked by the dregs of the mob? Beware that a false appearance of leniency does not seduce your mind from justice. What seems leniency will on closer inspection be the greatest cruelty.

While[383] you are merciful to one seditious and wicked man, you advance towards the destruction of all, for he is scurrying to arm them against your person. Imagine what must finally take place coming to pass—the fickle crowd roused to arms, the whole country ablaze with mournful war in sundry places, huge estates abandoned, cities fired, maidens forcibly raped, battle joined with uncertain outcome. When licence has broken the reins of the laws, too late will you then condemn this clemency of yours.

See[393] now, the source of this plague and bane draws near. Here is that well-known critic. Question him; if I am not mistaken, you will be told more by him than the tidings which rumour has spread abroad. I am not surprised that there are men who despise your rule when you yourself challenge the wicked by your leniency.

*HER.* It is the mark of good kings when the power is great to put limits on their use of force.

*QUEEN.* Is this how the matter stands? Will this man now impose limits on the royal sceptre? Is the kingship to be maintained at his discretion? If you had a king's spirit. . .

*HER.* Do go; leave these matters to me.

*QUEEN.* Yes, I go so that I may not suffer fresh insults against my person as before. When a queen yields unavenged to the lowest citizens, what hope of justice will encourage the rest?

HEROD   JOHN   CHORUS

*HER.* Has she now left? Yes, she has left. Let us discuss this matter meanwhile. There is nothing to cause you concern, nothing for you to consider strange in a slighted woman's being angrier than she should be when she is noble, rich, powerful and above all a queen.

You[410] yourself above all can be the best witness of how greatly I have always favoured your safety. The hatred of all the common folk seeks you out and demands that you stand trial to pay the penalty. Our leaders are angry, and the priests are seething. So I shall briefly recount the cause which fires this public complaint.

All[416] ranks of our society you openly savage in abusive speeches; and you deceive the common herd, ignorant of the old laws, by scattering abroad the deadly venom of new teaching. With your tempestuous words you confound the condition of the kingdom and the peace of the state. You hinder the soldiers from obeying their commander and the people from obeying Caesar as you promise the common folk a new kingdom. You promise that they will be free of the foreign yoke, and you rouse them with empty hope. You do not allow our rebellious nation to be at peace, and as if we had not borne sufficient calamities you seek in lunatic fashion to challenge Roman arms again.

I[429] have no doubt of your past recklessness out of my sight when in my presence you have openly censured me for an unchaste marriage, and have striven to fire the hatred of the people against me, and have tried to launch my brother in battle against me, so far as you were able. And as if you had not perpetrated sufficient crimes by venturing all things against the safety of all alike, you now prepare to make war on heaven, and try to abolish the rites which have been the means of this kingdom's continuing existence until now.

This[437] is what the whole people is growling. They complain that I am slow to avenge the ancestral laws. But no action of a harsher kind have I initiated against you; and now whatever the support of a friendly and well-disposed judge can confer will be generously bestowed on you by me. It was no Assyrian or Egyptian father who begot me to make me a tyrant eager for your blood. You and I share the same country as native land, wet-nurse, and mother. Whenever a person from the humblest of the common folk dies, I always regard it as a limb of my body torn away; it is my blood that seems to be shed.

In[449] Herod you will have a judge amenable and fair. If you can refute the other charges made against you, I pardon you for all that you have previously said against me and my kin. You will realise from the witness of the people that I ignore injury to myself, but punish injury to the state. I pray that you may dissolve the other charges against you in such a way that your innocence leaves me no occasion to exercise harshness.

*CHO*. Proceed by this path to win affection, and you will live famous in the eyes of posterity. Believe that kingdoms are safe not so much through gold or bands of soldiers, but when love and loyalty gained through fairness defend them.

*JOHN*. The man to whom God entrusts the wielding of reins over a people must listen to many things but need not believe them all. Gain, envy, partiality, fear, grief often repress the truth. If any individual from the common folk or the elders believes that I have uttered anything too unkind against him, he should condemn his manner of life before blaming my words.

It[469] has always been my way to censure public sins publicly. I neither do nor teach anything in secret; I do not seek hidden lairs. It is not men but sins which I rebuke. When the soldiers asked me how they could serve both king and God alike, I forbade them to strike, rob, assault, or encompass with guile the unwary. I bade them order their desires to the limit of their pay. No hope in revolution do I proclaim save that which you in your belief drawn from the ancient prophets share with me. Meanwhile from all these thousands not a single individual is adduced who at my prompting has despised his prince.

Whether[483] gossip has brought these charges, or blind anger has invented them in its headlong rage induced by zeal to harm, the naked truth will of its own accord readily refute them. I consider that there is no more certain proof of how devotedly I practise our ancient rites and customs than that the famed informer who lays charges against me does not come forward openly, but murmurs them in secret when an opportunity for falsehood readily occurs.

As[491] for my saying that it is not right for you to possess your brother's wife, you must ponder in your own mind whether it is juster to please yourself or God. Likewise I only wish that all who devote themselves to the friendship of kings had the disposition to prefer to utter what is true and healthy rather than the flattering words which will later be harmful. How numerous are the ills and troubles to which the way would then be barred!

You[499] are just and fair in what is just and fair, and as is just for a defender of justice, you must ponder any remarks I earlier uttered with greater frankness and truth. Set the limits to your power which the application of the laws has imposed on you. The rights which you here wield against others God who is king of all possesses against you and other kings. So whatever decision you will reach about my person you must believe that God makes about yours.

HER. Speak of matters heavenly when you reach the stars. As long as you dwell on earth, bear with earthly laws.

JOHN. I respect earthly kingdoms and I obey their kings; but the eternal kingdom I consider my native land, and its king I worship.

HER. The facts cry out how you obey kings, for you wish this king to obey your laws.

JOHN. If I could pass laws, I would decree that peoples should obey kings, and kings God.

HER. Enough of this disputation. Take this man back again. The matter is a tangled one. Until the whole situation is clear and becomes more certainly known, I am resolved to take no decision.

CHO. He who thinks that he can penetrate the secret thoughts of a king's mind from his words should surely know that he is trusting in a distorting mirror. I pray that the heavenly Father may order all things happily, but my mind trembles to presage what it fears.

HER. Words cannot express by speech nor the eye of the mind grasp by thought how wretched and troubled is the destiny of kings. The common herd believes that we alone are free and we alone happy; but in fact poverty besieges us, fear tortures us, wretched slavery oppresses us. The people venture to confess freely all that they love, desire or fear; they enjoy their modest wealth, for fear is far away. But when we go out of doors we must don the mask of respectability. We are compelled to make kindly promises with benevolent countenance, to utter just sentiments openly, to put off anger with feigning heart, to repress hatred until the appropriate time, to utter the greatest threats when the greatest causes of fear oppress the troubled breast.

The[539] common folk despises a moderate prince, and hates a harsh one. One must be both slave and commander to the fickle crowd. I do nothing at my own discretion. If I destroy this prophet, I shall displease the people; If I preserve him, I neglect the interests of my kingdom. What, then, must I do? Is there any doubt about this? I must take thought for my rule; I am my own neighbour. Granted that one must act the people's servant to preserve kingly power, what could be more foolish than to destroy the kingship through eagerness to please the mob? The common folk is capricious in embracing joy and anger, and likewise capricious in abandoning them.

Now[550] I am decided to buttress the king's authority with bloodshed. The crowd will be readily appeased thereafter. If I permit this present bane to infiltrate more widely, it will prevail over the remedies for it. He has manifestly dared to censure me for an unchaste marriage before my face. If I allow him this licence with impunity, the man's shamelessness will not halt there. Next he will seek to divert the royal power to conform with his own laws, next he will clap irons on his prisoners, next he will desire to rule rather than be ruled; he will impose laws on the royal house, and mingle what is highest with the lowest. This growing evil must at once be remedied; this new flame must be extinguished before it spreads. By enduring an existing evil one provokes new insults.

If[564] I can gain the favour of the people in exacting punishment, I shall not withhold gratitude for the people's support. But if I cannot gain it, it is my resolve to relegate everything to the kingship. I regard as no concern of mine the babblings of the rabbi Malchus about the laws, the meddlesome issues which he raises in accusations undefined, as long as the people realise that this one law is to be observed: to believe that for me anything contrary to the laws can be lawful.

CHORUS

Creator of this massive world, at whose nod all things tremble—the sky tricked with gleaming stars, the earth blossoming with diverse plants, the sea swelling with its lapping tides—has not the talk of men privy to a previous age brought to our ears the glorious deeds of this earlier era? Then it was that with the power of your strong right hand you yourself destroyed kingdoms proud with gold and riches, tearing them up by the roots so that you might implant us in their territory, a territory won not by our swords or darts, nor by our design or strength.

But[587] the almighty support of heaven led us safe through fierce armies. Are you not the famed king of the sons of Isaac, the God of the Hebrew race? Under your leadership we have destroyed the enemy, and trodden underfoot his treacherous army. Without trusting in our strength but with you as our leader and patron, we have often brought back splendid palms of victory to our native land.

Father,[596] you surely do not desert utterly the people whom you once loved? We are surely not abandoned to the enemy, as a mere whisper of the past? Devotion is despised, religion lies neglected, deceit rules in the empurpled hall. Your holy people offers as victim its devoted neck to the savage axe. Prophets die by the sword of the tyrant; the enemy takes joy in our griefs. Under the cloak of holiness men who deserve punishment are at the helm of the kingdom, whilst punishment constrains those deserving of the kingship.

Arise,[608] lend help to your people; arise, most noble father, and allow the enemy to see you as our fathers saw you, sinking the Egyptian chariots in the Red Sea, to see you as the servant of the presaging prophet once with open eyes beheld you, giving free rein to your fiery team, and scattering flames over the whole plain. Let him who keeps hidden the eyes of his human mind buried in blinding mist dispel the darkness of error and acknowledge you as the all-powerful One; likewise the land which grows warm at the first appearance of the sun, and that which sees the light of the sun's red fire plunge into the ocean.

MALCHUS    JOHN

*MAL.* Human affairs are undoubtedly so ordained that if God offers you a choice, you vacillate indecisively wondering what to refuse and what to desire. Do you long for wealth, distinctions, achievement for you and your kin? These things have often destroyed those who obtained their prayer. Do you pray for bonds, prison, flight for your enemy? These often bring him the greatest glory, and harm to you.

Indeed,[631] not to look for examples afar, I have found this to be true to my own despite. For when this new Baptist was dwelling on remote mountain ridges and was bewitching the mob, drawing with him the flock of the credulous common folk, I offered myself as the sole defender of the Pharisees' dignity while the rest hesitated. I did not cease to try every course until harsh bonds restrained those guilty hands and the public prison confined the enemy, and until I filled the whole palace with charges.

Yet[641] according to the evidence of my eyes bonds, prison, accusations are of no avail. The grim power of that wicked bane has so seized the minds of the common folk, and the hearts of all have so drained the deadly venom that they glorify his calamities and grieve at his hazards. Wherever I go they curse me, they point me out with their fingers, they gaze at me with hostile eyes. But favour is shown to that sacrilegious man who has removed all distinctions between situations and classes, and vigil is kept before his closed prison.

I[652] believe that there is nothing more wretched than we who abandon other matters and dedicate ourselves to the interests of the people. Whoever devotes himself to the people must know that his favours have been idly bestowed, since the people with malicious temper is always wont to support the debased and to despise the noble.

What[658] remedy shall I seek? What shall I complain of first? On whom should I concentrate my anger? To whom should I bring aid first? Our people wickedly cultivates a false prophet. The rabbis mutter, the king winks, the leaders ignore it. On these shoulders, yes, on these shoulders I alone sustain our tottering ancestral rites with none to lend a helping hand. I alone lament the fate of the state. What then shall I do? Shall I abandon the task? Shall I betray the laws and the dignity of our rank, and suffer myself to be a mockery to our enemies? Yes, I shall certainly suffer it, for what else could I do now? Shall I bear alone what all refuse to bear, and thrust myself in the path of the tumbling state? Let God defend his own possessions. Since now life's nature is such that every man fends for himself, I shall be my own neighbour. If I administer the state badly, its fall will turn against my person. Those who at present show me the greatest support whilst I am upright will be the first to grind me with their heels when I am prostrate. If I should run affairs well and incur unpopularity, I shall obtain for myself nothing but odium. Now at this late hour the strategy of Gamaliel appeals—

unless perhaps none can regain his senses so late. I prefer that they seek in vain my steadfastness here than that they punish my rashness after the deed is done.

Let[682] each man judge as he decides. I shall rid myself of my troubles and repair my good relations with this prophet; as a man of naive mind he will not, I think, refuse. If he shows himself more truculent towards me, I shall apply every technique so that the people may not believe that he has died through my devices. If I win over the people, the matter will not have turned out badly from every viewpoint.

Why,[690] he himself is here, I think; yes, he is certainly here. See what a crowd follows in attendance on the sacrilegious fellow! Meanwhile we sit idle in the middle of the city amidst empty chairs. But I should like to hear first what observations this master brings.

*JOHN.* Great ruler, creator, lord of the universe, all that the air contains in its yielding bosom, all that the earth brings forth, all that the sea nurtures beneath its waves acknowledges you as God, experiences you as parent, and follows your laws once given in unchangeable course. At your command the spring decks the fields with blossoms, summer proffers harvests, autumn pours forth wine, and winter clothes the mountains with whitening frosts. Winding rivers roll down to the sea masses of waters, the sea's tides ebb and flow, Diana fires the night and Phoebus the day as he traverses the world with his unresting torch. In short, there is nothing whatsoever in heaven or on earth which does not gladly obey its king, love its father, and declare its zeal for its founder with all the functions which it can achieve.

Only[712] man, for whom much more than for the rest of creation it would be fitting to rejoice in and to obey God's commands, amongst all and supremely registers contempt. He spurns God's commands, rejects the reins of the laws, and rushes headlong into every crime. He measures justice by wantonness, and weighs law by violence.

*MAL.* Your first remarks thus far are just.

*JOHN.* I am not so surprised at gentiles throughout the world leaving the path in wandering error as at the people who boast that they are God's heirs, and who assail others with rebukes, calling them wicked; whereas no race throughout the whole world, wherever sun gazes on earth, lives more licentiously.

*MAL.* True indeed are all your words thus far.

*JOHN.* This is not the fault solely of the fickle crowd. The Levite shining afar with gleaming robe, the scribe swollen with knowledge of the law, and you elders venerable in your full age—distorting delusion misleads you with its erroneous windings. At your platform the cause of the widow and of the orphan fails, and the rich man oppresses the poor. Things just and unjust are alike for sale.

*MAL.* I burst with anger. Am I to listen to this in silence?

*JOHN.* As for you, rabbis, who pretend to excel all others in holiness and knowledge, and you, consecrated rank of priests and chief bishop of the sacred college, you take your tithe of every vegetable which the earth brings forth. Anise, mint, rue, garlic do not escape you, nor nettles nor the hay still green. But certainly so far as reading and teaching the replies of the prophets and demonstrating the path of a holier life are concerned, your authority then is silent; in this you are silent watchdogs which do not bark, which do not drive off the wolves which howl around your sheep-folds. Why did I speak of the wolves? You yourselves are the wolves, you devour the flock; their wool clothes you, their milk slakes your thirst, their flesh relieves your hunger. You feed not the flock but yourselves.

*MAL.* Let harmony give place from here and to hell with it! Am I to endure further insults levelled impertinently like this against my rank? If God were to send me from heaven with the instruction that I must listen to these words, I would ignore the orders rather than hear these things said. I can endure them no further.

You[757] there, fine sir, sole teacher of the masses, is this, then, your teaching? Is this the instruction you give to simple folk?

*JOHN.* If you are honest, our words in no way apply to you.

*MAL.* Is it your job to ridicule a priest?

*JOHN.* I believe that censure of wicked men is well said.

*MAL.* It is fitting for a young man to obey his elders.

*JOHN.* It is more fitting for all to obey God.

*MAL.* Did God, then, bid you utter these sentiments?

*JOHN.* Truth bids all proclaim what is true.

*MAL.* It has often profited many to have left the truth unsaid.

*JOHN.* We have no time for profit linked with sin.

*MAL.* Do you consider it a sin not to speak of sin?

*JOHN.* I consider it a sin to watch all these thousands perish, when I could guide them back to the path.

*MAL.* Guide them back? Are we not the shepherds of the flock?

JOHN. Yes, if feeding and devouring are the same thing.

*MAL.* Concern yourself with your affairs, and relinquish ours.

*JOHN.* What is a neighbour's business is also mine.

*MAL.* Who then are you, pray, that you are endowed with this authority? Are you the Christ promised to our fathers?

*JOHN.* No.

*MAL.* Are you the expected prophet?

*JOHN.* No.

*MAL.* Are you Elias?

*JOHN.* Nor Elias either.

*MAL.* If you are none of these, neither our hope Christ nor a prophet nor Elias, how, pray, do you presume to be the instigator of the new baptism? Who, then, shall we say you are? Inform me.

*JOHN.* I am a voice crying on the distant ridges of the mountains: 'Prepare ye the way, make straight your paths, for the Lord is nigh. At his coming the hollow valleys will level themselves, and the mountains will bring low their rocky peaks to the ground.' I baptize the people with water in the name of him whose slippers I his servant would be unworthy to remove, of him whom no man acknowledges though he lives and continually roams amongst you.

*MAL.* What traps this fellow lays, how he deceives with ambiguities! By what miracle do you prove the authority which you claim for yourself in this way?

*JOHN.* I could ask you too in turn by what miracle you prove your authority.

*MAL.* How impertinent the man is! However you hide it, all none the less know what draws you into mad conduct. You surely long to advance yourself by the odium which we incur, to obtain profit and fame to our cost. You seek to become powerful by evil methods. You do not deceive us; it is yourself that you deceive. You are not the first to have attempted deception by these means. May you finally pay the allotted penalty, or rather may you change your attitude for the better at my prompting, and as you encouraged men to go astray, so may you change and encourage them to return to the path!

I[808] have seen men parading an austere sanctity in dress, so that they readily fostered the belief that they were moderate and

THE BAPTIST

simple in mind; then, when they had won positions and wealth by these means, they gradually revealed their nature, openly despised the honesty which they earlier successfully counterfeited, and gave free rein to their true characters. But if you seek to attain lofty distinctions by this path, ignorance of affairs deceives you in your inexperience. It is not by this way that one attains high fame. Unless experience, which is not the worst of masters, and old age, the mother of experience, have outrageously deceived me, you will better consult the interests of your reputation and profit if you seek what is safe rather than what is glorious.

*JOHN.* If I speak the truth and do what is right, why must anyone impose silence on me? But if I speak falsehoods, you who are learned must demonstrate this to me in my ignorance.

*MAL.* You will regret these words when you pay the penalty with death.

*JOHN.* That threat you must make to them that fear death.

*MAL.* If I live long enough, I will make you sorry for this impertinence. You will realise what it is to disregard the elders, to rend with rebukes the scribes, to challenge the rabbis with impudent words. And since you ignore the fact that we have friends, you will perhaps come to realise what power the hatred of the elders has.

CHORUS

The man who prepares himself for thieving avoids lights in the darkness. The assassin hates the torch which witnesses his madness. The child rejects the medicine which lurks in the bitter absinth. The wound reopened recoils from healing plasters.

The[841] man whose breast within is gnawed by the mind's secret ills finds troublesome the truth which exposes his unquiet heart. But as for you, stern hypocrites who take delight in wicked gain though manifesting severity on crabbed brow, however much you have hidden your secret crimes from the misapprehensions of the trusting crowd and though the foul dregs of your impious minds are concealed, none the less your conscience gnaws you in secret and finds you guilty. The hidden executioner enclosed within your entrails devours you, scourging you with his grim whip. Thrice blessed and more is the man chaste of mind who does not become the accused before the judges of his own house, and is not continually flogged in his heart by the torturer enclosed there!

## THE BAPTIST

#### MALCHUS　　CHORUS　　QUEEN

*MAL.*  No reliable hope lies in the king. By his base ambition he has betrayed both the state's cause and his own. In his eagerness to please the people, in his pursuit of the fair wind of favour by an appearance of gentleness, he has striven to consign me to the anger of the common folk, and has sought to compensate for the injuries done to him by exposing me to danger. Undoubtedly if he saw the people too discontented with the murder of the Baptist he was ready to appease them at once with my head; but should the people be untroubled by the slaughter of the leader of the new faction, he craftily sought it to be believed that he had avenged himself with the greatest fame.

In[875] this way kings mount for their enjoyment shows which exploit the blood of citizens from opposing sides, and sport with the slaughter we inflict on each other. Whatever plan the crowd approves they claim as their own, and proclaim that they have carried it out. They arrogate the diligence of our toil for their own praise. If the wind of popular favour veers away from what they were opining and demanding, they pass on the guilt to their ministers, and divert the effect of their sinning by spilling innocent blood and by destruction of life held cheap.

The[886] queen is the only one left who shares my resentment. She is like a raging tigress robbed of her cubs; this is because the Baptist did not approve the defilement of the compact of her previous marriage in the presence of the king, and because he openly condemned the marriage with his brother's wife which was forbidden by the law. Whilst this flame of her seething anger is still fresh and blazing, I shall thrust torches beneath her disturbed mind and feed them with appropriate words.

Why,[893] here she conveniently presents herself at the right moment.

*CHO.*  Now flame joins flame, poison now joins poison. The most extreme danger now looms.

*MAL.*  Hail, queen, shining glory of our race, sole lady worthy of the eminence of this great kingdom!

*QUEEN.*  Greetings to you likewise, rabbi Malchus. But why so sad?

*MAL.*  It is the same cause, I think, which pricks your mind.

*QUEEN.*  Perhaps, but you must reveal its nature more explicitly.

*MAL.* Can you endure without indignation contempt for your status, the cheapening of the sacred authority of the royal title throughout the world, and the subjection of the sceptre to the herd's whim?

*QUEEN.* What then can I do? Tell me what remedy there is.

*MAL.* Steel yourself to engender in your heart anger worthy of your spirit, your birth, and your marriage.

*QUEEN.* That has long been done. I am torn with anger. I weep, I rebuke, I shout, but I achieve nothing with anger and tears. The winds scatter my words.

*MAL.* If you had the appropriate authority with your husband, would he have endured unavenged the injuries to you, or to speak more truly, to himself?

*QUEEN.* Malchus, you yourself observe where the enthusiasm of the people lies. Perhaps the king believed that the man's eager spirit and boldness could be blunted and softened by this punishment.

*MAL.* If you believe that this brigand's fierce spirits are repressed by bonds and imprisonment, you are mistaken. The violence of wild beasts which have burst from a shattered cage rages more fiercely than that of those always reared by deep forest on trackless mountains.

What[922] will he not do when freed, since the people even now cherish his bonds? His anger when provoked is fired and not softened. His spirit borne aloft by insults is being driven to madness.

*QUEEN.* No; rather he will be softened by this kind treatment, because after being undone by his own obstinacy he has been freed by the king's mercy.

*MAL.* What you consider a kindness he thinks an injury, and he will recall more frequently your shackling him than your releasing him.

*QUEEN.* This is a harsh temperament which you describe.

*MAL.* A trait innate in almost all men is that gratitude for your kindness evaporates there and then, but none forgets your evil deed. Nearly everyone hates kindnesses when the recollection of them is associated with evil deeds. Realise that whenever the Baptist recalls your good deed, he remembers as often his own wickedness. He will believe that he has not been acquitted of his crime but is in your mind guilty, and freed because of base canvassing, that his punishment has been remitted but that your anger is only temporarily suppressed.

*QUEEN.* Good will softens savage tempers.

*MAL.* One can much more easily destroy than reform a habit which by long practice has continually developed for the worse.

*QUEEN.* Why then do you not offer me prior advice in my doubt about the appropriate action?

*MAL.* I shall do this readily and expeditiously if you trust me.

*QUEEN.* Just advise me; so far as I am concerned, there will be no delay.

*MAL.* Great deeds are done by investigation, action, foresight; not by idleness.

*QUEEN.* But if you achieve nothing by investigation, action, foresight, is it not better to remain inactive than to indulge in activity fruitless to yourself and to be a laughing-stock to others?

*MAL.* Often hard work prevails in something which violence does not achieve. A lofty oak is not felled suddenly at a blow; a battering-ram in war does not destroy walls at the first assault. Often time solves what you imagined could not be achieved. What reasoning frequently cannot attain, rude insistence seizes by storm. So do some soliciting. Mingle prayers with tears, anger with advice, soft words with rebukes. Diligently canvass your husband in every way, seize your opportunities on every occasion. If the deed cannot be carried through openly, stretch the net of wiles. For my part, it is my fixed intention not to relax in the slightest until the deed is done.

### CHORUS

At last malice and resentment, fired by unholy madness, have thrust forth the strength of their savagery against the devoted prophet. On the one side savage calumny joined to hideous tyranny fights in wicked deceit; on the other, guiltless truth with no supporter despises fearful threats. A single person is the target of all those darts, and as many wiles likewise level death at the young man. But he, like a hard oak battered by raging north winds, or a rock which the sea assaults with its resurging waves, is shattered by no fear.

Guileless[984] Truth, deity revered by all, whom neither the violence of war with its fear nor deceit with its ambush can dislodge from your unyielding stance, you alone do not fear the oppressive shifts of unsteady fortune. You are subject to no strokes of chance; you arm men's hearts with invincible strength.

You forbid the unsubdued power of the Fates, which is mistress of both life and death, to be oppressive to us.

But[997] do I hesitate to confront the prophet, to fill his ears with the most wretched possible tidings? Why, there he stands before the very doors of the prison.

Offspring holier than your holy parents, sole confirmation of their former innocence, look to your safety while time allows it. The rabbi Malchus secretly directs his wiles, and the queen bereft of any plan rages. The court fawns on the king, the king conceals his opinion; the rest fear to speak the truth. The time of the final danger is now at hand.

JOHN    CHORUS

*JOHN.*  What danger is there?
*CHO.*  Death's final moment looms.
*JOHN.*  Is this the sum of evil overhanging me?
*CHO.*  No greater ill could befall a man.
*JOHN.*  Even if the violence and guile of the tyrant were to vanish, length of days will of its own accord bring this upon me—an end to be feared by the base man, but desired by the innocent.
*CHO.*  Though you neglect your own safety, let thought for ours affect you. Put off this attitude for a while, soften the king's mind with prayers, I hope that he will not be obdurate when friends entreat him.
*JOHN.*  But am I not diligently doing this?
*CHO.*  May God foster this attitude in you.
*JOHN.*  There is no need for this prayer; this has for long been my disposition. The king hastens to sate his anger with my blood, and I do not oppose him. How could I appease the king more than by our wanting and not wanting identical things?
*CHO.*  Auspicious words, I pray.
*JOHN.*  What advice do you give me then? Two kings, one on each side, bid me do opposing things. The one is in heaven, and is merciful, kind, good; the other is earthly, and is uncontrolled, fierce, evil. One threatens death, the other forbids me fear death and promises a reward if I do not fear violence. One can destroy my body, but the other will be able to torture body and spirit in flames unavoidable. Since they are opposed to each other, advise me which I should obey.

*CHO.* There is no subsequent chance of appeasing Herod, if the chance now offered is let slip; but the anger of God can always be appeased.

*JOHN.* The slower God's anger rages, the more sternly it exacts punishment once roused.

*CHO.* Do you despise in this way the destined end which God has desired mortals to fear? He fastened spirit to body with a mutual bond of love so that no random reason which offers itself might separate the sacred association of body and spirit.

*JOHN.* I do not despise death, but I flee from the death which abides by espousing that which is momentary. The enjoyment of the light which God granted me I gladly return to him at his request.

*CHO.* Are you, a father, leaving your children orphaned in this way?

*JOHN.* One who believes that God is his father will never be orphaned.

*CHO.* Are you not influenced by your relatives or the tears of your friends, whom you are abandoning to an uncontrolled tyrant?

*JOHN.* I am not abandoning them, but rather being abandoned by them; for I am hastening to my end on the road established since the beginning of the world. All of us who enjoy the gift of kindly light are certainly born under this law, and one condition constrains us all; we advance towards death, and each day leads us to it.

God[1057] has willed that death be a punishment for the wicked and a harbour for the good—the end of a long journey, but the gate leading to the beginning of a longer life; the gate to direct us reborn more truly than dead to the shining house of enduring light. This is man's departure from prison, and the passage to a life without death. On this path the whole gathering of our fathers has preceded us, and all men will follow. What runner having left the starting-gate does not hasten in mind to the post? What man who wanders on a stormy strait in black darkness would refuse to lay up his vessel in a quiet harbour? What exile as he wandered through a deserted wilderness on foreign soil would grieve that he was returning quickly to his native land?

So[1071] I am joyful to think that I have run the course and am poised at the post. Now liberated from the straits of a life almost completed, I gaze upon land. I am returning home from foreign soil to behold for the first time the best of fathers. He is the father who separated the land from the waters, who clothed the land with sky, who governs the fixed changes of the moving heavens. He is the sole preserver, author, ruler of all things, for whom all things living and dead alike are alive.

As[1081] a flame of its own accord rolls upward its coils, as waters rush downwards with perpetual flow, as all things proceed to their own nourishment, so my spirit sprung from heaven has for long been panting for the father of the world who dwells in eternal light; for to gaze on him is life, and not to see him is death. Would I not hasten to go there even if the Caucasus bristling with its frosts, the air with its storms, the waters with their tempests barred the way? Must I not burst my way through, even if a thousand deaths confront me, to see all those holy leaders, kings, prophets and judges?

So[1093] my spirit is eager to fly free from the unbarred prison of the body to where the whole world will sooner or later pass. In my view a long life is nothing but lingering slavery in a grim prison. O death, alone the respite from harsh toil: death, harbour from grief and repose from evil, benefit which few appreciate, a source of fear for the debased but an aspiration to the good, receive in your bosom this shipwrecked, mean body, and conduct it into the home of everlasting rest where violence, guile and calumny will not attend it.

*CHO.* How blessed are you by reason of this stability of heart! How wretched are we, for sluggish fear of mind deprives us of this partnership in happiness! Since then you are firm on what you must do, we say hail and farewell for ever.

How[1110] unharmonious contention affects men's minds in different ways! He does not fear death who has done nothing to deserve it; but death has only to snap her fingers lightly with empty threats and the man who deserves to die turns pale and trembles with ignoble fear. The energy with which the wicked flee from death amidst flames, waters and remote rocks is matched by the eagerness for death with which good men urge on their glorious souls through all grim experiences. Surely death has advantages unknown to evil men, and the life which befriends death is happier.

We[1121] do not die in entirety, but the better part of us spurns the greedy pyre and climbs aloft to our ancestral heaven, where a fixed abode awaits innocent souls amongst the fiery dwellers of heaven. But the guilty shades are hounded in a pool of brimstone by the Furies with their hair of black snakes, by the hungry maw of greedy Cerberus, and by the abundance of Tantalus who is never filled. On the one side are the evil experiencing fear; on the other the good entertaining goodly hope, and hearts lavish with their frail lives in their haste to attain a life not frail.

O[1133] fleeting life, Siren-singer so powerful with your witch's enticements, hugging a deceitful good! With the soft allurements of evil you cut us off from the escape which is at hand, and you block the desirable harbour of enduring peace. In that harbour no rattle of war-terror is heard, and no trumpets reecho their harsh din; no grabbing corsair keeps the seas in terror, no fierce brigand haunts the silent grove. No crazy plunderer, impelled by wretched desire for domination, arranges destruction for his people, nor overwhelms the needy with disasters so that he may happily languish in solitary and peaceful leisure; there is none there to trade cheaply the lives of the wretched populace for empty honours. Instead, calm peace and fostering blessedness and ingenuous honesty control all things, and daylight which has learnt no passage to darkness, and life which knows no second death, and joys which know no complaining grief.

O[1153] sweet lodging of our bodily home, life's prison which we love too much, now at last strip of your sorcerer's bonds our heaven-born minds, which lie in the bosom of your embrace oblivious of their native land, intoxicated with the enervating poison of sleep-inducing forgetfulness, and happy with the yoke of that ignoble wedlock. Deceitful covering of our garment of clay, depart and disappear again into the ashes which you constitute, so that the mind may again be restored to its ancestral heaven, and become suffused with rays of clear light. By death free yourself from baneful toils, and the mind from troubles which bring anxiety.

#### QUEEN

So the Pharisee has deceived our hope, whilst the king has betrayed himself and me alike with equal futility in his fear of the tawdry gossip of the chattering crowd. I am wretchedly apprehensive about the activity of my daughter, to whom the king at a crowded banquet had recently promised whatever she asked as reward for her dancing. She stipulated that she would ask for the head of the Baptist on a dish, and she will obtain it, yes, she will surely obtain it, unless my knowledge of the king's mind is inadequate. He will be freed of the odium of the murder, and will gladly, I think, divert the hatred of the people on me. I shall gladly endure it if the deed is accomplished. Against the hatred I shall weigh the joy of vengeance; against the besmirching, the gain. It is base to be accounted a harsh woman, base if it were not baser for princes to go unavenged.

But[1181] both king and girl are stepping out from the house. The closer our hope comes, the more oppressively burns our fear. May God enable all to turn out well!

### HEROD    GIRL    QUEEN

*HER.* Does your request after careful thought now seem sufficient for you?

*GIRL.* Sufficient, if kings' promises turn out firm and kingly enough.

*HER.* Have no fear of what has been guaranteed with a firm promise in the presence of witnesses. Ask for half my kingdom, or if there is anything dearer to your heart than the kingdom, you will obtain it. No pressure will deter my compliance.

*GIRL.* We shall shortly see the nature of this willingness.

*HER.* Go on, ask; assent is certain.

*GIRL.* I have no need of your kingdom; whilst you are king I count it as much mine as if I myself possessed it. I ask for what is available and fair.

*HER.* It is not I but you who delay your obtaining it.

*GIRL.* Give me the severed head of the Baptist in this dish.

*HER.* What suggestion is this, my girl, which casually falls from your lips?

*GIRL.* Not casually.

*HER.* You beg a gift unfitting for a maiden.

*GIRL.* It is not an unfitting deed to destroy an enemy.

*HER.* Is this man, then, an enemy worthy of the king's anger?

*GIRL.* He is worthy of your anger since he deserved it by his crime.

*HER.* What cure shall I then find for the people's hatred?

*GIRL.* The people's role is to obey, the king's to command.

*HER.* The king's role is to command what is just.

*GIRL.* The king by his command can make just what was earlier unjust.

*HER.* But the law enjoins a limit to the king's commanding.

*GIRL.* If the law is what the prince has decreed, the law does not limit kings, but the king the laws.

*HER.* Rumour will brand me as tyrant, not as king.

*GIRL.* Yet rumour fears the royal power.

*HER.* It fears it, yet still gossips.

*GIRL.* Restrain it with the steel.

*HER.* Fear is a poor preserver of kingdoms.

*GIRL.* Failure to punish crimes causes easy destruction of kingdoms.

*HER.* He whom the citizens' loyalty preserves is safe.

*GIRL.* Kings must be feared; they need not be loved.

*HER.* Hatred oppresses the one who is cruel.

*GIRL.* Leniency in a king is despised amongst the common folk.

*QUEEN.* The trend of this whole discussion, in my view, is that promises vanish and are vain. You do not seem to me yet to know what a king's functions are. If you think that what the common folk believes honourable and base is honourable and base for a king, you are mistaken. Friends and neighbours, father-in-law and son-in-law, brothers and sisters, citizen and foe—bonds between these are accepted by common folk, but are titles empty in the eyes of kings.

Whoever[1225] once sets the diadem on his head should disregard all levels of obligation which the crowd observes. He should account nothing base which a king finds useful; he should regard as unfitting no deed which he performs for his own safety. The safety of the people depends on the king, so whoever is devoted to the king consults the interests of the people's safety.

Is[1232] the blood of this mere man of such value that in your anxiety you do not rest day and night? Remove from us this fear, this shame from the royal sceptre, this ruin from our city, this pillage from our army, this civil war from all. It is vital to establish by a great and fresh precedent that the kingship is sacrosanct before men. He has committed a crime; let that crime bring his destruction. If he has done no crime, let him die as a favour to your wife. Deliver this enemy to your wife; if you are indifferent to your wife, make good your promise as king and father to your daughter.

*HER*. I am determined to make good my promise with scrupulous faith. But if she takes my advice she will choose more wisely.

*QUEEN*. But if she takes mine, she must not change her design.

*HER*. Is this the situation? If this is the outcome, should I have sworn a rash oath, should I have pledged my promise to the girl, should I have entrusted my safety, kingdom and wealth, my life and death to a woman?

*QUEEN*. Let truth unwavering strengthen the promises of kings.

*HER*. Since I cannot refuse, I do what is now possible: I again urge and beg that anger should not compel you to carry out a deed unworthy of your blood, sex and royal dignity.

*QUEEN*. Give no thought to this; leave the rest to our care.

*HER*. If you decide on harsher treatment for the prophet, that will be your fault and your danger.

*QUEEN*. Now the royal dignity is freed from being exposed to any mockery henceforward. I shall now ensure that the headstrong people learns, even at its own cost, to speak of its kings with moderation; and whether kings enjoin just or unjust commands, the people must believe that they are all to be borne without resentment.

CHORUS

Kingdom of David, towers of Jerusalem, citadels of wealthy Solomon, what is the source of this rage so grim against prophets, of this savage thirst for the blood of the just? You ought to embody the norm of devoted care, but you are a singular example of wicked life. Theft, violence, slaughter, guile, plundering are the first training on your exercise-ground. Devotion does not induce the priest to restrain men's hands from sacrilegious deceits. The people have abandoned the Lord and Father of all things to worship an idol. Wood and stone are worshipped as a deity; for them the altars grow warm with the blood of steers and lambs, and the sculptor venerates the statues which his own right hand has made. Untrammeled by law, he begs a tree-trunk for life, he prays for eloquence from what is dumb. The rich man entreats the poor, the lord his servant. The ancient ritual is fading. The blood of innocent prophets drags you to the dais of the great judge. The poor cry out, the widows fill the heavens with their complaints.

So[1287] the punishment of just vengeance awaits you; no illusory punishment, unless my prophecy is mistaken. For the judge of heaven, sea and land, who restrains arrogant pride, gazes from on high and remembers both the tears of the folk and their sad prayers; and with avenging hand he will demand imminent punishment for their atrocious crime. A victorious foe will overturn the citadel in which you arrogantly boast. Barbarian soldiers will possess your estates; your vine-dresser will produce wine-harvests in plenty for a foreign lord. Where now the lofty temple of Solomon rises to heaven a foreign farmer will reap the harvest.

So[1301] while the benevolence of the deity affords you a respite for repentance, abandon the vices of a life basely lived, and cast out the images of a foreign cult. Restrain both your greedy thirst for a brother's blood and your unholy hunger for money. But you will not repent of your life wickedly spent, and you will not cast our from your holy temple the images of a foreign cult. You will not eschew the greedy thirst for your brother's blood, nor your unholy hunger for money. So foul plague will rend you; hunger, war, emaciation, poverty will overcome you until you pay the penalty with your deserving blood.

MESSENGER    CHORUS

*MESS.* Who will inform me if I can anywhere find the prophet's comrades to report my sad news?
*CHO.* Unless you happen to be in a hurry, stay a moment and report this briefly. We would like to know what news you bring.
*MESS.* You will not be pleased to know what you are eager to know.
*CHO.* However matters lie, do not begrudge a brief delay.
*MESS.* You know what request the girl made of the king?
*CHO.* That the severed head of the prophet be given her in a dish.
*MESS.* The severed head of the prophet she carried off in a dish.
*CHO.* How foul a deed is this! That divine vehemence and handsome face has withered in grim death; that mouth so recently full of God's sacred power foul violence has closed in enduring silence.

*MESS.* Why do you weep? Cease to pour out empty plaints.

*CHO.* I see and hear events worthy of tears; do you say I should not weep?

*MESS.* If death deserves tears, the dead must be bewailed by those whose hopes lie buried with the body, who do not believe that after a limit of most short-lived sleep our limbs will re-emerge, and that another life remains. Let the wretched bewail the dead, but only the wretched dead. Fortune can make no man wretched. Though the end of life awaits guilty and innocent alike, no man who has lived a good life will have a bad death. If you should account deaths wretched in general, you will consider wretched all the holy fathers whose life was cut off by cross or sword or water or fire. The man who dies as a supporter of the truth on behalf of religion and ancestral laws it is right to adorn with expressions of good omen, and in our prayers to ask for a similar end to life for ourselves.

*CHO.* All that you have said you have uttered with truth. But we are impelled by opinion and mistaken beliefs, and in fleeing from our due end we stupidly hasten to it. After fire has spared us, water drowns us. The man rescued from the sea is killed by the violence of unwholesome weather. The war-survivor dies wasted with disease. God allows us to postpone, not to avoid our destined end, and every day we borrow respites from death by paying in interest diseases, dangers, griefs and troubles. A long life is nothing other than a chain of protracted evils, fastened by unbroken links to the last stage of death. If we are not secured by these bonds we believe ourselves to be in wretched slavery. We tremble at the prospect of death rather than of slavery.

# EURIPIDIS
## POETAE TRAGICI
### MEDEA
#### GEORGIO BUCHANANO SCOTO
##### INTERPRETE

## AD ILLUSTRISSIMUM PRINCIPEM JOANNEM A LUCEMBURGO IVERIACI ABBATEM GEORGII BUCHANANI PRAEFATIO

Non dubito plerosque futuros, princeps clarissime, qui statim ubi haec in manus sumpserint meam admirentur impudentiam vel potius temeritatem, quod in tanto bonorum ingeniorum proventu id ego potissimum sim ausus aggredi quod aliorum vel pudor refugerat vel reformidarat audacia, atque Euripidi vertendo manum admoliri non pertimuerim; praesertim cum non ignorarem hanc a plerisque rem prius tentatam uni Erasmo ita successisse ut iuxta ab incepto me deterrere debuerit illorum casus atque huius felicitas; qui, praeterquam quod ad eam rem venerat tot bonarum artium praesidio instructus, etiam si qua erat in hac parte novitatis gratia eam praeoccupaverat. accedit et illud, quod praeter summam in choris obscuritatem (quae huic scriptori adeo familiaris est ut eam de industria sectatus esse videatur) haec ipsa quondam fabula ab Ennio prius versa fuerat, cuius non pauci versus adhuc in veterum commentariis passim leguntur, quorum comparatio his nostris alioqui obscuris plurimum sua luce officere posset. ego vero tantum abest ut his a scribendo rebus fuerim deterritus ut in utriusque fortunae qualemcumque eventum non mediocre praesidium hinc fore iam animo praeceperim, atque mihi ipsi quodam modo spoponderim. nam tametsi plausum a studiosorum theatro haec fabula non accipiat, si utcumque tamen steterit nec ignominiose explodatur, nunquam aeque moleste feram Ennii atque Erasmi auctoritate mihi tenebras offundi quam me post tam praeclara nomina qualemcumque saltem locum tenuisse. hoc vero quicquid est operae nos tibi, princeps clarissime, potissimum censuimus dicandum, non modo ut grati saltem animi professione tuam erga me summam testarer humanitatem, aut a vestrae familiae nobilissimae splendore contra calumniantium invidiam praesidium mihi peterem, sed ut meliori spe reliquorum doctorum suffragiis me committerem si tui iudicii praerogativa subnixus essem.

33 praerogativa *R*   praerogativo *1544*

qui cum in omni disciplinarum genere principatum teneas,
35  ac in hoc poeticae studio singulari quadam felicitate verseris,
soles tamen, ut inquit ille, 'meas esse aliquid putare nugas'.

# MEDEA

### ARGUMENTUM

Iason Medea comite Corinthum profectus cum Glauca Creontis Corinthiorum regis filia nuptias paciscitur. Medea vero indicto a Creonte exsilio unius diei moram exorat. idque beneficium ut remuneraretur, dono per filios ad Glaucam mittit vestem et coronam auream, quibus illa 5 induta exstinguitur; Creon quoque filiae adhaerens perit. Medea cum suos interfecisset liberos currum, quem a Sole acceperat alatis draconibus iunctum, conscendit atque Athenas profugit. ibique Aegeo Pandionis filio nubit. Pherecydes autem et Simonides aiunt Iasonem a Medea recoctum 10 iuvenem denuo factum. de patre vero eius Aesone is qui de Argonautarum reditu scripsit ita inquit:

> atque iterum blanda fecit revirere iuventa
> Aesona, subtili distringens arte senectam,
> plurima cum labris coxisset pharmaca in aureis. 15

Aeschylus in fabula quae Nutrices Bacchi inscribitur ait Bacchi nutrices earumque viros iuvenes ab eo denuo factos. Staphylus autem inquit Iasonem quodam modo a Medea peremptum. nam cum eius suasu sub Argus puppe obdormiret navisque iamiam vetustate solveretur, ruina puppis 20 oppressus periit.

### ALITER PER ARISTOPHANEM GRAMMATICUM

Medea, odio adversus Iasonem concepto propter nuptias Glaucae Creontis filiae, Glaucam Creonta ac suos etiam liberos interemit, relictoque Iasone Aegeo nupsit. 25

Fabula Corinthi fingitur agi. Chorus est e mulieribus Corinthiis. docuit eam Pythiodoro praetore circa octogesimam septimam Olympiadem.

27 Pythiodoro *R*   Pythodoro *cett*.

# MEDEA

## *PERSONAE*

Nutrix Medeae

Paedagogus

Medea

Chorus mulierum Corinthiarum

Creon Rex

Iason

Aegeus Rex Atheniensium

Nuntius

Filii Medeae

[Eur.]

NUTRIX

[1]  Utinam Pelasgis litus Argo ad Colchicum
non transvolasset cyaneas Symplegadas,
nec strata saltu pinus olim Pelio
cecidisset! acta nec virorum fortium
dextris, tulisset arietis spolium aurei                     5
Pelia imperante! non era excelsam mea
Medea Iolcon appulisset, Iasonis
amore saevo pectus aegrum saucia;
auctor puellis nec trucidandi patrem
Peliam, Corinthi degeret cum liberis                       10
viroque, gentis cuius exsul incolit
solum, favorem demereri sedula
et ipsa ubique morem Iasoni gerens.
felicitatem quam supremam existimo,
concors marito mulier ubi degit suo.                       15
nunc odia fervent, dissident carissimi
nuper. suorum liberorum proditor
eraeque Iason nuptiis regalibus
fruitur, tyranni filiam Corinthii
Creontis arto coniugem amplexu fovens.                     20
[20] at misera miseris habita ludibrio modis
Medea, pactam clamat infelix fidem,
pignusque fidei dexteram invocat datae,
testesque pacti conscios facit deos
non ita merenti quam rependat gratiam                      25
fallax Iason. inedia se macerans
iacet, doloris magnitudine obruta
flumine perenni lacrimarum liquitur.
ex quo mariti sensit in se iniuriam,
immota vultus, maesta terrae lumina                        30
figit; procellae similis aut scopulo, abnuit
surdis amicorum auribus solamina.
[30] nisi quod subinde colla flectens candida,

2 cyaneas *Walsh* Cyaneas *edd.*
23 datae *R* dati *1544*

171

[Eur.]

     secreta secum expostulat, deflens patrem,
35   patriam, penates patrios quos prodidit
     virum secuta cui modo contemnitur.
     at misera tandem iam suis didicit malis
     quam sit paternum suave non linquere solum.
     infensa natos odit, aspectu frui
40   non gaudet. illud vereor, ut ne quid novi
     excogitet. nam cum patitur iniuriam
     elatus animus, haud facile sibi temperat.
     hanc novi ego probe, trepidaque exanimor metu
     ne ferrum acutum condat in praecordia,
45   ingressa furtim tectum ubi torus sternitur;
     aut ne maritum perimat ac sponsam simul,
     dein maius ipsa subeat infortunium.
     metuenda sane est; nec facile victoriam
     referet, in illam si quis odia exerceat.
50   at cursu omisso iam reversi liberi
     non mente volvunt matris infaustae mala;
     puerilis animus gravibus haud curis patet.
     PAEDAGOGUS
     Antiquum erilis familiae peculium,     [49]
     quid sola stabas conquerens propter fores?
55   abs te relinqui sola Medea ut feret?
     *NUT.*   Senex minister liberorum Iasonis,
     mancipia frugi, si quid evenerit eris,
     aeque dolere suo decet ut incommodo.
     vis me doloris eo redegit ut solo
60   caeloque cogar evomere dominae mala.
     *PAED.* Quid? misera nondum luctui statuit modum?
     *NUT.*   A fine tantum luctus, o bone vir, abest
     ut haec doloris sola sint primordia.
     *PAED.*   O stulta, si quidem sic decet de eris loqui,
65   ut nil malorum comperit recentium!
     *NUT.*   Quid istud est? ne pigeat effari, senex.   [63]
     *PAED.*   Nil; extulisse me priora paenitet.
     *NUT.*   Amabo, me conservus haud celaveris.
     nam si necesse est spondeo silentium.
70   *PAED.*   Sacras ad undas abeo Pirenes, ubi
     sedere soliti sunt ad aleam senes.
     colloquia dum clam capto secreta, audio
     exigere pueros ut Corintho cogitet

## MEDEA

[Eur.]
    cum matre, regni sceptra qui hic tenet Creon.
    verusne rumor hic sit, haud certo scio;     75
    falsum esse mallem, ac falsus ut sit comprecor.
    *NUT.*   Et haec Iason liberis fieri sinet,
    iratus etsi dissidet cum coniuge?
    *PAED.*   Adfinitati vetus amor cedit novae,
    nec huic amicus perstat ille familiae.     80
    *NUT.*   Perimus igitur si malum accedit malo
    novum vetusto, donec exhaustum hoc erit.
    *PAED.*   At tu quiesce, et comprime haec silentio;
    nam tempus hauddum est, hoc erae ut fiat palam.

[82]
    *NUT.*   Audite, pueri, qualis in vos sit parens.     85
    perire nolim, dominus est enim meus,
    verum erga amicos perfidus deprenditur.
    *PAED.*   Publica querela est ista, iamdudum ipsa scis,
    sibi malle cunctos esse bene quam proximo;
    hunc iure, at alium commodo addictum suo.     90
    si caritati liberum sponsam pater
    praefert Iason, nil facit certe novi.

[89]
    *NUT.*   Introite, pueri, cuncta succedent bene.
    at tu seorsum hos contine, quantum potes,
    neve ad parentem propius accedere sinas.     95
    ira frementem nuper, oculis flammeis
    vidi minantem nescio quid istis; neque
    imponet irae frena donec quempiam
    feriat. in hostes potius utinam hunc impetum
    fortuna amicis incolumibus transferat.     100

[97]
    *MED.*   Infelix ego, miseris curis
    confecta, hei mihi quomodo perii!
    *NUT.*   Hoc, hoc ipsum est, cari pueri;
    aestuat ira animus genetricis,
    turget bilis; properate cito,     105
        tecta subite.
    neve accedite lumina propius,
    neve adieritis, sed vitate
    animumque ferum ac triste ingenium
    mentis praecipitis. iamiam ite,     110
    intro abscedite celeri passu.

90 addictum *1544*    adductum *1567, R*
110 mentis *1544*    mentes *R*

TRAGOEDIAE

[Eur.]

    nam luctus dubio procul olim
    nubes surgens subito ardebit
    maiore furore, ac patrabit
115    aliquid mentis vis infrenis
    et serie stimulata malorum.
    *MED.*   Heu, heu, toleravi misera,     [111]
    toleravi mala magnis deflenda
    luctibus. o nati scelerati,
120    vos male perdat miseranda parens
    cum patre, ac tota domus pereat.
    *NUT.*   Me miseram, cur natos patris
    peccato adscribis? cur illos
    odisti? hei mihi, pueri, misere
125    metuo ne quid secus eveniat.
    gravis est regum fastus, et irae
    nimium memoris, qui dare leges
    sunt soliti aliis, lege soluti
    ipsi. iudice me libertas
130    par et vitae aequatio praestat,
    seque adsuescere legibus aequis;
    si non regifico splendore, at
    tuto consenuisse licebit.
    nam popularibus aequi iuris
135    primum est nomen, et experiundo et
    usu longe praestabilius.
    at sublimia nunquam stabili
    perstant homini fixa pede diu, ac
    si quando sors laeva intonuit,
140    hoc ex fonte innumerae luctus
    undae in splendida tecta redundant.
    *CHO.*   Vocem audivi, audivi planctum     [131]
    miserae Colchidos; animi nondum
    aestus composuit. fare age, anus.
145    in vestibulo stans audivi
    intra atria clamorem. haud laetor
    vestrae, mulier, luctu domus,
    ac mihi minime grata geruntur.
    *NUT.*   Domus heu periit,     [139]
150    deserta omnia. detinet illum

---

134 popularibus *Walsh* (cf. Eur. 127) popularius *edd.*

MEDEA

[Eur.]     aula tyranni, ac contabescit
           luctu in thalamis era, amicorum
           nullo mollita animum hortatu.
[144]      MED.  Heu heu, ruat in caput hoc miserum
           fulmen ab aethere. quis mihi superest           155
           dehinc vitae usus, vivere ut optem?
           eheu, longis tristem curis,
           Parcae, miseram abrumpite vitam.
[148]      CHO.  Audisti, o Iuppiter, o tellus,
           o lux, quam vocem misera edat                   160
           mulier? quod tandem immoderatum
           thalami desiderium cogit,
           stulta, accelerare horam fati?
           istud ne expete. quod si coniunx
           conubio tuus alio fruitur,                      165
           id ne improperes illi crimen.
           hanc tibi iudex Iuppiter aequus
           dirimet litem. ne te afflictes
           socium lugendo tori.
[160]      MED.  O magna Themi atque Artemi sancta,       170
           cernitis, impius in me coniunx
           quale patrarit facinus, sancto
           mihi iureiurando adstrictus?
           quem cum sponsa utinam simul ipsis
           aedibus oppressos conspiciam,                   175
           qui immeritam laesere priores.
           o pater, o patria a me inhoneste
           germano deserta perempto!
[168]      NUT.  Quos vocet audis, quos imploret?
           Themin augustam cum Iove, praeses               180
           qui creditur esse sacramenti;
           nec cohibere era poterit facile
              pectoris aestus.
[173]      CHO.  Qui fiet, prodeat ut coram?
           auribus ut sermonis nostri                      185
           vocem hauriat ut, si pote fieri,
           acres animi leniat iras
           ac violentum ingenium ponat?
           NUT.  Haudquaquam sedulitas nostra
              deerit amicis.                               190
           CHO.  At abi, mea tu, dominamque foras

175

[Eur.]

    educ, atque adloquere. heus, propera
    ne designet quicquam asperius
    hos adversum, quos habet intus;
195  gliscit enim vis saeva doloris.
    *NUT.*   Effecta haec dabo. sed metuo ut erae    [184]
    persuadere queam. ista labori
    gratia vestro a me referetur,
    etsi fetae more leaenae
200  luminis acies flammea servis
    triste minetur, si quis propius
    ut compellet tentet adire.
    nil peccarit, veterum laeva ac
    praepostera qui vocet ingenia,
205  qui cantus ad sacra deorum,
    ad convivia festasque epulas
    instituere, illecebras gratas
    auribus; at suaviloquum carmen
    nemo invenit quo sedaret
210  tristes animi curas, unde
    mortes plurimaque mala erumpunt
    eversura domos. verum istis
    cantu medicari utilius erat.
    ad lautas epulas quid frustra
215  ilia tendunt, copia ubi dapis
    praesente animum laetitia explet?
    *CHO.*   Maesti luctus gemitus nostras    [204]
    perculit aures; clamat misera,
    illa, quam dolor edere cogit,
220  voce malum compellans sponsum,
    veteris desertorem thalami.
    laesa Themin Iove natam implorat
    arbitram iurisiurandi,
    quae illexit miseram ad solum Achivum
225  per mare saevum Scythiae adversum,
    per ponti immensi spumantes
    cano sale fauces angustas.

    *MED.*   Egressa tecto sum, Corinthiae nurus,    [214]
    de me querendi ne sit ulli occasio.
230  plerosque novi, quod seorsum degerent,
    habitos superbos; hos frequens praesentia

## MEDEA

[Eur.] fecit molestos; alius ingressus viam
vitae quietae, ignaviae subiit notam;
quia iudicandi certa veritas abest
oculis ab hominum, qui priusquam pectoris 235
norint recessus intimos, visos modo
odere nullis provocati iniuriis.
ergo urbis hospes moribus se accommodet;
nec laudo civem, contumax qui civibus
asperque agresti degit insolentia. 240

[225] at enim inopinum hoc quod mihi evenit malum
vitam abstulit vivae. pereo; vitae exui
iamdudum amorem, amore mortis percita.
in quo reposita cuncta habebam, pessimus
plane virorum me reliquit vir meus. 245
nihil miserius feminis terra, omnium
quaecumque vivunt menteque vigent, edidit.
primum necesse est opibus immensis virum
emere, suique accipere dominum corporis.
accedit aliud huic malo gravius malum, 250
in quo periclum maximum, frugi vir an
nequam; mulieri repudium infame est, neque
sponsae maritum ius recusandi est suum.
in iura moresque venientem opus est novos
plane hariolari, quippe quae haud didicit domi 255
quali marito serviendum sibi foret.
et ista recte cuncta cum curaveris,
si degat una sponte vir patiens iugi,
beata vita est; sin secus, praestat mori.

[244] domesticorum si quis offendat virum, 260
foras profectus sedat aegritudinem
caris amicis iunctus aut aequalibus;
at nos necesse est unius ab arbitrio
pendere, in unumque intueri. et interim
vitam periclis nos carentem degere 265
domi asseverant, ferre sese lanceam,
errore ducti. nam ter in acie prius
armata certem, liberos quam edam semel.
sed non utrasque haec spectat aeque oratio.
haec namque patria tibi, hic penates patrii, 270

233 subiit *R* subit *cett.*

                                                                                                                                                                        [Eur.]

|     |                                                                    |        |
| --- | ------------------------------------------------------------------ | ------ |
|     | praesidia vitae, grata conversatio                                 |        |
|     | inter sodales; contra inops ego, patria                            |        |
|     | extorris, aspra laesa contumelia                                   |        |
|     | a coniuge, solo advecta praeda barbaro.                            |        |
| 275 | non hic propinquus, mater, aut germanus est                        | [257]  |
|     | ad quos malorum afflicta tempestatibus                             |        |
|     | me veluti portum recipere in tutum queam.                          |        |
|     | tantisper igitur impetrare abs te velim,                           |        |
|     | dum mihi facultas aliqua ratiove suppetet                          |        |
| 280 | qua de marito expetere supplicium queam,                           |        |
|     | ob quae patravit immerenti, et plectere                            |        |
|     | illi locatam cum parente filiam,                                   |        |
|     | sis tacita. plena mulier alioqui metus,                            |        |
|     | infirma, ferrum contueri haud sustinet;                            |        |
| 285 | at in torum si quispiam peccaverit,                                |        |
|     | nullum cruoris pectus est sitientius.                              |        |
|     | CHO.   Id fiet. etenim iure poenas expetis,                        | [267]  |
|     | Medea; sortem nec dolere te tuam                                   |        |
|     | miror. Creonta sed video regem gradum                              |        |
| 290 | ferre huc, novorum consiliorum nuntium.                            |        |
|     | CRE.   Te, torva vultu taetrico, iratam viro,                      |        |
|     | Medea, monui regno ut extorris meo                                 |        |
|     | comitata geminis hinc abires liberis.                              |        |
|     | vetui morari. quando decreti arbiter                               |        |
| 295 | istius ego sum, non revertar hinc prius                            |        |
|     | domum, exsulem quam finibus protrusero.                            |        |
|     | MED.   Hei pereo, penitus undecunque miserrima!                    | [278]  |
|     | omnes rudentes explicant hostes mei,                               |        |
|     | mali nec usquam commodus datur exitus.                             |        |
| 300 | afflicta quamvis pessime, id quaeram tamen,                        |        |
|     | quae causa regno me exigere cogit, Creon?                          |        |
|     | CRE.   Te metuo—quorsum falsa opus praetendere?—                   |        |
|     | letale natae ne exitium struas meae.                               |        |
|     | causae timorem suggerunt hunc plurimae.                            |        |
| 305 | sagax es, artes gnara longe pessimas,                              |        |
|     | graviterque taedis orba fers divortium.                            |        |
|     | et nunc minari fama te refert malum                                |        |
|     | sponsoque sponsaeque et novae nuptae patri.                        |        |
|     | at id prius quam fiat, antevortere                                 |        |

273–4 contumelia/a coniuge, solo *interpunxit Walsh* (cf. Eur. 255f.)
contumelia,/a coniuge solo *1544, R*

MEDEA

[Eur.]
    volo cavendo. praestat autem odium tuum 310
    nunc ferre, sera quam peracto facinore
    hanc lenitatem luere paenitentia.

[292]   MED.   Non fama primum nunc nocet, Creon, mihi
    miserae, sed ante damna non semel dedit.
    quicunque vera praeditus prudentia est, 315
    ne disciplinis liberos impensius
    erudiat aequo, nec sapere doceat nimis.
    nam pigra praeter quae sequuntur otia,
    obliquus urget livor illos civium.
    apud imperitos scita si sophiae nova 320
    promas, ineptum rentur atque inutilem.
    at si putere denuo praecellere
    hos qui sophorum auctoritatem vindicant,
    eris molestus, idque adeo mihi evenit.
    perita cum sim, hos urit invidentia; 325
    his otiosa dicor; illis displicet
    diversa vitae ratio; nec desunt quibus
    obesse videar mediocri hac sapientia.

[306]   tu quoque vereris ne quid in te perpetrem;
    non hic mearum, ne time, rerum est status, 330
    reges ut a me metuere deceat, Creon.
    at tu quid in me perpetrasti iniquius?
    natam elocasti cui tibi lubitum est viro;
    at ego maritum prosequor odio meum.
    nec temere, opinor, ista gessisti, neque 335
    rebus secundis invideo. quin nuptias
    facite, beati vivite; latebras fugae
    permitte tantum hic. laesa licet, iniurias
    mussabo; discam cedere melioribus.

[316]   CRE.   Speciosa sunt haec blandaque auribus, tamen 340
    vereor repostum ne coquas animo malum,
    atque adeo tanto credo quam pridem minus.
    praecipitis irae mulierem aut etiam virum
    vites facilius quam modestum atque tacitum.
    desine morandi fando causas nectere, 345
    abi. statutum est ita; nec ars ulla faciet
    istic ut habites, me perosa hostiliter.

[324]   MED.   Per genua quaeso perque desponsam recens.
    CRE.   Ah, verba perdis; neutiquam persuaseris.
    MED.   Et me repelles haud reveritus supplicem? 350

[Eur.]
    CRE.    Equidem familiae non meae te praefero.
    MED.    O patria, subiit nunc recordatio tui!
    CRE.    Qua nil secundum liberos mihi carius.
    MED.    O amor, hominibus pestis exitiabilis!
355    CRE.    Perinde, opinor, res uti sese dabit.
    MED.    Quis auctor horum tu memento, Iuppiter!
    CRE.    Abscede, inepta, meque curis libera.
    MED.    Curae premunt me, nec egeo curis novis.
    CRE.    Hinc exigere subito servili manu.
360    MED.    Noli, obsecro, sed id te sine exorem, Creon.
    CRE.    Adhuc molesta, mulier, eris, uti video.
    MED.    Abibo; non hoc ut precibus impetrem ago.
    CRE.    Quorsum igitur urges, nec meo abscedis solo?
    MED.    Unum instruendae modo fugae indulge diem;  [340]
365    et quando curam hanc genitor abiecit, sine
me comminisci liberis opem ultimam.
miserescat horum; nam et tibi sunt liberi.
parens parentis calamitatibus fave.
nam nulla cruciat cura me exsilii mei,
370    sed liberorum miseriae me macerant.
    CRE.    Haud impotenti mente sum et tyrannica;  [348]
quin saepe damno mihi meus pudor fuit.
et nunc aperte, mulier, erratum meum
praevideo; verum vince, quod vis accipe.
375    praemoneo tamen id, si morantem crastinus
hic te videbit Phoebus ac natos tuos,
actum est, peristi. fixa stat sententia.
nunc si necesse est lucis unius moram
permitto; nam nil interim patraveris
380    horum, timore quae me habent nunc anxium.

    CHO.    Infelix mulier, misera malis  [357]
miseris obnoxia, quo tandem
te vertes? cuius amicitiam,
cuius tectum aut terram invenies
385    portum malis?
traxit ineluctabile fatum
in mare te, Medea, malorum.
    MED.    Male cuncta cedunt undecunque, quis neget?  [364]
sed ne putetis pessime hac succedere,

389 hac *1544:* hoc R

## MEDEA

[Eur.]
    sponsis adhuc mihi pugna superest cum novis;    390
    ingens futurus est labor cum adfinibus.
    credis tyranno quisse me palparier,
    ni subfuisset spes lucri vel spes doli?
    supplex fuissem? contigissem illi manum?
    at ille tanta praeditus vecordia est    395
    ut cum liceret obviam conatibus,
    si me expulisset, ire, siverit diem
    hunc me manere, tres ego hostes quo meos
    mactabo, patrem filiam meum virum.
    sed tanta leti cum facultas suppetat,    400
    unde inchoabo dubia, amicae, fluctuo.
    subdamne thalamis nuptialibus faces,
    an ferro acuto rupta fodiam pectora
    ingressa furtim tectum ubi torus sternitur?

[381]
    sed me moratur una res: si capta sim    405
    in tecta scandens, per dolum dum rem gero,
    perempta risus exhibebo malevolis.
    at usitatam praestat insistere viam
    cuius perita sum, necandi pharmacis.
    esto, perierint; quod recipiet me oppidum?    410
    quod erit asylum, fida quae fidi hospitis
    domus patebit protegetve perfugam?
    nusquam est. manebo paululum dum stabilia
    alicunde nobis praesidia sese offerent.
    dolis adoriar clamque perfungar nece.    415

[392]
    si pellat hinc me fors ineluctabilis,
    mucrone peragam facinus ipsa vel palam.
    lubens peribo modo queam illos perdere.
    ad culmen imus praecipitis audaciae.
    regina nobis culta semper unice    420
    Hecate triformis, artis adiutrix meae,
    te iuro, nostra quae colis penetralia,
    nostro e dolore nemo referet gaudium.
    his luctuosas atque acerbas nuptias,
    adfinitatem funebrem et meam fugam    425
    reddam. eia, cunctis utere simul artibus,
    Medea, cuncta convoca consilia. age
    aggredere facinus; nunc opus constantia

    397 siverit *R*   permisit *1544*

[Eur.]

      animoque forti. quae feras vides. cave
430   ut ne propines risui nepotibus
      te Sisyphaeis nuptiisque Iasonis,
      te patre claro Soleque proavo editam.
      perita es ipsa, deinde nata femina,
      ignava quibus est mens honesta ad omnia,
435   ad turpe superest facinus omne audacia.

         CHO.   Retro ad fontes sacra feruntur
         flumina; ius et fas vertuntur.
         hominum plena dolis consilia,
         nec pacta fides dis sat certa est.
440      audiet ex hoc muliebre bene
         genus, accrescet gloria nobis.
         non iam deinceps fama sinistra
         traducet femineum sexum.
         ex hoc mutabit Musa modos
445      vatum priscorum, qui cantu
         muliebrem celebrant perfidiam.
         at si caeleste melos citharae
         nos docuisset carminis auctor
         Phoebus, paria audisset
450           progenies virum.
         sed multa potest longior aetas
         nobis exprobrare virisque.
         at tu patriam deseruisti                  [431]
         animi vecors, vecta gemellos
455      trans scopulos ponti, ac peregrinam
         habitas terram, orbata cubilis
         taedis vidui, ac misera hinc exsul
         eiciere ignominiose.
         periit reverentia iurisiur-
460      andi; nullus superest Grais
         pudor, in caelum sed revolavit.
         tibi vero nec patria domus est,
         infelix, in quam ceu portum
         perfugias e thalami curis;
465         sed regina potentior
            occupat aulam.

         IAS.   Non nunc sed ante saepe perspectum est mihi  [446]
      quam sit malum impotens et inmedicabile

MEDEA

[Eur.]
ira aspra. licitum fuerat et terra et domo
hic tibi frui, si quidem tulisses molliter                    470
potentiorum imperia, quae nunc exulas
ob vana verba quae molestiam mihi
minime facessunt. perge, uti facis, dicere
longe virorum pessimum esse Iasonem.
at quae in tyrannos blaterasti, si exsul es                   475
ob haec, recense pro lucro iussam fugam.
ego saevientum molliebam principum
animos feroces, ne exsulares; tu tamen
stulta esse pergis, prodigens convicia
dirisque reges devovens. itaque exulas.                       480
nec ista amicos me movent ut deseram;
adsum tuisque commodis, mulier, vaco
ut ne recedas hinc inops cum liberis
egensve rerum. multa secum incommoda
ferre fuga suevit. sed nec indigne fero                       485
nec velle possum male tibi, etsi me oderis.

[465]
MED.   O pessime undequaque! nam imbecillitas
conviciari me sinit tantum mea.
me adisti, adisti, maxime mortalium
exose disque mihique cunctisque hominibus?                    490
non fortitudo est ista, non fiducia
laesos amicos contueri cominus,
sed morbus unus omnium gravissimus
additus hominibus, impudentia. id tamen
abs te probe actum est quod adieris; ego ut levem             495
animum dolore, iurgia in te congerens,
et tu vicissim sentias molestiam.

[475]
et primum, ut a primis initiis ordiar,
salutis auctor tibi fui, ut Grai sciunt
quoscumque tecum vexit Argo Pelias.                           500
flammam vomentes iussus es tauros iugo
supponere, et letale sulcis condere
semen; draconem saepe in orbes nexilem,
circumvolutum vellus auro fulgidum, et
sopore nunquam fessa victum lumina                            505
fallere. perempto tibi dedi illo cernere
vitale lumen. prodito patre et domo,

475 exul es *1544:*   exules *R*

[Eur.]

applicui Iolchon te secuta, tibi nimis
hic obsecundans ac mihi parum providens.
510 Peliam peremi, morte qua nulla gravior,
manu suorum liberorum; sustuli
tibi metum omnem. tu tot ob beneficia [488]
nos prodidisti, praedo perfidissime,
novas secutus nuptias post liberos
515 de me creatos; orbus etenim si fores,
veniam dedissem coniugis cupido novae.
dein peieratis dis fides fluxa, ac satis
statuere nequeo quos putabas tum deos
regnare credas nunc quoque, an potius novum
520 ius esse fasque traditum mortalibus,
ut qui tibi ipsi es conscius periurii.
o tacta saepe dextera, o saepe genua
frustra prehensa tibi manu infidissima!
ut spes fefellit! age, velut amicum adloquar [499]
525 sperantis instar aliquod abs te commodum;
etenim rogando detegam scelus tuum.
quo nunc revertar? spreta quo me conferam?
an ad penates patrios ac patriam
quam te secuta prodidi? an potius petam
530 Peliae misellas filias, quae me hospitem
tractent benigne patris ob necem sui?
sic est, amicos perdidi domesticos;
quos non decebat afficere me iniuria,
te propter hostes universos reddidi.
535 ergo beatam inter Pelasgidas nurus [509]
me reddidisti pro his beneficiis virum
sum singularem nacta fidumque misera.
si profuga cogor hoc solo egredier inops,
deserta amicis, sola, solis liberis
540 comitata, pulchrum elogium erit sponso novo
mendica proles exsulans cum coniuge
cui debet, aura quod fruitur. o Iuppiter,
adulterini indicia cur certa hominibus
auri dedisti, sed virum in corpore nota
545 impressa nulla est unde noscantur mali?
CHO.   Gravis ira res est et malum insatiabile, [520]
amici amicis conserunt cum iurgia.
IAS.   Me, ut video, oportet eloquendi esse haud rudem,

[Eur.]       verum gubernatoris instar callidi
             effugere summa linteorum margine                    550
             loquacitatem, mulier, istam futilem.
             ego, beneficium quando nimium exaggeras,
             Venerem salutis autumo auctorem meae
             ducemque cursus, nec deum aut hominum alteri
             debere ob illa sentio me gratiam.                    555
[529]        ingenii acumen acre suppetit tibi; at
             orationis arrogans iactantia est,
             ea cum recenses quae coacta feceras
             amore, duris nos ut e laboribus
             eruere posses. illa tamen examine                    560
             librare nolo exactiore; sicubi
             profueris, agnosco libens beneficium.
             at, ut docebo te, incolumitate ex mea
             plus quam dedisti ad te redundat commodi.
[536]        primum Pelasgam patria pro barbara                   565
             terram colis, ubi lex et aequitas vigent,
             nec iura cedunt gratiae vel viribus;
             omnesque doctam te esse Grai intellegunt
             famaque flores. finibus si in ultimis
             orbis habitares, mentio haud fieret tui.             570
             mihi nec aurum sit domi aggestum neque
             Orphea canendo suavitas quae vicerit,
             splendore si non sortis haec decoret favor.
             haec dicta nostra sint super laboribus,
             contentionem quando ad hanc me provocas.             575
             at quae exprobrasti regiis de nuptiis,
             primum reperies hic sapere me, dein virum
             et temperantem et tibi meisque liberis
             fidelem amicum. sed quiesce tu interim.
[551]        ut me Corinthon ex Iolcho contuli                    580
             cumulo malorum inexplicabili obrutus,
             quid comminisci commodum potui magis
             quam si puellam regiam exsul ducerem?
             non, quod tibi aegre est, quod torum odissem tuum,
             sponsaeque amore saucius forem novae,                585
             nec numero ut ulli liberum contenderem
             —sat liberorum est, de subole nil conqueror—
             sed, quod putandum plurimi est, ut splendide
             aevum exigamus neve penuria premat

590 (quippe indigentes qui fugere procul sciam [Eur.]
cunctos amicos) utque familiae meae [562]
pro dignitate liberos educerem
ex teque natis gignerem fratres, pares
quos simul honorum per gradus producerem,
595 meamque postquam constabiliissem domum,
felix ut essem. liberis sane tibi
haud est opus aliis; mihi vero utile est
consulere natis per futura pignora.
num cogitasse videor absurde? torus
600 modo ne angat animum, haud istud ipsa dixeris.
at eo mulierum crevit impotentia:
si coniugalis salva sit fides tori,
tum cuncta recte creditis succedere;
sin hac sinistre parte quidquam evenerit,
605 quae cara fuerant sunt statim inimicissima.
at quam fuisset procreasse liberos
aliunde melius, nec fuisse feminas!
exempta quantis vita foret hominum malis!
CHO.   Haec pulchre, Iason, perpolita oratio est; [576]
610 at mihi videre—invita quamvis, proloquar—
egisse inique, coniugem cum proderes.
MED.   Quam nostra vulgo dissidet sententia!
orationis qui probus erit artifex
factisque iniquis, hunc reor gravissima
615 poena esse dignum. nam quae iniqua comere
se gloriatur lingua, non maleficio
ullo abstinebit, ac vacua sapientiae est.
igitur omitte splendidis coloribus
fucare verum et eloquendi viribus;
620 verbo quidem uno te subito confecero.
si quidem fuisses vir bonus, te oportuit
non haec amicis clam peregisse, at prius
me persuasa nuptias facere novas.
IAS.   Quin paruisses mihi suadenti probe
625 si quidem indicassem nuptias, quae nec modo
tumidi minuere pectoris bilem potes.
MED.   Non haec movebat causa te, sed barbaras [591]
taedas senectam adusque fore putaveras

614 iniquis *edd.*   iniquus R *dubitanter*

MEDEA

[Eur.]
parum decoras. *IAS*. Tibi velim id persuadeas, 
non me secutum regiis his nuptiis 630
cupidinem uxoris; sed, uti dixi prius,
tuae saluti consulebam, ac liberis
meis uti de stirpe fratres regia
domui futuros praesidia progignerem.
*MED*.   Ne mihi dolori iuncta sit felicitas 635
opesque, quae cor triste curis ulcerent.
*IAS*.   Haec vota vertes tibique melius consules
precando, ne quod utile est triste id putes,
nec cum secundae res erunt, te esse miseram.
*MED*.   Illude. perfugium tibi inventum est; ego 640
deserta cogor his profugere finibus.

[605]
*IAS*.   Tibi auctor ipsa es, ne alteri id des crimini.
*MED*.   Quinam? novis quod prodidi te nuptiis?
*IAS*.   Diris tyrannos exsecrandis devovens.
*MED*.   Et exsecratur vestra me invicem domus. 645
*IAS*.   Quot his supersunt plura, quae haud redarguo?
at si qua poscis praesidia tuae fugae
natisve nostris ex opibus accipere, age
profer parato liberali dextera
donare, nostros tesseras ad hospites 650
dare ut exsulantem recipiant humaniter.
haec si recuses, mulier, haud recte sapis.
iram remitte; consules tibi melius.
*MED*.   Tuis nec uti volumus hospitibus neque
accipere quicquam, nec dederis aliquid mihi. 655
nam quae mali dant dona prosunt nemini.

[619]
*IAS*.   At ego deorum sancta testor numina
natis paratum cuncta me dare tibique.
sed tu recusas optima, et ferocia
fugas amicos, ac malo id quidem tuo. 660
*MED*.   I, sponsam amatam vise. nimium demoror
ab eius oculis te procul. agite, nuptias
facite; faventes forte si respexerint
nos di, pigebit apparasse nuptias.

[627]
*CHO*.   Si iusto amores acrius 665
humana corda vulnerent,
virtus facessit, deperit
famae decus; sed si Cypris

[Eur.]

gradu modesto venerit,
670  nemo deorum est gratior.
regina Cypris, aureo
ex arcu inevitabilem
in me sagittam haud torseris
amoris unctam nectare.
675  mi grata temperantia,
munus deum pulcherrimum.
infrenis iracundia
rixosaque aemulatio
mentem mihi ne saucient
680  ulla dolentem paelice,
O sancta Cypris, quae toros
amas carentes litibus,
parata prompte expendere
lecti iugalis crimina.
685  O patria, o aedes meae, [642]
nunquam exsul et consilii inops
aevum moleste transigam,
confecta miseris luctibus.
o fata, fata, tollite
690  ex hoc prius me lumine!
inter molesta cuncta nil
molestius cognovimus
pelli solo quam patrio.
nec id relatu didicimus
695  alterius. haud te civitas
miseratur aut aequalium
quisquam gravissimis malis
pressam. male pereat miser
miserabilisque nemini,
700  qui cum licet nullo colit
officio amicos, nec aperit
sincera claustra pectoris.
mihi quidem amicus nunquam erit.

*AEG.* Medea, salve. hoc pulchrius prooemium [663]
705  nemo habet, amicos quo salutarit suos.
*MED.* Salve, propago providi Pandionis,

680 *sic interpunxit 1544*

## MEDEA

[Eur.]
Aegeu. unde in istud contulisti te solum?
AEG.  Phoebi vetustum deserens oraculum.
MED.  Cur umbilicum faticanum adisti soli?
AEG.  Prolis cupido consulere adegit deum.                 710
MED.  Et subolis orbus, per deos, aevum exigis?
AEG.  Orbus, voluntas quando sic tulit deum.
MED.  Caelebsne, vinctus an iugali copula?
AEG.  Haud nuptialis fuimus expertes tori.
MED.  Quid tandem Apollo rettulit de liberis?              715
AEG.  Carmen facultatem supra humani ingeni.
MED.  Responsa nobis nosse num fas est dei?
AEG.  Fas est; peritae namque mentis indiget.

[678]
MED.  Quid ergo dixit? scire si fas est, refer.
AEG.  Utri eminentem solvere vetuit pedem.                 720
MED.  Nempe antequam facias quid, aut quem adeas locum?
AEG.  Prius paternam quam adiero rursus domum.
MED.  Tu cuius ergo ad hancce tellurem venis?
AEG.  Pittheus tyrannus quispiam est Troezenius. . .
MED.  Pelopis ut aiunt filius sanctissimus.                725
AEG.  Communicare oraculum cum illo volo.
MED.  Sane peritus talium et gnarus vir est.
AEG.  Mihique amicos inter acceptissimus.
MED.  Sit auspicatum quicquid animo destinas.
AEG.  Cur corpus oculusque ita tuus contabuit?             730

[689]
MED.  Aegeu, maritus pessimus hominum est meus.
AEG.  Quid ais? aperte profer aegritudinem.
MED.  Immeritam Iason afficit me iniuria.
AEG.  Quinam? profare quicquid est apertius.
MED.  Habet supra me coniugem domus eram.                  735
AEG.  Nempe ausus istud facinus est foedissimum?
MED.  Sic est. priores nunc amicos despicit.
AEG.  Amore captus an torum exosus tuum?
MED.  Ingenti amore, nec suis fidus manet.
AEG.  Valeat, malitia si modo est qua praedicas.           740
MED.  Adfinitatem concupivit regiam.
AEG.  Quis coniugem illi dederit, hoc edissere.
MED.  Is qui Corinthi sceptra moderatur, Creon.
AEG.  Veniam meretur, mulier, iste tuus dolor.
MED.  Ad haec et exsul hoc misera pellor solo.             745
AEG.  A quo? recens hoc denuo narras malum.
MED.  Regno exsulare me Creon isto iubet.

[Eur.]
AEG. Sinit hoc Iason? nec equidem hoc facinus probo.
MED.   Verbo repugnat, exigi re non vetat. [708]
750   sed te per istud oro mentum, per tua
te genua supplex, supplices tendo manus,
miserere, miserere mulieris miserrimae,
nec orbam amicis exsulemque despice;
regno domoque contubernalem excipe.
755   sic efficacem sortiantur exitum
quae a dis petisti liberis super, ipseque
moriare felix. comminisci haud alteram,
qualis reperta est sponte, potuisses viam.
dehinc faxo ne sis sterilis, et subole domum
760   fundabo vestram; tale novi pharmacum.
AEG.   Permulta sunt cur facere tibi gratum hic velim, [719]
primum deorum, liberum dein gratia
quos polliceris; muneri namque huic ego
inefficax sum totus. ita profecto habet.
765   tu si Cecropium adveneris solum, hospitem
recipere nitar, cultor ut iusti unice.
praemoneo tantum id te, mulier; ex hoc solo haud [725]
te duco; verum sponte si perveneris
nostras ad aedes, tuta mecum manseris.
770   nec vim time; te neutiquam dimisero.
quin effer ipsa sponte gressum hinc; nam id velim,
me criminandi ne sit hospitibus locus.
MED.   Id fiet. at si dederis ita fore haec fidem,
votis abunde satis erit factum meis.
775   AEG.   Mihine parum credis? quid hic est scrupuli?
MED.   Credo, sed odit me domus Peliae et Creon, [734]
nec me ut revellant hi tuo sinus solo
iuratus ac vinctus sacramento mihi.
verbis ligatus testibusque dis meus
780   fies amicus, nec fidem praeconibus
qui me reposcent facile habebis. namque ego
infirma sum; illis regna vires oppida
large supersunt ac opes tyrannicae.
AEG.   Probe elocuta es, mulier, atque provide,
785   et quando visum est sic tibi, non abnuo.
adversus hostes hunc tuos praetendere
potero colorem, tutiusque istud reor.
praesidia muni, verbaque ac deos praei.

MEDEA

[Eur.]
  *MED.* Iura solum Terrae, patremque mei patris
Solem, deorumque universum adice genus.  790
  *AEG.* Quid praebiturum vel negaturum? refer.
  *MED.* Quod non repelles exsulem regno tuo,
nec si meorum quispiam velit hostium
educere, haud id vivus et volens sines.
  *AEG.* Tellurem et almum deiero Solis iubar  795
deosque cunctos, firma fore quae postulas.
  *MED.* Sat est. quid autem poenae erit si peieres?
  *AEG.* Quae peierantes poena consequi solet.
[756]  *MED.* Avibus secundis perge; cuncta recte habent.
ego te revisam protinus, ubi fecero  800
quae destinavi, et quae volebam ubi adsequar.

[759]  *CHO.* At te pacifer hinc Mercurius
incolumem ad tua tecta reducat;
quaeque agitas animo, perficere
det tibi. nam generosus  805
mihi vir visus es, Aegeu.

[764]  *MED.* O Iuppiter, Iovisque Fas, faxque aurea
Phoebi, tropaeum nunc feram illustrissimum!
nunc recta ad ipsam tendimus victoriam;
spes expetendi de hoste supplicii datur.  810
nam qua pericli supererat vel plurimum,
portus repertus natus est Pandionis.
posthac rudentem principem ligabimus,
cursum tenentes recta ad urbem Palladis.
nunc cuncta prodam, mente quae celaveram,  815
ac dicta crede serio quae proloquar.
[774] mittam e ministris quempiam qui Iasonem
accersat ad me. post ubi pervenerit,
oratione blandiore colloquar:
recte videri nuptias et ordine  820
factas, quibus me bene merentem prodidit.
nec parva secum ferre dicam commoda;
petamque natis hic licere vivere,
non quod relinqui liberos velim meos
et hostium hic exponier ludibrio,  825

800 ego *1544* (cf. Eur. 757) ergo *R*
818 accersat *1544* arcessat *R*

[Eur.]

sed ut puellam regiam perimam dolo.
nam dona sponsae quae ferant natis dabo,
subtile peplum cum corona nexili
ex auro, ut istoc munere redimant fugam.
830 quod si recepta dona corpus tetigerint,
peribit ipsa et quisquis admorit manum;
sic imbuentur efficaci pharmaco.
atque hic loquendi de his mihi statuam modum. [790]
sed corda maeror obruit cum cogito
835 quantum supersit perpetrandum dehinc scelus.
mactabo natos, nec manu quisquam mea
hos liberabit. post ubi turbavero
penitus Iasonis domum, vertam solum
profuga peremptis liberis carissimis,
840 caede inquinata dexteram nefaria.
non est ferendum, feminae carissimae,
risus ut hosti materia sim. sic eat;
quid enim relictum est cur iuvet dehinc vivere?
nam nec patria nec mihi domus nec miseriae
845 perfugia restant ulla. tunc insanii,
patrios penates cum reliqui, credula
homini Pelasgo, qui favente numine
poenas rependet; nam nec ex me liberos
vivos videbit dehinc, nec e sponsa nova
850 gignet, venenis sed mala peribit malis.
me nemo posthac insimulet ignaviae
aut imbecillem desidemve censeat;
quin contra amicis benevolam, hostibus gravem.
nam quisquis istis praeditus erit moribus,
855 aevum perenni laude clarum transiget.
*CHO.* Arcana nobis quando credis pectoris, [811]
prodesse cupio tibi, ac tueri publicum
mortalium ius fasque; quare suadeo
ne tam nefando scelere te contamines.
860 *MED.* Haec fixa perstant; ac tibi ignosci potest
istaec loquenti, quae pari haud premeris malo.
*CHO.* Mactare subolem mulier audebis tuam?
*MED.* Id nempe coniunx maxime indigne feret.
*CHO.* Et tu miseriis maximis cumulaberis.
865 *MED.* Sic eat. inanis omnis est oratio,
ab instituto quae refrenet. verum age—

MEDEA

[Eur.]
opera fideli semper utimur tua
ad cuncta, tectam quae fidem desiderant—
adduc maritum; at ne revela regibus
consilia nostra, si sapis et es femina. 870

[824] *CHO.* Cecropidae quondam felices
et sancta deum suboles,
arva invicta ac sacra colentes,
aurea quos sapientia pascit,
lucida purae per spatia aethrae 875
traducentes molliter aevum,
ubi castas quondam Pieridas
fama novem peperisse
narrat flavam Harmonien;
ubi pulchriflui flumina propter 880
Cephisi Venerem aiunt fessam
mollibus exhalando flabris
et blandum spirantibus auris
campos adflavisse beatos,
dum nectit purpuream roseo ac 885
suaveolenti e flore coronam
  ambrosiae comae;
in quam, ut referunt, comites sophiae
misit amores, omnigenae essent
ut virtutis opitulatores. 890

[846] quinam sacrorum fluviorum
urbs et cunctis hospita tellus
te venientem accipiet, subolis
exsecranda caede cruentam?
quin expende hic inter amicos 895
quantum aggrediare nefas; animum
refer ad tristia funera prolis.
ne, per genua oramus pariter
cunctae, ne progeniem perimas.
unde haec cruda audacia cordi? 900
unde haec caeca temeritas? natis
nempe inferre manum pote propriis?

[862] quinam immunes fletibus oculos
in natorum funere habebis?
cum procumbet suboles supplex 905
inter caedem, miseranda animi
sanguine poteris tingere dextram?

193

[Eur.]
*IAS.* Advenio iussus; quamlibet succenseas [866]
hic tibi deesse nolui. sed expedi
910 ecquid requiras modo novae ex nobis rei.
*MED.* Iason, oro, quicquid in te dixerim
ignosce. nostra si quid iracundia
asperius egit, te remittere id decet
beneficiorum memoriae communium.
915 namque ipsa mecum sola dum ratiocinor,
meme reprendi: 'Misera, cur insanio?
infensa cur sum recta consulentibus?
hostis tyrannis sum viroque, qui facit
quod utilissimum est mihi, sociam tori
920 dum rege natam ducit, ac natis meis
fratres creabit? non furoris impetum
frenare par est? quid fero, cum praebeant
di cuncta abunde? non mihi sunt liberi?
orbos amicis video nos et exsules.'
925 haec mente volvens, quanta vis insaniae [882]
me tenuit iramque immerentem intellego.
quin laudo nunc te providumque iudico
qui tam potentem adfinitatem adiunxeris.
ego stulta certe, consili quae particeps
930 istius esse, quae ministra debui
adstare lecto coniugis novae, atque ei
gratum quod esset facere. verum nos sumus
non dico pestis quanta, certe feminae.
sed te malorum non decet fieri aemulum
935 et stulta stultis dicta dictis reddere.
insaniebam, fateor, ante; cedo nunc,
consultius deliberavi. o liberi,
o liberi, huc accedite, exite huc, domo [894]
prodite, complectamini adloquamini
940 cum matre patrem; pristinum deponite
odium in amicos cum parente pristinos.
iam foedus ictum est, ira cessit; dexteram
prehendite. hei mihi, subit animum mali
memoria tecti. o liberi, an superstites
945 exporrigetis dexteras caras diu?
hei misera, lacrimis nuper obsita et metu,
odium paternum tempus ubi iam leniit,
rigare fletu cogor ora denuo.

## MEDEA

[Eur.]

[908]

CHO.   Et nostra liquidis ora fletibus madent,
praesente maius ne quod accidat nefas.                            950
IAS.   Haec laudo, mulier; illa nec graviter fero.
par est profecto femina uti succenseat
novas marito contrahenti nuptias.
at saniora consilia tuus animus
admisit, ipsaque admonente tempore                                955
fideliorem percipis sententiam;
quod esse munus feminae arbitror probae.
nec oscitanter, filii carissimi,
vestrae salutis inita ratio est a patre,
si quidem faventes habeat inceptis deos.                          960
nam spero terrae vos adhuc Corinthiae
olim futuros principes cum fratribus.
sed crescite modo; cetera expediet pater
divumque quisquis nos benignus aspicit.
utinam ex ephebis exeuntes vos probe                              965
videam institutos superioresque hostibus!
sed cur tenellas uda lacrimis genas
maeres, retrorsum flexa vultus candidos,
nec haec libenter auribus verba imbibis?

[925]  MED.   Nil; liberorum memoria animum perculit.             970
IAS.   Bono animo es; istis ego probe prospexero.
MED.   Fiet, tibi parebo. verum femina
sum; natus autem sexus hic ad lacrimas.
IAS.   Cur tantopere vero ingemiscis pignora?
MED.   Ea nempe peperi; cum precarer prospere                     975
his, me subibat tacita commiseratio

[932]  an certa sint haec vota. sed qua gratia
huc te vocavi, ex parte dictum; cetera
ego in memoriam suggeram. cum regibus
visum sit isto me relegare e solo                                 980
(id esse video commodissimum mihi,
principibus ut ne sim impedimento et tibi
hic commorando, quippe cum infensa videar
aulae), exsulatum propero; verum liberi
ut educari patria possint manu,                                   985
roga Creontem ne iubeat esse exsules.
IAS.   Certum experiri, at nescio an persuasero.

981–4 *sic interpunxit Walsh* (cf. Eur. 934–7)

MED. At tu iubeto sponsa genitorem ut roget, [Eur.]
hinc exsulatum ne releget liberos.
990 IAS. Fiet; et opinor impetraturam, nisi
a ceterarum discrepabit moribus.
MED. Et ego laboris huius adiutrix ero. [946]
nam dona mittam, pulchrius quibus nihil
nunc inter homines est, sat id scio, peplum
995 tenue ferentes filios, et aureum
orbem coronae. sed ministrorum ilico
aliquem necesse est ferre mundum hunc muliebrem.
felicitate non fruetur simplice,
sed mille sane commodis cumulabitur
1000 te nacta thalamo coniugem virum optimum,
adepta cultus quos patris mei pater
Phoebus ferendos posteris dedit suis.
haec capite manibus dona nuptialia,
nati, ac beatae ferte sponsae regiae;
1005 non respuenda capiet utique munera.
IAS. Cur ipsa tete stulta spolias his? putas [959]
ullis egere regiam peplis domum
aurove? serva, ne dederis haec. sat scio,
alicuius esse si putabit me preti,
1010 auro maritum sponsa longe praeferet.
MED. Omitte; flecti muneribus aiunt deos. [964]
oratione qualibet potentius
apud homines aurum est. fovet felicior
illam aura sortis; cuncta fortunat deus
1015 illi. puella regnat, ego fugam haud modo
auro sed anima liberum redimam lubens
at vos propinquas, filii, ingressi domos,
novam parentis coniugem, dominam meam,
orate, deprecamini ne vertere
1020 solum necesse sit, offerentes in manum
haec dona. multum namque nostra id interest,
illius istaec munera accipi manu.
ite, et peracta re probe ex sententia,
matri referte nuntium qualem cupit.

1025 CHO. Nulla dehinc superest spes pueros [976]
victuros; ad caedem properant.
sponsa coronam fulvam accipiet,

## MEDEA

[Eur.]
 misera accipiet miserum exitium,
 flavaeque comae dirum ornatum
 acceptum capiti imponet.          1030
 gratia pepli et nitor ambrosius
 auro tempora cingere coget;
 sponsa ornabitur Orco.
 tales cadet in laqueos,
 misero et fato defungetur;          1035
 nec mortis patet exitus usquam.
 tu vero, o miser, o infelix
 sponse, adfinis dum vis regum
 esse, calamitatem imprudens
 accersis natis, ac sponsae          1040

[996]
 miserum exitium. o miseranda parens
 puerorum, tua lugeo fata,
 quae thalamos geniales propter
 dulcia prives pignora vita;
 quos tibi vir linquens iniuste          1045
 nuptae thalamo alterius fruitur.

[1001]
 *PAED.* Natis remissum est, o era, exsilium tuis.
 regina munus in manum accepit lubens.
 tranquilla pueris cuncta sunt illinc tuis.
 *MED.* Hei! *PAED.* Quid gemiscis, cuncta cum feliciter 1050
 cedant? quid ora vertis illuc candida,
 meum nec audis mente laeta nuntium?
 *MED.* Ae, ae!
 *PAED.* Haec cum relatis nuntiis haud congruunt.
 *MED.* Vae denuo, vae! *PAED.* Num fefellit opinio  1055
 mea me, malumque nuntium invitus fero?
 *MED.* Quae nuntiata, nuntiata; haud culpo te.
 *PAED.* Deiecta vultus ergo quid fletu mades?
 *MED.* Huc multa cogunt, o senex; namque et dei
 huc impulere et stultitia simul mea.       1060
 *PAED.* Animo bono es; per liberos potentiae
 adhuc prioris magna superest portio.
 *MED.* Alios quidem prius misera deducam ego.
 *PAED.* Non sola natis segregaris. calamitas
 modice ferenda est tibi, genita cum sis homo.   1065

[1019]
 *MED.* Id fiet. at tu protinus in aedes abi

1040 accersis *1544*   arcessis *R*

TRAGOEDIAE

[Eur.]

puerisque solitum praepara diarium.
iam parta vobis civitas, o filii,
filii, domusque quam colatis me sine
1070 orbi parente sempiternum. at exsulem
me capiet alia terra, fructus antequam
capiam expetitos, quam beatos videro,
lectos priusquam nuptialesque thalamos
sponsasque vobis praeparem, ac tollam facem.
1075 o iam sinistram contumaciam meam!
frustra educavi, filii, vos, pertuli
frustra labores, anxia incassum fui,
frustra dolores passa sum puerperi.
o spes inanes saepe de vobis meas                    [1032]
1080 fore vos senectae praesidia nostrae, et manu
vestra sepulcro mortuam me contegi,
quae prima ferme vota sunt mortalibus.
exstincta nunc est dulcis exspectatio.
nam maesta, vobis orba, vitam transigam
1085 et luctuosa; nec deinceps cernere
vobis parentem suavibus oculis licet
ad institutum transeuntibus novum.
eheu, quid in me respicitis, o filii,
risu renidentes mihi novissimo?
1090 hei misera quid agam? mulieres, mihi deficit
cor, intuendo blanda lumina liberum.
nequeo. priora consilia valeant; solum
mecum relinquent. quid? dolore dum patrem
afficio, duplo gravius accersam malum
1095 mihi ipsa? minime. consilia valeant. mihi
quid contigit cur torpeam? ludibrio
me patiar esse meis inultis hostibus?
audenda sunt haec. sed meae est ignaviae            [1051]
hoc crimen; animo molliora suggero
1100 verba. introite; si quis est cui non licet
his interesse sacris, ipse viderit.
meam profecto dexteram non polluam.
ah, facinus, anime, ne istud admittas cave;
ipsos omitte, misera, parce liberis!
1105 fugae levamen exsulantes una erunt
nostrae. per atrae noctis ultores deos
non sic abibit, ut meorum ego hostium

MEDEA

[Eur.] natos relinquam obnoxios libidini.
vitare mortem non queunt. quo nos trahit
fatum, sequamur; sortiantur terminum                    1110
hinc lucis, unde ceperint primordium.
peracta sunt haec; fixa stat sententia.
hanc nemo reddet inritam. iam vertice
haeret corona, sponsa peplis regia
[1067] perit involuta; sat scio. ingrediar iter           1115
miserrimum iam, miserius etiam meos
missura natos per iter. adloqui lubet:
date, date matri dexteram, amplectamini
[1071] nati parentem. o mihi manus carissima, o
carissimum os, o forma grataque facies!                 1120
felicitatem, sed ibi, vobis comprecor,
nam quicquid hic supererat abstulit pater.
o molle corpus, grataque amplexatio,
blandumque spirans suavis oris halitus!
abite, abite, contueri non queo                          1125
vos iam. malorum cedo magnitudini,
videoque quantum perpetrabitur nefas.
sed pessimorum facinorum genitor furor
ratione maior me retrorsum distrahit.

[1081]   *CHO.* Mecum saepe exactius                     1130
sum conata expendere ac
subtili librare examine
num deceat disquirere feminas
de rebus subtilibus anxie.
nec nobis Musarum aliena                                 1135
sunt commercia; sunt sapientiae
corda capacia, non tamen omnibus,
sed rara inter copia feminas
indulget studiis sapientiae.
illud vero ausim contendere,                             1140
his iam longe actum felicius
quibus aevum penitus transigere
contigit orbis subolis
quam quibus est numerosa propago
sorte data, orbi quod inexperti                          1145
ignorent an dulce an amarum

1141 his iam *Walsh dubitanter*   his cum *edd.*

199

## TRAGOEDIAE

[Eur.]

sit genuisse, anxietatibus
vacui innumeris vivant. suboles [1099]
quis numerosa est, anxia curis
1150 degunt miserae tempora vitae,
primum ut honeste educant vitae-
-que necessaria subsidia parent.
deinde accedit ad alias curas
illud, sintne futuri, incertum,
1155 male compositis moribus an boni.
id quoque postremum mortalium
nulli non grave proloquar: etsi
cetera vitae commoda suppetant,
et pubentes iam perveniat
1160 corpus ad annos moribus optimis,
exculto ingenio, dea inutilis
tum si illa incumbat Mors, dulces
ac mittat sub tartara liberos,
qui fuit utile pignora propter
1165 hunc adiectum a dis mortalibus
intolerandum luctus cumulum?

MED. Iamdudum, amicae, opperior exitum rei, [1116]
fortuna quo se vertat illic, praestolans.
atqui e ministris cerno quendam Iasonis
1170 gressus ferentem ad nos anhelo spiritu;
mali videtur fore recentis nuntius.
NUN. O perpetratrix facinoris nefarii
Medea, fuge, fuge; classe seu cita licet
seu vecta curru, corripe celerem fugam!
1175 MED. Quae digna causa cogit ad properam fugam?
NUN. Regia puella modo periit atque genitor
Creon, venenis illiti pariter tuis.
MED. Gratum attulisti nuntium; deinceps meos
inter benevolos ac amantes nostri eris.
1180 NUN. Quid? mente sana mulier es an desipis?
domum tyranni funditus cum verteris,
audire gaudes, nec facinus istud paves?
MED. Non deest ad ista quod queam rependere. [1132]

1150 degant *R dubitanter*
1151 educant *R* educent *1544*
1162 incumbat *R* incumbet *1544*

200

MEDEA

[Eur.]
    sed ne gravere tantulum nobis morae
    dare, pereundi donec explices modum.    1185
    nam morte functos si sciam miserrima,
    cumulabis animum gaudio duplice meum.

[1136]  *NUN.*  Ut gemina proles cum patre advenit tua
    et coniugalis attigit limen domus,
    famuli, dolori quibus erat tuus dolor,    1190
    gaudemus; aures omnium cito pervolat
    rumor maritum teque pacto foedere
    consopiisse pristinam discordiam.
    hic tangere manus, ille flavum verticem
    mulcere pueris. ipse quoque prae gaudio    1195
    pueros gynaeceum usque laetus prosequor.
    at era colenda quae tui nobis loco
    successit, antequam puerulos viderat,
    vultu renidenti intuens Iasonem
    haerebat; at post maesta tristis lumina    1200
    abscondit, ora retro flectens candida,
    quippe puerorum graviter adventum ferens.
    sed leniebat molliter puellulae
    iras Iason, disserendo talibus:

[1151]  'Adversum amicos ne fueris aspera; animum    1205
    compone. rursus flecte vultus, ac puta
    hos esse amicos quos maritus diligit.
    et dona suscipe et patrem exora tuum
    hinc ne releget pignora meam in gratiam.'
    at illa mundum ut vidit, haud viro amplius    1210
    negare quicquam sustinuit. ac antequam
    tectis abessent genitor et nati procul,
    ornata peplis ipsa versicoloribus,
    mollem corona pressit aurea comam,
    sese nitentis ante specli splendidum    1215
    aequor refingens; ac renidens suaviter,
    spectabat umbram corporis inanimem sui.
    dein sede sese sublevans e regia
    per tecta graditur laeta donis, molliter
    eburna terrae collocans vestigia    1220

[1167]  et colla fixo saepe spectans lumine.
    at triste post haec incidit spectaculum.
    colore mutato subitus iterum tremor
    obliqua membra vexat, ac aegre throno

## TRAGOEDIAE

[Eur.]

1225 praeoccupato potuit efficere ne humi
prolapsa rueret. tum pedisequa quaedam anus
iram esse Panos aut deum cuiuspiam
rata, eiulavit lugubre, ante candidis
quam tincta spumis ora vidit et oculis
1230 circumrotari pupulas et sanguinis
inane corpus. eiulatum flebilem
dein excipit ploratus. alia ipsum ad patrem
festinat, alia calamitatem coniugis
novum ad maritum currit ut recenseat.
1235 tota in tumultus versa varios regia
strepebat. et iam cursor accelerans gradum
lassus citatum ad terminum pervenerat.
haec muta clauso quae iacebat lumine,
suspiria trahens graviter, expergiscitur.
1240 misera gerebat cum duplice bellum malo.
nam quae premebat verticem auro tortili      [1186]
corona, mirum, flammeam scaturiginem
voracis ignis evomebat; at pepli
tenues, tuorum liberorum munera,
1245 niveum exedebant corpus et miserae cutem.
porro illa surgens e throno comam igneam
rotat, huc et illuc usta iactans tempora,
quaerens coronam excutere; at insolubilis
aurum tenebat nexus, et quoties comam
1250 quatiebat, ignis saeviebat acrius
duplo. mali tum victa magnitudine
cecidit, parenti cognitu tantum suo
facilis; nec oculis forma constabat sua,
decor nec oris. vertice e summo cruor      [1198]
1255 stillabat igne mixtus; avulsa ossibus
caro venenis per genas tacitis fluit
ceu taeda lentis laesa sudat lacrimis,
res dira visu; terror omnes occupat,
tangere cadaver nemo ut ausit. scilicet
1260 magistra sors adversa nos erudierat.
ignarus autem genitor infelix mali,      [1204]
ut tecta primum contigit, cadaveri
infusus ingemuit, et ulnis comprimens

---

1229 quam *Walsh* (cf. Eur. 1173 πρίν)    nam *1544*, R

MEDEA

[Eur.]
atque osculatus solvit ora talibus:
'O nata misera, quis deorum perdidit 1265
sic morte foeda te? quis orbavit senem
capulo propinquum tristeque silicernium?
utinam liceret, nata, tecum commori!'
ut lacrimis et luctibus fecit modum,
senile corpus adlevare dum cupit, 1270
peplis adhaesit tenuibus, uti laureis
ramis adhaeret hedera. tum certaminis
horrenda facies oritur; ille tollere
genua experitur, illa contra nititur.
sin vim parabat, viva vellens viscera 1275
nudabat ossa. deinde sensim languit;
fugiente vita spiritum tandem miser
efflavit impar invalescenti malo.
iam iuncta genitor nataque cadavera iacent,
dignum profecto lacrimis spectaculum. 1280

[1222]
de te quid opus oratione? senties
poenae expetitae iam vicissitudinem.
haud primitus nunc esse res mortalium
umbras fugaces credo; nec dubitaverim
hos qui videntur sapere, verborum aucupes 1285
hos curiosos, asseverare omnium
iure esse habendos optimo stultissimos.
certe beatus nullus est mortalium.
ut adfluunt res, ille fortunatior
illo putetur, haud beatus sit tamen. 1290

[1231]
CHO. Iure, ut videtur, plurimum hodie congeret
deus malorum in Iasonem; infortunii
tui misertum est, o Creontis filia
misella, thalamis quae procul ab Iasonis
ad tecta Ditis functa fato duceris. 1295
MED. Certum est, amicae feminae, celerrime
natis peremptis hoc solo discedere,
nec otiose desidendo dexterae
infestiori dare necandos filios.
mori necesse est liberos penitus meos. 1300
quando id necesse est, nos trucidemus utique
qui progenuimus. verum age, anime, accingere.
ecquid moramur dira patrare scelera,
et quae necesse est perpetrare? age, o manus

203

[Eur.]

1305 mea misera, ensem cape cape, ac ad carceres
progredere vitae tristis, ac ne defice;
nec subeat animum liberorum memoria
quos edidisti, o cara, et obliviscere
fuisse natos breviculum hunc diem tuos.
1310 post deinde luge. nam tametsi occideris,
cari fuerunt; mulier autem misera ego.

  CHO. O terra lucidumque   [1251]
  Phoebi iubar, videte,
  aspicite pestilentem
1315  hanc feminam et cruentam,
  manum trucem priusquam
  in liberos verterit
  qui de tua stirpe aurea
  ducunt originem.
1320  quam metuo, deum
  ne imbuat hominum sanguis dextram!
  at tu, caeligenae moderator
  lucis, cohibe reprime furiam,
  pelle cruentam et miseram tectis
1325  e feralibus. in cassum labor
  deperit ob natos susceptus;
  pignora frustra cara genueras.
  o Symplegadum inhospita saxa   [1263]
  quae deseruisti, angustas fauces,
1330  misera, unde tibi furor hic animi?
  unde atrox caedes cumulatur?
  quisquis consanguinea terram
  imbuerit caede, ac macularit
  sanguine dextram, vindicta comes
1335  urget saeva, ac di mala plurima
  hinc domibus caelitus inmittunt.

 PUER Quid agam? parentis quomodo hei fugiam manus?
 ALTER Ignoro, frater care; perimus utique.

  CHO. Audis puerorum, audis vocem?
1340  o misera, o infelix mulier!
  tectum ingrediar, pignora rapiam e
  caede nefanda.

1338 perimus *R* periimus *1544*

## MEDEA

[Eur.]   *PUER*   Per o deorum numen opitulamini,
         dum licet; in ipsis paene retibus sumus!

[1279]   *CHO.*   Misera, aut ferrum aut silicem gestas          1345
         pectore, quae propria mactabis
         dextra pignora quae peperisti.
         unam saecula memorant, unam
         Ino, quam foedasse cruore
         sui recensent pignoris caram manum,                      1350
         nec sponte, diro sed furore percitam,
         insanientem Iuno cum miseram domo
         exegit. oblita caede natorum impia,
         periit peremptis liberis mortis comes
         progressa litus ultra, in aequor decidens.               1355

         quid sceleris iam restat inausum?
         o feminei thalami curae
         pleni anxiferae, quanta e vobis
         homines torquet Lerna malorum!

[1293]   *IAS.*   Quae statis hasce propter aedes feminae,        1360
         estne intus auctor facinoris nefarii
         Medea, sese an abripuit alio fuga?
         tellure sese ni recondat obrutam
         pennave liquidas aetheris findat plagas,
         domui rependet capta poenas regiae.                      1365
         an se interempta stirpe regum credidit
         impune tectis hisce posse evadere?
         nec illius me cura sed subolis coquit.
         namque illa poenas solvet his quos laeserat;
         sed liberorum huc venio vitae ut consulam,               1370
         ne scelera matris vindicantes impiae
         genere propinqui adversus illos saeviant.
         *CHO.*   Nescis malorum quo redactus sis, miser
         Iason; alias ista nunquam diceres.
[1308]   *IAS.*   Quid est? an etiam me interimere cogitat?       1375
         *CHO.*   Caesi occiderunt liberi matris manu.
         *IAS.* Hei mihi, quid ais? ut me iugulasti, femina!
         *CHO.*   Ut luce cassis cogita de liberis.
         *IAS.*   Ubi eos peremit? intus an foris refer.
         *CHO.*   Foribus reclusis funera intuebere.              1380
         *IAS.*   Auferte vectes, tollite hinc repagula

205

[Eur.]

    statim, ministri, scelus ut aspiciam duplex,
    illos peremptos, hanc uti poenam exigam.
    *MED.*   Quid frustra in istas arietas pulsans fores,
1385  caesosque meque caedis auctorem petens?
    laborem omitte hunc, meque si qua in re est opus
    adfare; manibus haud licebit tangere.
    talem parentis Sol pater currum mihi
    quo me tuerer e manu hostili dedit.
1390  *IAS.*   O dira, dis o mulier immortalibus    [1323]
    exosa mihique et omnibus mortalibus,
    quae sustinebas liberorum pectori
    inserere ferrum mater, orbum et perdere
    me! et his patratis intueri sustines
1395  solem solumque, facinus ausa pessimum?
    male peri. ego resipisco nunc; insanii    [1329]
    tum, cum paternis aedibus te barbaro
    Graias ad urbes e solo advexi malum
    pestemque, patris proditricem et patriae
1400  quae te educavit. supplicia de me expetunt
    scelerum tuorum vindices Erinyes.
    nam fratre caeso sanguinis socio ratem
    mecum decoram ingressa es Argo Peliam.
    hinc orsa es, inde coniugali copula
1405  mihi iuncta de me sustulisti liberos;
    offensa taedis quos peremisti novis,
    quod Graia nulla perpetrasset femina,
    quibus ego spretis praetuli thalamos tuos
    adfinitate pestilente me inligans
1410  saevae leaenae, haud feminae, quae pectore
    Scyllae cruentos ferreo vincis canes.
    sed nulla mentem commovent opprobria;    [1344]
    ita impudenti obduruisti audacia.
    pereas, cruenta liberorum carnifex.
1415  lugere superest mihi meum infortunium,
    qui nec recenti perfruar conubio,
    nec quos creavi et educavi liberos
    iam morte raptos adloqui vivos licet.
    *MED.*   Quam multa contra suppetunt quae redderem
1420  si non utrimque testis esset Iuppiter
    quam debuisti ac rettulisti gratiam!
    spretisne nostris nuptiis tu molliter

# MEDEA

[Eur.]
    vitam perageres, mihi miserae inluderes?
    regiaque virgo et qui dedit nuptum hanc Creon
    impune an umquam me expulissent hoc solo?     1425
    igitur leaenam me voca aut Scyllam, ut lubet,
    Tuscum obsidentem litus; ut par est, tuum
    animum vicissim perculi molestiis.
    *IAS.* Angeris et ipsa, et es malorum particeps.

[1362]
    *MED.* Modo ne dolentem irrideas, iuvat dolor.     1430
    *IAS.* O matre nati filii nefaria!
    *MED.* O filii, ut vos perdidit scelus patris!
    *IAS.* Non hos peremit nostra certe dextera.
    *MED.* Sed culpa lectumque in iugalem iniuria.
    *IAS.* Torumne propter ausa es illos perdere?     1435
    *MED.* An hunc dolorem mulieri reris levem?
    *IAS.* Si qua est modesta; tu undequaque es pessima.
    *MED.* Illi occiderunt; hoc habet te pessime.
    *IAS.* Capiti imminebunt vindices umbrae tuo.
    *MED.* Dis primus auctor notus est iniuriae.     1440
    *IAS.* Dis nota mens est exsecrabilis tua.
    *MED.* Mihi es molestus, et odiosa oratio.
    *IAS.* Et tua vicissim mihi. sed hac molestia
    facile carebis. *MED.* Quomodo? id namque unice
    cupio. *IAS.* Remitte flenda mihi cadavera     1445

[1378]
    ac sepelienda. *MED.* Minime; eos namque hac manu
    Iunonis alto sepeliam sanctae sacro,
    sepulcra ne forte hostis insolentia
    violet superbi; Sisyphique posteris
    caedis nefandae sacra dabo piamina,     1450
    festaque dicabo in posterum sollemnia.
    at ipsa Erechthei propero ad urbem, ubi Aegeo
    iungar marito filio Pandionis.
    tu vero, ut aequum est te, peribis pessime
    Argus reliquiis tempora effractus tuae,     1455
    finem nefastum sentiens thalami mei.
    *IAS.* At te cruentae filiorum Erinyes
    perdant, et ultrix iustitia caedis ferae.
    *MED.* Ecquis deorum te audiet vel daemonum,
    periure, fallax, hospitumque proditor?     1460
    *IAS.* Ah ah, nefanda liberorum carnifex!

1455 tuae *1544* tua *R*

                                                    [Eur.]
*MED.* Proficiscere domum, conde tumulo coniugem.
*IAS.* Natis orbus geminis abeo.
*MED.* Nondum luges; senium exspecta.

1465    *IAS.* O carissima pignora! *MED.* Matri        [1397]
cara profecto, patri minime.
*IAS.* Tamen exstinxti. *MED.* Te ut cruciarem.
*IAS.* Heu me miserum! tangere cara
cupio natorum ora meorum.

1470    *MED.* Nunc adloqueris, nunc amplecti
optas, dudum quos repulisti.
*IAS.* Per o deorum numen id tribue mihi
ut molle corpus liberum tangam manu!
*MED.* Minime; in cassum verba profundis.

1475    *IAS.* Iuppiter, hocne ut spernimur audis,       [1405]
quaeque scelesta patraverit in me
lea natorum caede cruenta?
quod licet unum fleo, vociferor
testesque deos advoco, natos

1480    quod me attingere manibus prohibes
abs te occisos, quod mihi tollis
funeris arbitrium. quos utinam
nunquam ego genuissem, abs te ut caesos
cernere cogerer ipse superstes.

1485    *CHO.* Dispensat mortalia cuncta
caelo Iuppiter; inopina dei
plurima peragunt, spes eventu
fraudant saepe suo; quae credas
fieri haud posse, expediet deus, ut

1490    finem haec nunc sortita est fabula.              [1419]

Acta fuit Burdegalae an. MDXLIII

# EURIPIDIS
## POETAE TRAGICI
### ALCESTIS
#### GEORGIO BUCHANANO SCOTO
#### INTERPRETE

## AD ILLUSTRISSIMAM PRINCIPEM DOMINAM MARGARITAM HENRICI SECUNDI FRANCORUM REGIS SOROREM, IN ALCESTIN PRAEFATIO

Alcestin Euripidis, ante aliquot annos a me Latinam factam, ad te potissimum, Margarita principum optima, censui mittendam. nec id ea modo causa feci qua ceteri fere solent, qui hoc tempore in scribendo aliquid aut possunt aut audent—ut videlicet hac praerogativa freti aliorum iudicia minus reformident, et auctoritate nominis tui adversus calumniantium malignitatem se tueantur; sed quod huius fabulae lectionem tibi multis de causis non ingratam fore sperabam. est enim orationis genere leni et aequabili, et, quod Euripidis proprium est, suavi; parricidii vero et veneficii et reliquorum quibus aliae tragoediae plenae sunt scelerum nulla prorsus hic mentio, nullum omnino vestigium. contra vero coniugalis amoris, pietatis, humanitatis et aliorum officiorum adeo plena sunt omnia ut non verear hanc fabulam comparare cum libris eorum philosophorum qui ex professo virtutis praecepta tradiderunt; ac nescio an etiam praeferre debeam. actio enim rerum sermone et spiritu paene animata acrius quam nuda praecepta sensus impellit, et facilius in animos influit et illabitur; atque ubi illapsa fuerit, firmius haeret et quasi radices agit. quod si quis minus ad te pertinere credat ista, quod eo iam in omni virtutis genere sis progressa ut non sis alienis exemplis confirmanda sed alios tuo exemplo ad virtutem provoces, fallitur vehementer meo quidem iudicio; praecepta enim officiorum et rerum praeclare gestarum memoria aliis fortasse utiliora erunt qui ea legunt, ut velut ad normam suos mores eo dirigant; illis certe iucundissima esse debent qui iam perfuncti discendi et imitandi laboribus sub aliena persona suas laudes citra omnem adulationis suspicionem

19 illapsa *R*    illapsum *1557*

## TRAGOEDIAE

30 legunt. habet enim haec fabula, quantum ego quidem iudicare possum, earum virtutum quas in te non minus libenter agnoscimus quam in Alcestide legentes miramur adeo expressam imaginem, ut quoties eam in manus sumas toties tuarum tibi virtutum in mentem veniat necesse sit. eam cum
35 laudari audies, de tuis moribus iudicium fieri existimes. eam igitur ad te, ut dixi, mittimus. quod si audacius a me factum videatur, eam tu potissimum culpam praestes oportet, quae me tua auctoritate ad scribendum impulisti, et in arenam productum omni favoris genere prosequeris et foves. Vale.

### ALCESTIDIS ARGUMENTUM

40   Cum iam moriturus esset Admetus, Apollo a Parcis impetravit ei ut quantum vixisset alterum tantum viveret, si alium daret qui pro se moreretur. parens autem uterque cum hanc pro filio moriendi condicionem recusasset, Alcestis uxor se obtulit. paucos vero post dies cum ea incidisset calamitas,
45 Hercules advenit. is edoctus ab uno ministrorum quae Alcestidi contigerant, ad sepulcrum profectus Mortem abegit, mulierem veste obnubit, atque Admetum orat ut eam a se acceptam servet; affirmabat enim sibi, cum lucta vicisset, eam praemio datam. id cum abnueret Admetus, detectam ei
50 quam lugebat ostendit uxorem.

### PERSONAE TRAGOEDIAE

| | |
|---|---|
| Apollo | Servus |
| Thanatos | Admetus |
| Chorus | Eumelus |
| Semichorion | Hercules |
| Ancilla Alcest. | Pheres |
| Alcestis | |

---

34 sit *R*   est *1557*

[Eur.]

APOLLO

O tecta cara regis Admeti, in quibus
convictor esse pertuli servis deus!
huc me coëgit, filium Aesculapium
flammis trisulcis cum peremit, Iuppiter.
ego impotenti saevus ira fulminis 5
fabros Cyclopas perimo; poenas ut darem,
mortalis esse me viri servum pater
voluit. profectus igitur huc, pecus hospitis
pavi, domumque praestiti incolumem hactenus,
ut sancta sancto quae Pheretis filio 10
pareret. ipsum liberavi e faucibus
leti imminentis, praeoccupans Parcas dolo.
namque adnuerunt mihi deae ut subducerem
Admetum ab Orco, et funus in praesentia
aliud loco eius manibus supponerem. 15

[15] cumque ambiisset ille amicos, omnium
expertus animos, patris ac matris senis
quae peperit ipsum, nemo praeter coniugem
inventus unam est, sponte quae prior mori
voluit, nec alma luce postea frui. 20
ea baiulatur nunc manus inter domi
frigente sensim corpore; haec etenim dies
decreta fato est, morte vitam ut exuat.
sed funus hic ne polluat me, desero
caros penates. mortuorum sed prope 25
Thanatos sacerdos advenit, sub Tartara
rapturus illam. tempori vero huc adest,
hunc praestitutum mortis observans diem.
TH. Ha, ha, ha, ha.
quid tibi tandem hic, Phoebe, negotii? 30
quid oberras haec limina propter?

[30] iterum iniurius es diis Stygiis,
quorum aboles ac tollis honores.
non sat erat tibi morti Admeti
iniecisse moram, arte dolosa 35

[Eur.]

        circumventis Parcis? iterum
        arcitenentem cur modo dextram
        armatus ades, Peliae observans
        natam, quae pro coniuge caro est
40     pollicita mori?
        *AP.*  Bono animo es; aequum iusque fasque poscimus.  [38]
        *TH.*  Quorsum igitur arcu, iusta si petis, est opus?
        *AP.*  Haec arma semper ferre consuetum est mihi.
        *TH.*  Opemque ferre praeter aequum his aedibus?
45   *AP.*  Hominis amici mihi dolori est calamitas.
        *TH.*  Etiam hoc secundo fraudor abs te funere?
        *AP.*  Atqui nec illud abstuli invito tibi.
        *TH.*  Cur vivit ergo nec apud inferos agit?
        *AP.*  Sponsae redemptus morte, quam tu nunc petis.
50   *TH.*  Et quam silentes mortuam ad manes agam.
        *AP.*  Perge, aufer; etenim nescio an persuasero.
        *TH.*  Mi? munus ipsum cuius est occidere?
        *AP.*  Minime, morantes morte sed tollere senes.
        *TH.*  Quo verba spectent et voluntas tua, scio.
55   *AP.*  Alcestidi ergo non licet senio frui?  [52]
        *TH.*  Non licet; honores, Phoebe, nos etiam iuvant.
        *AP.*  Nil praeter animam poteris unam tollere.
        *TH.*  Ex morte iuvenum maius accedet decus.
        *AP.*  At vetula moriens ditius tumulabitur.
60   *TH.*  Lex haec rem habentes, Phoebe, solos respicit.
        *AP.*  Quid? tu sophistes insciis nobis eras?
        *TH.*  Res ampla quibus est, redimerent mortis moras.
        *AP.*  Non ergo visum est tibi facere gratum hic mihi?
        *TH.*  Minime. ipse morum non meorum ignarus es.
65   *AP.*  Quos nec deorum nec hominum ullus diligit.
        *TH.*  Haud cuncta poteris praeter aequum consequi.
        *AP.*  At reprimetur ista saeva immanitas,  [64]
        quamlibet acerba; talis accedet domum
        Pheretis hospes, imperante Eurystheo
70   Thrace ab nivosa quadriiugos abducere.
        acceptus hospes ille in Admeti domum
        vi tollet istam feminam tibi. neque
        hanc a me inibis gratiam; et cum ingratiis
        eadem peregeris, odio esse haud desines.
75   *TH.*  Ut multa dicas, nil tamen profeceris.
        haec mulier Orci pallidam viset domum.

| | |
|---|---|
| [Eur.] | properoque ad ipsam ut ense delibem comam.<br>damnatus ille manibus deis erit,<br>cuicumque ferrum hoc verticem libaverit. |
| [77] | CHO.   Quae pro foribus taciturna quies?     80<br>Cur conticuit domus Admeti?<br>SEM.   Nullus adest qui narret amicus,<br>an lugenda est filia Peliae<br>Alcestis ceu mortua, an aura<br>fruitur supera, quae optima longe     85<br>mihique et cunctis femina visa est<br>in coniugem fuisse.<br>SEM.   Auditne quisquam lacrimarum aut planctuum<br>sonum per aedes, flentium aut suspiria?<br>SEM.   Minime. sed neque famulum quisquam     90<br>ad vestibulum est. utinam, o Paean,<br>auxiliator in hac clade adsis,<br>atque salutifer aspiciare.<br>SEM.   Nec tacita domus defuncta esset<br>domina, nec clam condita tumulo est.     95 |
| [95] | SEM.   Unde? haud video quid te recreet.<br>SEM.   Tamne probam clam populo Admetus<br>coniugem humasset funere vili?<br>SEM.   Nec ante portas conspicor<br>fontanae aquae lavacra, ceu     100<br>ad mortuorum ianuas |
| [101] | adsuevit; haud propter fores<br>abscissa coma est, posita in luctu<br>quae funereo caeditur, usquam<br>neque virgineum perstrepit agmen.     105<br>SEM.   Atqui haec fuerat praescripta dies,<br>qua tenebrosum viseret Orcum.<br>SEM.   Quorsum haec memoras?<br>SEM.   Pupugisti cor, pupugisti animum. |
| [109] | CHO.   Cum bonos Parcae rapiunt severae,     110<br>qui bonus vixit teneris ab annis<br>iure eos luget. neque enim Chimaerae<br>arva si remis adeas, vel aestu<br>semper arentes Garamantum arenas<br>templaque Ammonis, miserae prece umbras     115<br>faucibus taetri rapies ab Orci. |

TRAGOEDIAE

[Eur.]

  mors gradu tristis properat citato;
  nec focos iuxta video deorum
  quem sacerdotem precibus fatigem.
120  si modo argutis oculis decorus       [122]
  filius Phoebi hac frueretur aura,
  illa, desertis Stygiis tenebris,
  Noctis et portis, Acheronte ab ipso
  viva rediret;
125  namque defunctos revocabat Orco,
  antequam telo trifido timendus
  Iuppiter saevos iaculatus ignes
  perculit illum.
  nulla spes vitae reliqua est. peregit
130  cuncta rex; omnes pecudum cruentis
  stragibus divum cumulantur arae.
  nec mali est usquam fuga certa certi.

  sed uda lacrimis quaepiam egreditur domo  [136]
  ancilla. miserum me! quid adferet novi?
135  veniam meretur luctus hic, si quicquam eris
  accidit acerbum. scire at illud gestio,
  vita fruatur mulier an iam perierit.
  ANC.  Vivam vocare et mortuam pariter licet.  [141]
  CHO.  Qui poterit idem vivus esse et mortuus?
140  ANC.  Vix ducit aegra spiritum ad thalami fores.
  CHO.  Uxore quali qualis orbabere miser!
  ANC.  Iam coniuge orbus dominus istud sentiet.
  CHO.  Nec spes salutis ulla restat amplius?
  ANC.  Fati prementis instat illi terminus.
145  CHO.  Ergo apparantur iusta rite funeri?
  ANC.  Mundus paratus est, quem humo condat simul.
  CHO.  Praestante sese coniuge orbatum sciat,  [150]
  sub orbe caeli nulla qua melior fuit.
  ANC.  Quidni? quis aliter sentiat? qui femina
150  potuisset ulla facere gloriosius
  suumque amorem prodere manifestius
  erga maritum, quam suam si impenderit
  vitam illi? at ista cuncta novit civitas.
  at obstupesces si modo audies, domi
155  quae perpetrarit. destinatum cum diem

119 sacerdotem *R* (cf. Eur. 121)  sacerdotum *1557*

## ALCESTIS

[Eur.]
    adesse sensit, lauta vivo flumine
    corpus decorum, cedrino ex armario
    effert amictum; compta deinde splendide
    mundo superbo, constitit domesticam
    Vestam ante, tales ora solvens in preces:     160
[163] 'o dea, ego tristes abeo ad umbrarum domos.
    tibi advoluta te precor novissimum,
    orbos tuere liberos; huic coniugem
    caram, maritum filiae da splendidum.
    nec, velut acerbo rapta mater funere est,     165
    praecipitet illos Parca praecox, sed sua in
    patria beati transigant ac suaviter
    iucunda vitae spatia.' cunctas regiae
    accessit aras, supplicavit, singulas
    festa corona myrteae cinxit comae,     170
    nec ora fletu madida nec suspirio
    indice doloris; vis nec instantis mali
    vultus decori pristinum carpsit decus.
    at coniugalem ut attigit thalamum ac torum,
    lacrimis profusis solvit ora talibus:     175
[177] 'o lecte, ubi mihi morte quem redimo mea
    solvit pudorem virginalem vir, vale!
    nec te quidem odi, me tametsi exstinxeris,
    nam dum recuso coniugem et te prodere,
    morior. at alia te tenebit femina     180
    non castior, fortasse fortunatior.'
    tum devoluta exosculatur lectulum,
    totumque inundat lacrimarum flumine.
    ubi tandem abunde fletuum profuderat,
    revoluta strato ex aedibus se proripit;     185
    ac saepe thalamo egressa rediit denuo,
[189] supraque lectum denuo incubuit. peplos
    flebant tenentes liberi; illa amplexibus
    modo hunc, modo illam comprimebat, scilicet
    moritura iamiam. flebili tota domo     190
    famuli tumultu fata lugebant erae.
    at illa dextram singulis dedit, neque
    quisquam inter omnes adeo contemptus fuit
    quem affata non sit mutuis sermonibus.
    atque ista turbant nunc domum Admeti mala     195
    quae morte poterat fugere; mortem dum fugit,

[Eur.]

nunc sempiternum sibi dolorem arcessiit.
CHO.　His ingemiscit igitur Admetus malis, [199]
quem fata nupta dividunt ab optima?
200　ANC.　Luget profecto, coniugem caram tenens
ulnis, rogansque morte ne se deserat—
absurda poscens, quaeque fieri non queant.
tabescit illa, et languidum manus onus
proiecta inertis, debilem etsi spiritum
205　vix fessa ducat, intueri solem avet,
almaeque lucis ultimo aspectu frui,
visura nunquam splendidum posthac iubar.
sed abeo, teque adesse nuntiavero.
nec semper omnes regibus cives favent,
210　nec rebus adsunt turbidis alacriter;
at tu vestustus amicus es meis eris.

CHO.　O di, quae fuga superest cladis? [213]
quae fuga sortis quae imminet aulae?
exitne aliquis? laceremne comam?
215　pullone tegam corpus amictu?
ANC.　Certa res est, certa, amici; [218]
sed precemur numina.
nam potestas est deorum
visque longe maxima.
220　o Apollo sancte, cladis
exitum huius inveni.
affer, affer remedium nunc,
ut prius commentus es.
nunc ades salutifer;
225　pelle fatum lugubre.
Ditis implacabilis
pectus atrox mitiga.
CHO.　Heu, heu, vae, vae. [226]
o nate, nate Pheretis, Admete o miser,
230　qua clade premeris orbus ista coniuge!
pateris ferro rem fugiendam
et graviori clade piandam,
quam si laquei de trabe celsa
tereti nectas vincula collo.
235　non enim caram modo, at
coniugem carissimam

## ALCESTIS

[Eur.]
    hac morientem luce videbis.
[233]    sed iam maritus ipse progreditur domo.
    Pheraea tellus, ingemisce, illacrima.
    optima longe femina morbo           240
    contabescens, Ditis ad umbras
    sub cava rapitur viscera terrae.
[238]    nunquam thalamos plus laetitiae
    quam tristitiae ferre fatebor;
    partim id veteris casibus aevi           245
    doctus, partim hac clade recenti
    regis, quem longe optima coniunx
    morte relinquens, non sinet unquam
    dehinc vitalem vivere vitam.
[244]    *ALC.* O sol luxque diurna,           250
    caelestesque rotatae
    celeri turbine nubes!
    *ADM.* Me teque miseros aspicit duos, tua
    nil promerentes morte dignum caelitus.
    *ALC.* O tellus, o atria, thalami           255
    o geniales patriae Iolci!
    *ADM.* Sustolle teipsam, o misera, neu me deseras,
    sed flecte precibus omnium dominos deos.
[252]    *ALC.* Biscalmam video, video ratem;
    atque umbrarum portitor haerens           260
    conto accersit me propere Charon.
    age festina, quae causa morae?
    praesto cetera cuncta; moraris
    nos sola. gradu celeri propera.
    *ADM.* Heu, navigationem acerbam istam mihi           265
    memoras. malorum quanta nos moles premit!
    *ALC.* Eripit, eripit quidam tibi me—
    nonne vides?—ad tecta silentum.
    fronte subnigra lumina Pluto in-
    tentat celer huc. quid facis? aufer.           270
    quod miserabilis iter insisto!
[264]    *ADM.* Acerbum amicis, ac mihi atque liberis,
    queis luctus hic est proprius, miserrimum.
    *ALC.* Iam dimittite, dimittite me.
    genua labant. iam deponite me.           275
    oculos densae condunt tenebrae.
    pueri, o pueri, iam vestra parens

nulla est, nulla est iam vestra parens. [Eur.]
valete, nati, et lumen almum cernite.
280 *ADM.* Hei mihi! tristis vox ferit aures [273]
ac morte mihi durior omni.
ne me desere, ne per superos;
tolera. nam te lumine cassa
vivere acerbum est. pendet ab una
285 te mea mors ac vita; ita nobis
tui amor penitus fixus inhaeret.

*ALC.* Admete, cernis quo in loco res sint meae. [280]
quae sentit animus, ante mortem proloqui
volo. salutem praetuli meae tuam,
290 per fata lucem cum liceret cernere;
morior, fuisset cum integrum haud pro te mori
sed mihi maritum quem luberet Thessalum
eligere, sedes et beatas regio
incolere luxu; abs te revulsa vivere
295 renui orphanis cum liberis. vitae meae
minime peperci, aetate quamvis integra,
cum qui genuerat te pater quaeque peperit
te prodidisset mater; auras linquere
quibus decorum iam per aetatem foret,
300 et gloriosa morte vitam filio
suo redimere, quippe quibus unicus eras
nec spem relictam procreandi liberos
te functo haberent. viveremus tu ac ego, [295]
nec tu doleres solitudinem tori
305 vidui, nec orbos educares liberos.
sed haec, deorum quando quispiam gradu
hoc ire voluit, sic eant; at gratiam
hanc tu referto quam peto, haud meritis parem
—nam par rependi pretium animae nullum potest—
310 sed quam ipse iustam dixeris. cum diligas
aeque atque ego istos, si sapis, pueros, meae
domini face isti sint domus; nec liberis [305]
induc novercam feminam minus probam
parente, natis quae manum impingat meis
315 tuisque, livor tristis ubi stimulos ciet.

282 *sic interpunximus*
294 te *suppl. R om. 1557*

## ALCESTIS

[Eur.]
    utique cave istud faxis, oro. prioribus
    inimica natis cum noverca inducitur,
    nihilo cruenta vipera est clementior.
    in patre magnum filius praesidium habet,
    sermone cum quo mutuo possit frui.     320

[313]
    tu, nata, vero quomodo educaberis
    in virginali aetate honeste? quam tuo
    nuptam parenti sors dabit, quae nec nota
    te foedet ulla, nec tuas ipso in aditu
    florentis aevi nuptias contaminet?     325
    neque elocabit mater unquam te, neque in
    dolore partus adsidens solabitur,
    ubi nil parentis caritate est suavius.
    mori necesse est me; timori nec malum
    cras istud, aut in tertium est mensis diem.     330
    iamiam inter umbras luce cassas censeor.
    valete, laeti vivite. at tu, vir, potes
    te gloriari coniugem nactum optimam,
    et vos, parentis optimae vos filios.

[326]
    *CHO.*   Bono animo es; huius polliceri hoc nomine     335
    ego nil verebor, mente ni prorsus caret.
    *ADM.*   Ne metue, fient ista, fient. nam mea
    viva ut fuisti sola, sola mortua
    dicere coniunx; nec tuo ulla me loco
    suum vocabit sponsa Thessalis virum,     340
    quamvis superbos generis enumeret avos,
    formae decore quamlibet praefulgeat.
    sat liberorum est; liceat istis modo frui
    deos precamur, quando te frui haud licet.
    nec finietur luctus hic spatio annuo,     345
    sed omne in aevum, quod supererit dehinc mihi,
    lugebo. matrem quae peperit odio ac patrem
    habebo, amici quando verbo non re erant.

[340]
    tibi ego salutem debeo, quae pro mea
    anima dedisti quod homini est carissimum.     350
    non iure, tali quando privor coniuge,
    dura inter aevum transigam suspiria?
    nec coetus aut aequalium convivia
    post me iuvabunt, nec coronae floreae
    cantusve dulces, nostra nec citharam manus     355
    dehinc tanget unquam, nec Libyssae ad tibiae

[Eur.]
    sonos canoros animus oblectabitur;
    nam cuncta vitae tu abstulisti gaudia.
    quin et periti dextera artificis tua               [348]
360    in lecto imago ficta collocabitur.
    amplectar illam manibus, illi procidens
    tuum vocabo nomen; ulnis coniugem
    caram tenere, non tenens, fingam tamen.
    est ea voluptas frigida, at molestiam
365    animi levabit. umbra me per somnia
    utinam reversa oblectet; etiam lurida
    sub nocte amicos suave vultus cernere,
    quocumque sese in tempore offerent. mihi
    si lingua adesset Orphei et blandum melos,
370    furvae canendo pectus ut Proserpinae
    duri vel Orci flecterem ac reducerem
    te, promptus irem; centiceps nec me canis
    nec qui silentes portitor manes vehit
    prohiberet, almum viva per me denuo
375    donec videres lumen. illic mortua               [363]
    nunc praestolare, donec illuc mortuum
    me fata mittent, ac domum ambobus para,
    una ut habitemus. nam sepulcro corpora
    uno imperabo collocari, et conseri
380    lateri latus te propter extensum meum;
    nec ipsa mors me poterit abs te avellere,
    quae sola nobis usque fida inventa sis.
    *CHO.* Maerore digna est. itaque luctus particeps    [369]
    huius ero, amicum velut amico convenit.
385    *ALC.* Ipsi haec loquentem, filii, audistis patrem.
    nullam deinceps spondet aliam coniugem
    sibi fore, nec me luce cassam negleget.
    *ADM.* Nunc assevero id, atque perfectum dabo.
    *ALC.* Cape pignus horum de mea pueros manu.
390    *ADM.* Accipio carum pignus e cara manu.
    *ALC.* His tu puellis mater esto meo loco.
    *ADM.* Te morte rapta cogit id necessitas.
    *ALC.* Intereo, nati, par fuit cum vivere.
    *ADM.* Quaenam futura est vita mihi superstiti?     [380]
395    *ALC.* Te mitigabit temporis longinquitas;
    qui periit autem, in posterum iam fit nihil.
    *ADM.* Duc, duc me ad Orcum, per deos, tecum simul!

## ALCESTIS

[Eur.]
    *ALC*. In morte nostra sat superque cladis est.
    *ADM*. Sors saeva, quali viduor abs te coniuge!
    *ALC*. At at tenebrae iamiam oboriuntur oculis.      400
    *ADM*. Perii profecto, si modo abs te deseror!
    *ALC*. Nil me putaris iam, velut nusquam forem.
    *ADM*. Attolle vultus, liberos neu deseras!
    *ALC*. Non sponte certe, sed valete, liberi.
    *ADM*. Oculos ad illos tolle, tolle et aspice!      405
    *ALC*. Sum nulla posthac. *ADM*. Quid agis? ita me deseris?
    *ALC*. Valeto. *ADM*. Miseris heu pereo miser modis!
    *CHO*. Periit, nec usquam est uxor Admeti amplius.

[393]
    *EUM*. Hei mihi misero, periit mater.
    o pater, adiit manes, neque iam      410
    dulci fruitur lumine solis;
    me deseruit, me orbum, infelix.
    languidulos cerne oculos, rigidas
    cerne manus. o genetrix, audi
    audi, genetrix! ego te appello,      415
    tua proclivis ad oscula pullus.
    *ADM*. Nil audientem, nil videntem adfare. ego
    vosque ambo saeva clade perculsi sumus.

[406]
    *EUM*. Puer, o genitor, matre orbatus
    solus deseror. o me miseris      420
    pressum aerumnis, teque sororem
    quam premit eadem sors! o genitor,
    infrugiferos, infrugiferos
    thalamos nactus es; haud tetigisti
    hac cum coniuge claustra senectae.      425
    prius erepta est. te pereunte,
    genetrix, pariter domus eversa est.

    *CHO*. Admete, clades has necesse est perpeti.
    nec primus es nec ultimus mortalium
    uxore viduatus proba. atque id cogita,      430
    nos universos esse morti obnoxios.

[420]
    *ADM*. Scio, nec ista me repente perculit
    aerumna; pridem praescius malo premor.
    sed efferendae funus huic parabitur.
    adeste, et alternante planctu lugubri      435
    date iusta; Diti dicite implacabili
    paeana. sceptris Thessalum quisquis meis

[Eur.]

    paret, mulieris huius ergo publice
    lugere iubeo rasili tonsos coma
440  pulloque amictu. quadriiugosque iungite
    currus; superbam sonipedum e collo iubam
    tondete ferro. tibiae nusquam sonus
    strepat per urbem vel suaviloquae lyrae,
    bis luna senos donec orbes impleat.
445  nam neque cadaver hoc sepeliam carius
    ullum, nec in me paribus officiis; neque
    honoribus eam prosequi dignis queam,
    quae me redemit sola morte vicaria.

    *CHO.*  O Peliae mihi nata, vale,     [435]
450  quae Orci habitas sine sole domos.
    at sciat arbiter hoc Stygius
    nigricomans deus, atque senex
    portitor exanimem populum
    qui vehit et subigit residens
455  puppe ratem celerem: mulier
    optima longe Acherontis aquas,
    optima femina transvehitur
    rate biscalma.
    Pieridum tu carmen alumnis     [445]
460  decantabere diu; montigena
    te testudine septem nervis
    resonante canent, ac sine cithara
    memores repetent carmine laudes,
    cum redeuntis circulus anni
465  mensem Spartae Carneium iterat,
    lunaque pernox vere benigno
    pleno pernitet orbe decora.
    inque beatis divitis agri
    decantabere semper Athenis.
470  tales mors tua sufficit hymnos
    vatibus. o revocare liceret     [455]
    si te superas rursus ad auras
    e tenebrosis sedibus Orci,
    e Cocyti fluctibus, alno
475  e fluminea quae vehit umbras.
    tu feminei gloria sexus
    sola reperta es, coniugis Orco

[Eur.]
quae mutata anima animam eriperes.
terra levis tibi sit super ossa.
[463] quod si taedis vir tuus aliis 480
captus erit, mihi iure invisus
natisque tuis deget, quando
nec tua mater, nec qui genuit
te senior pater, abdere vellent
pro nato sua corpora terra, 485
nec servarint, etsi seris
candida sparsi tempora canis.
[471] at tu primo in flore iuventae
iuvenis redimens fata mariti
deseris auras. o mihi talem 490
vitae sociam di date sponsam,
quae iucundum transigat aevum
mecum! at vitae cognita paucis
est mortalibus ista voluptas.

[476] *HER.* Cives Pheraeam qui colitis urbem, an domi est 495
Admetus?  *CHO.*  Intus est Pheretis filius.
at quae te ad urbem causa adegit Thessalam,
hospes Pheraeas advenires ut domos?
*HER.*  Obeo laborem Eurystheo Tirynthio.
*CHO.*  Quo tendis? error quis vagabundum trahit? 500
*HER.*  Diomedis ut Thracis quadrigas huc agam.
*CHO.*  Qui poteris? hospes an vetus forsan tibi est?
*HER.*  Minime, nec unquam Bistonum attigi solum.
[486] *CHO.*  Potiare ut illis, ferro oportet cernere.
*HER.*  Sed nec labores refugere ut velim licet. 505
*CHO.*  Caeso redibis rege, vel caesus cades.
*HER.*  Discrimen istud non adeo nunc primitus.
*CHO.*  Quid promovebis, dominum ubi deviceris?
*HER.*  Captos tyranno tradam equos Tirynthio.
*CHO.*  Frenare captos alter haud facilis labor. 510
*HER.*  An forte flammas evomunt e naribus?
*CHO.*  Avidis virorum membra laniant dentibus.
*HER.*  Memoras ferarum non equorum pabulum.
*CHO.*  Praesaepe tabo sordidum intuebere.
*HER.*  Quo patre iactat educator se editum? 515
*CHO.*  Marte, et opulentam frenat armis Thraciam.
[499] *HER.*  Fatis laborem debitum agnosco meis,

[Eur.]

per aspra semper quae petunt sublimia.
cum Marte natis optimum fuerat manum
520  non contulisse, primitus Lycaone,
ac deinde Cygno; tertius porro hic mihi
cum domino equisque exhauriendus est labor.
mortalium sed nullus intuebitur
hostis paventem dexteram Alcmena satum.
525  CHO.  Atqui ipse dominus huius Admetus soli    [507]
huc tecta linquens dirigit recta gradum.
ADM.  Iove nate, salve, Persei clarum genus!
HER.  Admete, salve, rector inclite Thessalum!
ADM.  Utinam! benevolum te mihi certo scio.
530  HER.  Tonsura vero quid sibi haec vult lugubris?
ADM.  Hodie cadaver efferendum est hinc mihi.
HER.  Avertat istud fors malum a natis tuis.
ADM.  Vivunt creati liberi de me domi.
HER.  Maturus annis forte genitor occidit?    [516]
535  ADM.  Et ille superat atque mater, Hercules.
HER.  An igitur uxor periit Alcestis tua?
ADM.  De uxore nobis sermo sese offert duplex.
HER.  Fatone functam dicis, an superat adhuc?
ADM.  Obiit, nec obiit; meque luctu conficit.
540  HER.  Perplexus es; iuxta ac pridem intellego.
ADM.  Fatine nosti quae premat necessitas?
HER.  Pollicita mortem nempe pro te occumbere.
ADM.  Si pepigit istud, quomodo hanc vivam putas?
HER.  Lugendo clades interim ne praeveni.
545  ADM.  Cui mors propinqua est, iam perisse illum puto;
qui periit autem, vivere nusquam dixeris.
HER.  Non esse et esse discrepant longissime.    [528]
ADM.  Sic tibi videtur, Hercules; aliter mihi.
HER.  Quid ergo luges? quisnam amicorum occidit?
550  ADM.  Mulier. mulieris mentio facta est modo.
HER.  Aliena vobis an propinqua sanguine?
ADM.  Aliena, quamvis iuncta necessitudine.
HER.  Quinam ergo vitam finiit domi tuae?
ADM.  Hic educata est orba patre mortuo.
555  HER.  Utinam dolore comperissem liberum!
ADM.  Exspecto quorsum tendat ista oratio.

546 vivere *Walsh* iure *1557, R*

ALCESTIS

[Eur.]
HER. Alterius hospes hospitis domum petam.
ADM. Bona verba; facinus istud avertat deus.
HER. Ingrata lugenti hospitis praesentia est.
ADM. Ingredere tu aedes; mortui sint mortui.  560
HER. Hospiti epulari turpe funesta in domo.
ADM. Ducam seorsum te hospitum ad cenacula.
HER. Sine abire; inibis gratiam a me maximam.

[545]
ADM. Minime; nec alios hospes accedes lares.
heus tu, praeito, reclude posticum aedium,  565
iube atrienses adparare largiter
hospitibus epulas; limen autem claudite
quod medium ab aula separat cenacula.
non est decorum, luctus ut convivio
obstrepat, et aures hospitum offendat dolor.  570
CHO. Admete, quid agis? tanta cum te calamitas
premat, recipies hospites? ita desipis?

[553]
ADM. Atqui domo illum si expulissem et moenibus
hospitii egentem, an id probares? neutiquam.
minus hospitalis, non minus miser forem.  575
ad calamitates illud etiam accederet,
ut hospitum hostis mea vocaretur domus.
nunc hospitem illum habebo rursus optimum,
siticulosum quando ad Argos venero.
CHO. Cur ergo, amicus siquidem is est, uti tu ais,  580
hunc esse passus nescium aerumnae es tuae?
ADM. Siquidem ille nostrum scisset infortunium,
nunquam subisset atrium domus meae.
at facere stulte me ille forsan rebitur,
nec haec probabit. mea sed aula haud hospites  585
huc ventitantes scit repellere turpiter.

[568]
CHO. O viri hospita liberi
semper atria, qua incola
se dignatus Apollo
est Phoebus citharae sciens.  590
nec deum puduit domus
huius lanigeros greges
curvis pascere vallibus,
et per prata virentia
pastoralia carmina  595

588 qua *Walsh* quae *1557, R*

227

TRAGOEDIAE

[Eur.]

    blanda pangere fistula.
    quin et versicolorum                 [579]
    lyncum turba suavibus
    emollita modis, gregi
600  iunxit intrepido latus;
    armentumque leonum
    venit fulvicomantum
    ex Othryi nemoroso.
    ad tuae strepitum lyrae
605  adplausit maculosus
    pictorum hinnuleum chorus,
    pernici pede deserens
    abietum alticomum nemus,
    docto carmine concitus.
610  ergo tu pecoris domum              [588]
    fertilissimam colis
    limpidum propter lacum
    Boebiae, arvi et iugera,
    et patentibus soli
615  terminos convallibus,
    qua iubar solis cadens
    nube currus induit;
    ad Molossos pertinet
    et freta Aegaei maris,
620  aestuosa et litora
    celsum ad usque Pelion.
    nunc apertis aedibus,                [597]
    umidis fletu genis
    hospitem recipit tamen,
625  coniugis modo mortuae
    flens adhuc funus recens.
    nam pudori pronus est              [600]
    candor ingenuus; neque
    ulla pars sapientiae
630  abest, cum probitas adest.
    et mentem bona spes habet,
    successura homini pio
       omnia recte.

    *ADM.*   Cives Pheraei qui hic adestis sedulo,   [606]
635  famuli cadaver rite compositum ad rogum

[Eur.]     sublime portant ac sepulcri ad aggerem.
at vos supremam prodeuntem iam viam
de more defunctam ultimum adloquamini.
*CHO.*   Atqui senili cerno genitorem gradu
huc se ferentem, coniugi et mundum tuae     640
portare famulos, manibus donaria.

[614] *PHE.*   Maeroris adsum particeps, fili, tui;
proba et pudica sane es orbus coniuge.
sed ista quamvis dura perpessu, tamen
feras necesse est. accipe hunc mundum, ac humi     645
una reconde. honore corpus prosequi
illius aequum est, quae prior pro te mori
sustinuit, ac ne subolis orbus degerem
tristem senectam et luctuosam te sine,
perfecit una, ceterisque feminis     650
tam illustre facinus ausa peperit gloriam.
o sospitatrix filii, quae mortuos
nos suscitasti, iam vale; ac manes tibi
placidos bonosque sub Acheronte imo precor.
tales hominibus utiles taedas reor     655
aut vincla nunquam nosse coniugalia.

[629] *ADM.*   Nec has rogatu nostro ad inferias ades,
praesens amicum nec mihi in numero es; neque
hunc induetur illa mundum, aut indiga
rerum tuarum sepelietur. tum aequius     660
dolere fuerat, fata cum me tollerent.

[634] an qui stetisti tum eminus, quique alteram,
senex puellam, siveris pro te mori,
illacrimabis funeri huic? nec mihi pater
verus fuisti, nec peperit ea me parens,     665
falso parentem quae meam se dictitat,
sed stirpe servili editum in lucem tua
me admovit uxor uberi furtim suo.
et tu quis esses prodidit periculum—
nam nec patrem te existimo vere meum,     670
aut si es, pavore nemo te mortalium
superat inerti, qui supremo in limine
vitae, senecta languidus, nec volueris
nec fueris ausus emori pro filio,
sed has mulierem hanc exteram in se sumere     675
partes tulistis, quam genetricem et patrem

[Eur.]
    solam vocare iure possum aequissimo.
    at te facinoris tam decori gloria     [648]
    ingens manebat, filium superstitem
680 si morte genitor liberavisses tua,
    cum posset aevi reliquus haud longus tibi
    restare cursus; quod supererat temporis,
    mecum ista vivo viva consenesceret,
    taedis nec orbus macerarer luctibus.
685 at tu, beata vita quicquid parturit
    fructus, tulisti, sceptra qui florentibus
    tenueris annis, meque regni filium
    heredem habueris, orbus ut ne liberis
    vacuam alienis dissipandam linqueres
690 domum. nec illud dixeris, te a filio     [658]
    prodi, senectam quod tuam contempserit,
    ut qui reveritus semper unus maxime
    te sim; rependis gratiam hanc contra mihi
    cum matre genitor. sed nec alios liberos
695 dehinc gignere potes, qui senectutem tuam
    alant et ornent. neque enim humabere hac manu.
    etenim quod ad te pertinet, sum mortuus     [666]
    iamdudum. at alium si salutis vindicem
    sum nactus, atque intueor eius munere
700 hoc lumen almum, me illius natum puto,
    vicesque senii huic educandi debeo.
    vane profecto postulant senes mori,
    et de senecta longiore expostulant;
    si mors propinquet, nemo iam cupit mori,
705 nemo senectam queritur amplius gravem.
    CHO.   Absque his malorum iam sat est; quiescite,
    nec tu paternam, nate, bilem exaspera.
    PHE.   O nate, probris quem lacessis arrogans?     [675]
    venaliumne de grege aut Lydum aut Phryga?
710 an Thessalum me Thessalo nescis patre,
    planeque stirpe generis ingenui satum?
    nimis insolenter contumeliosus es,
    et verba iuvenis in patrem petulantia
    iactas. at istic haud procax gratis eris.
715 dominus familiae te edidi ut fores meae,
    deinde educavi, non prior ut exstinguerer.
    nec hanc habemus traditam a maioribus     [683]

## ALCESTIS

[Eur.]
    legem, ut parentes morte servent liberos,
    nec Graius hic mos. sive felix seu miser,
    tibi natus uni es. cuncta ego officia patris     720
    tibi cumulate praestiti: late imperas
    populis, et agri fusa late iugera,
    quae mihi reliquit genitor, haec linquam tibi.
    qua fraudo te in re? quamve facio iniuriam?
    ne morere pro alio, nec ego pro te. cernere     725
    tibi dulce lucem est? dulce patri itidem puta.

[692]
    nam reputo mecum quot manendum saecula
    sit inter umbras, quam brevibus angustiis
    sint clausa vitae spatia, sed blandula tamen.
    at tu recusas impudenter emori,     730
    ultraque fato destinatum terminum
    uxore caesa vivis; ac redarguis
    dein me pavoris, femina, timidissime,
    inferior ipse, quae tuam iuvenis vicem
    formose functa periit. at enim callide     735
    rationem inisti qua perenne viveres,
    si, ut quamque nactus coniugem sis, ne mori
    pro te recuset persuadere poteris.
    deinde ipse timidus impetis conviciis,
    qui facere renuant haec, amicos; heus tace,     740
    tecumque reputa, vita ceu dulcis tibi est,
    dulcem esse cunctis. si ingeras opprobria,
    haud falsa rursum et plura forsan audies.

[706]
    *CHO.*   Iam fit malorum superiorum accessio;
    senex, omitte exasperare filium.     745
    *ADM.*   Ceu me locuto cuncta prome. veritas
    si audita te urit, abstinendum iniuria.
    *PHE.*   Pro te fuisset gravius erratum mori.
    *ADM.*   Nil ergo refert iuvenis obeat an senex?
    *PHE.*   Una anima oportet, non duabus vivere.     750
    *ADM.*   Quin vive, saecla donec anteas Iovis.
    *PHE.*   Sic immerentes, hem, parentes devoves?
    *ADM.*   Te nempe vitae longioris amor tenet.

[716]
    *PHE.*   At pro te, opinor, hoc cadaver efferunt.
    *ADM.*   Quod te pavoris arguit, timidissime.     755
    *PHE.*   Pro me perisse hanc haud opinor dixeris.

739 deinde *1557*   dein *R*

TRAGOEDIAE

[Eur.]

 *ADM.* Utinam aliquando tibi opus opera sit mea!
 *PHE.* Saepe esto coniunx, efferas ut plurimas.
 *ADM.* Tibi hoc pudendum, qui recusaris mori.
760 *PHE.* Suave lumen hoc, suave cernere.
 *ADM.* Ignavus animi es, nec viri quicquam tenes.
 *PHE.* Non funus effers laetus ac ridens senis.
 *ADM.* Utcumque moriere, moriere inglorius.
 *PHE.* Audire male post fata non curae est mihi. [726]
765 *ADM.* Ohe, senectus plena ut impudentiae est!
 *PHE.* Haud impudens haec, illa sed stolida fuit.
 *ADM.* Abi, atque humare me cadaver hoc sine.
 *PHE.* Abeo. ipse humabis, quippe qui ipse occideris.[730]
 at tu propinquis coniugis poenas dabis.
770 posthac Acastum nemo censebit virum,
 germanae inultam si ferat tacitus necem.
 *ADM.* Nunc apage tuque et uxor orbi liberum
 vivente nato; digni ut estis, carpite
 miseram senectam, nec eadem mecum domus
775 vos capiet. ite. patrium praeconio
 siquidem liceret tibi larem interdicere,
 nihil moratus hunc tibi interdicerem.
 at nos—ferendum quippe praesens est malum—
 eamus ignem mortuae supponere.
780 *CHO.* Fortibus o miserabilis ausis, [741]
 o generosa atque optima longe,
 salve! sit tibi bonus ac placidus
 Atlantiades, Plutoque facilis
 te suscipiat. si qua bonorum
785 illinc praemia, cum Persephone
 vitae fructus carpe bene actae.

 *SER.* Plerosque memini plurimarum gentium [747]
 domoque et epulis hic ab Admeto hospites
790 olim receptos; hospite isto at nequior
 se in hos penates nullus unquam contulit.
 funesta primum tecta non exhorruit
 intrare, luctu squalidum cernens erum.
 dein fortuitos apparatus insolens
795 non consulebat, clade perspecta, boni.
 si quid deesset, immodeste clamitans

785 illinc *1557* illic *R (cf. Eur. 744* κἀκεῖ)

[Eur.]
[756]  id flagitabat. cymbium et manibus capax
tollens, meraco ingurgitat se sanguine
nigrae parentis, usque dum adfusa undique
calfecit artus flamma vino exaestuans.
deinde impeditus fronde myrtea comam,                    800
agreste latrat; dissonos licet sonos
[761]  audire pariter. ille, securus animi
in clade nostra, cantitat. nos autem eram
lacrimis profusis flemus optimam; haud tamen
spectante fletu commadescimus hospite,                   805
quando ita voluntas fert erilis. interim
ego peregrinum hunc excipio dapibus domi,
furem scelestum et impium sicarium.
[767]  effertur illa; funeri nec prodii
comes, manuve nuda planxi pectora,                       810
dominamve luxi quae parens fuerat mihi
servisque cunctis, quae mariti mollibus
frangebat iras vocibus, mille et malis
nos eruebat. itaque iure hunc odero,
qui tecta subiit in calamitate, hospitem.                815
[773]  HER.  Heus tu, severum cur tuere et taetricum?
haud esse torvo erga hospites vultu decet
servum, sed animo excipere laeto comiter.
tu domino amicum suscipis supercili
severitate tristi et ore turbido,                        820
intentus animum cladis in luctum exterae.
accede propius huc, uti sapientior
reddare. nosti lege qua mortalia
natura genuit? haud opinor; unde enim
id nosse posses servus? at de me accipe.                 825
[782]  mori necesse est omnibus mortalibus,
nec ullus hominum novit an sit crastinae
visurus ortum lucis; etenim lubrica
fortuna caecas temperat rerum vices,
quae nec doceri aut arte comprendi queant.               830
haec doctus ex me, genium age exhilara; bibe.
quodcunque vitae singuli adferunt dies,
id crede nostrum, sortis esse cetera.
praeterea hominibus caelitum suavissimam
longe, Dionem cole; benigna etenim dea est.              835
haec alia omitte, et mihi monenti obtempera,

si quidem videntur vera quae tibi consulo.  [Eur.]
atque adeo, opinor, exsolutus his malis  [794]
comamque vinctus flore, nobiscum bibes,
840 istius inanis liber aegritudinis.
nec dubito quin, si proluat semel scyphus
inversus hic te, ex vultuoso et taetrico
effingat alium. quando mortales sumus,
ex usu opinor sapere nos mortalia.
845 nam taetricorum et tristium aerumna potius
quam vita, vita me putanda est iudice.
*SER.* Haec scimus. atqui familiae praesens status  [803]
nihil habet aptum risui et conviviis.
*HER.* Mulieris obitum ne exterae supra modum
850 defle, familiae quando salvi sunt eri.
*SER.* Salvi? fugit te quanta clades nos premit.
*HER.* Nisi forte dominus me fefellerit tuus.
*SER.* Nimis ille, nimis est hospitalis omnibus.
*HER.* Minime; nec ad eum funus externum attinet.
855 *SER.* Nimis hoc profecto familiare funus est.
*HER.* Fors me malorum quidpiam celaverit?
*SER.* Perge esse laetus; nos eri tangant mala.
*HER.* Hic sermo luctus exterae haud exordium est.
*SER.* Nec tibi epulanti maestitudinem adferam.
860 *HER.* Iniuriam tuli haud ferendam ab hospite.
*SER.* Alieno adisti hanc hospes aulam in tempore;  [817]
nam luctuosa cuncta cernis, rasile
caput et amictum lugubrem *HER.* Num liberum
decessit aliquis, an gravis senio pater?
865 *SER.* Exstincta coniunx, hospes, Admeti occidit.
*HER.* Quid ais? deinde me recepit hospitem?
*SER.* Suis pudebat te repellere ab aedibus.
*HER.* O quali es orbus, o miserrime, coniuge!
*SER.* Quae clade eadem pariter omnes perdidit.
870 *HER.* Quin sentiebam id, uda cernens lumina
tristemque vultum rasilemque verticem.
tamen exterum illi funus esse credidi,  [827]
ac vi coactus hanc subivi ianuam;
atque in statu isto turbido rerum bibi,

843 effingat *Walsh*   effinget *edd.*
857 tangant *1557*   tangunt *R dubitanter* (cf. Eur. 813)
858 exterae *1557*   exteri *R dubitanter* (cf. Eur. 814)

[Eur.]
    et hospitalis hominis adsedi in domo 875
    conviva demens, flore vinctus tempora.
    sed culpa, qui non indicaveris, tua est.
    aerumna tanta cum familiae incumberet.
    sed ubinam humatur? qua profectus reperiam?
[835]   SER.   Larissae ad alta nobilis qua moenia 880
    recta itur, urbis ante portam protinus
    tumulum videbis artifice factum manu.
    HER.   O anime corque exercitum molestiis,
    ostende qualem Electryonis filia
    Alcmena subolem procrearit te Iovi! 885
    subtrahere fato feminam exstinctam est opus,
    suosque rursus ad penates ducere
    Alcestin, Admeto ut rependam gratiam.
[843]   ibo, et nigrantis squalido ferrugine
    stolae tyranno manium insidias dabo. 890
    atque illum, opinor, deprehendam ad aggerem
    tumuli bibentem victimarum sanguinem.
    quod si e latebris clanculum inruens eum
    prendam, et lacertis strinxero circumdatis,
    utcunque latera verset, eripiet mihi 895
    hunc nemo, donec coniugem Admeti auferam.
[850]   sin aucupantem haec praeda me fefellerit,
    nec ad cruoris adsit haustus, inferum
    reges adibo et regna solis nescia,
    poscamque, nec non impetraturum reor, 900
    Alcestin, ut eam coniugi tradam in manum
    qui me recepit hospitem nec reppulit,
    quamvis acerbo sauciatus vulnere;
    animo sed alto id me reveritus abdidit.
    quis Thessalum est in hospites benignior 905
    Graiumve? certe sordido non dixerit,
    generosus animi cum sit, beneficium datum.

[861]   ADM.   Heu maestum aditum, tristem aspectum
    vidui tecti. quo feror? ubi sum?
    quid loquar, aut quid taceam? 910
    qui peream? o me misero fato
    genitum! functos morte beatos
    duco; his gratulor, hos amo, cum illis
    degere dehinc libet. haud libet auras

[Eur.]

915 cernere superas; haud iuvat almae
dehinc vestigia figere terrae.
obside tali despoliatum
mors me saevo pignerat Orco.
CHO.   Subi, subi tenebras [872]
920 tecti; subi. tulisti
digna lacrimis, tulisti
calamitatem lugubrem.
conditos nil lacrimae
coniugis manes iuvant.
925 ADM.   Hoc, hoc verbo vulnera renovas. [878]
quae magis homini est aspra calamitas
quam spoliari coniuge fida?
utinam taedae thalamique exsors
socia haud ulli tecta habitassem!
930 lectos vacuos coniuge et orbam
subolis vitam duco beatam.
unam in vitam impendere curas
est moderati sarcina luctus;
at languentia pignora morbo, et
935 deformati funere thalami,
intolerandi est cumulus luctus;
praesertim cum coniugis orbam et
subolis liceat ducere vitam.
CHO.   Sors, sors ineluctabilis [889]
940 premit, nec ullus lacrimis
modus est. acerba fers, tamen
perfer. etenim nec coniuge
tu primus orbus es. alios
mortalium alia calamitas
945 dolore saevo conficit.
ADM.   Longi o luctus, o amicorum [895]
desideria luce carentum!
cur vetuisti me praecipitem
triste sepulcri mittere in antrum,
950 et cum coniuge fida pariter
tumuli unius mole recondi?
accepisset geminas pro una
animas Pluto, transque fretassent
duo fidissima pectora pariter
955 Stygias undas.

## ALCESTIS

[Eur.]

[903] CHO.  Mihi vir quidam sanguine iunctus
puerum amisit lacrimis dignum,
solam generis spem; moderate
tamen aerumnam hanc pertulit, etsi
orbus subolis vertice cano                               960
et praecipiti languidus aevo.
[911] ADM.  O mutati facies tecti!
quinam ingrediar, quinam habitabo
versis fatis? hei mihi, quantum
distat ab illa domus haec, olim                          965
quam Peliacae lumine taedae
et festis ululatam hymenaeis
ingrediebar dexterae inhaerens
carae coniugis, ac multisono
convivarum strepitu a tergo,                             970
qui beatos dicerent
meque et illam mortuam:
[920] quippe utrosque nobiles,
et utrimque ex optimis
editos maioribus,                                        975
coniugali vinculo
copulatos. at modo
nuptialis carminis
luctus occupat locum,
proque candidis peplis                                   980
pulla vestis ad toros
me reducit caelibes.
[926] CHO.  Mali inexperto tibi fortunae
dolor hic cursum rupit amicae.
at servasti vitam animamque;                             985
mortua coniunx liquit amantem;
quae nova mentem turbat imago?
multos coniuge mors orbavit,
solvens socii foedera lecti.

[935] ADM.  Etsi aliter aliis visum, amici, coniugis    990
feliciorem duco quam sortem meam;
erepta namque plurimis molestiis
cum laude summa, triste nil dehinc sentiet.
at ego, perisse quem fuerat aequum, meo
fato superstes vitam agam inlaetabilem;                  995

[Eur.]

    quod adeo iam nunc sentio. nam qui domum
    subire potero hanc? quem adloquar? cuius fruar
    sermone, mentem quo domi oblectem? gradum
    quo vertam? ubique solitudo in aedibus
1000  maerore mentem conficit, cum coniugis
    vacuum cubile cerno, cum vacuam throni
    sedem relictam et squalidum situ solum,
    circaque genua procidentes liberi     [947]
    deflent parentem lacrimantes, servi era
1005  sese queruntur destitutos optima.
    atque is domi rerum est status mihi; at foris
    me Thessalorum nuptiae, me feminis
    coetus frequentes enecabunt, different
    dolore miserum uxoris aequales meae.
1010  quas quo intuebor ore? tum si quis male
    animatus in me est, solvet ora talibus:
    'En, quem cupido foeda vitae detinet     [955]
    metusque mortis, qui redemit coniugis
    se morte ab Orco ignavus—ac vir postea
1015  sibi videtur! tum parentes proprios
    infensus odit, ipse non ausus mori.'
    hic rumor inter improbos me differet.
    ecquam ergo vita mihi voluptatem feret,
    quem fama lacerat et calamitas obruit?

1020  *CHO.*  Ego ignota profano     [962]
    per compendia vulgo
    Musarum comes ivi,
    et sermonibus aurem
    doctis applicui meam
1025  non raro. at remedi genus
    nondum ullum reperi, cui
    cedat dura necessitas.
    hanc contra medicamina
    docti nec dedit Orphei
1030  Thressis in tabulis manus;
    nec cum Asclepiadis pater
    Phoebus pharmaca proderet
    ut mortalibus aegris
    morbo membra levarent,

1018 ecquam *R*   ecquem *1557*
1025 remedi *R*   remedii *1557*

[Eur.]

　　　　hanc adversus opem tulit. 1035
[972]　solas huius ad aras
　　　　non est ire deae, neque
　　　　ad simulacra; nec ulla
　　　　est placabilis hostia.
　　　　o diva, o, violentior 1040
　　　　ad me ne solito veni!
　　　　nam tu consiliis comes
　　　　quicquid Iuppiter adnuit,
　　　　certum ducis ad exitum;
[980]　tu dextra facili domas 1045
　　　　duri robora ferri.
　　　　nec fastum tibi mentis
　　　　infrenem cohibet pudor.
[984]　et dextrae infragili suae
　　　　vinclo te implicuit dea. 1050
　　　　perfer; nam neque fato
　　　　functos aethereas trahes
　　　　flendo rursus ad auras.
　　　　mors etiam notha pignora
　　　　divum falce metit sua. 1055
　　　　dum nobiscum erat omnibus
　　　　cara, et mortua cara erit.
　　　　tu lecti tibi comparem
　　　　supra omnes generosam es
[995]　sortitus. neque coniugis 1060
　　　　bustum ullus numeret tuae
　　　　inter funereas specus,
　　　　aggere quae tumuli premunt
　　　　vita functa cadavera;
　　　　divinis sed honoribus 1065
　　　　aequet religio hospitum
　　　　manes. atque aliquis via
　　　　flectens dixerit olim:
　　　　'Haec moriendo viri sui
　　　　vitam sponte redemit; 1070
　　　　nunc auget numerum deum.'
　　　　salve, o sancta; ope sospita
　　　　nos praesens. ita votis
　　　　illam atque ominibus bonis
　　　　longum posteritas colet. 1075

                         TRAGOEDIAE
                                                              [Eur.]
         sed visa fallunt me nisi Alcmena satus,              [1006]
         Admete, ad aedes dirigit gressum tuas.
         HER.   Admete, amicos libere eloqui decet,
         nec in recessu pectoris silentio
1080     abdere quod aegre est. amici haberes me ut loco,
         dignus videbar, clade cum in tua adforem;
         at tu, propinquo coniugis iam funere                 [1012]
         non indicato, me recepisti hospitem,
         ceu cura premeret te doloris exteri.
1085     at ego coronis tempora evinctus, deis
         libavi apud te in lugubri laetus domo.
         irascor equidem, irascor hac iniuria
         adfectus abs te, sed tuis iam luctibus
         acerbitatis nolo quicquam adponere.
1090     causamque cur huc sum reversus denuo,                [1019]
         narrabo. mulierem interim hanc serva mihi,
         dum, rege caeso Bistonum, huc redux agam
         Thraces quadriiugos. sin, quod absit, accidat
         (nam me ut reducant sospitem precor deos)
1095     hanc dono dicoque familiae ancillam tuae,
         quae parta nobis est labore maximo.
         proposita namque publico in certamine                [1029]
         sudore digna deprehendi praemia,
         unde hanc reporto victor. e certamine
1100     leviore munus erant equi victoribus.
         maiora sed qui vicerant, ut caestibus
         luctave fortes, dona referebant boum
         armenta; post haec ultimo femina loco.
         cumque incidissem forte, turpe sum ratus
1105     cum laude pariter praemium contemnere.
         sed, ut ante dixi, feminam curae tuae
         commendo, quam non praedo per vim sustuli,
         sed comparatam maximis laboribus
         adduco. fors factum ipse post laudaveris.
1110     ADM.   Quod clam te habuerim calamitatem coniugis, [1037]
         ne interpretere contumeliae, Hercules,
         id ergo factum, aut quod sinistre sentiam
         de te. dolori sed dolorem adieceras,
         alterius aedes si subisses hospitis;
1115     nam flere clades sat mihi fuerat meas.
         sed hanc puellam, si pote, obsecro, iube             [1042]

[Eur.]

ALCESTIS

        adservet alius Thessalum, quem non pari
        sors calamitate perculit; multi hospites
        tibi sunt Pheraei. memoriam cladis meae
        renovare omitte. non potero siccis domi        1120
        oculis tueri hanc. vulneri vulnus novum
        ne adpone; satis est cladium quod nunc premit.
        qua parte poterit aedium servarier
        caste puella? vestis adulescentulam
        cultusque loquitur; an virum in commercio?        1125

[1052]   qui poterit inter assiduo iuvenes agens
        castam tueri se? nec in promptu, Hercules,
        regere iuventam est; ac mihi cura est tui.
        functaene fato coniugis thalamo hanc alam?
        et qui in cubili collocabo hanc illius?        1130
        offensionem hic metuo duplicem, et civium
        ne criminetur quispiam me, et optime
        de me merentis proditorem coniugis
        dicat puellae alterius amplexu frui;
        sponsamque vereor mortuam, cuius mihi        1135
        esse sacrosanctam memoriam merito decet.

[1061]   me multa circumspicere par. o femina,
        quaecumque tandem es, es profecto Alcestidi
        modo et statura corporis simillima.
        me miserum! ab oculis per deos procul meis        1140
        apage mulierem hanc, neve perdas perditum.
        namque intueri coniugem videor meam
        cum intueor istam; pectus horror obsidet,
        fontes ab oculis lacrimarum profluunt.
        nunc calamitatis huius heu miser, miser,        1145
        acerbitatem luctuosam sentio.

[1070]   *CHO.*   Laudare sortem non equidem possum tuam;
        tamen ferendum, quisquis es, quod dant dei.
        *HER.*   Si mihi potestas esset haec divinitus
        concessa, ab umbris coniugem ut reducerem        1150
        eamque possem tibi referre gratiam. . .

[1075]   *ADM.*   Scio referres promptus; at cuinam hoc datum?
        nec luce cassis luce post frui licet.
        *HER.*   Perfer modeste, neve te adflictes nimis.
        *ADM.*   Lenire verbis facile quod durum est pati.        1155
        *HER.*   Quid promovebis, perpetim si lugeas?
        *ADM.*   Scio; dolendi sed voluptas me huc rapit.

[Eur.]

|      |      |                                                          |        |
|------|------|----------------------------------------------------------|--------|
|      | HER. | Exstinctam amare lacrimandi occasio est.                 |        |
|      | ADM. | Etiam miserius quam loquor me perdidit.                  |        |
| 1160 | HER. | Uxore es orbus optima, quis id neget?                    |        |
|      | ADM. | Nullo ut fruatur pectus hoc post gaudio.                 |        |
|      | HER. | Tempus levabit quod recens nunc est malum.               | [1085] |
|      | ADM. | Tempus profecto, si mori tempus vocas.                   |        |
|      | HER. | Te mitigabit uxor ac taedae novae.                       |        |
| 1165 | ADM. | Au, quid ais? ex te haud istud exspectaveram.            |        |
|      | HER. | Expers iugalis exiges vitam tori?                        |        |
|      | ADM. | Nulla accubabit mulier unquam huic pectori.              |        |
|      | HER. | Prodesse reris posse te sic mortuae?                     |        |
|      | ADM. | Ubi ubi sit, illam honore semper prosequar.              |        |
| 1170 | HER. | Haec laudo sane, laudo; sed stulte facis.                |        |
|      | ADM. | Sponsum nec ulla me vocabit femina.                      |        |
|      | HER. | Quin coniugem erga laudo nimirum fidem.                  |        |
|      | ADM. | Si neglegam etiam mortuam, peream male.                  |        |
|      | HER. | Nunc recipe tecto hanc stirpe nobili satam.              |        |
| 1175 | ADM. | Per qui creavit te Iovem istud deprecor!                 |        |
|      | HER. | Hoc si recusas, perperam tibi consulis.                  |        |
|      | ADM. | Hoc ni recuso, macerabor luctibus.                       |        |
|      | HER. | Obsequere, et huius non pigebit gratiae.                 |        |
|      | ADM. | Utinam haud tulisses praemium hoc certaminis!            |        |
| 1180 | HER. | Et mecum es huius particeps victoriae.                   |        |
|      | ADM. | Probe es locutus, sed recedat femina.                    |        |
|      | HER. | Si quidem est necesse; at num necesse sit vide.          | [1105] |
|      | ADM. | Necesse, nisi ob id forte tu succenseas.                 |        |
|      | HER. | Non temere id a te tantopere contenderem.                |        |
| 1185 | ADM. | Age, vince, quamvis grata minime postules.               |        |
|      | HER. | Factum probabis postea; pare modo.                       |        |
|      | ADM. | Si quidem hanc subire tecta oportet, ducite.             |        |
|      | HER. | Servis mulierem hanc neutiquam commisero.                |        |
|      | ADM. | Quin ipse in aedes ducito illam, si lubet.               |        |
| 1190 | HER. | Tibi profecto mulierem tradam in manum.                  |        |
|      | ADM. | Ego haud tetigero. tecta subeunti patent.                |        |
|      | HER. | Tuae stat uni dexterae hanc concredere.                  |        |
|      | ADM. | Coactus istud atque nolens perpetro.                     |        |
|      | HER. | Protende promptus dexteram; tange hospitam.              |        |
| 1195 | ADM. | Protendo veluti Gorgonis sectum ad caput.                |        |

HER. Tenesne? ADM. Sane teneo. HER. Serva iam, et Iove
natum fatebere generosum olim hospitem.
ipsam intuere, similis uxori an tuae

ALCESTIS

[Eur.]
    sit, ac beatus luctuum iam desine.
    *ADM.*   O di boni, o miraculum inopinum ac novum!   1200
    oculis profecto coniugem intueor meam,
    aut me deorum quispiam ludibrio
    recreat, inani corda lactans gaudio.
    *HER.*   Non ita, sed ipsam coniugem cernis tuam.
    *ADM.*   Ne larva ab umbris missa sit, circumspice.   1205
    *HER.*   Cave esse credas hospitem tuum magum.

[1129]
    *ADM.*   Sed quam sepelii coniugem intueor meam?
    *HER.*   Sic. at fidem tu, et iure, sorti non habes.
    *ADM.*   Tango adloquorque coniugem ut vivam meam?
    *HER.*   Adloquere; votis quicquid optabas habes.   1210
    *ADM.*   O corpus, ocule o coniugis carissimae!
    spem praeter habeo te, videre postea
    quam non putaram posse me? *HER.*   Ne dubita; habes.
    modo ne deorum quispiam invideat tibi.
    *ADM.*   O clara suboles maximi Iovis, utinam   1215
    beatus aevum transigas, ac sospitem
    te servet idem qui creavit Iuppiter!
    nam me iacentem solus erexti. e Styge
    quonam reduxti ad lumen hanc rursus modo?

[1140]
    *HER.*   Deproeliatus cum tyranno manium.   1220
    *ADM.*   Ubi nactus illum proelio congressus es?
    *HER.*   Propter sepulcri dexteram inieci aggerem.
    *ADM.*   Quid muta, tandem, perseverat femina?
    *HER.*   Nondum tibi fas eius adloquio frui,
    dis antequam sese expiarit manibus,   1225
    terrisque lucem tertia ostendet dies.
    duc coniugem intro iam tuam; ac in posterum,
    Admete, iusti cultor atque in hospites
    pius esse persta. vale. ego Stheneli filio
    abeo imperatum mihi laborem ut exsequar.   1230
    *ADM.*   Mane, ac penates et dapes adi sacras.
    *HER.*   Id fiet alias. nunc celeritate est opus.

[1153]
    *ADM.*   Di rem secundent, teque reddant sospitem.
    edico cunctis civibus regni mei,
    ob res secundas ut choris indulgeant,   1235
    et victimarum sanguine aras imbuant.
    mutata vitae in melius est facies modo,

1226 ostendet *1557*    ostendat *R*

felicitatem nec tego ingratus meam. [Eur.]

      *CHO.* Fortuna vices lubrica versat
1240    varias docilis sumere formas.
      inopina dei plurima peragunt.
      non succedunt quae fore speras; [1161]
      quae fore nemo posse putaret,
      saepe expediunt numina, qualem
1245    haec sortita est fabula finem.

# NOTES

## *JEPHTHA*

This play was composed after *Medea,* which was mounted by Buchanan's pupils in 1543 at Bordeaux. There is dispute whether it was written at about that time or during a second visit to Bordeaux in 1545–7 (so Trinquet). On this controversy, see the Introduction, p. 4, and McFarlane, 94 and 190ff. There was in any case a considerable interval between performance and publication at Paris in 1554.

The theme is the sacredness of a vow, and the circumstances under which a vow could be abrogated. This was a burning sixteenth-century issue; in particular the celebrated dispute between Bucer and Masson, which made its way into print in 1544–5 (see Introd. 14 and McFarlane, 194n. 42) was certainly preoccupying Buchanan shortly afterwards (see 977n). But Buchanan is not concerned to defend a *parti pris* so much as to exploit the tragic implications of the hero's struggle with his conscience.

The structure of the play is much superior to that of *The Baptist,* revealing Buchanan's greater maturity as a dramatist. The scene is carefully set at the moment of Jephtha's triumph, so that the action follows the prescribed Aristotelian pattern. The development from good fortune to ill-fortune is achieved by a carefully-pondered series of dialogues—with his daughter Iphis (who cannot be told the truth), with his military comrade Symmachus (the voice of commonsense), with the *sacerdos* (representing religious authority), and finally with his wife Storge (personifying the demands of kin). Little of this is to be found in the brief Old Testament account. Buchanan has exploited the similarity of situation between Jephtha's daughter and Iphigenia as treated by Euripides, Lucretius and others; but there is also considerable originality in the characterisation of the main *personae.*

*Praefatio*

1  *Carolum Cossaeum*  Charles de Cossé, comte de Brissac (1505–64), distinguished himself in campaigns in Piedmont and the Low Countries,

became *maréchal de France,* governor of Picardy and then of Paris. See McFarlane, pp. 162, 174ff.

30f.   *gaudet enim* . . .   Claudian 23.5f. (=*De cons. Stilichonis tertio*).

34f.   *et quae natura* . . .   B. is adapting Ovid, *Met.* 15.63f., 'et quae natura negabat/visibus humanis, oculis ea pectoris hausit'; the person being described by Ovid is Pythagoras.

48f.   Cf. Virgil, *Georg.* 3.8f., 'qua me quoque possim/tollere humo . . . ; Virgil is evoking Ennius, *Epigr.* 10 Warmington.

52f.   So Sallust, *Cat.* 2.9, 'is demum mihi vivere atque frui anima videtur, qui aliquo negotio intentus praeclari facinoris aut artis bonae famam quaerit.'

58f.   *Philippi Cossaei fratris*   See Ch. Marchand, *Charles Ier de Cossé* (Paris 1889) for details of the bishop and other members of the Count's family.

62f.   Cf. Ausonius 26.1.6f., 'qui proelia Musis/ temperat et Geticum moderatur Apolline Martem'.

64   *filium*   Timoléon de Cossé (1543–69), son of Charles, had Buchanan as his tutor; he took part in various battles in the religious wars, and was killed at the battle of Mucidan in Périgord.

71   *qui antea* . . .   For the earlier history of the composition of *Jephthes,* see Introduction, p. 2, and McFarlane, p. 190.

*Argumentum*

1   *Libro Iudicum* Cf. *Judges* 11.
There is a second summary of the plot composed in verses by Charles Utenhove; it does not appear in the 1554 edition. It runs as follows:

    Forte Galaddidae, patris post funera, fratres
       dicere 'cede domo' non habuere nefas;
    iure coheredem sibi scilicet esse negabant
       supposita fratrem de genetrice nothum.
    ille latrociniis inopem traducere vitam
       coepit, et in castris aera merere novis.
    iamque sui specimen cum terque quaterque dedisset
       roboris, et dextrae Martis ad arma bonae,
    dux et ab Isacidis consanguineisque creatus
       fertur in adversos protinus Ammonidas,
    iam prope vicenis hos qui crudeliter annis
       compulerant famulo subdere colla iugo.
    ergo profecturus, si victor ab hoste rediret,
       'victima victrices imbuet illa manus,

quisquis erit' (voti fuit haec sententia) 'primus
ille domo qui fors egredietur' ait.
prima revertenti ruit obvia filia Iephthae
unica, victori victima fitque patri.

The author of these verses, Charles Utenhove, was a scholar from the Low Countries who spent some time in France and associated closely with humanists and poets, especially Ronsard, Du Bellay and Dorat. He was tutor to the three daughters of Jean de Morel, Camille (the most learned and celebrated), Lucrèce, and Diane or Anne; it was in the house of Jean de Morel, a man of great learning and culture, that B. was able to meet the French poets. In 1568 Utenhove's *Xenia* was published by Thomas Guarinus in Basel, along with poems by Buchanan, Turnèbe, L'Hospital and Dorat. Cf. McFarlane, pp. 226ff.

1–72. PROLOGUE. The device of the angel's-eye-view, which acquaints the audience not only with the *mise-en-scène* but also with a summary of the future action, is an imitation of the practice in Classical tragedy. Euripides deploys a deity in *Alcestis* and a ghost in *Hecuba*, plays familiar to Buchanan; Seneca introduces the action with a ghost in *Agamemnon* and with a deity in *Hercules Furens*. Sypherd notes the parallel with Mercury in the Prologue of Plautus' *Amphitruo*.

1 *Tonantis* The opening words make evident the classicising style of the biblical play. 'Tonans' is used at the beginning of Seneca's *Hercules Furens* ('Soror Tonantis') and is a cliché in classical poetry; it is taken over by Christian poets like Prudentius (*Apotheosis* 171, *Psychom.* 640, *Peristeph.* 6.98) and Paulinus of Nola (*Carm.* 22.149).

*aliger* Used of Mercury by Statius, *Silv.* 3.3.80f., 'summi Iovis aliger Arcas/nuntius' and of Cupid in Erasmus, *Iphigenia* 708, 'Cupido deus aliger'.

2 *Isaci ad lares* This mention of Isaac prefigures the theme of sacrifice.

5 *sacri . . . foederis* This reference to the O.T. covenant may likewise hint symbolically at Jephtha's vow; see below, 480.

6 For oppression by the Ammonites, see *Judges* 10.7–9.

10 The reading of the 1597 edition and of Ruddiman (see *app. crit.*) may well represent B.'s own attempt to remove the awkwardness in the change of gender from the neuter *solum* to the feminine *docta* (sc. *gens*); but we retain the earlier reading.

10–14 See *Judges* 10.16.

15 *mens* The same hint of the limitations of the human reason is

found in the Prologue of the *Baptistes*, 35f., 'sincerum nihil/humana gignit mens'.

23  *lupatis*  Cf. Ovid, *Amores* 1.2.15, 'asper equus duris contunditur ora lupatis'; Virgil, *Georg.* 3.206ff., 'namque ante domandum/ingentis tollent animos prensique negabunt/verbera lenta pati et duris parere lupatis'.

27–9  *novos deos . . . ritibus . . . sacra*  The phrases referring to Jewish infidelities would have a striking contemporary significance in the context of the Reformation; cf. 37, 'pristinisque ritibus'.

42  *liberatorem*  In the ensuing detail of Jephtha as liberator sent by God, B. appears to depict him as a type of Christ, to whom this word is often applied in Christian Latin.

47  *vili*  *Judges* 11.1 stresses this maternal obscurity ('filius mulieris meretricis'). Though Jephtha's father Gilead is not a well-known figure, B. later repeatedly stresses the proud lineage of the hero.

56–9  See *Judges* 11.30f.

60f.  *heu . . . miserande*  An obvious reminiscence of Virgil, *Aen.* 6.882 (Anchises lamenting the future death of Marcellus): 'heu, miserande puer, si qua fata aspera rumpas'.

71f.  A slight inconsistency is notable here. Only the mother should be gloomy, for the daughter must be unsuspecting and cheerful throughout the first part of the play.

73–146. ACT I.  This consists of a dialogue between mother and daughter. B. himself supplies the names Storge ('Dutiful love') and Iphis, which ingeniously has two points of reference. It is cognate with Iephthes, but it is also a late form (found in Lycophron) of Iphigenia. The name thus evokes the sacrificial daughter in Euripides' play *Iphigenia at Aulis,* in which Agamemnon is urged by Menelaus to seek calm weather for the Greek expedition to Troy by the ritual slaughter of Iphigenia. B.'s handling of his theme owes much to Euripides; this scene has a counterpart in Euripides' dialogue between Clytemnestra and Iphigenia (*I.A.* 607ff.). B.'s creative hand is seen in the characterisation of Storge, whose earlier career and the dream which she describes do not appear in the biblical account.

82f.  *familiae solacium . . . senectae columen*  Cf. Terence, *Phormio* 287, 'columen familiae'; Ps-Seneca, *Octavia* 168, 'puer columen augustae domus'.

91  *oberrat*  Cf. Seneca, *H.F.* 1279ff., 'iamdudum mihi/monstrum impium saevumque et inmite ac ferum/oberrat'.

92  *blanda . . . quies*  Compare Andromache's dream in Seneca,

*Troades* 440ff., which B. echoes at several points. In addition to the parallel at this line (440f., 'ignota tandem venit afflictae quies/brevisque fessis somnus obrepsit genis'), compare also 82f. with 462, 'spes una Phrygibus, unica afflictae domus', and 81 with 488, 'omen tremesco misera feralis loci'.

93   *mutumque*   Cf. Ovid, *Met.* 7.184, 'mediae per muta silentia noctis'.

101   *sinu*   With this passage (98–102) compare Erasmus, *Hecuba* (ed. Waszink, Amsterdam 1968) 99ff.: 'vidi siquidem cervam variam ... nostro e gremio vi direptam,/quam laniat lupus ungue cruento.' B. knew both the original and this translation.

103   *vaga*   Cf. Statius, *Theb.* 3.63, 'noctis vaga lumina testor'. Storge's emotional turbulence at the dream is denoted by the metrical change from iambic senarius to anapaestic dimeter.

106   *nigris*   See Erasmus, *Hecuba* 77f., 'o sacra tellus,/gignens atris somnia pennis'.

108   *fata*   The language of B. throughout the play is in terms of classical fate (cf. 123, Parca) rather than of Jewish or Christian providence.

123ff.   The theme of the unremitting calamities in Storge's earlier history lends depth and originality to the characterisation of the mother, and an aura of gloom to the action.

126–30   See *Judges* 10.7ff.

130   *profana sacra mixta*   Cf. Horace, *Epist.* 1.16.54, 'miscebis sacra profanis'.

131   *portio*   Cf. Juvenal 9.126–8, 'festinat enim decurrere velox/flosculus, angustae miseraeque brevissima vitae/portio'.

142   *secundis rumoribus*   So Virgil, *Aen.* 8.90, 'ergo iter inceptum celerant rumore secundo'.

144   *salva familia*   A good example of dramatic irony. The audience is aware that though her first two wishes will be realised, the third will not. It is important too that Iphis sees no danger to herself. The repetition of *salvum*, likewise at the beginning of the line, at 146 intensifies the irony.

147–219. FIRST CHORAL ODE.   In this first entr'acte the Chorus of Jewish women, speaking according to classical convention in the first person singular, deploys first the Lesser Asclepiad (147–72) and then the Lesser Sapphic (173–218), with occasional insertion of the Adonius (176, 183, 194, 219). The chorus reveals by its ignorance of future events that it was not on stage during the Prologue. After an invocation to the river

NOTES

Jordan, they bewail the divine displeasure which has brought suffering to the nation. The conviction that the Ammonites are soon to pay the penalty (205ff.) springs from the utterances of the prophets and not from the angel's intimations.

147   *vitreo gurgite*   Cf. Erasmus, *Iphigenia* 1015f., 'ilicet sacrum Simoentis amnem,/vitreo qui gurgite vorticosus'.

151   *Solymae*   The abbreviation for Jerusalem, normally neuter, is made feminine because Hierosolyma is feminine in the Vulgate.

151   *palmiferae*   Cf. Ovid, *Amores* 2.13.8, 'palmiferamque Pharon'. B. often uses compound words favoured by Ovid; here there are two other such words within twenty lines (*falciferis* 159; *nubiferis* 169). A similar grouping is found at *Silvae* 7.66–71 (*palmifer, letifer, falcifer, gemmiferos*).

158ff.   158–9 refers to the pursuit of the Israelites by the Pharaoh (*Exod.* 14.6ff.), 160–61 to the crossing of the Red Sea (*Exod.* 14.21ff.), 162 to the trek across the Sinai (*Exod.* 15.22ff.), and 163–4 to the tower of Babel (*Gen.* 11.1ff.).

160   *purpurei*   So Propertius 2.26.5, 'purpureis . . . fluctibus'.

161   *refluis*   Silius Italicus 5.624: 'ac super haec reflui pugnarunt montibus amnes,/et retro fluctus torsit mare'.

164   *mancipium*   The singular suggests that the Israelites are the collective property of Ammon.

165   *malo* implies *active* wickedness.

166   *sub turpi domino*   Discussions on tyranny and tyrannicide became common mainly in Protestant writing later in the century, especially in the 'seventies, e.g., Hotman, *Franco-Gallia* (1573); Bèze, *Du droit des magistrats sur leurs sujets* (1574); La Boétie, *La servitude volontaire ou Le Contr'Un* (1576); Du Plessis-Mornay, *Vindiciae contra Tyrannos* (1579); and Buchanan's own *De iure regni apud Scotos* (1579).

184–94   The Chorus proclaims that Israel would prefer the visitation of God's anger directly by fire (as at Sodom and Gomorrha, *Gen.* 19.24ff.) or by earthquake (as happened to the conspirators against Moses, *Num.* 16.31ff.) or by flood (*Gen.* 6.5ff.) rather than indirectly through neighbouring nations.

185   *Phari*   Pharus is occasionally found for Egypt in classical poetry, as Statius, *Silv.* 3.2.102, 'regina Phari'.

188   *trisulci*   Cf. Ovid, *Met.* 2.848, 'ille pater rectorque deum, cui dextra trisulcis/ignibus armata est'.

193   *superfusis*   See Seneca, *Thyestes* 584, 'ne superfusis violetur undis/ignis aeternis resonans caminis'.

207f.   *citato . . . cursu*   So Seneca, *H.F.* 178ff., 'properat cursu/vita citato volucrique die/rota praecipitis vertitur anni'.

208ff. *levis hora . . . tempus properat*  See Ovid, *Met.* 15.180ff., 'neque enim consistere flumen/nec levis hora potest . . . tempora sic fugiunt pariter'.

215  *pollui*  An ironical touch in view of the later fate of Iphis.

221  *huc venit*  It seems impossible that B. committed the metrical solecism of writing merely *venit*. See 229 for possible support for *huc*.

223–340. ACT II.  The lamentations of the Chorus are now transformed to joy by the messenger's report of Jephtha's victory. The tragedy thus proceeds on Aristotelian lines; 'the change of fortune must be from good to bad' (*Poetics* 1453a). As Sypherd observes, there is a general similarity between this account of Jephtha's victory in battle and that of Sosia recounting the victory of Amphitruo in Plautus' comedy of that name (186ff.).

239  *perfudit*  Cf. Silius Italicus 3.332, 'aurorae lacrimis perfusus'.

244  *curvis*  So Virgil, *Georg.* 1.508, 'et curvae rigidum falces conflantur in ensem'.

249  *foetus*  Ruddiman adopts the Steph. (1566) reading, 'corda, fretus', but 'corda foetus' in the 1554 edition can be paralleled in Paulinus of Nola, *Carm.* 25.162, 'feta uterum'.

264  *terrae Niloticae*  So Martial 6.80.1, 'Nilotica tellus'.

271  *Arnon et Jabocus*  See *Judges* 11.13, 'a finibus Arnon usque Iaboc atque Iordanem'; cf. 11.22.

285  *Chamos*  See *Judges* 11.24, 'nonne ea quae possidet Chamos deus tuus tibi iure debentur? quae autem Dominus Deus noster victor obtinuit, in nostram cedent possessionem'.

292  *rauci*  Cf. Virgil, *Georg.* 4.70f., 'morantis/Martius ille aeris rauci canor increpat'.

294  *Fremitus . . . boat*  See Virgil, *Aen.* 11.607, 'adventusque virum fremitusque ardescit equorum'; Plautus, *Amph.* 232, 'boat caelum fremitu virum'.

295  *remugit*  So Virgil, *Aen.* 9.504, 'sequitur clamor caelumque remugit'.

300  *pulverea*  Cf. Virgil, *Aen.* 8.593, 'pulveream nubem et fulgentis aere catervas'.

306f.  *refulsit . . . fragor*  The climax to the battle with its pervasive Virgilian echoes is clearly inspired by *Aen.* 8.524ff., where Venus signals support for Aeneas: 'vibratus ab aethere fulgor . . . iterum atque iterum fragor increpat ingens.' Aeneas, like Jephtha here, breaks into speech to proclaim the inevitable defeat of the enemy through this divine intervention.

## NOTES

310   *gelidumque*   Cf. Seneca, *H.F.* 414, 'gelidus per artus vadit exsangues tremor'.

318   *instat*   For this and 325 below ('resument . . . vires'), cf. Ovid, *Met.* 9.59, 'instat anhelanti, prohibetque resumere vires', and 9.193, 'geminasque resumere vires'.

341–430. SECOND CHORAL ODE. The Chorus celebrates the tidings of victory with an extended song. In the first section (in iambic dimeters, 341–60) there is a flavour of Christian hymnology mingled with echoes of choral odes from Classical tragedy; the Ambrosian hymn is recalled both by metre and diction. The second and longer section (361–430) is in glyconics, a metre familiar to Buchanan through such poems as Catullus 61.

341   *o aurei* Cf. Prudentius, *Cath.* 2.25 (as in Walpole, *Early Latin Hymns,* 22), 'lux ecce surgit aurea'; cf. Seneca, *H.F.* 592.

342   *recursu*   Cf. Seneca, *Phaedra* 1061, 'praepeti cursu evolat'.

343   *vices . . . temperas*   So Ambrose (Walpole, 17.1), 'rector potens, verax deus,/qui temperat rerum vices'.

344   *flammifer*   Cf. Seneca, *H.F.* 593.

347f.   *iubar . . . fundis*   Cf. Ambrose (=Walpole 3.7f.), 'iubarque sancti spiritus/infunde nostris sensibus'.

353   *praedo*   So Plautus, *Truc.* 106, 'de praedonibus praedam capere'.

354f.   *Scythico . . . nervo*   Cf. Ovid, *Met.* 10.588f., 'quae . . . Scythica non setius ire sagitta/Aonio visa est iuveni'.

359   *densae phalanges*   Likewise Virgil, *Aen.* 12.662f., 'phalanges/stant densae'.

362f.   *non lapis, non lignum*   The content of this section with its attacks on the idolatry of the Ammonites, recalls *Isa.* 44 and 46; the language is inspired by Prudentius, *Per.* 5.34, 'tu saxa, tu lignum colas'.

370   *arces . . . igneas*   So Horace, *C.* 3.3.10, 'arces attigit igneas'.

371   *rerum sator*   So also Sil. Ital. 4.430.

373ff.   *nec cerni,* etc.   Cf. Ausonius, *Ephem.* 3.4ff., 'cuius formamque modumque/nec mens complecti poterit nec lingua profari;/cernere quem solus coramque audire iubentem/fas habet . . . ipse opifex rerum'.

377f.   *impia vota*   There is dramatic irony here in the reference to Jephtha (376–9) and to Storge and Iphis (380–82).

384   *olidi gregis*   So Horace, *Ep.* 1.5.29, 'olidae convivia caprae'.

385   *sceptra aurea*   Likewise Ovid, *Fasti* 6.38.

389   *terrae daedala machina*   Lucretian evocation, for both *daedala* (cf. 1.7, 'daedala tellus') and *machina* are favourite words of L.

396   *Tagum*   Used as a western location to contrast with the eastern

regions. The golden sands of the Tagus in present-day Portugal were a commonplace in Latin literature; cf. Seneca, *Thyestes* 353ff., 'non quicquid . . ./unda Tagus aurea/claro devehit alveo'. There are other references to the Tagus at *Elegy* 5.56, *Silvae* 1.14; the connexions between Coimbra, where B. resided after 1547, and Bordeaux (see McFarlane, 123ff.) may have brought the Tagus to mind.

408 *tinnula cymbala* Cf. *1 Cor.* 13.1, 'cymbalum tinniens'.

409 *nablium* is the classical form (cf. Ovid, *A.A.* 3.327); in the Vulgate *nablum* is regular (*1 Par.* 15.16, *1 Macc.* 13.51).

412 *multiforae* Cf. Ovid, *Met.* 12.157f., 'non illos carmina vocum/ longave multifori delectat tibia buxi'; Seneca, *Ag.* 358f., 'tibi multifora tibia buxo/solemne canit'.

413 *terram pede libero* So Horace, *C.* 1.37.1f., 'nunc pede libero/ pulsanda tellus'.

417 With this further dramatic irony Iphis is recalled to our attention; the victim is not to be the *dux gregis,* but the daughter of the *dux exercitus,* the 'magni spes generis' (422).

425 *amplectere* It is ironical that the Chorus urges Iphis on to her own destruction; the critical moment is delayed by their sending her out of the way.

431–592. ACT 3. This falls into two parts. In the first, Jephtha enters alone to offer a homecoming prayer to the God of might and mercy, who has punished the Israelites for past errors but who has now shown mercy by routing their enemies. He promises appropriate sacrifice, reminding God (and thereby the audience) of the nature of his vow. The dramatic irony of his speech becomes clear to him when Iphis is the first creature to emerge. In his ensuing dialogue with Iphis which forms the second part of the scene, the father's ambivalent utterances recall the similar scene in Euripides' *Iphigenia at Aulis* between Agamemnon and his daughter (631ff.; in Erasmus' Latin version, with which B. was familiar, 838ff.). But in Euripides Clytemnestra is also present and has to be beguiled with the fiction of a prearranged marriage with Achilles; in our play Symmachus ('War-comrade'), a trusted family-friend, promises Iphis to elicit the reason for her father's unhappiness.

431 *regnator* Is Buchanan thinking of Tacitus *Germ.* 39, 'eoque omnis superstitio respicit, tamquam inde initia gentis, ibi regnator omnium deus'? It is the Semnones in Tacitus who make human sacrifice to the gods. But cf. also Prudentius *Contra Symm.* 2.170, 'quis mihi regnator caeli, quis conditor orbis?'

432–7   B. here expresses pithily the paradox of the God of stern justice who is also the God of mercy; this is the classic Christian contrast, nobly expressed for example in Thomas of Celano's *Dies Irae* ('rex tremendae maiestatis . . . salva me, fons pietatis'). In the Old Testament it is the characteristic of the *propitium numen* to lay waste the enemy.

441   *fonteque perennis boni*   Cf. Prudentius, *Apoth*. 885, 'summumque bonum de fonte perenni'; Prudentius favours the word *perennis*.

442f.   *saxa . . . lignis*   For the parallel with Prudentius, cf. 362f. The emphasis on idolatry here and elsewhere suggests that a point is being made about contemporary Catholic excesses; cf. Calvin's *Institution de la religion chretienne*, 1.10–11.

450   *Idume*   B. thinks of the attacks by the Edomites under Joram (*2 Kings* 14.7) and the capture of Jerusalem by Nebuchadnezzar; this is of course an anachronism.

450   *Palestinae manus*   The bands with which the immigrant Israelites came into collision, beginning with the Amalekites (*Exod*. 17.8f.).

463f.   *arcu . . . remisso*   So Horace, *C*. 3.27.67f., 'et remisso/filius arcu'.

469   *creator*   Though classical in origin, the word is much more frequent in the Vulgate and in Christian Latin; cf. Prudentius, *Per*. 13.55, 'creator orbis'.

471   *victimis*   For the irony, cf. 417.

474ff.   Cf. *Exod*. 14.21ff.

478   *vitreus*   Cf. 147 and Horace, *C*. 4.2.3f., 'vitreo daturus/nomina ponto'.

479   *muro*   See *Exod*. 14.22, 'et ingressi sunt filii Israel per medium sicci maris; erat enim aqua quasi murus a dextra eorum et laeva'. The previous verse describes how the waters were turned back.

480   Note the connexion between the covenant and Jephtha's vow (see line 5).

482   *exigua*   Ironical; the audience already knows the outcome of the vow.

484   *quod primum*   B. misrepresents the sense of the Vulgate text; cf. *Judges* 11.31, 'quicumque primus fuerit egressus de foribus domus meae, mihique occurrerit revertenti . . . eum holocaustum offeram Domino'. Though the verse has troubled commentators, the sense is clear; the Septuagint has ὃς ἂν ἐξέλθῃ . . . . But Castellio's translation has '*quod mihi extra fores . . . obviam prodierit*'; this appeared in 1551. It seems that B., like Castellio, attempts to attenuate the meaning of the passage so that it might include an animal. At least one contemporary commentator, Ioannes Arboreus in his *Theosophia* (Paris 1540), had seen the

# JEPHTHA

absurdity of earlier attempts to press such an interpretation: 'neque enim est aut fuit consuetudinis ut redeuntibus cum victoria de bello ducibus pecora occurrerent' (257v°). But the choice of this interpretation by B. has obvious dramatic advantages.

497 *sine frui* There is a similarly affectionate gesture by Iphigenia in Euripides, 631f.

508f. *misera peccavi, pater . . . misera, peccavit pater* Such pointed repetition in stichomythia is a device borrowed from Greek drama.

509 *peccavit* Though the present verse does not necessarily imply guilt for wrong done to Iphis ('I have sinned against you' means 'The oath I took has brought you harm'), Jephtha's sense of sinning now intensifies; cf. 717.

513 *aequo animo* The ideal of filial virtue is one to which B. often returns; cf. 1175n.

519 *gaudia . . . contamines* Cf. Terence, *Eun.* 552, 'ne hoc gaudium contaminet vita aegritudine aliqua'.

521 *absentiam . . . praesentia* As at Erasmus, *Iph.* 873f. ('etenim haec dies praesens absentiam mihi/tibique pariet, nata, quam longissimam') the absence will be the daughter's.

526 *familia* conveying the sense of both household and family, picks up Storge's words at 144. Jephtha is aware that the family is *not* safe though the household is; the household (and land) have been saved from the enemy, but his daughter is to be a victim.

531 *votaque* The further dramatic irony is notable.

532 *cum reflavit* Cf. Cicero, *Off.* 2.19, 'cum prospero flatu eius (sc. fortunae) utimur ad exitus pervehimur optatos, et cum reflavit affligimur'.

538 *propitium* Cf. 432 and 643.

543 *puellares* So Tacitus, *Ann.* 14.2, 'puellaribus annis'.

549 *sacrificio* The irony here is heavy, but Jephtha shows delicacy in trying to delay Iphis' realisation of the situation. B. is exploiting the exchange between Agamemnon and Iphigenia at Euripides 673–5, translated by Erasmus 916f. as 'spectabis ipsa; nam futurum est uti sacris/ adstes et adsis tu lavacris proxima'.

551–3 *liberos . . . liberorum* The rhetorical plurals jar on the ear in view of the emphasis on Iphis as *sola generis . . . spes* (727).

554 *taetricus tristis* So Livy 1.18.4, 'disciplina taetrica ac tristi veterum Sabinorum'.

562 *dente* Cf. Horace, *C.* 4.3.16, 'et iam dente minus mordeor invido'.

569ff. The character of Symmachus as wise war-comrade and trusty

NOTES

family-friend is established by a sequence of prudent *sententiae*.
572   *repostos . . . sensus*   The thought is from *1 Kings* 16.7, 'homo enim videt ea quae parent, dominus autem intuetur cor'.
573   *purus*   Iphis' purity is comparable with John's in the *Baptistes*.
575   *iniuria*   Cf. 513n.
582   Just as the Chorus encouraged Iphis to be first to meet her father, so they now precipitate the discovery and execution of her fate.
590   *caecos*   A good description of Jephtha's mind, encompassing not only his present confused motivation, but also his state of mind after the revelations have been made.

593–617. THIRD CHORAL ODE.   This ode is composed in Pherecrateans, a metre not used by Seneca but familiar to B. from Euripides and from Horace, who uses it as the third line of the Fifth Asclepiad (e.g., 'grato, Pyrrha, sub antro' at *C*. 1.5.3). The theme of malice is dominant; the Chorus fears that Jephtha's displeasure at Iphis may have been aroused by the malicious gossip of slave or neighbour. But this theme of *livor* is not central to the play, and the ode's brevity indicates the author's eagerness to resume the main theme.
604   *praeceps*   This favourite word of Seneca is often used by B. to express emotional and irrational attitudes or activities.
610   *tenebrosi*   Cf. Ovid, *Met*. 1.113, 'tenebrosa in Tartara'.
611   *Averni* recalls Jephtha's words at 494.

618–783. ACT 4.   After a leisurely discussion on the blessings and evils of high estate, in which Symmachus again indulges his sententious generalisations, Jephtha at last recalls his vow. The level-headed friend urges consultation and delay rather than precipitate action, but Jephtha denounces his guilt yet proclaims his stubborn resolve to discharge his promise.
625   *festis*   Cf. Ovid, *Met*. 3.528, 'festisque fremunt ululatibus agri'.
628   Symmachus' advice is convincing, but Jephtha disregards him as he disregards his family. His recourse to moral commonplaces (so frequent in Seneca) reveals him justifying himself to himself as well as to others by the consolation of traditional recipes for happiness. The theme of the happiness of the insignificant is prominent in Euripides, *I.A.* 16ff.; cf. Horace, *Epodes* 2.1ff.
632   The observations of Symmachus at 632–41 closely echo Sallust's philosophic preface to the *Catiline;* 1.1, 'omnes homines qui sese student praestare ceteris animalibus summa ope niti decet ne vitam silentio transeant velut pecora. . .' . 1.3, 'quo mihi rectius videtur ingeni quam virium opibus gloriam quaerere . . . et memoriam nostri quam maxume

longam efficere; nam . . . virtus clara aeternaque habetur.' 2.7, 'sed multi mortales dediti ventri atque somno indocti incultique vitam sicut peregrinantes transiere . . . eorum ego vitam mortemque iuxta aestimo, quoniam de utraque siletur'.

633  *vera virtus*  This is what the play is about. Does true virtue lie in Jephtha's faithful adherence to his vow, or in Iphis' unquestioning obedience, or in the reasonable attitude of the priest? Compare *Baptistes* 337, 1149.

637  See the Prologue to the *Baptistes*, 23, 'ipsique somno dediti ac ignaviae'. For the echo of Sallust, see 632n.

645  *gratus*  Symmachus' appeal to Jephtha to be grateful is ironic since the whole problem arises from Jephtha's being too insistent on giving thanks; the tragedy is the direct result of his gratitude.

648  *memor animus*  Perhaps the parable of the lepers (Luke 17.12) was in B.'s mind.

649  *praeclara*  It is strange that Jephtha should enter this debate about ethical commonplaces. He shows no real sorrow, anguish or doubt except at the end (660, 'miseriae quem premunt certissimae'). The scene is too long drawn out, since the drama is concerned with the particular case more than with the general principles. And Jephtha does not describe his motives and state of mind accurately; whatever he feels, he does not manage to show Symmachus exactly what is wrong.

651  *fronte prima*  Quintilian uses the phrase regularly for *prima facie*.

654  *fortuna . . . refulsit*  Cf. Livy 30.30.15: 'et mihi talis aliquando fortuna adfulsit'.

680f.  *altum vertice pulsas Olympum*  Cf. Ennius, *Ann.* fr.1 Warmington, 'Musae quae pedibus magnum pulsatis Olympum'.

691ff.  Note the further homespun *sententiae* in the development of the character of Symmachus.

699  *aedesque laxas*  Cf. Velleius Paterculus 2.81, 'laxior domus'.

712  *pharmacis vulgaribus*  A striking description of these ethical commonplaces.

717  *culpa . . . errorem*  The first admission of culpability for the rash vow.

722  *prudentior*  The admission that he should have been more cautious reflects a growing awareness of his rashness.

727  *sola*  In spite of his intransigence, Jephtha shows concern for his family and for Iphis. The use of the imperfect tense (*supererat*) is poignant.

737  *corusci*  Cf. Cicero, *Tusc.* 2.21, 'iace, obsecro, in me vim coruscam fulminis', where Cicero gives a free rendering of a passage of Sophocles' *Trachiniae*.

## NOTES

738 *terra*, etc., recalling Jephtha's words at 494.
741 *dexter* Cf. Ovid, *Fasti* 1.6, 'dexter ades'.
745 *noxiam* Cf. 717n.
749 *trisulcis* Cf. 188n.
750 *scelestum parricidam* The note of self-condemnation rises higher.
755 *temere* Symmachus' advice to proceed cautiously, prompted by Jephtha's deranged attitude, contrasts with Jephtha's regret that he had not been cautious earlier.
758 *liber* At 679 Symmachus had said that Jephtha was 'liber e servo', but now he regards him as a prisoner of his own principles.
759 *amicis* Symmachus is aware of the isolation of Jephtha which is comparable to that of John in the *Baptistes;* as elsewhere Symmachus plays the role of prudent and sympathetic *raisonneur*.
774 *ineluctabile* So Virgil, *Aen.* 8.334, 'fortuna omnipotens et ineluctabile fatum'.
776 *probabunt* The language of this passage (cf. 760 and 777) is that of the moral theologian.
783 *temere* Cf. 755n.; the Chorus repeats the warning of Symmachus to avoid rash action.

784–841. FOURTH CHORAL ODE. A meditation on the wretchedness of Jephtha and Iphis, followed by general reflexions on the mutability of fortune. The ode is composed in anapaestic dimeters, the commonest of Buchanan's lyric metres.

788 *consilio . . . aut precibus* The Chorus searches for some solution to the dilemma which they themselves have precipitated.
793–6 *error exsors consilii    impietas* These sentiments represent the traditional Christian attitude as summarised by Aquinas (Introdn., 16).
793 *compede* Cf. Horace, *C.* 4.11.22ff., 'puella . . . tenetque grata/ compede vinctum'.
794 *error* Not because he has made a rash vow, but because he intends to fulfil it.
802 *dira lues* So Ovid, *Met.* 15.626, 'dira lues quondam Latias vitiaverat auras'.
803 *mactatu* The only classical passage in which this word is found (as a variation of *mactatio*) is at Lucretius 1.99, and there can be no doubt that this celebrated condemnation of the evil effects of *religio* was in B.'s mind here. Lucretius cites as a conspicuous example the ritual murder of Iphigenia, and offers an affecting description of the scene with the sad father and fellow-Greeks standing impotently by; Iphigenia

is brought to the altar not for marriage but (*ut*)
>
> hostia concideret mactatu maesta parentis . . .
> tantum religio potuit suadere malorum.

The technique of evocation is reminiscent of Montaigne's deployment of Classical quotations to convey less palatable ideas.

805 *vice brutae pecudis* In the sacrifice prepared by Abraham, divine intervention ensured that Isaac was replaced by a ram; and in the later versions of the Iphigenia-legend, a hind was substituted for the girl (e.g., Ovid, *Met.* 12.29ff.). Here there is an ironical reversal of that pattern.

806 *sanguinis . . . undam* Cf. Statius, *Theb.* 9.747, 'stat faucibus unda/sanguinis'.

809 *feritas ursae* Is Buchanan thinking of the boy torn to pieces by the bear in Apuleius, *Met.* 7.24ff.?

821 'dormitavit Buchananus' (W. S. Watt). Harsh winter does not follow warm spring.

830 *remeabilis* The word is rare (but cf. Statius, *Theb.* 4,537, 'saxum remeabile'), and it is possible that the use of *irremeabilis* as at Virgil, *Aen.* 6.425 or Seneca, *H.F.* 548 inspired it.

831 *Cauri . . . protervi* Cf. Horace, *Epodes* 16.22, 'protervus Africus'.

832 *freta . . . spumea* Cf. Claudian, 18.266, 'mergique fretis spumantibus orat'.

837–9 For the image of evanescent fire in straw, cf. Ovid, *Tr.* 5.8.20, 'flammaque de stipula nostra brevisque fuit'.

842–1055. ACT 5. After the dialogues with Iphis (Act 3) and Symmachus (Act 4), the crucial issues are posed still more tautly in this discussion between the scrupulous, unbending Jephtha and the *sacerdos* who carries the authority of religious orthodoxy. The priest's categorical arguments are 1) Ritual sacrifice of a daughter is unnatural and therefore against the law of God, who in any case finds bloody offerings unacceptable. 2) Though vows are acceptable to God in general, and once undertaken should be carried out, any vow which would contravene God's unchanging law is impious and must be abandoned. Jephtha challenges these arguments as the sophistry of the learned which undermines religious practice, and proposes the thesis that it is sincerity of intention which God respects. The rabbi replies that private judgment induces fatal frailties and undermines the objective status of the moral law.

846 *tellus, hisce* Cf. Ovid, *Met.* 1.546, 'tellus, ait, hisce'.

NOTES

855 *lamentabili* Cf. Cicero, *Tusc. 2.32,* 'adflictusne et iacens et lamentabili voce deplorans'.

858 *recusat* The priest adds his voice to that of Symmachus urging Jephtha to rely on the help and advice of his friends; once more we are made to see the loneliness of Jephtha in his decision.

870f. *alis aëra findit* So Ovid, *Met.* 4.667, 'et liquidum motis talaribus aëra findit'; cf. *Met.* 8.832.

887ff. The motif of the preferability of bloodless sacrifice is strong in the Old Testament; cf. 924n., Ps. 50.18, Isa. 1.11–15, 66.3; Osee 6.6 (evoked at Matt. 9.13 and 12.7); Mich. 6.6ff. The Christian Fathers in condemnation of pagan Roman ritual echo the doctrine that the sacrifice of pure hearts and minds is preferred by God. See Paulinus of Nola, *Ep.* 11.7: "We can slay a goat by excizing our sins in which is the stench of death. We can kill a bull by abandoning our pride, we can sacrifice a sheep if we expel effeminacy and idleness by the heat of our love and our burning spirit. We can offer within ourselves a lamb if our lives are spotless, and a steer if we become as children strangers to wickedness, so that we can reproduce the purity of the lamb by our chastity, and the stupidity of the steer by our simplicity." Cf. also Paulinus, *Poem* 32.24, and other passages quoted in *Patrologia Latina,* 61.691.

888ff. *Aegyptus ... Assyria* B. probably adverts to the Egyptian practice of treating certain animals as sacred, but there is no doubt that their official worship included animal-sacrifice; cf. Herodotus 2.39 with How and Wells' *Commentary;* Herodotus further asserts (2.45) that there were human sacrifices on occasion. The Assyrians also practised blood-sacrifices; B. may have in mind here the later effects of Zoroastrianism.

896 *bubulove sanguine* Cf. Prudentius, *Perist.* 10.1007, 'meus iste sanguis verus est, non bubulus'.

899 *conscientia* Echoing Iphis at 568.

899 *offerenda ... conscientia* Cf. Prudentius, *Epilogus* 1–3, 'immolat deo patri ... dona conscientiae'.

901–3 The Genesis account of Abraham and Isaac is clearly in the author's mind.

904 *nuncupata* Cf. Paul. ex Fest. 173 Müll., 'vota nuncupata dicuntur quae consules praetores cum in provinciam proficiscuntur faciunt; ea in tabulas praesentibus multis referuntur. at Santra ... nuncupata colligit non directo nominata significare, sed promissa et quasi testificata circumscripta recepta, quod etiam in votis nuncupandis esse convenientius'.

915 *sanus* Jephtha seems curiously aware that there are some actions which only a madman could do, yet simultaneously unaware that the

260

same could be said of his own rash vow. He does not however claim that the madman who had vowed to burn his state's laws would be absolved of his vow.

920 *Abramum* The story of the sacrifice was popular in the late middle ages and the Renaissance, especially as a subject for carvers and sculptors. Théodore de Bèze's *Abraham Sacrifiant* appeared in 1550.

924 *oboedientiam* Cf. *1 Kings* 15.22, 'et ait Samuel: numquid vult Dominus holocausta et victimas, et non potius ut obediatur voci Domini? melior est enim obedientia quam victimae: et auscultare magis quam offerre adipem arietum'.

932 *stultis* An apt description of Jephtha's mental state; he is the victim of his own obsessive imagination.

933f. *deum crudelitati . . . adscribere* Cf. Ovid, *Met.* 15.127ff., 'nec satis est quod tale nefas committitur; ipsos/inscribere deos sceleri, numenque supernum/caede laboriferi credunt gaudere iuvenci'. B.'s well-stocked mind can assemble protests against the ritual slaughter of animals not only from biblical but also from Classical sources.

942 *scopum* A word rare in classical Latin, usually written in the Greek form (the reading at Suetonius, *Domit.* 19 is doubtful). B. uses it also at *Franciscanus* 23 and *Baptistes* 171.

943 *ab una lege* Cf. *Ps.* 1.2.

947 *lucerna* Cf. *Prov.* 6.23, 'mandatum lucerna est'; *Ps.* 118.105, 'lucerna pedibus meis verbum tuum'.

952 *cumulabit* Cf. Cicero, *Cat.* 1.14, 'alio incredibili scelere hoc scelus cumulasti'.

961 *moribus* The final argument of the priest's speech, the attack on the value of individualism in religious practice, goes beyond the context of Jephtha's vow to attack his whole attitude.

962 *sapere* This passage echoes contemporary discussions about priestly learning, which was often equated with sophistry; cf. Rabelais, *Garg.* ch. 14 ('Comment Gargantua feut institué par un sophiste en lettres latines'; the earliest editions had 'théologien' for 'sophiste'); ch. 21 ('L'estude de Gargantua selon la discipline de ses précepteurs sophistes'; originally 'précepteurs Sorbonagres'). See also Marot, 'Au Roy, du temps de son exil à Ferrare' (*Les Epîtres*, ed. Mayer, 1958, 197); and B.'s own poems, *Franciscanus* and *Fratres Fraterrimi*.

966 *mysteria* This Greek word is frequently used for 'sacraments' in Christian contexts, and B. may visualise Jephtha here as an antireforming figure.

977ff. This play was mounted in the Collège de Guyenne at Bordeaux, 'destined to become the leading seminary of the liberal arts in France'

## NOTES

(D.F.S. Thomson, *Phoenix* (1950), 81); these lines and the retort of the *sacerdos* will have been the distillation of an argument familiar there. At his later trial by the Inquisition, B. claimed that in this play his view is that 'vota *quae licite fiunt* omnia servanda'; see J.M. Aitken, *The Trial of George Buchanan*, 12.

980f.  *peritior . . . neglegentior*  The rhyme at the conclusion of a lengthy speech is more characteristic of Renaissance than of Classical drama; cf. 493f., *Baptistes* 456f., 1182f.

988  *consensio*  The priest's argument, that the popular attitude to which Jephtha has made appeal does not justify an immoral action, counters the claim of Jephtha that common folk abide firmly by a promise solemnly made.

999  *diiudicandi*  This sounds like criticism of the typical Catholic attitude to reformers.

1001  *dogma*  Though this is essentially a criticism of the traditional Catholic standpoint, Jephtha always manifests the simplicity and integrity which evokes the attitude of John in the *Baptistes;* it is the two-sidedness of the presentation which lends the drama its strength.

1006  *perusta*  So Pliny, *Ep.* 7.1.4, 'perustus ardentissima febre'.

1009  *vos*  The plural (cf. 1025, 1052 for further examples) indicates that the participants regard the issue of simple faith versus moral theology as an argument between groups.

1014  *religio*  In this key-passage true religion is linked with strictures on the practice of sacrifice; B.'s contemporaries would doubtless relate this to current controversy on the sacrifice of the mass (Introduction, p. 18), though we need not assume that B. here sets down his own opinion on the subject.

1024  *curva . . . corrigit*  Cf. Seneca, *Apocol.* 8, 'hic nobis curva corriget'.

1051  *apicem*  Cf. Matt. 5.18, 'amen dico vobis, donec transeat caelum et terra, iota unum aut unus apex non praeteribit a lege donec omnia fiant'; cf. Luke 16.17.

1054  *stultam*  Recalling the Pauline idea of the folly of the Christian faith centred on the cross; cf. *1 Cor.* 1.25, 3.19.

1056–1125. FIFTH CHORAL ODE.  The Chorus sings in anapaestic dimeters of the sudden reversal of fortune as evidenced in the case of Jephtha, and then of the dark clouds surrounding the human intelligence which make it difficult to acknowledge the truth or to tread the path of virtue.

1056  *Isacidas*  For the allusive use of the patronymic, cf. 2n.

1064  *vitet in horas*  So Horace, *C.* 2.13.13f., 'quid quisque vitet, nunquam homini satis/cautum est in horas'.

1073  *retractans*  Cf. Ovid, *Met.* 10.288, 'rursus amans rursusque manu sua vota retractat'; cf. 7.714.

1075f.  *taetris . . . tenebris*  Cf. Cicero, *Agr.* 2.44, 'taetris tenebris'.

1080f.  *virtutis nudae*  So also Petronius, *Sat.* 88, 'priscis . . . temporibus cum adhuc nuda virtus placeret'; see 1094n.

1082  *maligna*  An echo of the famous Virgilian passage, *Aen.* 6.270f., 'quale per incertam lunam sub luce maligna/est iter in silvis'.

1088  *praeterpropter*  Just as at 803 *mactatu* points to the famous Lucretian discussion of Iphigenia, so here this archaic expression is an evocation of Ennius' *Iphigenia,* itself an adaptation of Euripides' *Iphigenia at Aulis.* Several fragments of Ennius' version survive (see Warmington's *Remains of Old Latin* (Loeb series) 1.300ff.), amongst them the fragment of a choral ode preserved by Gellius 19.10.12, 'imus huc, hinc illuc; quom illuc ventum est, ire illinc lubet./incerte errat animus, praeterpropter vitam vivitur'. The passage has clearly inspired B.'s thought here.

1090  *venalem funere laurum*  The laurel was often planted round tombs; cf. Propertius 2.13.33.

1094  *captatores . . . captans*  This second example of wayward behaviour seems irrelevant to the theme of the play, and to have been included merely to evoke Petronius, *Sat.* 116f., a romance later exploited to good effect by a fellow-Scot in France, John Barclay, in his *Euphormionis Satyricon* (1603). In the passage of Petronius cited, Eumolpus decides to impersonate an heirless millionaire to deceive the legacy-hunters of Croton. 'in hac urbe . . . aut captantur aut captant.' (cf. 1094). 'in hac urbe nemo liberos tollit.' (cf. 1095). 'adibitis oppidum tamquam in pestilentia campos, in quibus nihil aliud est nisi cadavera quae lacerantur aut corvi qui lacerant.' (cf. 1098).

1099  *murmura blanda*  Cf. Ovid, *A.A.* 3.795, 'nec blandae voces iucundaque murmura cessent'.

1103  *rutilas Hermus*  Cf. Juvenal 14.298f., 'aurum/quod Tagus et rutila volvit Pactolus harena'; Virgil, *Georg.* 2.137, 'auro turbidus Hermus'.

1107  The shorter line, the Adonius, is deployed to indicate a change of subject, the arrival of Iphis and Storge.

1113  *Olympum*  Cf. 680f.

1117f.  *pulveris . . . turbine*  Cf. Horace, *Sat.* 1.4.31, 'fertur uti pulvis collectus turbine'.

1126–1330. ACT 6.  The obdurate attitude of Jephtha extends into a

NOTES

dialogue with an increasingly bitter wife, but the intervention of the saintly Iphis, who unquestioningly accepts her fate and begs her parents not to let her death sow discord, causes the hero's resolve to break down. He proposes his own death in place of his daughter's, but the masterful meekness of Iphis dismisses the suggestion. The influence of Euripides' characterisation of Iphigenia and Clytemnestra (*I.A.* 819ff.) is again manifest in this scene.

1126 *festa nuptialia* There has been no specific mention of marriage previously (though cf. 82), but in Euripides' play a story of marriage with Achilles is the pretext for summoning the girl to Aulis for sacrifice, and her mother Clytemnestra attends her; the marriage-motif is likewise present in the affecting description of Lucretius (I 96ff.; 803n.).

1132 *falsa* Storge's false dreams about Iphis' future happiness are to be contrasted with her true dream at the beginning of the play (73ff.).

1137 *o ter beatos* A reminiscence of Virgil, *Aen.* 1.94ff., 'o terque quaterque beati/quis ante ora patrum Troiae sub moenibus altis/contigit oppetere!'. Cf. *Baptistes* 858.

1142ff. *liberorum . . . victimis* The rhetorical plurals intensify the note of protest. Cf. 551–3n.

1156 *sceleris* See 750n.

1159 *solusque* Jephtha concludes with a clear statement of his own dilemma, his obligations, his solitude.

1160 *sponte* Storge sums up succinctly the objective view of Jephtha's responsibility, already expressed by others in preceding scenes.

1161 *arbitrii* Here a link is made between contemporary discussions on vows and those on the freedom of the will; cf. Introduction, p. 17.

1176 *legeret* The question of the rights of parents in the marriage of their children was of great topical interest at the time B. was writing. See Rabelais, *Tiers Livre* (1546), ch. 48, 'Comment Gargantua remonstre n'estre licite es enfans soy marier sans le sceu et adveu de leurs peres et meres'. An account of contemporary opinion on the subject may be seen in Michael Screech's edition of the *Tiers Livre* (Geneva 1974), 318f.

1211 *doloris* Storge points to her husband's apparent indifference to her; is he to be played as a saint or a madman? But see 1226n.

1215ff. The contrast between the tender understanding of the daughter and the bitter recrimination of the wife is an impressive technique of the characterisation.

1226 *vertis* Jephtha shows that he is capable of some emotion, perhaps even great emotion; we are reminded of Iphis' first meeting with him (498, 'cur, genitor, a me torva vertis lumina?') which produced this tragic outcome.

JEPHTHA

1241 *renuente* This appears to be almost an admission of the opposite point of view, yet Jephtha is unable to change his mind; he has convinced himself that God showed approval of his vow by giving him victory.

1245 In spite of his obstinacy Jephtha shows a certain nobility here, especially at the end of the speech.

1253 *patratur* Jephtha's reply is logical and apt. He remains calm in revealing his sense of duty in sacrificing Iphis and no-one else.

1254 *sanctitas* There is a mixture of sarcasm and agony in the bitterness of this ironic couplet, a telling comment on Jephtha's sense of sin.

1256 In this saintly expression of *pietas* the Iphigenia of Euripides (*I.A.* 1368ff.) is discernible.

1261 *necessitas* It is ironic that Iphis is the only one who accepts that her father is *compelled* to carry out the sacrifice; Storge, Symmachus, the priest all believe that the fault is his own.

1289 *votum* Though the sense is 'prayer', there is a deliberate contrast between the word here and Jephtha's vow made to attain victory.

1295 *aras piemus* Cf. Propertius 3.10.19, 'ubi ture piaveris aras'.

1299 *temere* Jephtha at last uses the word which others had used to describe his action.

1305–6 *ultima sub spatia* For the suggestion that *Alcestis* inspired this motif, see *Alcestis* 1010n.

1308 *auram gloriae* Cf. Virgil, *Aen.* 7.646, 'ad nos vix tenuis famae perlabitur aura'.

1309 *patriam* Iphis has already made clear the link between her obedience to her father and her duty to her country (cf. 1268; also 1318, 1348 below). The motif is likewise present at Euripides, *I.A.* 1554.

1314 *innectere* See Statius, *Theb.* 5.743f., 'atque utinam plures innectere pergas,/Phoebe, moras'.

1316 *fas* There is no reason for him to die; the vow would still be unfulfilled, and he would have added another crime while remaining guilty of a failure to fulfil the vow.

1319 *nec ulla ... redarguet dies* Cf. Virgil, *Aen.* 11.687f., 'advenit qui vestra dies muliebribus armis/verba redarguerit'.

1331–60. SIXTH CHORAL ODE. A celebration in anapaestic dimeters of the future fame of Iphis coupled with brief condemnation of those who lack such altruistic patriotism.

1333 *animi ... virilis* Cf. Paulinus of Nola, *Ep.* 29.6, 'si feminam dici licet tam viriliter Christianam'. Paulinus elsewhere calls the lady referred to here (the elder Melania) 'Melanius'. But Erasmus, *I.A.* 2000, 'beata es tam virili pectore', is the likely inspiration.

## NOTES

**1335–7** *abscidit . . . carpserit* The combination after *licet* of indicative (a post-classical construction) and subjunctive is clumsy.

**1341** *rutilae* Cf. Ovid, *Met.* 12.294f., 'rutilasque ferox in aperta loquentis/condidit ora viri, perque os in pectora, flammas'.

**1342** *posteritas sera* Cf. Ovid, *Pont.* 4.8.47f., 'carmine fit vivax virtus, expersque sepulcri/notitiam serae posteritatis habet'.

**1344f.** *curru Sarmatico . . . per Istrum* This is a literary cliché in Augustan poetry (cf. Virgil, *Georg.* 3.361f., Ovid, *Tristia* 3.10.53f., *Pont.* 4.7.9f.) but the direct influence is from Ovid, *Tristia* 3.12.29f., 'nec ut ante per Histrum/stridula Sauromates plaustra bubulcus agit'.

**1361–1450.** ACT 7. In this final act the Messenger acquaints Storge with the manner of her daughter's end. B. was inspired here not only by Euripides, *I.A.* (in which the maiden was miraculously rescued) but also by the similar scene in Euripides, *Hecuba* 484ff., in which the herald reports the moving death of Polyxena to her mother Hecuba. Erasmus' version of this play was familiar to B.

**1368** *callum* Cf. Cicero, *Tusc.* 2.36, 'ipse labor quasi callum quoddam obducit dolori'.

**1372** *staret aras* Cf. Seneca, *Oed.* 303, 'opima sanctas victima ante aras stetit'.

**1374** *pudor* Cf. Tibullus 1.4.13f., 'at illi/virgineus teneras stat pudor ante genas'; Erasmus, *Iph.* 225, 'suffundit ora purpureus pudor'.

**1375** Note the crowd of men present as in Euripides, *Hec.* 521 and *I.T.* 1546; their attendance is less appropriate in this case.

**1376f.** *ut si . . . liliis* An evocation of the beauty of Lavinia at Virgil, *Aen.* 12.67ff., 'Indum sanguineo veluti violaverit ostro/si quis ebur, aut mixta rubent ubi lilia multa/alba rosa; tales virgo dabat ore colores'.

**1378–80** *sola* Cf. Seneca, *Troades* 1099f., 'non flet e turba omnium/qui fletur'.

**1384-95** Cf. Seneca, *Troades* 1144ff., 'hos movet formae decus,/hos mollis aetas, hos vagae rerum vices;/movet animus omnes fortis et leto obvius'. It seems clear that Seneca's *Troades* has exercised a strong influence on this final act.

**1389** *fidem* There is a contrast between the faithlessness of fortune and Iphis' fidelity (see 1379).

**1391** *auro* Cf. Erasmus, *Iph.* 926, 'o pares auro comae'.

**1392** *constantiam* This traditional Roman and Stoic virtue was much praised at this time; cf. Montaigne, *Essais* 1.12.

**1395** *viraginis* So Virgil, *Aen.* 12.468 of the deity Iuturna; B. uses the word to emphasise the virile courage of Iphis. Cf. *virilis* at 1333, 1410.

**1396f.** *aequor in Tartessium Phoebi* Cf. Ovid, *Met.* 14.416, 'sparserat occiduus Tartessia litora Phoebus'.

1400   *fati . . . in limine*   Cf. Statius, *Silv.* 5.3.72ff., 'mihi limine primo/fatorum . . . Tartara dura subis'.

1413   *parens*   The address to the divine father emphasises by contrast the natural father Jephtha's unnatural attitude. At Euripides, *I.A.* 1552, Iphigenia addresses her human father, and proclaims that she sacrifices herself for Argos and Hellas.

1414   *gentis*   Iphis goes beyond the thought that she is dying for her country as the result of a vow, to the idea that her death is in expiation of the people's sins.

1424   For the invitation to strike, cf. Euripides, *Hec.* 562ff.

1425   *gelido*   Cf. Ovid, *Heroides* 11.82, 'torpuerat gelido lingua retenta metu'.

1433   *meatus*   So Pliny of the death of his uncle at *Ep.* 6.16.13, 'nam meatus animae, qui illi propter amplitudinem corporis gravior et sonantior erat, ab iis qui limini obversabantur audiebatur'.

1444   It is significant that there is no description of the actual death of Iphis. The playwright seeks to end the play on a note of serenity and edification.

# THE BAPTIST

This was the first of the two biblical dramas to be composed by B., as the Introduction (p. 2ff.) has indicated. The Preface calls it *primus foetus;* the *Vita* claims that it was 'prima omnium . . . conscripta', and explains that it was written for performance at Bordeaux in the early 1540s. But it was not published until 1577.

The inexperience of the novice-playwright is reflected in both the structure and the characterisation. Too often the action does not proceed smoothly from one act to the next, but has been composed in static and self-contained sections. The result is that the characterisation of Herod and Herodias does not develop consistently or convincingly, as our notes indicate.

The central theme of John's religious challenge to the corruption of the Sanhedrin encourages the reader to detect numerous sixteenth-century echoes, to which we draw attention (e.g. 46, 130, 138, 173–4, 213, 479, 493, 718, 738, 1236, 1274, 1282, 1305, 1342, 1344nn.). On the question whether the play should be envisaged as a *pièce à clé* with sixteenth-century counterparts to the main characters, see the Introduction, p. 10ff.

At some points of the play, sentiments with a sixteenth-century resonance seem more appropriate to the conditions of 1577 than to those of 1540 (see 232, 1236, 1305nn.) and B. may have undertaken some revision in places. This would go some way to explain a greater stylistic and metrical virtuosity than is evinced in *Medea;* but we have also to consider the likelihood that *Medea* is in essence a school-composition (Introduction, p. 3).

*Praefatio*

2f. *postquam . . . appositus* For the circumstances in which B. became tutor to James VI of Scotland, see McFarlane, p. 445.
6 *quamquam abortivus* See Introduction, p. 3.
20 *Sallustium* See *Jug.* 85.9, 'bene facere iam ex consuetudine in naturam vortit'.

1–51. PROLOGUE. The prologue handles two themes; first, the reception accorded to plays by contemporaries, and second, the place of the *Baptistes* within the classifications of ancient and modern literature.

The use of the Prologue by authors not for explanation of the *mise-en-scène* but for attacks on critics goes back to Terence, who rebutted accusations of weaknesses of style in the *Phormio* (compare 32ff. in this play) and charges of plagiarism and help from friends. It is curious to find B. so vehement about the acidity of critics in this his first play, but we must remember that publication followed long after performance, and that in the meantime *Jephthes* had also appeared (see Introduction, p. 5). The Prologue has been added for publication.

The controversy about plots ancient versus modern has a long history. When Horace (*Ars Poetica* 119ff.) advises Piso to go to Homer's *Iliad* for a dramatic theme rather than to create a new plot, he is pronouncing on a subject already well-aired (see Aristotle, *Poetics* 1451b). The controversy was revived in 16th- and 17th-century France; see below 13n.

1 *Protea* The passage appears to be modelled on a combination of Ovid, *Met.* 8.730ff. ('sunt quibus in plures ius est transire figuras/ .. nam modo te iuvenem, modo te videre leonem,/nunc violentus aper, nunc quem tetigisse timerent,/anguis eras ..') and *A.A.* 1.761f. ('utque leves Proteus modo se tenuabit in undas,/nunc leo, nunc arbor, nunc erit hirtus aper.'), together with the celebrated episode at Virgil, *Georg.* 4.387ff. (note especially 411, 'sed quanto ille magis formas se vertet in omnis . . .', and 441, 'omnia transformat sese in miracula rerum'). Ruddiman suggests that B. knew the poem which Licentius sent to Augustine (Baehrens, *Fragmenta Poetarum Romanorum*, 413: 'spumat aper, fluit unda, fremit leo, sibilat anguis . . .'). B. refers to Proteus also at *Franciscanus* 328, *Epigr.* 1.40, 2.6.

4 *liquentes . . . undas* Again the Virgilian influence; *Georg.* 4.442, 'fluviumque liquentem'.

9 *Sibyllae . . . oraculis* This further commonplace of Virgilian and Ovidian epic purposefully indicates that the biblical theme will be treated in the traditional classical style.

*veriorem* Though B. has used the normal word *fabulantur* to express the fiction of poetic statement, he is anxious to stress that the myths embody a deeper psychological truth.

13 *calumniis* The entire play is on the theme of calumny, as the subtitle states. Here B. connects this central preoccupation with the calumny emerging from his unsettled times and the tensions caused by changing aesthetic standards. Apart from official censorship of the theatre, there was great difference of opinion amongst critics about the nature of drama. The whole of the passage 15–51 describes succinctly the reaction of critics to triteness and innovation in the theatre; this is of

particular interest at this moment when the theatre was emerging from one form into another, but the same problem affected all literature at the time, as can be seen from the radical changes which took place in attitudes to the writing of poetry. In France these can be traced from Sebillet's *Art poétique françois* (1548), Du Bellay's *Deffence et illustration de la langue francoyse* (1549), Peletier's *Art poétique* (1555), and Ronsard's *Abregé de l'art poétique* (1565). What we have here is perhaps the most vital moment of the Querelle des Anciens et des Modernes, when the Renaissance introduced innovation by looking back beyond the Middle Ages to ancient classical culture.

23  *somno dediti*  Cf. Sallust, *Cat.* 2.8, 'mortales dediti ventri atque somno'.

27  *Lyncea*  The classical cliché of the sharp-sighted Argonaut; cf. Horace, *Epist.* 1.1.28, 'non possis oculo quantum contenderet Lynceus'.

28  *notaque . . . censoria*  The Roman technical term for censure of senators or equites for dereliction of duty or immorality again lends a classical flavour.

30  *severa supercilia*  So Ovid, *Tr.* 2.309, 'supercilii matrona severi'.

32  *aestimator candidus*  Cf. Seneca, *Suas.* 6.22, 'candidissimus . . . aestimator'.

39  *Baptista*  In the following three verses B. sets out tersely the theme of the play and the outcome of the story, already completely familiar to his audience. There can be no question of suspense in a play like this, which deals with such a well-known story, and it was unthinkable at the time that the author should alter the basic facts, though he does change some of the details. *Baptista* is a Vulgate form (cf. Matt. 3.1, etc.) which is common in Christian Latin.

46  *recenti memoria*  Although no explicit detail is given, B. claims that the story has contemporary relevance; it is not merely that deceit, calumny and envy lend the play a universal relevance, but recent events may have given topicality to the theme; cf. Introduction, p. 10ff.

52–280. ACT I. B. skilfully develops this dialogue between two rabbis of differing religious attitudes to reveal the two-sided nature of the Jewish tradition from which John springs. Malchus the inflexible conservative is a non-historical figure, his name perhaps taken from that of the servant of the High Priest whose ear Peter severed (Luke 22.50, John 18.10); Gamaliel is an historical person, the moderate on the Council who advises against the execution of the apostles at *Acts* 5.34ff., and who is the preceptor of Paul at *Acts* 22.3. It is of interest that Malchus appears in *The Golden Legend* as one of the Seven Sleepers of Ephesus; Gamaliel comes into the same work as the person who with

Nicodemus buries Stephen. Malchus appears in the late 15thC *Mystère de la Passion* of Jean Michel, and both Malchus and Gamaliel in the *Passion d'Auvergne* of the same period. See *The Baptism and Temptation of Christ; the First Day of a Medieval French Passion Play*, ed. and tr. by J.R. Elliott Jr. and G.A. Runnalls (Yale 1978).

57 *profana* Like the *Jephthes,* the *Baptistes* is much concerned with this topic of the relation between sacred and profane which so exercised B.'s contemporaries; see Mme de la Garanderie's book on Guillaume Budé, *Christianisme et lettres profanes* (Lille 1976).

59 *Gabinii* After holding the consulship in 58 BC, Gabinius became governor of Syria and reorganized Judaea, treating the Jews with more equity than Malchus suggests; see R. Syme, *The Roman Revolution* (Oxford 1939), 67.

60–62 *Antonii . . . Cleopatrae* Mark Antony controlled the eastern provinces from Syria after 37–6 BC. He awarded Cleopatra queen of Egypt the balsam-groves near Jerusalem, and the monopoly of the bitumen from the Dead Sea. She repeatedly sought to obtain portions of the kingdom of Herod the Great, coveting the whole of his kingdom (cf. Josephus 15.75ff.; Syme, *The Roman Revolution,* 260).

64 *rex Antipatri . . . pronepos* The Herod of the play is Herod Antipas, tetrarch of Galilee and son of Herod the Great who had died in 4 BC. As B. correctly states, Herod Antipas was the great-grandson of the elder Antipater, who was appointed by Alexander Jannaeus to be governor of Idumaea. His son was the more famous Antipater, father of Herod the Great. Ruddiman's suggestion that *nepos* should be read in this line for *pronepos* is misguided.

*Semiarabis* The elder Antipater was an Edomite (and hence an Arab), but became Jewish by religion. The form (not attested) is by analogy with *Semigaetulus,* etc.; B. himself uses *Semimaurus* ('sub Semimauro Caesare', *Misc.* 8.17).

79 *Baptistes* The Greek form (not in *TLL*) is preferred here for metrical reasons.

80 *non e profanis,* etc. The source for this section on John's origins is Luke 1.5–25, 39–80, which contains the account of Zachary and Elizabeth, and of the Visitation and the birth of John.

83 *dicatus* In the account of Luke 1.15, John already in the womb 'erit magnus coram Domino'. But B.'s characterisation of Malchus demands that he is ignorant of or disregards the peculiar circumstances of John's birth and circumcision (the recitation of the *Benedictus* by Zachary acknowledges his son as forerunner of the Messiah and prophet of the Most High).

NOTES

91 *pellibus* See Matt. 3.4, 'zonam pelliceam circa lumbos suos'; cf. Mark 1.6.

97 *proceres* Cf. *In quandam praesulem* (in *Fratres Fraterrimi*) 3, 'quod non te proceresque colant et vulgus adoret'.

100 *lymphis* Malchus implies that baptism is an innovation by John, whereas it was a ritual regularly practised by the Jewish prophets. Cf. John 1.25, 'quid ergo baptizas si tu non es Christus neque Elias neque propheta?' Maimonides and the Babylonian Talmud state that the admission of a proselyte involved baptism as well as circumcision and sacrifice. The language used to describe the ritual here has a classical rather than a Jewish or Christian ring.

101 *ritibus* The emphasis upon the introduction of new ritual suggests that B. is here as in *Jephthes* presenting the drama with a sixteenth-century flavour.

102–5 *furor . . . furentis* Virgil in his epic continually dwells on the *furor* of Dido and Turnus (and of Juno at the celestial level) as the cause of disorder and anarchy; B. repeatedly ascribes to John's opponents the view that he is consumed by *furor* and therefore incapable of *ratio* or reason.

118 *quam . . . sciam* Malchus is criticised for the same defect as that shown by B.'s detractors; see the Prologue 20, 'et priusquam noscere queant exigunt'.

126f. *sectas novas novosque ritus* See 101n.

130 *in nos severi* Gamaliel's stance of self-criticism may be visualised as similar to that of some of B.'s contemporaries attempting to reform the Church from within; the most important attempts came from Lefèvre d'Etaples and his disciples, and from Briçonnet, Bishop of Meaux, and his followers.

138 *praesuli* Though this word means a leader in some post-classical texts, the most common meaning is that of bishop; *praesul Romanus* is the Pope. Once again the sixteenth-century spectacles are notable.

139 *plebs audiat* A commonplace of sixteenth-century political and social thinking, which Gamaliel queries at 144, 'et tibi videtur aequa lex haec?'

143 *cernat et plectat* Cf. 1291–4, 'spectat ex alto . . . exiget poenas'.

154 *parentum stemmata* Cf. Juvenal 8.1, 'stemmata quid faciunt, quid prodest, Pontice, longo/sanguine censeri . . .'

158 *templo* Cf. *1 Cor.* 6.18f., 'fugite fornicationem . . . an nescitis quoniam membra vestra templum sunt Spiritus Sancti . . . ?'

166 *iuvenis furentis* See 102n. At the Reformation the debate about tradition and innovation was often a matter of generations, and the

272

reformers were often seen as youthful hotheads. John, like the reformers, appeared to threaten the overthrow of the established political and religious order.

167  *lucri*  Malchus shows his true character here; just as he assumed that John's motives were unworthy, so he does not credit Gamaliel with other than materialistic concerns.

171  *scopo*  Cf. *Jephthes* 942n.

173  *fastu . . . superbia*  This characterisation of the Pharisees is in line also with sixteenth-century attacks on the pomp and arrogance of the Church.

174  *non haec*  An argument often used by reformers both outside and inside the Catholic Church at the moment of the Reformation, suggesting that the traditionalists were not true to their tradition. One has the impression that this dialogue is coloured by the typical interchanges of B.'s day.

175–6  *Vetusta,* etc.  There is unconscious irony here, since Malchus the traditionalist now appears as a dishonest opportunist, basing his conduct on the *mores* of his own day.

181  *crudelitas*  The sixteenth century was a violent and intolerant period, especially in matters of religion, and often with the official approval of the Church authorities. Yet in spite of the atrocities in which both sides indulged, there were some who spoke out against violence; the humane attitude of Gamaliel is an echo of the sentiments of men like More, Erasmus, Colet and Rabelais.

185  *redarguis*  Gamaliel's is the voice of reason against intransigence, and against all totalitarian practices; his appeal to Malchus' desire for glory through rhetorical persuasion shows that he realises that the appeal to reason will not be psychologically sufficient.

195  *ante*  Cf. Matt. 18.22.

200  *servare . . . omnes*  Is there a possible reference here to current debate about the doctrine of *Extra ecclesiam nulla salus*? Not that John is an outsider in this sense in the Jewish religious context.

208  *quin potius*  Once again Gamaliel confronts violence with reason, maintaining the tension which runs through the play.

213  *divinus . . . spiritus*  One senses the impact of contemporary debate, though the notion of God's spirit is frequently present in Old Testament passages; cf. *Job* 33.4, 'spiritus Dei fecit me', etc.

215  *apud vos*  The plural suggests 'you and your ilk'; and since Malchus threatens to seek royal help, the implication is that the Sanhedrin or Council, of which Gamaliel was an influential member, was unwilling to persecute John.

## NOTES

216 *regium* The prologue summarised the action as the oppression of the Baptist 'regia libidine et invidorum subdolis calumniis' (39–40). The *calumniae* are those of Malchus; the *regia libido* is now to become a positive force in the action. In the context of the sixteenth century, the parallel is the appeal of one religious leader against another to the authority of the king.

219 *obnubilat* The word is commonly found in Augustine and Gregory in this sense; see *TLL*.

220 *auremque . . . obstruit* So Virgil, *Aen.* 4.440, 'placidasque viri deus obstruit auris'.

223 *furentem* There is a splendid irony here; the Malchus who believes that John's *furor* will bring anarchy is himself stigmatized as the embodiment of the same madness.

228 *coetus* Though Malchus and Gamaliel are both rabbis, the word probably embraces the whole Jewish 'establishment' of elders, priests and scribes who composed the Sanhedrin.

232 *auro,* etc. Throughout this speech, and especially in lines 231–51, Gamaliel paints a vivid picture of what the realities of everyday life must have been like at certain periods of the Reformation; yet if B. is speaking from experience and not just from hearsay or imagination, the scenes described seem more appropriate to the later period, the time of the civil and religious wars. It is possible that this speech was added (or modified and augmented) when he came to revise the speech for publication. It seems at any rate to reflect the conditions of 1577 more closely than those of 1540. The speech develops the theme of the manipulation of the royal power by religious leaders, whose calumnies find fertile soil in the king's fearful predispositions.

249 *concoqui* Cf. Livy 40.11.2, 'clandestina concocta sunt consilia'. The whole of this sentence describes the conspiratorial preparations in terms of Sallust's account of the Catilinarian conspiracy.

257 *delatoribus* The theme of the corrupting effects of *delatio,* so prominent in the religious courts of B.'s day, is obsessively present in Tacitus, Pliny and others who document the history of the Julio–Claudian emperors and of Domitian; Trajan's well-publicised discouragement of such practices was a main plank of his popularity.

266 *prophetam* Gamaliel accepts the popular idea of John which Malchus rejects; see Luke 1.76 and Matt. 11.9.

274–5 *innocuo . . . sancti* The adjectives suggest that Gamaliel rejects the second possibility (in 270f.) that John is a trickster.

275 *prodigus* So Ovid, *Amores* 3.9.64, 'sanguinis atque animae prodige Galle tuae'.

278 *immanitatis* Malchus stigmatized Herod's reign as cruel (cf. 65); Gamaliel stresses even more strongly the king's savage nature, and the final line prepares us for a character whose madness is uncontrolled. But Herod fails to give this impression on his appearance. There are bewildering inconsistencies in the characters of both the king and the queen; B. gives the impression of having written his play in self-contained acts.

281–344. FIRST CHORAL ODE. This ode in the sapphic metre reflects on the events of the first act by psychological observation of the character of Malchus. In the contrast drawn between the surface manifestations and the hidden demons lurking beneath, the Chorus immediately indicates its *parti pris* in support of John.

290 *unicum ... specimen* So Tacitus, *Ann.* 3.4, 'unicum antiquitatis specimen'.

291f. *aestuat,* etc. In these two lines B. evokes Virgil's celebrated psychological picture of Turnus at *Aen.* 12.666ff., 'aestuat ingens/uno in corde pudor mixtoque insania luctu/et furiis agitatus amor ...'

293 *Aetnaeis* Seneca adverts repeatedly to Aetna and Vesuvius in his letters and in his *Natural Questions,* and this interest spills over into his tragedies, especially the *Phaedra,* which has probably inspired B. here; cf. 102, 'qualis Aetnaeo vapor/exundat antro'; at 177ff. the speech of Phaedra uses the image in a discussion of *furor,* as here.

296 *Vesevum* for the form, cf. Statius, *Silvae* 4.8.5, Valerius Flaccus 4.507.

297 *caecus furor* So Horace, *Epod.* 7.13, 'furorne caecus ... ?'

299 *nudam* The image of truth (and virtue) unadorned is pervasive both in this play (cf. 485) and in *Jephthes* (898, 938, 1054, 1080n.). It is also prominent in the poems. B. may be recalling Christian sentiments such as that of Lactantius, *Inst.* 3.1.3, 'veritas ... ornamentis additis fucata corrumpitur'.

302 *vano ... fastu* Martial 4.11.1 'dum nimium vano tumefactus nomine gaudes'; Claudian 26.551, 'vanos fastus'.

306 *blandis ... venenis* Sil. Ital. 3.580 'blando veneno'; cf. also Statius, *Silvae* 3.2.119, 'blando qua mersa veneno' (of Cleopatra).

308 *pectoris aulam* The image is frequent in the Fathers as a result of the Pauline view of the pure heart as the temple of the Spirit; so Leo, *Serm.* 19.1, 'anima ... in aula mentis'.

310–11 *quae ... hospes* The literary allusion has here made for ambiguity. Juvenal 6.1–20 suggests that *pudicitia* is the virtue that stayed latest ('credo pudicitiam Saturno rege moratam/in terris

NOTES

. . . paulatim deinde ad superos Astraea recessit/hac comite . . .'). But *pudor* has already been mentioned in 309, and B. is more probably thinking here of *iustitia* as it is evoked in Virgil, *Georg.* 2.472f., 'extrema per illos/iustitia excedens terris vestigia fecit'. Moreover, *fides* and *iustitia* are always closely associated ('fundamentum iustitiae est fides', Cicero, *Off.* 1.23).

316 *penetrale mentis*   The phrase is in Ambrose, *In Luc.* 1.5.105. The combination of *penetrale* and *penitus* (315) intensifies the image of the depths of the subconscious at which these monsters operate.

317 *variata*   Cf. 1n.

318 *stabulare*   Cf. Ovid, *Met.* 13.822, 'multae stabulantur in antris'.

320–21 *Libyeque . . . feta*   Cf. Varro Atacinus fr. 19M. 'feta feris Libye'.

322 *Caucasus*   Cf. Ennodius, *carm.* 43.23, 'cautibus horrens/Caucasus', an imitation of Virgil, *Aen.* 4.366f., 'sed duris genuit de cautibus horrens/Caucasus, Hyrcanaeque admorunt ubera tigres'. Mention of *tigris* here in 323 suggests that the Virgilian passage is in B.'s mind.

323–4 *tigris . . . leaenae*   Cf. Virgil, *Georg.* 2.151f., 'at rabidae tigres absunt et saeva leonum/semina'.

327–9 *basiliscus . . . aspis*   The combination suggests that *Ps.* 90.13, 'super aspidem et basiliscum ambulabis', inspired these lines. Pliny, *H.N.* 29.66 writes 'olfactu necantem' of the basilisk, which is similar to 'venenata aura' here. These monsters are assembled also in B.'s Ode to Queen Elizabeth (*Fratres Fraterrimi* 5.29ff.): 'super dracones fortis inambula,/saevam leonum frange ferociam;/per aspides erra, et per oras/quas Libycus basiliscus afflat.'

328 *ferens soporem*   So Lucan 9.701, 'aspida somniferam'.

329–30 *caudae . . . telo*   Cf. Ovid, *Met.* 15.371, 'scorpius exibit caudaque minabitur unca'.

330 *lacrimisque fictis*   The cliché of crocodile tears is not mentioned by Pliny or Isidore, but it was widespread in the 16thC. Cf. Erasmus, *Adagia* 2.4.60, 'Crocodili lachrymae', but with no specific source-citations ('sunt qui scribant . . . alii narrant'). Also Francis Bacon, Essay 23 ('It is the wisdom of the crocodiles, that shed tears when they would devour.').

332–3 *fallax ludus hyaenae*   The hyena was thought to change its sex annually; cf. Pliny, *H.N.* 8.105, 'alternis annis mares, alternis feminas fieri'. So also Ovid, *Met.* 15.410; Tertullian, *Pall.* 3.

334 *ficta crudeles*   The catalogue of monsters lying deep within the heart epitomises the cruelty and duplicity of a king like Herod; the reason why B. introduces the bizarre images of crocodile and hyena is because with the fox they offer a trinity of deception.

335  *stola fimbriata*  The fringed robe is the dress of Jewish priests; cf. 2 *Macc.* 3.15, Matt. 23.5, 'dilatant enim phylacteria sua, et magnificant fimbrias'.
336  *in panno tenui*  So Juvenal 7.145, 'rara in tenui facundia panno'.
337  *nuda . . . virtus*  299n. For the Horatian inspiration, see *C.* 3.2.21, 3.5.29; cf. *Jephthes* 633, 1085, and below, 1149.
339  *insanosque fori tumultus*  The following lines are inspired especially by Virgil's praise of country life at *Georg.* 2.458ff.; for this phrase, cf. 2.502, 'insanumque forum'.
340  *popularis aurae*  So Horace, *C.* 3.2.20, 'arbitrio popularis aurae'.
341–2  *cliens . . . adsidet*  Cf. Juvenal 10.161, 'mirandusque cliens sedet ad praetoria regis'; Virgil, *Georg.* 2.461, 'foribus domus alta superbis'.

345–572. ACT II. This second act consists of two main scenes. In the first, a dialogue between Herod and his second wife (and niece) Herodias, the king is depicted as the more moderate figure who is the victim of pressure from an unscrupulous spouse. B. has made this inference from Matt. 14.8–9. The second scene is the dialogue between Herod and John. Though Herod is at pains to appear reasonable and benevolent, his speech after John's departure shows that he is motivated wholly by the desire to preserve his power.
354  *conventicula*  In this derogatory sense the word is found chiefly in the Fathers to describe heretical groups; see *TLL* s.v.
361  *hypocritis*  The word is frequent in the Vulgate in this secondary sense of 'hypocrites'.
363  *gramineum torum*  So Iuvencus 3.84, 'gramineisque toris'; Ausonius, *Ep.* 2.15, 'gramineos nunc frango toros'; cf. Ovid, *Fasti* 1.402.
371  *tyrannus . . . regi*  The classic distinction on these lines is given by Cicero at *Rep.* 2.47ff.
377  *concitatur*  Since there is little or no foundation for the queen's argument, we are reminded of Gamaliel's words, 'falsis regias rumoribus/implemus aures' (234f.).
387  *lugubri*  Cf. Horace, *C.* 2.1.33f. 'aut quae flumina lugubris/ignara belli?'.
391  *frena legum*  Cf. Lucan 2.145f., 'tum data libertas odiis resolutaque legum/frenis ira ruit.'
393  *atque ecce*  It is at this point that John makes his entry on to the stage. There is perhaps some dramatic weakness in the fact that he has to wait until the queen's exit and the end of Herod's long speech before he speaks himself. Yet this does mean that he is shown in a position of

# NOTES

inferiority and humility in the presence of those who are to decide his fate.

406   In this long speech of Herod and in his dialogue with John we see the king's weak and vacillating character; in defending himself to John he changes his attitude, showing that he is a time-server who talks differently to different people.

412   *universae plebis odium,* etc.   This trinity of allegations, that John has incurred the hatred of the common folk, the anger of leaders, and the annoyance of the priests, is the exact opposite of the complaint of Malchus at 97–8. The ordering of the syntax in these two passages indicates that Herod is being characterised either as a credulous man relying on calumniating advisers or (more probably) as a man of duplicity, in keeping with the sentiments of the previous chorus.

414   See 97n.

417   *laceras*   An echo of Malchus' *lacerat* at 104.

420   *regni*   Again this argument has already been used by Malchus (169–70). In this speech John is repeatedly depicted as a Christ-figure who suffers the attacks which Christ suffered.

422–3   *parere . . . parere*   These charges, rebutted by John in the ensuing speech, form part of the calumnies directed at his person.

429   *absens*   This takes up the point made by the queen at 354 concerning John's secret plotting.

430   *impudicas . . . nuptias*   Herod had divorced his wife, the daughter of Aretas king of the Nabataeans, to marry Herodias, wife of his half-brother Philip (the *fratrem* of 432). This was contrary to *Leviticus* 18.16 and 20.21. Cf. Matt. 14.1–12, Mark 6.14–29.

438   *lentumque*   Once again Herod echoes the word of the queen (cf. 345).

444   *Assyrius*   Malchus had already (64) mentioned that Herod was half-Arab; but since his ancestor embraced the Jewish religion, Herod claims to be a compatriot.

445   *et patria*   There is a striking parallel at Cicero, *Flacc.* 26, 'eorum eadem terra parens, altrix, patria dicatur'.

463   *cuncta credere*   It is striking that the first words uttered by John warn Herod of the falsehoods to which he is occupationally exposed.

471   *occulte*   This rebuts the charges made not only by Herod (429) but also by his queen at 354.

472   *latebras*   Cf. Virgil, *Aen.* 3.424, 'at Scyllam caecis cohibet spelunca latebris'.

474   *milites*   See Luke 3.14, 'interrogabant autem eum et milites dicentes: Quid faciemus et nos? Et ait illis: Neminem concutiatis neque

## THE BAPTIST

calumniam faciatis: et contenti estote stipendiis vestris.' It is surprising that B. does not reproduce the word *calumniam,* which is rendered by 'dolo circumvenire improvidos'.

475 *servire* Cf. Matt. 22.21, where Christ answers a similar question.

479 *novarum . . . rerum* The immediate sense which this phrase registers is that of revolution; John is rebutting the charge made by Herod at 424ff. But it may be possible for the reader to interpret the king's words in the sixteenth-century sense of a religious renewal resting on the Christian equivalent of the authority of the prophets, namely the gospel.

485 *nuda . . . veritas* See 299n.

489 *praeclarus index* John was not present when Malchus denounced him to Gamaliel, but the audience is to assume that John knows of his hostility.

489 *palam* It will be remembered that Gamaliel had urged Malchus to speak out openly; cf. 185.

491 *negavi* Cf. Luke 3.19, 'cum corriperetur ab illo de Herodiade uxore fratris sui . . .'

493 *tibi . . . an deo* It is at this point of the play that the resemblance between John and Thomas More is especially notable; Introduction, p. 11f. Roper in his life of More recalls that Thomas reminded Henry of 'the most virtuous lesson that prince ever taught servant: willing him first to look unto God, and after God unto him'.

500–501 *aequum . . . aequitatis . . . aequi . . . aequus* John repeats the claim which Herod makes about himself (449, *aequum iudicem*) but the accumulation of four citations in two lines reveals an ironical purpose.

502 *fines* John quotes with devastating effect Herod's own words to his wife at 398f.

511 *patriam* The notion of heaven as our true *patria,* so pervasive in Christian and medieval writing, has its forebears in such passages as Cicero, *Tusc.* 1.51, where heaven is described as our *domus.*

515 *populos . . . deo* Cf. Horace, *C.* 3.1.5f., 'regum timendorum in proprios greges,/reges in ipsos imperium est Iovis'.

517 *perplexa* John's appeal to the authority of God does not seem to touch Herod at all. The complexity is rather political, since Herod does not know how far he can disregard the wishes of the people (v. 542).

518 *nihil decernere* Herod conveys the impression of wise caution though in a sense he is simply following Gamaliel's advice at 109 and 267; but the ensuing comment of the Chorus counsels against taking this at surface value. *abditos* (520) contrasts with the ingenuous openness of John (471); there is irony in the fact that the man who accuses John of

NOTES

secret plotting is himself a master of hidden wiles. These words of the Chorus are to be envisaged as spoken out of Herod's hearing.

524   *quam misera*   The theme is handled also in *Jephthes;* see there 628n. John has now returned to prison, and in soliloquy Herod becomes more self-revealing.

533   *persona honesta*   The whole of this sentence lays bare Herod's true interests, and provides the key to his purposes in the dialogue with John.

545   *ipse mihi sum proximus*   This is Herod's cynical answer to the question posed to Christ and answered with the parable of the Good Samaritan (Luke 10.29ff.). Though the issue has not been in serious doubt in the minds of the bystanders, this is the moment of decision at which Herod decides that John must die (550 *nunc stat cruore* . . .). When he is later appalled by the request of his wife's daughter for John's head, it is not the murder to which he is opposed, but to the manner of it, which would stigmatise him as a murderer for trivial reasons.

552   *serpere malum*   The phrase is a cliché in Cicero, but usually with *longius;* Livy frequently writes *serpere latius* (e.g., 28.15.16).

558   *captis*   Presumably Herod and the royal entourage.

567   *garriat*   The contempt which the king entertains for the bruised susceptibilities and religious niceties of Malchus is an important thread in the characterisation of Herod; he reveals his single-minded obsession to be the retention of power.


573–623. SECOND CHORAL ODE.   As has been noted in *Jephthes* (341n.), B. in such invocations to the Creator is inspired partly by the classical tragedians (notably Seneca), partly by Christian hymnology. In this ode in anapaestic dimeters, the Chorus reviews the previous history of the divine protection accorded to Israel, and begs God to renew it.

575   *caelum . . . aptum*   So Virgil, *Aen.* 11.202, 'caelum stellis fulgentibus aptum', in imitation of Lucretius 6.357.

577   *tumidum . . . aequor*   Cf. Ovid, *Met.* 14.544, 'tumidum subitis concursibus aequor'. Cf. also Virgil, *Aen.* 3.157.

594   *duce et auspice*   See Horace, *C.* 1.7.27, 'nil desperandum Teucro duce et auspice Teucro'.

598   *fabula*   For the sense of 'has been', cf. Terence, *Hec.* 620f., 'nos iam fabulae/sumus, Pamphile'.

601   *victima*   In this sense John's impending death will symbolise the sacrifice of the Jewish people.

611–12   *aequore . . . Rubro*   See *Exod.* 14.15ff.

613–14   *vatis fatidici . . . puer*   The reference is to the servant of the prophet Eliseus (Elisha) at *4 Kings* 6.8ff., esp. 17–18: 'cumque orasset Eliseus, ait: Domine, aperi oculos huius ut videat. Et aperuit Dominus oculos pueri, et vidit: et ecce mons plenus equorum et curruum igneorum in circuitu Elisei. hostes vero descenderunt ad eum . . .'. B. characteristically describes the prophet in the terms of Roman epic; for *vatis fatidici,* cf. *Aen.* 8.340, 'vatis fatidicae', and Ovid, *Met.* 3.348.

615 *igniferis . . . quadrigis* Cf. Seneca, *Medea* 33f., 'committe habenas, genitor, et flagrantibus/ignifera loris tribue moderari iuga'.

617 *caligine . . . erroris* Cf. Cicero, *Tusc.* 5.6, 'hic error et haec indoctorum animis offusa caligo'; Jerome, *Ep.* 100.11, 'animas . . . ab omni errorum caligine separantes'. Images of light and darkness were very often used by humanists and reformers alike to denote the passage from the Middle Ages to the new enlightenment.

618–20 *qui . . . et quae* The curious combination of subjects is clumsy; B. may be saying that men in both east and west should acknowledge the one God, but *qua . . . qua* would have been clearer.

622 *rutilae . . . flammae* Cf. Ovid, *Fasti* 3.285, *Met.* 12.294f.

624–832. ACT 3. Malchus is alone on stage when the act opens. In his soliloquy he reveals the ineffectuality of his attempt to silence John, and the unpopularity which he has incurred in imprisoning him. He determines to attempt a reconciliation. John's prayer of praise to the Creator, glorifying the order of the natural world and lamenting the infidelity of man (especially of the Jewish nation) meets with Malchus' approval; but when John turns his attack against priests, scribes and elders, Malchus threatens reprisals.

Malchus appears in this speech as self-seeking, cruel and provincially-minded, yet aware that evil-doing does not always succeed. He is worried that his wicked treatment of John will misfire, and he even sees that it is already clear that he has not achieved his aims. He firmly believes that he is right, and shows considerable courage (*ceteris cunctantibus* 637) in defending the old Jewish tradition (*solus his umeris ego* 662). (This isolation is perhaps comparable with that of orthodox Catholics during the reformation years.) Yet in spite of these good qualities we are left with an impression of his selfishness (672 *ego sum mihi proximus,* echoing Herod at 545). This selfishness of Malchus contrasts with the selflessness of John and the *caritas* which the Chorus has just been advocating.

625 *optionem* This may be an echo of the controversy about free will which took place in the 1520s; cf. Erasmus, *De libero arbitrio* (1524); Luther, *De servo arbitrio* (1525). B. may also have known Charles de Bovelles, *De voto, libero arbitrio ac de differentia orationis* (1529).

## NOTES

627 *opes honores* Juvenal *Satire* 10 ('The vanity of human wishes') will be in B.'s mind.

633 *remotis . . . iugis* Matt. 3.1, 'praedicans in deserto Iudaeae'.

634 *fascinaret* Matt. 3.5, 'tunc exibat ad eum Ierosolyma et omnis Iudaea . . . et baptizabantur ab eo . . .' The use of the verb *fascinare* equates the activity of John with the witchcraft with which the Inquisition was frequently concerned in B.'s own day.

636 *Pharisaeae dignitatis* Matt. 3.7, 'videns autem multos Pharisaeorum . . . venientes ad baptismum suum, dixit eis: Progenies viperarum . . .'

638 *nec . . . desii* In the account of Matthew (14.3) there is no suggestion that John was imprisoned for any reason other than his criticism of Herod's marriage to Herodias; one wonders therefore whether this fictitious suggestion that Malchus had contrived the arrest was inspired by the part played by Cranmer in the arrest of More.

645 *letale virus* Echoing the words of Herod at 419.

660 *pseudoprophetam* A word taken over from the Vulgate (Zach. 13.2, Luke 6.26).

661 *rabini* The form Rabbi ('master', 'teacher') is used at John 3.26 in an address to John the Baptist, and Rabboni at Mark 10.51 in words to Christ; *rabini* does not seem to have appeared in Latin before the sixteenth century (so Latham's *Revised Medieval Latin Word-List*).

672 *mihi sum proximus* Cf. 545n. Though Malchus is a very different character from Herod, B. repeatedly attributes to them the same sentiments, as if to indicate an identical pattern of self-interest achieved by devious means.

678 *Gamalielis consilium* It is out of self-interest that Malchus at last comes round to Gamaliel's position, and is prepared to make peace with John. But this resolve does not survive the plain speaking which he is soon to endure from the prophet, and in any case the royal house is engineering John's death.

681 *re peracta* The murder of John.

684 *animi simplex* A convincing tribute, but there is some inconsistency in Malchus' view of John, whom he has labelled deceiving (*fefellit*, 90) and wild (*furens*, 166, etc.).

686 *machinas* Cf. Plautus, *Miles* 813, 'quantas res turbo, quantas moveo machinas!' In spite of his change of heart Malchus is just as ready to scheme.

688 *populum* Once again Malchus echoes the sentiments of Herod; cf. 551, 'vulgus facile post placabitur'.

694 *magister* Heavily ironical; Malchus retires out of sight to hear

this sermon. John's speech shows how the harmonious ordering of nature is shattered by man's rebelliousness, his self-will and his recourse to violence, all of which have a direct bearing on the plot of the play.

695 *O magne*  A clear reminiscence of Seneca, *H.F.* 205, 'O magne Olympi rector et mundi arbiter'.

696 *laxo sinu*  This is a cliché of Augustan poetry; cf. Tibullus 1.6.18; Ovid, *Rem.* 680, *Fasti* 4.436.

703 *albicantibus*  So Horace, *C.*1.4.4, 'nec prata canis albicant pruinis'.

705 *reciprocat*  Cf. Silius Italicus 15.226, 'refluusque reciprocat aestus', and see above, 577.

715 *frena legum*  Cf. 391n.

718 *principia*  It is clear from 734 and 757 that Malchus' comments of approval here and at 725 are asides; Malchus accepts John's general strictures on the sins of the chosen people, but bursts out angrily as soon as John attacks the priests. It is impossible not to see this also in the light of sixteenth-century events.

720–21 *die hereditatem*  Cf. *Ps.* 27.9, 'salvum fac populum tuum, Domine, et benedic hereditati tuae'; *Ps.* 32.12, 67.10, etc.

727 *Levita*  The regular form in the Fathers; cf. Prudentius *Peristeph.* 2.39, 5.30; Paulinus of Nola, *Ep.* 23.14, etc. The three groups impugned by John (priests, scribes and elders) are often associated in the gospels; they together interrogate Christ (Luke 22.66) and question the apostles (*Acts* 4.5ff.). Together they form the Sanhedrin or Council.

727  As Ruddiman notes, there is an anacoluthon here. It is explicable by the fact that B. thinks of the three groups as one, and addresses all in the vocative, leaving *vos* to be understood.

731 *viduae orphanique*  A common biblical combination (*Ps.* 67.6, Jer. 49.11); B. may be thinking of Matt. 23.14 (cf. Mark 12.40, Luke 20.47), where Christ attacks the scribes and pharisees for devouring 'the houses of widows'.

738 *pontifex*  Though this is an attack on the High Priest, it would certainly have been taken by B.'s contemporaries as a reference to the Pope and College of Cardinals.

739 *decimatis*  Cf. Matt. 23.23, 'Vae vobis Scribae et Pharisaei hypocritae qui decimatis mentham et anethum et cyminum, et reliquistis quae graviora sunt legis, judicium et misericordiam et fidem. haec oportuit facere, et illa non omittere.' The catalogue of plants has been taken over from the Elder Pliny's *Natural History* 19–22 as well as from Matthew.

741 *viride faenum*  Cf. Cassiodorus, *In. Psalm.* 101.5, 'tamquam viridia faena vegetamur'.

743f.  *sanctioris orbita . . . vitae*   Cf. Juvenal 14.37, 'veteris . . . orbita culpae'.

745   *canes*   Cf. Isa. 56.10, 'canes muti non valentes latrare, videntes vana, dormientes et amantes somnia'.

747   *lupos*   Cf. Matt. 7.15, 'attendite a falsis prophetis, qui veniunt ad vos in vestimentis ovium, intrinsecus autem sunt lupi rapaces'; cf. Matt. 10.16, Luke 10.3, *Acts* 20.29 ('lupi rapaces . . . non parcentes gregi'). There is also a reminiscence of the famous Virgilian simile at *Aen.* 9.59 ('pleno lupus insidiatus ovili/cum fremit ad caulas'); cf. *Georg.* 3.537.

748   *deglubitis*   This is a favourite image of B.; see e.g. *Franciscanus* 155. Cf. Suetonius, *Tib.* 32, 'praesidibus onerandas tributo provincias suadentibus rescripsit: "boni pastoris esse tondere pecus, non deglubere".' Even more striking is the parallel with Erasmus, *Adages* (Amsterdam 1650) pp. 518–19: 'hodie vulgo celebratum durat, ubi quis est exactor durior atque instantior. quid? num et pellem vis? quasi conveniat lana contentum esse. tondent igitur qui ita spoliant ut cutem relinquant unde res possit crescere, deglubunt qui nihil reliqui faciunt. nam lana detonsa renascitur: cute detracta nihil est quod deinde possis auferre.'

749   *sitim sedat*   So 362, 'unda cui sedat sitim'.

751   *maximam malam crucem*   This colloquial expression is Plautine; e.g., *Men.* 66 and 328.

754   *Olympo*   The Classical flavour is again notable.

758   *magister*   694n.

761   *sacerdotem*   The word is occasionally found in Christian Latin of the Jewish High Priest, but more commonly of a Christian priest, so that as at 738 the sixteenth-century reader could see a contemporary relevance.

766   *veritas*   299n.

770   *tot perire*   The basic premise of the Inquisitors.

776   *auctoritate*   B. stays close to the biblical account; cf. Matt. 3.1ff., Mark 1.1ff., Luke 3.1ff., and especially John 1.15ff. for the questions about John's identity.

778f.   *propheta . . . Helias*   Cf. Matt. 16.14, 'quem dicunt homines esse Filium hominis? at illi dixerunt: alii Joannem Baptistam, alii autem Eliam, alii vero Jeremiam aut unum ex prophetis'.

783   *vox sum*   The quotation from Isa. 40.3 is given more fully in Matt. 3.2, Mark 1.3, Luke 3.4.

792   *laqueos nectit*   Cf. Horace, *Epist.* 1.19.31, 'nec sponsae laqueum famoso carmine nectit'.

794   *miraculo*   It will be recalled that Christ was often asked for such

a sign of his authority (cf. Matt. 12.38, 16.1, 24.3, etc.). The present passage owes much to Matt. 21.23ff.: 'accesserunt ad eum docentem principes sacerdotum et seniores populi dicentes: In qua potestate haec facis? et quis tibi dedit hanc potestatem? respondens Iesus dixit eis: 'Interrogabo vos et ego unum sermonem: quem si dixeritis mihi, et ego vobis dicam in qua potestate haec facio. baptismus Ioannis unde erat? e caelo, an ex hominibus?'

798 *furorem* 102–5n.

800 *gloriamque* So also at 85, *cupitae gloriae*.

811 *honores et opes* Cf. 627n.

812 *nudare . . . ingenia* So Horace, *Sat.* 2.8.73f., 'ingenium res/ adversae nudare solent, celare secundae'.

814 *frena . . . permittere* Cf. Statius, *Theb.* 10.703, 'ne frena animo permitte calenti'.

818f. *non pessimus magister* Proverbial; cf. Pliny, *Ep.* 1.20.12, 'usus, magister egregius'; 6.29.4 'usum . . . optimum dicendi magistrum'.

822 *vera* Cf. John 8.46, 'si veritatem dico vobis, quare non creditis mihi?' and 18.23, 'si male locutus sum, testimonium perhibe de malo: si autem bene, quid me caedis?'

827 *longum . . . laetabere* So Orodes to Mezentius at Virgil, *Aen.* 10.740, 'nec longum laetabere'.

833–62. THIRD CHORAL ODE. This brief ode in iambic dimeters visualises Malchus as a man plunged in moral darkness and festering with hidden guilt. Brevity is appropriate as we approach the climax of the action; significantly Malchus remains on stage as the message is enuntiated.

837 *pharmaca* Used also at *Jephthes* 712.

838 *absinthio* The child's dislike of absinth is mentioned by Lucretius (1.935ff.), a favourite author of B.'s.

846 *fronte . . . taetrica* Cf. Martial, 10.64.2, 'non tetrica nostros excipe fronte iocos'.

854 *secreta rodens* B. has already used this phrase twelve lines earlier.

856–7 *exest . . . flagellans* The mixture of metaphors is not happy; an executioner may whip but not devour.

858 *o ter beatum* Cf. Virgil, *Aen.* 1.94, 'o terque quaterque beati/quis ante ora patrum Troiae sub moenibus altis/contigit oppetere'. Cf. *Jephthes* 1137.

859 *purus animi* An allusion to John's innocence; cf. 274–5, 684.

862 *tortore* The whole of this passage is inspired by Juvenal

NOTES

13.192ff., '. . . quos diri conscia facti/mens habet attonitos et surdo verbere caedit/occultum quatiente animo tortore flagellum'.

863–965. ACT 4. Malchus is disillusioned with Herod's Machiavellian tactics, and turns to the queen as his main hope for destroying John. In the dialogue which follows he seeks to convince her that the prophet's imprisonment and subsequent release will not achieve the desired end of quelling the threat to the royal house. It is perhaps a weakness in the construction of the play that Malchus was not present to overhear Herod's resolve to dispose of John (550) whilst pouring scorn on Malchus' own concerns; the events of this act do not proceed from what has gone before.

865–6 *gratiae . . . auram* Cf. Cicero, *Sest.* 101, 'honoris aura', etc.

867 *supponere* Malchus had earlier shown exactly the same desire to keep the blame off himself (cf. 687).

873 *factionis* Malchus clings to his view of John as political revolutionary; 249n.

876 *alterna* The political scene is visualised in Roman terms as a struggle of the two orders, with John leading the *populares* and the Sanhedrin representing the *optimates* or *boni*. Herod is described as playing off one against the other.

881 *popularis aura* Cf. 340n.

886 *tigris orba* Cf. Statius, *Silv.* 2.1.8f., 'citius me tigris abactis/ fetibus orbatique velint audire leones.'

888 *non probaverit* See 430n.

893 *commode* The queen's entrance is rather *too* convenient! The chorus visualises the combination of Malchus' and the queen's intrigues as the *ultimum periculum*. It is not necessarily a dramatic weakness that there is no historical evidence for such a development in the action; but the influence of Malchus is hardly mentioned in the later denouement.

In this dialogue the queen is initially non-committal and forces Malchus to declare himself. The gradual unfolding of their respective attitudes soon leads to their agreement. Malchus makes clear his attitude towards the weakness of the king by saying that she alone is worthy to rule; the queen simulates a state of doubt quite out of character with her earlier anger, allowing herself to be persuaded by Malchus, whose deviousness remains constant throughout the play.

918 *latroni* The derogatory label, combined with the subsequent image of John as a caged beast, reveals that Malchus himself is deranged and captive to the *furor* of which here (919, 925) and so often earlier he accuses John.

926   *quin lenietur*   Such argumentation, which is wholly inconsistent with the earlier character and motivation of the queen and with her later attitudes, is perhaps explicable by the queen's desire not to appear vindictive or hate-filled before a subject; Herod's description of the trials and tribulations of a monarch in cloaking his feelings (532ff.) would support this interpretation.

933   *quod bene*   Cf. Sallust, *Jug.* 31.28, 'multo praestat benefici quam malefici immemorem esse'.

940   *pravo ambitu*   Malchus has already used the phrase of Herod's desire for popularity at 864; when he repeatedly uses *tuus* (937, 939) in this speech, he associates the queen with the royal crown.

944   *fregeris quam flexeris*   Cf. Quintilian 1.3.12, 'frangas enim citius quam corrigas quae in pravum induruerunt' (*induruit* in 943 shows that this is in B.'s mind); Ovid, *A.A.* 2.179f., 'flectitur obsequio curvatus ab arbore ramus;/frangis, si vires experiare tuas.'

953   *labor*   Cf. Virgil, *Georg.* 1.145f. 'labor omnia vicit/improbus'; this was often quoted by Renaissance educationalists, and was the motto of Peter Ramus.

957   *tempus expedit*   A cliché of ancient as of modern thought; B. may have in mind Ovid's poem about time's healing hand at *Tristia* 4.6.

965   *desistere*   At the end of the scene the queen passes no comment on Malchus' final advice; we are left with the assumption that she has been expecting it throughout, but that her royal position does not allow her to lend open assent. Death is not mentioned, but the intended outcome of her persuasion of Herod is not in doubt.

966–96.   FOURTH CHORAL ODE.   In this sequence of glyconics, the Chorus brings out the unholy alliance of Malchus' calumny and the despotic power of the royal house, and contrasts with this the innocence and impregnable devotion to truth of John.

966f.   *livor . . . dolor*   The malice is that of Malchus, the resentment the queen's; compare 408.

970   *calumnia*   The chorus clearly regards the falsehoods of Malchus as the more reprehensible; hence the alternative title of this play (cf. 13n.).

973   *innoxia veritas*   The faces of truth, as B. frequently suggests (299n.), can differ; his emphasis on the truth which is without armed support or worldly pomp may obliquely reflect on the apparatus of the Inquisition.

979   *tunsa*   At Horace, *C.* 4.4.57f. we read 'duris ut ilex tonsa bipennibus/nigrae feraci frondis in Algido'. B. has adapted the motif and

changed the verb, combining the image of the wind-beaten oak with that of the rock, familiar from such passages as Virgil, *Aen.* 5.124ff., 'saxum . . . quod tumidis submersum *tunditur* olim/fluctibus'.

981   *remeabili*   Cf. *Jephthes* 830n.

985   *candida Veritas*   For the personification, cf. Martial 10.72.11, 'siccis rustica Veritas capillis', where the image of Truth unadorned harmonises with B.'s conception.

997–1109. ACT 5.   In this brief scene John expresses to the Chorus his longing to escape from this world; nothing could be in greater contrast to the picture of the ambitious demagogue painted by Malchus.

1004   *inops*   The queen has successfully given this impression on her last appearance with Malchus rather than earlier.

1006   *mussant dicere*   So Virgil, *Aen.* 11.344f., 'cuncti se scire fatentur . . . sed dicere mussant'.

1007   *tempus instat*   The chorus repeats for the benefit of John what it has already said at 895.

1014   *salutem*   There may be a play on the double sense of *salus* here as 'safety' and 'salvation'; John neglects his personal safety, but the Chorus begs him ponder their eternal welfare, which will be endangered if his prophetic role is cut off.

1017   *flecte*   The same advice which Malchus gave to the queen (cf. 961). *per amicos* must refer to advisers with the attitude of Gamaliel.

1024   *auctor*   The idiom is common in popular speech; cf. Plautus, *Pseud.* 231; *Poen.* 410.

1030   *corpus . . . perdere*   Cf. Matt. 10.28, 'et nolite timere eos qui occidunt corpus, animam autem non possunt occidere; sed potius timete eum qui potest et animam et corpus perdere in gehennam.' This text was often used by B.'s contemporaries as a proof of the immortality of the soul.

1036   *placabilis*   See *Nehem.* 9.17; cf. *Jephthes* 436.

1044   *momentanea*   Cf. *2 Cor.* 4.17, 'id enim quod in praesenti est momentaneum et leve tribulationis nostrae, supra modum in sublimitate aeternum gloriae pondus operatur in nobis'.

1045   *deus lucis*   Cf. 1. John 1.5, 'quoniam deus lux est'; James 1.17, 'deus luminum'.

1048   *nunquam orphanus*   So John 14.18, 'non relinquam vos orphanos'.

1053   *fata*   A classical expression for Christian providence (cf. *Prov.* 8.23, 'ab aeterno ordinata sum, et ex antiquis antequam terra fieret'; *2 Thess.* 2.13). To the sixteenth-century reader this would have a ring of predestination about it.

## THE BAPTIST

1054   *lucis . . . almae*   A cliché in Augustan poetry; cf. Virgil, *Aen.* 1.306, 3.311, etc.

1055   *tendimus*   These sentiments may be inspired by those of Orpheus to the gods below at Ovid, *Met.* 10.33f., '. . . serius aut citius sedem properamus ad unam./tendimus huc omnes, haec est domus ultima'.

1061   *renatos*   Cf. John 3.5, 'Amen, amen dico tibi, nisi quis renatus fuerit ex aqua et spiritu sancto, non potest introire in regnum Dei.'

1065   *carceres*   There is a successful play here with *carcer* in 1062; the body is the prison of the soul, but it is also the starting-barrier from which the soul hastens to the *meta* of heaven.

1070   *tesca*   So Horace, *Ep.* 1.14.19, 'deserta et inhospita tesqua'. It is used by B. also at *Miscell.* 3.11, 'per tesqua Maurorum'.

1071–2   *tramite decurso*   Cf. *2 Tim.* 4.7, 'cursum consummavi'.

1078   *mobilis caeli*   Cf. Virgil, *Georg.* 1.417, 'caeli mobilis umor'.

1087   *horrens Caucasus*   Cf. 322n.

1094   *liber*   The word is repeated from 1073, and with the powerful imagery of 1097 depicts John's longing to be rid of the encumbrance of the body.

1095   *quo cunctus . . . serius ocius*   So Horace, *C.* 2.3.25ff., 'omnes eodem cogimur, omnium/versatur urna serius ocius/sors exitura, et nos in aeternum/exsilium impositura cumbae.'

1102   *sinu recepta*   Cf. Lucan 7.810f., 'placido natura receptat/cuncta sinu'.

1109   *salve valeque*   Recalling the poignant address of Catullus to his dead brother (101.10), 'atque in perpetuum, frater, ave atque vale'.

1110–65. FIFTH CHORAL ODE.   This is an extended meditation, in the metre of the lesser asclepiad, on the blessings which death brings, and on the illusory attractions of continuing life.

1121ff.   *nec toti morimur,* etc.   There is a sustained reminiscence of Horace, *C.* 3.30.6f. here: 'non omnis moriar multaque pars mei/vitabit Libitinam . . . dum Capitolium/scandet . . . pontifex'. This celebrated epilogue to *Odes* I–III was imitated by Ovid in the epilogue to his *Metamorphoses* 15.871ff., and B. at 1122ff. (et aethera . . .) clearly has in mind *Met.* 875f., 'parte tamen meliore mei super alta perennis/astra ferar . . .'. For *rogos . . . avidos,* cf. Ovid, *Amores* 3.9.28, 'diffugiunt avidos carmina sola rogos'.

1127–9   *Eumenides . . . Cerberi . . . Tantali*   The celebrated passage of Lucretius pouring scorn on these imaginary figures of Hell is clearly in B.'s mind; Lucretius 3.966, 'nec quisquam in barathrum nec Tartara deditur atra', may lie behind 1126 'sulphureo in lacu', and Lucretius has Cerberus and the Furies together at 3.1011. But Tantalus a little earlier (3.980f., 'nec miser impendens magnum timet aëre saxum/Tantalus') is pictured differently. Ovid, *Met.* 4.450ff. likewise has Cerberus and the Furies together, and Tantalus ('tibi, Tantale, nullae/deprenduntur aquae', 458f.) follows shortly afterwards. Ovid's description evokes the punitive Hell of Virgil's *Aeneid* (6.548ff.). It is safe to say that B. has all three descriptions in mind when he composes these lines.

1133   *Siren*   The symbolism of the Sirens in earlier classical and Christian literature is well treated by H. Rahner, *Greek Myths and Christian Mystery* (London 1962), ch. 7. In general they represent the twin hazards of sensual pleasure and knowledge. Although the dangers which they symbolise were already signalled in Greek literature, B. may have in mind such passages from Roman satire as Horace, *Sat.* 2.3.14 and Juvenal 14.19.

1133   *magicis illecebris*   So Apuleius, *Apol.* 34, 'ad illecebras magicas'.

1139   *rauco reboant*   Perhaps recalling Lucretius 4.546, (tuba) 'reboat raucum . . . bombum'.

1144f.   *otio torpescat*   So Sallust, *Cat.* 16.3, 'ne per otium torpescerent manus'.

1148   *almaque faustitas*   So Horace, *C.* 4.5.18, 'nutrit rura Ceres almaque Faustitas'.

1149   *simplex probitas*   This recalls the character of John as described throughout the play.

1158   *Lethes somniferae*   Cf. Ovid, *Trist.* 4.1.47, 'utque soporiferae biberem si pocula Lethes'.

1161   *vanesce*   Cf. Tacitus, *Hist.* 5.7, 'velut in cinerem vanescunt'.

1165   *anxiferis*   Cicero uses this word twice in his verses, once in his *De consulatu* quoted at *Div.* 1.22, 'tu tamen anxiferas curas requiete relaxas'. B. uses the word also in *Medea* 1358; *Franciscanus* 464.

1166–1263. ACT 6. The long speech of John (1051ff.) and the Choral Ode which follows may have heightened the suspense by delaying the resolution of the action, but the philosophical and theological generalisations are long drawn-out and weaken the impact of the sequence of events. By contrast the queen's speech here returns to the simplicity of the familiar gospel account (Matt. 14.1–12, Mark 6.14–29, Luke 3.19–20, 9.7–9), and the tempo immediately picks up. But it is here above all that the gospel-story appears inadequate for Aristotelian demands of drama, because the action which now ensues does not develop inevitably from what precedes, but is the result of a whim of the queen's daughter—encouraged, it is true, by the queen, but opposed by Herod in spite of his earler resolution to remove John.

1166 *Pharisaeus . . . fefellit* It is hard to see the queen's reason for this judgment on Malchus, who in the exchange at 863ff. has urged her to persuade the king to execute John. But she has perhaps hoped that Malchus would personally intervene with the king, or mount an agitation to have John removed.

1168 *timet* So Matt. 14.5, 'et volens eum occidere, timuit populum; quia sicut prophetam eum habebant'.

1168 *rumusculos* Cf. Cicero, *Clu.* 105, *Leg.* 3.35.

1179 *atrocem* A favourite Tacitean epithet for the woman of violence; cf. *Ann.* 4.52, 14.61.

1202 *remedium* Herod's weakness (cf. 1167) is seen in the fact that he immediately thinks of the reaction of the people.

1205 *aequum* Herod himself has already said much the same thing; cf. 571f.

1214 *timeri, diligi* Cf. Cicero, *Off.* 1.97 (quoting from a lost play), 'oderint dum metuant'.

1219 *videre* The queen addresses Herod and not the girl, as is clear from what follows.

1223 *civis hostis* In the three other pairs the bonds are obvious, but this final pair have a relationship with each other rather than a bond.

1227 *turpe . . . utile* These are the staple terms of moral philosophy as discussed by Cicero, *turpe* being the antonym of *honestum;* see, e.g., *Off.* 2.9, 'consuetudo . . . eo deducta est ut honestatem ab utilitate secernens constitueret esse honestum aliquid quod utile non esset, et utile quod non honestum, qua nulla pernicies maior hominum vitae potuit afferri.'

1236 *civicum bellum* These suggestions of destruction, pillage and civil war seem outrageously irrelevant in the biblical context; B.'s vision must be affected by contemporary events. This sentence raises interesting possibilities of a revision of the text between composition and publication; at the time the play was produced the remark could have been only prophetic, but at the time of publication it was quite apposite.

1241 *da coniugi* B. thus provides an interconnexion between the acts of the play, with Malchus putting persuasion on the queen, and the queen pressurising the king. But since the playwright simultaneously seeks to be faithful to the gospel accounts, the links between the acts seem half-hearted; the queen's intervention here is given less emphasis than the king's promise to her daughter. Yet that promise is extraneous to the main themes of Malchus' calumny and the tyranny of the royal house.

1247 *iurasse temere* This recalls the whole situation of the *Jephthes*. Like Jephtha, Herod admits that his promise was rash, but there is no going back on it.

1250 *veritas* There is a heavy irony here; John, who is truth incarnate, falls to another species of truth, fidelity to a rash vow. In an important passage in his *De officiis* (3.95f.) Cicero discusses the morality of such rash vows; amongst his *exempla* is the vow of Agamemnon to sacrifice Iphigenia, on which he comments: 'promissum potius non faciendum quam tam taetrum facinus admittendum fuit. ergo et promissa non facienda non nunquam, neque semper deposita reddenda.' The irony is all the more pronounced in the mouth of the queen, who has just proclaimed the priority of *utile* over *honestum* (1227f.).

1257 *vestra illa culpa* This recalls Pilate's statement to the Jews at Matt. 27.24, 'innocens ego sum a sanguine iusti huius: vos videritis'. Herod's final words characterise him not as tyrant but as weak and timorous; again the facts of the gospel accounts outweigh the theme of cruel tyranny for which we were earlier (65, 278ff., 334, etc.) prepared.

1262 *iniquave* In this her final utterance the queen drops any pretence that she has been concerned with justice; her sole concern is the upholding of the dignity of the royal house. In this sense B. rescues the theme of the cruel tyranny of the royal house; it is wielded not so much by Herod as by the queen.

1264–1315. SIXTH CHORAL ODE. Here the Chorus declaims in sapphics the vices of fellow-Jews, and prophesies the future destruction of Jerusalem. An appeal for repentance is choked with the despairing realisation that it will be disregarded.

1264 *Solymaeque* See *Jephthes* 151n.

1267 *sanguinis iusti sitis* For the theme of the spilling of just blood, see especially Matt. 27.4, where Judas says 'peccavi tradens sanguinem iustum', and the O.T. passages (*Ps.* 93.21, Isa. 59.7, etc.) with which the Matthew passage is linked. For the Classical formulation of the idea, cf. Ovid, *Met.* 13.768, 'caedis amor feritasque, sitisque immensa cruoris'.

1269 *unicum ... specimen* Cf. 290n.

1274ff. *cultor idoli* This section of the Ode incorporates themes and language already noted in the *Jephthes* (362n.) where it is much more obviously relevant to the idolatry of the Ammonites. It is difficult to see why such idolatry should be incorporated amongst the sins of first-century Jerusalem. It is accordingly reasonable to infer that B. is exploiting the stock Christian arguments against the religious practices of pagan Romans to pass oblique criticism on religious practices of his own day. One may compare *Fratres Fraterrimi,* 'Imago ad peregre venientes religionis ergo', 'Ad idolorum cultorem', 'In eundem'.

1276   *Lignum . . . lapisque*   See *Jephthes* 362n.

1278   *simulacra adorat*   B. may have in mind the commands at *Exod.* 34.15, 'ne ineas pactum cum hominibus illarum regionum; ne, cum . . . adoraverint simulacra eorum, vocet te quisquam ut comedas de immolatis'.

1282   *ritus . . . vetusti*   An ambiguous phrase in the context of the Reformation, when there was much discussion about what were to be considered the old rites. But the preceding lines suggest that these words are reinforcing charges of idolatry, and that the phrase harks back to the practices of the early Church.

1283   *cruor*   Cf. Matt. 23.29ff., 'vae vobis scribae et Pharisaei hypocritae, qui aedificatis sepulchra prophetarum, et ornatis monumenta iustorum, et dicitis: Si fuissemus in diebus patrum nostrorum, non essemus socii eorum in sanguine prophetarum. itaque testimonio estis vobismetipsis, quia filii estis eorum qui prophetas occiderunt.' B. has already made use of this chapter at 739.

1284   *tribunal*   Cf. *Rom.* 14.10, 'omnes enim stabimus ante tribunal Christi'; *2 Cor.* 5.10.

1285   *viduaeque*   731n.

1288   *nisi fallor augur*   Cf. Horace, *C.* 3.17.12, 'nisi fallit augur/ annosa cornix'.

1295–6   *insolens victor . . . barbarus miles*   There is a clear reference here to the fall of Jerusalem after the siege of 66–70 AD, when Titus captured it. There may also be a contemporary reference to the threat of invasion by the Turks.

1298   *vinitor*   Cf. Isa. 61.5, 'et filii peregrinorum agricolae et vinitores vestri erunt'; also *Deut.* 28.30, Jer. 5.17, Amos 5.11. For scriptural prophecies of the destruction of Jerusalem, see Jer. 26.6, Luke 21.20ff.

1305   *fraterni*   The Chorus appeals to the Jews to heed John's call for repentance, and to renounce amongst other sins the thirst for a brother's blood. This has specific reference to the impending murder of John, but also resumes the theme of civil war (1236n.). Since in the context of the sixteenth century this phrase was more appropriate to the time of publication of the *Baptistes* than to the time of writing, it is possible that B. has added to or revised the original version at this point.

1311   *famem argenti*   So Horace, *Ep.* 1.18.23, 'quem tenet argenti sitis importuna famesque'.

1337f.   *insontem . . . sontemque*   Cf. Sallust, *Cat.* 16.3, 'insontes sicuti sontes circumvenire'.

## NOTES

1341 *patres* Within the context of the play this refers to the deaths of OT prophets, but it is clear that both the early Christian martyrs and those who died in the name of religion at the Reformation are in B.'s mind.

1344 *legibus* John himself has scarcely died 'pro patriis legibus', but for attempting to change them. Perhaps B. is here intentionally ambiguous, leaving open a possible identification of John with Thomas More, and at the same time making him appear a Protestant martyr.

1345 *ominibus bonis* Cf. Livy, *Praef.* 13, 'cum bonis potius ominibus'.

1353 *differre non vitare* Cf. Virgil, *Aen.* 7.314f., 'immota manet fatis Lavinia coniunx;/at trahere atque moras tantis licet addere rebus'.

# MEDEA

As is mentioned in the Introduction p. 3, this was B.'s first attempt at translation of Greek drama. In a letter to Daniel Rogers dated 9 November 1579 (Ruddiman-Burman, II 755) he claims that he did not translate it for publication, but to improve his knowledge of Greek; and that he agreed to publish it only after considerable pressure from friends when he was teaching at Bordeaux. Here and again in the *Vita* (text now conveniently in McFarlane, App. G) he states that this was one of the plays performed at Bordeaux by the boys. In the *Vita* he deprecatingly suggests that he composed his other translation 'paulo diligentius'; and the longer interval between the performance of *Alcestis* and its publication would have allowed him more leisured perusal of his text for purposes of revision. The result, as these notes suggest, is that *Medea* contains more errors of translation than *Alcestis;* such errors are, however, not numerous, and we must be careful always to examine the Greek text as it appears in the early editions before condemning B.'s version. There is also a more confident handling of metres in *Alcestis;* the *conspectus metrorum* (334ff. below) reveals the wider range there, and one finds also closer observance of Senecan canons. So, for example, his use of the anapaestic dimeter in *Medea* reveals almost a hundred lines without a caesura after the second foot, whereas in *Alcestis* this solecism is virtually expunged.

*Praefatio*

1   *Joannem a Lucemburgo*   On B.'s relations with John of Luxembourg, bishop of Pamiers 1540–48, see McFarlane, 93, 118f.
8   *Erasmo*   See the Introduction, p. 6f.
15   *Ennio*   Q. Ennius (239–169 BC) of Rudiae in Calabria wrote at least twenty tragedies, all of them probably close adaptations of Greek tragedies like *Medea*. The authoritative collection of the fragments is that of Vahlen, *Ennianae Poesis Reliquiae* (1903); but readers of this volume may find it more convenient to consult the text and translation by Warmington in the Loeb series (*Remains of Old Latin,* I, 1935). The general study of H.D. Jocelyn, *The Tragedies of Ennius* (1967) is recommended.

## NOTES

36 *meas esse* . . . Cf. Catullus 1.4.

*Argumenta and Personae* These have been taken over directly by B. from the edition of Euripides which he used. C. Fries, 'Quellenstudien zu George Buchanan', *N.Jb.f.d.klass. Altertum* II 4 (1900) 177–192, II 5 (1900) 241–261, esp. 180n.1, claims that he probably used the Basel Hervagius 1537 edition, but this is merely a reprinting of the Aldine, and we prefer to refer to the Aldine edition throughout these notes.

1 *Utinam Pelasgis* Ennius frr. 253ff. Warmington begins: 'utinam ne in nemore Pelio securibus . . .' but B.'s version is subsequently quite different. *Pelasgis* is an adjective ('Greek') to be taken with *Argo*.

2 *cyaneas* Cyaneae and Symplegadae are *alternative* titles for the 'clashing rocks' at the entrance to the Euxine Sea; hence it is better to take *cyaneae* here not as a proper name but as an adjective ('dark blue'). Compare Euripides at 1263.

8 *amore saevo . . . saucia* Cf. Ennius, fr. 261W, 'Medea animo aegro amore saevo saucia'.

14 *felicitatem* Euripides' version here has 'safety', and the next line in the Greek is expressed negatively (= 'when a woman is not at odds with her husband').

26 *fallax* The adjective, not in the Greek, strengthens the characterisation.

28 *flumine perenni* The metaphor is not in the Greek. The adjective is particularly frequent in the Roman historians in descriptions of seas and rivers.

31 *procellae* Euripides has 'a billow of the sea'; a storm is not so appropriate as an image of indifference.

41ff. Though this appears to be a generalisation in B., in the Greek it is addressed to Medea's temperament, and B. probably intends the same particularity.

46 *maritum . . . ac sponsam* The Greek seems to have been misinterpreted or emended by B. The Aldine has ἢ καὶ τυράννων (*sic*) τόν τε γήμαντα κτάνῃ, 'or that she may kill both king (τύραννον) and bridegroom'.

50 *cursu omisso* The Greek (ἐκ τρόχων) implies 'games' rather than 'course'.

60 *dominae* The Aldine has Μηδείας here, not δεσποίνης, which suggests that B. consults other texts from time to time besides the Aldine.

64 A good example of a clumsy line attributable to B.'s seeking fullness of translation.

68   *amabo*   B.'s intimate acquaintance with comedy leads him fittingly to use the word ('pray') for πρὸς γενείου ('by your beard').
74   The unnatural order of clauses imitates the Greek.
76   An example of a line which B. has had to pad out.
90   *hunc* does not refer to or justify Jason; *hunc . . . alium* translates οἱ μέν . . . οἱ δέ ('some act justly in putting their interests first, others do it for gain').
92   *nil facit certe novi*   Explanatory elaboration of the Greek.
101ff.   It has frequently been noted that in this play 99 out of 369 anapaestic dimeters have no caesura after the second foot. By contrast in *Alcestis* only one line is defective in this way.
101–2   ἰώ (96) is in the O.C.T. but not in the Aldine. The Greek here expresses *a desire* to die where B. has *perii;* cf. Fries, 180.
107   *lumina*   'Your mother's eyes'.
113   *nubes . . . ardebit*   The image, taken over from the Greek, is suggesting a lightning-shaft from the cloud.
115   *aliquid*   Fries castigates this as a mistranslation of τί (interrogative).
116   The interrogation-mark in Murray's O.C.T. text is not in the Aldine.
119   *scelerati*, etc.   The Greek means 'Accursed children of a hateful mother, may you perish . . .'. B. has perhaps translated κατάρατοι ('accursed') by *scelerati* because of the nurse's ensuing remark. But the sense of the Greek, 'Why in your eyes do the children share in the father's sin?', does not necessarily suggest that Medea holds them guilty, but only that she foresees that they will suffer the consequences of what he has done.
126   *gravis . . . fastus*   Stronger than the Greek (= 'Strange is the temper of princes').
129f.   *libertas par* introduces an anachronistic political note not in the Greek, which says: 'Being accustomed to live on equal terms is better'; nor is there any mention in Euripides of 'equal laws' (131 below).
132   *si non*   The mss and the Aldine have εἰ μὴ μεγάλως (123).
134   *popularibus*   Our emendation appears necessary to correspond with βροτοῖσιν ('mortals') in the Greek at 127.
137f.   The Greek means 'Overweening power spells no profit to men'; B.'s rendering, 'High position never continues firmly based for long for men' makes too much of καιρόν.
139–41   B. has completed the nurse's sombre reflexions more poetically. *sors laeva* represents δαίμων ('god' or 'fortune'), *innumerae undae* has no equivalent in the Greek, and modern editors take οἴκοις (B.:

'splendida tecta') with ὀργισθῇ ('When fortune is angry with a house, it brings greater disasters').

148 *minime grata* This represents the sense of the Aldine, which reads μὴ φίλα at 137 ('for things unhappy have come to pass') where the O.C.T. has μοι φίλον.

151 *aula* Corresponding with the Aldine reading which has δῶμα ('house'); the O.C.T. has λέκτρα ('bed').

158 *Parcae* The apostrophe to the Fates, who traditionally spin and hold the threads of mortal lives (hence *abrumpite*, 'break off') is imaginative elaboration by the translator.

161 *immoderatum* The mss reading ἀπλήστου in the Aldine ('Whatever is this desire of yours for an insatiate bed?) is behind this; modern editions prefer Elmsley's ἀπλάτου.

165 *fruitur* is more prosaic than Euripides' σεβίζει ('reverences'); likewise *improperes* in the following line is not as strong as χαράσσου ('scratch').

171–3 It is worth noting that B. has changed the emphasis by making Jason the subject of the subordinate clause ('Do you see the nature of the sin which my wicked husband, bound to me by a sacred oath, has committed against me?'). In the Greek we have: 'Do you see what I suffer, bound by mighty oaths to that accursed husband?'

180 *cum Iove* But Medea has not called on Jupiter at 170. The same problem is found in Euripides, where modern editors attempt to solve the difficulty by adding an invocation to Zeus at 144.

189–90 The equivalent lines in the Greek are attributed to the nurse in almost all the mss and in the Aldine, but modern editors allot them to the chorus.

191 *mea tu* The Aldine Euripides (182) has . . . ἔξω φίλα καὶ τάδ' αὔδα, which B. translates ('Bring her out, dear lady, and address her') by ignoring τάδε. Modern editions read . . . ἔξω·φίλα καὶ τάδε. . . ('tell her we too are friendly').

197 *labori* B. may have misread the Greek at 186, where the nurse says not 'I shall confer this favour on your toil', but 'I shall confer the favour of this toil on you'.

203 *laeva* The Greek word for 'left-handed' also means 'foolish'; this sense is occasionally found in Latin with *laevus* (e.g., Virgil, *Ecl.* 1.16, *Aen.* 2.54), so that 'foolish' rather than 'unpropitious' is the meaning here.

215 *ilia tendunt* A lively expression for the strain of loud singing; no parallel from classical poetry comes to mind.

218–20 This is the punctuation of the 1544 edition; we are to take *illa* with *voce*.

# MEDEA

228–435.

231   *frequens praesentia*   Perhaps B. has not grasped the sense of the Greek at 217, 'among the domestics'.

241   *at enim*   An unfortunate use, since the reader is led to expect an anticipated objection, which this is not.

245   *reliquit*   The Greek ἐκβέβηχ' actually means here 'has turned out' (Fries, 180).

250   *gravius malum* should denote 'suique accipere dominum corporis' (249), and not the hazard of whether your husband is honest or wicked, if B. were following the sense of the Greek; the punctuation of the Aldine edition is identical with that of the O.C.T. So B. has erred here.

251   *periclum*   Not quite the same as ἄγων, 'issue'.

255   *hariolari*   B.'s fondness for the diction of Roman comedy is frequently observable in this play.

262   The equivalent line in the Greek is excised by modern editors for metrical reasons.

267   There may be a hint of Ennius' version (frr. 269–70W) here: 'nam ter sub armis malim vitam cernere/quam semel modo parere'.

269   *utrasque*   i.e. Medea and the leader of the Chorus.

271   *praesidia vitae*   The equivalent Greek phrase (254) suggests enjoyment in comfort rather than protection.

273–4   The Aldine Euripides supports our change of punctuation here.

281–2   *et plectere . . . filiam*   The equivalent line in the Greek is excised by modern editors, who regard it as too early in the developing drama for Medea to indicate that her revenge will encompass the new bride; but cf. 307f. (=Eur. 288f.).

287   In view of the previous note it is interesting to observe that the Greek (267) says: 'You will justly take revenge on *your husband*'; B. does not limit the threat in this way.

298   The metaphor of letting out the ropes for full sail is reproduced from the Greek.

313   B. dispenses with Medea's expression of grief (φεῦ, φεῦ) at the beginning of this speech.

318   *pigra . . . otia*   The sense of ἀργία in the Greek (296) is 'unprofitability' rather than 'idleness'.

323   *sophorum auctoritatem*   Though the basic idea is in the Greek (300), there is a hint here of sixteenth-century controversies; see *Jephthes* 962n.

325   *invidentia* is distinguished by Cicero (*Tusc.* 4.17) from *invidia*; it is envy of others' prosperity which is doing no harm to those who grudge it.

327   *diversae vitae*   The Greek is equally vague; presumably the implicit meaning is 'the tendency to be meddlesome'.
328   The Aldine Euripides here (305) has no distinct colon after προσάντης, though the sense requires it; the Hervagius edition has a full-stop. B. assumes that there is no stop.
337   *latebras fugae*   B. strengthens the expression of the Greek (313f.): 'Let me dwell in this land'. B. intensifies Medea's elaborate self-humiliation before the king.
344   *modestum*   The Greek has σοφός, 'shrewd'.
355   The elliptical sense is: 'Love is deadly or beneficial according to the circumstances.'
358   *novis*   Though this is not in the Greek, B. is justified in filling out the sense. Medea means that the loss of her marriage is enough pain without exile's being superimposed.
363   *solo*   The manuscripts in the Greek (339) have χθόνος, which B. renders from the Aldine, but modern texts incorporate the conjecture of Wilamowitz, χερός ('refuse to release my hand'); cf. 394 (Eur. 370).
368   B. intensifies the pathos; the Greek states 'It is right for you to show good will'.
373   *erratum*   It is an inherent part of the tragedy, in Euripides as in B., that Creon realises that his clemency is dangerous; but he reassures himself (379f.) that a day's delay can bring no harm.
386   *ineluctabile fatum*   The Virgilian phrase (cf. *Aen.* 8.334) renders θεός ('a god') in the Greek. On the other hand *in mare malorum* is weaker than the Greek's 'into a billow beyond escape' (362–3).
389   *hac*   This, the 1544 reading, translates ταύτῃ at 365 in the Greek; *succedere* is used impersonally, as often.
394   The rhetorical questions are the elaboration of B.; in the Greek these are statements.
406   *scandens* translates the reading of the mss and the Aldine ὑπερβαίνουσα; Housman's emendation, ὑπεσβαίνουσα ('secretly entering') is rightly adopted in the O.C.T. by Murray.
410–11   The punctuation here follows that of the Aldine Euripides.
421   *triformis* The conventional Latin adjective (cf. Horace, *C.*3.22.4, Ovid, *Met.* 7.94), which denotes the roles of the goddess in heaven (Luna), on earth (Diana), and in Hades (Proserpina), is an addition by B.
430–1   *nepotibus . . . Sisyphaeis*   Sisyphus was the founder of Corinth, so 'Sisyphaean descendants' are Corinthians. In the Greek the adjective Σισυφείοις is to be taken with γάμοις, 'by reason of your Corinthian marriage', but in the Aldine Euripides a comma is inserted (τοῖς Σισυφαίοις, τοῖς τ''Ιάσονος) and this has misled B.

## 436–66.

440ff.  *audiet . . . bene*  B. has done well to realise that the Chorus sings here not of itself but of the female sex in general; he elaborates upon the Greek to make the meaning explicit.

447–50  Again here B. renders the correct general sense while departing from the literal meaning of the Greek, which is: 'For Apollo, leader of lays, did not instil the inspired song of the lyre in our minds, for I would have hymned a song in answer to the race of men.'

452  *exprobrare*  B. boldly interprets πολλὰ . . . μοῖραν εἰπεῖν ('can say much of our lot and that of men') as rebuke.

457  *misera*  In the Greek τάλαινα (437) is taken as vocative by modern editors; in the Aldine it is not clear-cut.

464  *e thalami curis*  The O.C.T. has a comma after μόχθων πάρα, and τῶν τε λέκτρων goes with κρείσσων (= 'governing your bed'). The Aldine has no comma after πάρα, but one after τῶνδε (*sic*) λέκτρων; hence B.'s rendering.

## 467–664.

475  *blaterasti*  B. has doubtless recalled this prosaic word from Horace, *Sat.* 2.7.35.

476  *pro lucro*  As in the Greek, the thought here is: 'regard it as gain that exile, and nothing worse, is your punishment'.

479–80  *prodigens . . . devovens*  Another example of B.'s flights into rhetorical elaboration. The Greek merely speaks of constantly abusing princes.

487f,  *imbecillitas . . . mea*  The Greek which B. translates here—"This is the greatest reproach one can utter against your unmanliness"—has been criticised as making unsatisfactory sense. B. has tried to make it mean 'My weakness allows me only to reproach you', which is clearly an impossible rendering.

490  The equivalent line of the Greek (468) is excised by modern editors. The two lines 467–8 appear as a question in the Aldine, and clearly B.'s version gains from our adopting this punctuation.

492  *laesos*  The Greek (470) emphasises that the beholder is also the one who inflicts harm.

505–6  *sopore . . . fallere*  The only equivalent in the Greek is ἄυπνος ὤν (= 'being sleepless').

508–9  *tibi . . . providens* is again B.'s elaboration; the Greek has 'with more eagerness than sense'.

512  *metum*  The Aldine Euripides has φόβον ('fear') not δόμον ('house').

## NOTES

517 *peieratis dis*   For the expression, cf. Ovid, *Amores* 3.11.22; the Greek has 'all trust in oaths is gone'.

525 *aliquod*   In the Greek (500), τί is interrogative in the O.C.T. ('but what do I think to obtain from you?'), but the Aldine has indefinite τι; hence B.'s version.

527–30   Perhaps B. recalled the words of Ennius fr. 284W here: 'quo nunc me vortam? quod iter incipiam ingredi?/domum paternamne anne ad Peliae filias?' As in the Ennius version, so in B. there is rhetorical elaboration at 527.

531 *benigne*   The note of irony is well captured from the Greek.

537, 540   The punctuation follows that in the Aldine Euripides.

540 *elogium*   The ironical words in the previous lines (*beatam, singularem, fidum*) are all taken over from the Greek. B. intensifies the effect by this further ironical word *elogium* for ὄνειδος ('rebuke').

550 *summa ... margine*   As in the Greek, Medea's onslaught is visualised as a storm; sailors rolled up the sail to the yard so that only the edge was exposed to the wind.

552 *exaggeras*   Predominantly an oratorical word, frequent in Cicero.

557 *orationis ... iactantia*   B. seems to have misunderstood Euripides 529ff., where Jason states that it would be invidious (ἐπίφθονος λόγος) to recount how Love compelled Medea to save him.

559 *duris e laboribus*   B. translates the πόνων ἀφύκτων of the Aldine (τόξοις ἀφύκτοις in the O.C.T.).

566–7 *lex et aequitas*   The irony in the Greek (Medea's treatment is a travesty of justice) is intensified in B.'s version. The Greek says: "You are acquainted with justice and with the use of laws which do not favour violence." *et aequitas* and *gratiae* are B.'s additions.

571   B. does not make it clear that he is translating the expression of a wish: 'May I have neither gold in my house nor the ability to sing a finer lay than Orpheus, if my fortune be not famed' (Euripides, 542ff.). Compare 635 for a wish similarly vaguely expressed.

590 *indigentes*   Euripides says that all friends shun poverty; B. makes the point more explicitly by saying that they shun poor men.

596 *essem*   Euripides has used the plural here to indicate that Jason and his first family might be happy.

607–8   The exclamations are further rhetorical elaboration by B.

610 *invita*   The Greek (577) has παρὰ γνώμην = 'indiscreetly' rather than 'unwillingly'. Fries, 181 is however too severe here.

620 *confecero*   The Aldine Euripides has οὖν κτένει ('will kill you') for the ἐκτενεῖ ('will prostrate you') of modern texts.

623 *me persuasa*   One of the very few transgressions of grammatical

norms in B.'s Latin. *persuasa* is scanned here as quadrisyllabic (cf. Lucretius 4.1157, *sŭādent*).

624   *probe* is to be taken with *paruisses* in an ironical sense, as the Greek indicates.

635   See 571n.

637   *vertes* Modern texts of Euripides have Elmsley's reading, the aorist imperative μέτευξαι (600), but the reading of the mss and the Aldine is the future indicative μετεύξῃ which B. renders.

645   B. has misunderstood the sense of the Greek at 608. Euripides says 'And I perchance am a curse on your house', not 'I am in turn accursed by your house', as B. takes it.

649   *profer* = 'state it to me, for I am ready. . .'

664   *apparasse* The Greek has: 'Your marriage will be such that you will deny its existence.'

665–702.

667   *facessit* B. is fond of this colloquialism ('retires').

675   *mi grata* Modern texts of Euripides have Wecklein's στέργοι (635) expressing a wish, but the mss and Aldine have the indicative στέργει which B. follows.

677   The Greek has: 'May dread Aphrodite never direct disputatious anger and unsated contention, ravaging my heart with desire for another's bed. . .'. The introduction of *paelex* is more rhetorical intensification by B.

683   *parata* 'ready as she is eagerly to assess the sins of the marriage-bed'. Modern texts of Euripides have the optative expressing a wish, but the Aldine followed by B. has the indicative κρίνει.

702   *sincera* The mss and Aldine have καθαράν (660) agreeing with κλῇδα, and B. renders this.

704–870.

709   *faticanum* is appropriated from Ovid, *Met.* 9.418.

720   The neck of a leather bottle (*utri*) was made from the foot of an animal. The cryptic injunction not to loose the foot was actually a ban on sexual intercourse.

741   *concupivit* In the Greek (700) there is continuing play on ἐρᾶν from 697–8 ('he *loved* obtaining kinship with royalty'). Such nuances are always difficult to achieve in translation, and B. has not attempted to render the play on words.

749   *exigi . . . vetat* There is an element of irony in the Greek (708:

'Not according to what he says, but he consents to endure it!') which again the translation has difficulty in expressing.

752 The alliterative force is not in the Greek at 711, but there is a similar effect there at 712. B.'s rendering of εἰσίδῃς (= 'look idly on') is much stronger ('despice' 753).

755 *sortiantur* The Greek (714) makes it clear that this is a wish.

766 *unice* a line-filler not in the Greek.

767 Another example of a clumsy line, the result of incorporating two lines of Greek (725–6).

780 *praeconibus* The Greek in the Aldine Euripides (738) has κἀπὶ κηρυκήμασιν οὐκ ἂν πίθοιο, which is what B. has translated.

782–3 *oppida*, etc. The Greek (740) speaks merely of wealth and a royal house; the mention of towns is anachronistic.

788 *muni* B. takes ἄραρε (745, Aldine ἄρηρε, = 'is fixed') as if it were an imperative.

795 *almum . . . iubar* The Aldine Euripides has λαμπρὸν ἡλίου τε φῶς, 'gleaming light of the sun'.

799 *avibus secundis* For the phrase, cf. Livy 6.12.9.

802 *pacifer* Not in the Greek (759), but an epithet of Mercury at Ovid, *Met.* 14.291.

807 *faxque aurea* Decorative addition to the Greek.

813 *posthac* misinterprets ἐκ τοῦδ' (770) which means *'on him* shall I secure the rope of my prow'.

820–1 *ordine factas* translates the Aldine reading εἰργασμένα.

830 *tetigerint* 'touches' makes the poison more baneful than the Greek, which means 'wraps it round'.

838 *vertam solum* The technical expression for emigration in Cicero and Livy.

840 A much stronger sentiment than the Greek (796), which says: 'Having dared a most impious deed'.

859 As at 854–5 (where there are two Latin lines for the one in the Greek at 810) B. has introduced more striking vocabulary for the δρᾶν τάδε of 813.

866 *quae refrenet* The Greek (819) speaks of 'words in between' (i.e., between now and the deed) as being superfluous.

869 *ne revela regibus* B. misunderstands the Greek at 823, which means: 'If you are well-disposed to your superiors' (i.e., Medea) 'say nothing'.

871–907. B.'s rendering contrives to be both faithful to the sense and a splendid poem in its own right.

872 *sancta deum suboles*   The Greek (825) has 'children of the blessed gods'; an echo of Virgil's 'cara deum suboles' (*Ecl.* 4.49) reverberates in B.'s rendering.

875–6   Creative translation of the Greek's 'Treading delicately through the clearest air'.

880 *pulchriflui*   Another example of B.'s addiction to compounds; this is not a Classical form.

891 *quinam*   Here, and again at 907, this is to be taken as 'how, I ask. . . ?' 'The city of sacred rivers' is B.'s noble attempt to cope with the corrupt Greek at 847.

893 *te venientem*   The Aldine has πομπιμόν, which B. seems to render here. The reading of the mss, πομπιμός, means (a land) 'which allows passage' to friends.

895 *inter amicos*   The difference in punctuation between the Aldine and modern texts of Euripides explains the rendering. The Aldine has τὰν οὐχ ὁσίαν, μετ'ἄλλων/σκέψαι τεκέων πλαγάν ('the unholy; ponder with others the murder of children'), whereas the sense of the O.C.T. is: 'How will the land receive you, the child-murderer, one whose presence with others is unholy? Think on the murder of children. . .'.

899 *cunctae*   The mss and the Aldine edition of Euripides have πάντες, which would mean 'all here' (not merely the female Chorus), but B. restricts the meaning (ungrammatically) to the Chorus.

900 *unde*   The Aldine Euripides here has πῶς δέ for the πόθεν of the mss. It therefore seems likely that B. is not translating the Aldine here.

901ff.   The equivalent Greek lines (856–9) seem beyond redemption, and B. has boldly offered an approximate version. In the Aldine Euripides we read at 862 σχήσεις; whereas the Hervagius 1537 text punctuates with a stop. B. follows the Aldine.

908–1024.

921 *creabit?*   It is better to punctuate with a question-mark (as in the Greek at 878 and in Ruddiman) than with a full stop (as in the 1544 edition).

924 *orbos*, etc.   B.'s translation reproduces the Greek cryptically. The implied sense is: 'I should not show anger when I have no allies here, and the children need support.'

932 *gratum . . . facere*   Euripides has: '. . .should have rejoiced at the alliance of your bride.'

943–4 *hei mihi . . . tecti*   Spoken as an aside.

944–5 *O liberi*, etc.   B. has not quite understood Euripides here. In the Greek play, Medea tries to cover up her involuntary grief, and says: 'My children, will you after living many years stretch out your dear hands thus?' In the translation *diu* should go with *superstites,* but clearly does not.

948   *ora*   More pathetically in the Greek 'tender eyes' (905).
950   *ne*   The Greek expresses a wish, not a fear.
953   *novas . . . nuptias*   B. translates the Aldine reading, γάμους παρεμπολῶντι γ'ἀλλοίους πόσει.
956   *fideliorem*   The Greek has τὴν νικῶσαν (912: 'the counsel that prevails').
975   *precarer* translates the reading of the mss and Aldine ἐξηύχουν; the O.C.T.'s ἐξηύχου ('when *you* prayed') is Scaliger's emendation.
979ff.   The main clause following the causal clause *cum . . . visum sit* is at 984, *exsulatum propero;* the intervening lines are in parenthesis as in the Greek at 934ff. Our punctuation seeks to make this clear.
990–1   *nisi . . . moribus*   The equivalent line in the Greek (945) is allotted in some mss and in the Aldine to Jason, and they are followed by B. here. Others, followed by the O.C.T., allot them to Medea.
1011   *deos*   The line is obscure without the aid of the Greek, which says 'The saying is that gifts persuade *even* gods' (964).
1016   *redimam*   subjunctive, not future indicative, as the Greek indicates.
1017   *propinquas*   B. translated πλησίους, read by the Aldine, as against πλουσίους preferred by the O.C.T.
1024   *referte*   The Greek has the optative to express a wish ('May you bring good tidings'). B. may have mistaken the form for an imperative.

1025–46.

1030   *acceptum* renders λαβοῦσα from the mss and Aldine; Nauck later excised it.
1041   B. does not attempt to render Eur. at 995: 'Wretched in your fate, how great is your ruin!'

1047–1129.

1050   *hei*   In the O.C.T. of Euripides as emended by Kirchhoff it is the paedagogus who utters ἔα, an exclamation of surprise, not grief, at Medea's troubled countenance. The mss and Aldine, however, allot it to Medea, and B. follows this version.
*quid gemiscis?*   The misrendering (the Greek says 'Why do you stand there, worried?') is attributable to B.'s mistranslation *hei.*

1051–2  *quid . . . nuntium?*  The equivalent lines in the Greek, 1006–7, were excised by Valckenaer, and do not appear in modern texts.

1061–3  *per liberos . . . deducam ego*  At 1015 in the Greek, the reading of the mss and of the Aldine is κρατεῖς, and B. attempts to translate this ('A large part of your previous power remains'). But Porson's emendation κάτει, universally adopted, lends real point; it means 'You will come back from exile' (with the help of your children). Medea then plays on the two senses of the Greek word, which literally means 'you will go down'; she replies 'I shall drive others down first', meaning that she will consign her children to Hades. All this is inevitably lost in B.'s rendering.

1070  *sempiternum*  Found occasionally in comedy as an adverb; cf. Plautus, *Aul.* 147.

1081  *contegi* follows *spes inanes,* 'empty hopes that I may be covered. . .'.

1087  *institutum . . . novum*  Here as throughout the speech the ambivalence of the Greek (1039) referring to the future abode of the children is admirably reproduced.

1091  *blanda*  Perhaps not the *mot juste* for φαιδρόν ('bright' and hence 'cheerful').

1093  *relinquent*  The children, not *consilia,* are the subject.

1095  *mihi,* etc.  This reinforced resolution to kill the children, and the uncertainty preceding it, are less subtly expressed than in Euripides (1049), where the break after the end of the line allows a longer pause for cogitation.

1099  *suggero*  B. must mean: 'I utter words softer than (the resolve in) my heart.' The mss and the Aldine Euripides have πρόεσθαι ('What cowardice is mine to utter soft words from the heart') but Badham's emendation πρόσεσθαι ('to admit soft words to my heart') is accepted by Murray in the O.C.T.

1102  *polluam*  B. misunderstands the Greek at 1055, where διαφθερῶ must mean 'weaken' rather than 'pollute'.

1106  *per atrae,* etc.  Once again by beginning a new thought in mid-line, B. makes the vacillation of Medea less pronounced than does Euripides.

1109–11  In the Greek text, lines 1062–3 have been excised by Pierson because they are a doublet of 1240–41, but they are in the Aldine. B.'s translation, however, departs from the Greek in a most uncharacteristic way. 'quo nos trahit fatum, sequamur' is an evocation of Virgil *Aen.* 5.709, 'nate dea, quo fata trahunt retrahuntque, sequamur', and it is the Virgilian thought which seduces B. here.

## NOTES

1110–11  *sortiantur terminum,* etc.  A free rendering of Euripides 1063, which merely says: 'We who begot them will kill them'.

1112–13  *fixa stat sententia. hanc nemo reddet inritam* misunderstands the Greek (1064), where Glauce is the subject of ἐκφεύξεται ('she will not escape').

1118  *dexteram*  The Greek (1070) adds 'to kiss'.

1120  *grataque*  The Greek has εὐγενές ('noble').

1123  *amplexatio*  The word is found in Jerome, Cassiodorus and other late writers (see *TLL*).

1129  *me retrorsum distrahit*  Elaboration of the Greek (1080).

### 1130–66.

The version by B. is rather obscure and considerably less inspired than his previous renderings, perhaps because the ode of Euripides is without obvious unity and is rather prosaically written.

1139  *indulget*  The Greek text is corrupt, but B. offers the general sense.

1141  *his iam*  It is difficult to force sense out of *his cum*, the reading of all the editions.

1149  *numerosa*  A prosaic rendering of γλυκερὸν βλάστημα (1099).

1151  *educant*  As Ruddiman explains in his appendix on metres, *edūcant* is demanded here rather than *edŭcent,* which early editions print.

1160–61  *moribus optimis, exculto ingenio* elaboration upon χρηστοί (1109).

1161ff.  The Euripidean passage is notoriously difficult, but at 1110 in the Greek the meaning must be: 'But if fortune turns out thus, death vanishes to Hades, bearing the bodies of your children.' *dea* (1161) accordingly should be Fortune, not Mors, as B. has it (1162); *inutilis* is B.'s rhetorical addition.

1164  *pignora propter* is a literal rendering of the Greek, and the sense is vague. B. means: 'How was it profitable that this intolerable load of grief should be imposed on mortals merely so that they might have the dear pledge of children?'

### 1167–1311.

1172  *perpetratrix*  Perhaps coined by B.; *perpetrator* is used by Augustine and Sidonius Apollinaris.

1193  *consopiisse*  Likewise used metaphorically by Ammianus 22.5.3, 27.5.1.

1196 *gynaeceum* Frequent in Roman comedy for 'women's quarters'.
1203 *leniebat molliter* An imaginative addition to the Greek ἀφῄρει (1150).
1205–9 These commands are framed as questions in the O.C.T., but not in the Aldine which B. follows.
1213ff. In the equivalent lines of the Greek, as Verrall notes, Euripides ironically presages the coming death and burial of Glauce by the language with which he describes her attire; B. achieves something of this at 1217 (*umbram . . . inanimem*) but inevitably much is lost in translation.
1215 *sese* The Aldine Euripides here has κόμην ('her hair'); B. appears to be translating the reading of the ms V, δέμας ('her form').
1221 *colla* The Greek (1166) means 'gazing at the straight sinew (of her foot)'; she has laid aside the mirror. B. mistranslates.
1223–4 *tremor obliqua membra vexat* The picture is unclear. The Greek (1168ff.) has: 'Losing her colour she staggered back, her limbs trembling'.
1228 *eiulavit lugubre*. B. has erred here; see Fries, 181. The Greek cry ἀνωλόλυξε (1173) is an acknowledgment of the god's presence, not a cry of distress; cf. 1231 below. It is perhaps notable that *pedisequa* (1226) and *eiulare* both occur in Plautus, *Aul.* 796–807.
1229 *quam* All the editions of B. have *nam,* but the Greek at 1173 has πρῖν which is more appropriately rendered by *ante . . . quam.*
1230 *circumrotari* The Greek means 'turning the pupils upwards from her eyes'; i.e. they disappear under the upper lids. The word *circumrotare* is found in Classical literature only once in Statius and once in Apuleius.
1231f. *eiulatum flebilem* The sense of the Greek is: 'Then she let out a great wail, *contrasting with* her ecstatic cry' (1176). Cf. 1228n.
1236f. *et iam* It seems that B. has not fully grasped the meaning of the Greek. Euripides says (1181ff.) that Glauce lay senseless for as long as a swift walker covers a *stadion* (=600 feet), but B. does not indicate this.
1242 *scaturiginem* The word occurs only in the plural in Classical Latin.
1245 *niveum* The Aldine (1189) preferred the reading λευκήν, which B. translates; the O.C.T. has λεπτήν, 'her delicate flesh'.
1256 *per genas* Euripides here (1201) with a striking metaphor speaks of the flesh flowing off the bones through 'the hidden jaws of the poison' (γναθμοῖς ἀδήλοις φαρμάκων); the Aldine, however, reads γναθμῶν, taking it (as B. does) with σάρκες, 'the flesh of her jaws'.

## NOTES

1267   *capulo propinquum*   The sense is as at Lucretius 2.1173f., 'omnia paulatim tabescere et ire/ad capulum spatio aetatis defessa vetusto'.

1267   *silicernium*   Used of an old man in Roman comedy, from where B. draws so much of his colloquial vocabulary. Cf. Terence, *Adelphi* 587: 'ego te exercebo hodie, . . . silicernium.' The whole of this line is notable elaboration of the single word τύμβον in Euripides (1209).

1275   The alliterative effect is a vividly original touch by B.; the whole of this speech is brilliantly rendered.

1287   *stultissimos*   B. is reproducing the meaning of the Aldine, which has μωρίαν against the reading of the mss ζημίαν.

1305   *ad carceres*   B. takes over the metaphor of the starting-gate (and finishing-post) from the Greek.

1308   *o cara*   The Aldine Euripides distressingly reads ὦ φίλτατ', and B. seeks to translate as self-address; the true reading is ὡς φίλτατ' ('how dear they are').

### 1312–1359.

1320–21   *quam metuo*   B. makes a brave attempt to cope with the corrupt Greek (1256–7), which as it stands must mean: 'that the blood of gods should be spilt at the hands of men is terrible'.

1324–5   *tectis e feralibus*   The Greek 1259–60 means: 'Drive from the house the fury, bloodied and made wretched by avenging spirits'; B. seems to take ὑπ' ἀλαστόρων with οἴκων.

1328   *o Symplegadum*   B. omits from the Greek the adjective 'dark blue' which he uses at line 2. In the Aldine this apostrophe (*o . . . quae deseruisti*) is taken with the preceding line (1262; 'In vain did you bear your dear brood, O you who left. . .') as in the O.C.T.

1330–31   *unde . . . cumulatur*   B. follows the text as in the Aldine, which has (1266f.) καὶ δυσμενὴς φόνος ἀμείβεται; Murray in the O.C.T. has καὶ δυσμενὴς φόνος· ἀμείβεται.

1332ff.   A creditable attempt at the corrupt Greek of 1268ff., which roughly means: 'Defilement of one's own kin falls harshly in turn on mortals over the earth; griefs that harmonise with the slaughter falling from the gods on their houses.'

1337–40   In the O.C.T. of Euripides the lines allotted to the Chorus here (1339f.) are placed before the cries of the children (1337f.), but B. has followed the traditional order of the mss and the Aldine.

1341   *tectum ingrediar*   Since the Chorus does not enter the house, the O.C.T. at 1275 punctuates with a question-mark, but this does not appear in the Aldine.

1344   *retibus*   The Greek (1278) speaks of the children being 'almost in the sword's net'; the mixture of metaphors is too much for B., who omits the sword.

1350   *caram*   If the Latin text is sound, this is a surprising lapse by B. The Aldine has: φίλοις χέρα προσβαλεῖν τέχνοις. To reproduce this sense B. should have written *cari* rather than *caram*.

1355   *litus ultra*   Ino threw herself over a projecting cliff, but neither Euripides nor B. makes this clear.

1358   *anxiferae*   The adjective is found only in Cicero amongst Classical writers.

1359   *Lerna*   This is the name of the Argive forest which was the haunt of the monstrous Hydra; it is used here with *malorum* in the sense of 'morass of evils'.

1360–1490.

1378   *luce cassis*   Virgil, *Aen.* 2.85 uses *cassus lumine* for a corpse, transforming the sense of the phrase from Lucretius 4.368, where it means a shadow. Cf. also *Aen.* 11.104, 'aethere cassis', of men killed in battle.

1383   *hanc*   In the Greek (1316), Jason's emotion is signalled by an anacoluthon: 'that I may see a double evil, my children dead, and as for her—that I may take revenge.' B. achieves the same effect skilfully with *hanc*.

1384   At this point Medea appears above the house in a chariot drawn by winged serpents.

1384   *arietas*   The word appears in comedy (cf. Plautus, *Truc.* 256) and often in Seneca.

1393   *mater*   The position of the word in the sentence corresponds exactly with that of τεκοῦσα in the Greek, stressing the unnatural nature of the deed.

1400f.   *Erinyes*   Euripides states, rather differently: "The gods have directed against me the spirit who was to take vengeance on you" (1333).

1405   *sustulisti* 'raised' here, but perhaps the ambivalence ('removed' also) was intended.

1411   *canes*   Euripides merely says that Medea has a nature wilder than Scylla's.

1422f.   *spretisne . . . inluderes?*   The note of interrogation is in the Aldine Euripides but not in the O.C.T.

1427   *Tuscum . . . litus*   The equivalent Greek phrase (1359) is obelised by Murray as corrupt in the O.C.T.

## NOTES

1430 *iuvat dolor* It appears that B. has misconstrued the Greek (1362), which means: 'Your failure to mock relieves the pain'; the subject of λύει is the clause which follows, not ἄλγος.

1432 *scelus* The Greek has νόσος, illness. By being more specific, B. loses the taunt in the original.

1434 *culpa* Similarly here, where the Greek has ὕβρις, B. loses the precise sense.

1435 The Aldine puts the Greek (1367) in the form of a question; the O.C.T. does not.

1440–41 *dis . . . dis* in imitation of similar repetition by Euripides (1372–3), though B. has ignored the earlier use of the technique in the previous two lines.

1442 *mihi es molestus* The Euripides mss here (and the Aldine) have στυγῇ, (= 'You are hated'); the O.C.T. incorporates the emendation of Weil, στύγει, 'hate all you like'.

1453 *iungar marito* The Greek (1385) merely says: 'to dwell with Aegeus son of Pandion'. The story that Medea married Aegeus and had a son by him called Medus (Hyginus 26.1; see also the *argumentum* of the play) emerges from the later tradition; Euripides does not imply such a marriage here.

1455 *Argus* is genitive as at Propertius 2.26.39. The story goes that as Jason slept in the shade afforded by the Argo, it fell on him and killed him.

1457 *Erinyes* As at 1401 B. converts the singular in the Greek (1389) into a plural.

1484 *ipse superstes* B.'s own elaboration.

1488 *fraudant* The subject is *dei;* 'The gods often cheat hopes of their outcome'.

# *ALCESTIS*

This translation was originally made by B. for performance by his pupils at Bordeaux. It was composed after the translation of *Medea* and after *Baptistes* (see Introduction, 2ff.), probably in the mid-1540s. But it did not appear in print until a decade later, in 1556, and it is likely that B. was able to subject his version to more careful revision than that applied to *Medea*. This version of *Alcestis* achieved a notable *succès d'estime*. It was reprinted at Paris within a year, and thereafter, at many other centres (details in McFarlane, *Buchanan,* App. A). But McFarlane's suggestion that the play was performed at Elizabeth's court, and that the queen requested a repeat performance, seems to rest on a misreading of Charles Utenhove's *In Alcestin Epigramma,* which appeared as a frontispiece to many early editions. (The play actually performed seems to have been Richard Edwards' *Damon and Pythias* (1571).)

B.'s more careful revision and greater experience of translating Euripides makes his version of *Alcestis* technically superior to that of *Medea.* There are fewer mistakes of rendering, and a more ambitious range of metrical effects.

## *Praefatio*

1 *ante aliquot annos* The Paris edition dated 1557 was printed in December 1556; before that, the royal authority giving Vascosan the sole rights of publishing the play for a decade, is dated 1553. B. claims here to have finished his text 'several years before'; for the controversies surrounding the date of the performance of the play (either during his period at Bordeaux in the early 1540s, or during a second visit in 1545–7) see Introduction, 4f. and McFarlane, 94.

2 *Margarita* Marguerite de France (1523–74), daughter of François I, married in 1559 Emmanuel Philibert, Duke of Savoy. She was a great patroness of the arts, celebrated by Ronsard, Du Bellay, Dorat and others. See McFarlane, 175.

15 *philosophorum* Seneca above all is in B.'s mind.

## NOTES

*Argumentum*

This is a translation of the first of the two Greek versions printed in the O.C.T.; the second does not appear in the Aldine.

<u>1–79.</u>

4 *flammis trisulcis* Perhaps Ovid's phrase used of Jupiter's thunderbolt, *trisulcis ignibus* (*Met.* 2.848f.) is the inspiration of this elaboration of 'flame' in the Greek. Cf. *Jephthes* 188, 'ignis armatus potius trisulci . . . iaculis'.

10 "Since it (the house) piously obeyed the pious son of Pheres." The Aldine Euripides has ἐτύγχανε for ἐτύγχανον, and B. has tried to render that reading. The Greek actually means: "I took on the role of pious servant of a pious master, Pheres' son."

13–15 *subducerem . . . supponerem* B. gives Apollo a more active part in the proceedings than does Euripides, who speaks of Admetus' escaping death by his provision of another corpse for the shades below.

16–17 *omnium . . . patris ac matris* reproduces the awkward verbal pattern of the Greek.

21 *baiulatur* In the passive common only in late and Christian Latin, following upon its use in the Vulgate (*Acts* 3.2).

22 *frigente sensim corpore* The Greek word ψυχορραγοῦσα means 'letting the soul break loose'.

29 *ha, ha, ha, ha* Reproducing the four exclamations in the Aldine Eur.; there are only two in the O.C.T.

37 It is tempting to insert a note of interrogation at the end of this line, but the Aldine Euripides does not contain one.

37 *arcitenentem* B. is fond of such compounds; this word appears at Virgil, *Aen.* 3.75, Ovid, *Met.* 1.441, 6.265.

41 *iusque fasque* Not quite the 'trusty tidings' of Euripides.

44 The mark of interrogation is in both the 1557 edition of B. and in the Aldine Euripides.

47 *invito tibi* See Fries, 180 n.1, for a defence of this rendering against O. Dähnhardt.

49 *redemptus morte* The instinctive rendering of ἀμείψας by the Christian translator.

52 The interrogation-mark at the end of the line is not in the 1557 edition nor in the Aldine Euripides, but it clearly improves the sense.

53 *senes* is added by B. to accentuate the meaning.

61 In the years during which B. was writing, 'sophiste' was commonly used to refer to the theologians of the Sorbonne. Cf. *Jephthes* 962n.

61   We have added the mark of interrogation here, following the Aldine Euripides (58).

70   *quadriiugos*   An intelligent rendering of Euripides ἵππειον . . . ὄχημα, for Hercules was sent for the man-eating horses and not the chariot.

73   *hanc*   B. must mean: 'You will get no thanks from me for this' (i.e., for being forced to surrender Alcestis).

   *ingratiis*   A word common in Roman comedy, with which B. is closely familiar.

76   *pallidam*   A rhetorical addition to the Greek.

77   *ense delibem comam*   The Greek (74) has 'ὡς κατάρξωμαι', 'to make a beginning of the sacrifice', and this was regularly the cutting of the hair (cf. Herodotus 2.45, Aristophanes, *Birds* 959), so that B. is expanding the sense of the Greek according to the information provided by Euripides at 76.

80–135.   B.'s allocation of lines to the Chorus and to the half-chorus follows the arrangement in the Aldine Euripides, which has XO. and HMI. as headings.

89   *flentium*   A strange rendering or omission of the Greek ὡς πεπραγμένων, 'as if all were over'.

92–3   The meaning of Euripides here is 'Would that you would appear, Paean, to calm the disaster'. *auxiliator . . . atque salutifer* is elegant elaboration, for which Statius, *Silvae* 3.4.24ff. is the inspiration: '. . .ubi maximus aegris/*auxiliator* (sc. Aesculapius) adest, et festinantia sistens/fata *salutifero* mitis deus incubat angui.'

95   *nec clam. . .*   This translates the Greek as in the mss and early editions; the division of the three lines into three separate utterances by different members of the Chorus was proposed by Kirchhoff.

96   *haud video quid* renders the text of the Aldine Euripides, οὐκ αὐχῶ τί σε θαρσύνει; the O.C.T. has a full-stop after αὐχῶ.

105   *virgineum . . . agmen*   This is a careful rendering of Euripides' strange phrase νεολαία χείρ, 'a youthful band' of women; why they should be youthful is not clear.

107–8   B. translates lines 106–7 of Euripides in the order in which they appear in the Aldine; the O.C.T. follows the mss *VB* in reversing this order.

110   *Parcae . . . severae*   This is B.'s rhetorical elaboration upon the phrase 'when the good are destroyed' in the Greek.

112–13   *Chimaerae arva*   Euripides speaks merely of Lycia; B. airs his knowledge of mythology in his rendering. Lycia was the home of the

## NOTES

Chimaera (Ovid, *Met*. 6.340 may be in B.'s mind); but Euripides has introduced Lycia here because he thinks of the shrine of Apollo at Patara.

113–15   *vel aestu . . . Ammonis*   The Greek speaks merely of the abode or shrine of Ammon; B. exploits the romanticism of African names after the fashion of Catullus 7, which is in his mind here. For *arentes*, cf. Horace, *C*. 3.4.31f., 'arentes arenas/litoris Assyrii'.

116   *faucibus . . . ab Orci*   Another imaginative addition by B.

117   *gradu . . . citato*   A cliché in the poetry of the Silver Age to which B. is partial.

119   *sacerdotem*   A general rendering of the more specific 'sheep-sacrificer' in the Greek (121).

122–4   *desertis . . . viva*   The Greek merely has 'leaving the dark abodes and gates of Hades'.

126   *telo . . . timendus*   The alliterative ts carefully represent the πς in 127–8 of the Greek, the phrase being B.'s own elaboration. For *trifidus*, see *trifida . . . flamma* at Ovid, *Met*. 2.325, etc.

129–31   The equivalent lines in Euripides (132–5) have often been condemned as spurious, but the arguments are not wholly secure.

134   *miserum me*   The phrase has no equivalent in the Greek.

### 136–211.

140   *ad thalami fores*   B. is here guilty of an error in translation; he has rendered προνώπιος 'before the door', in mistake for προνωπής, 'drooping'.

141   This line is printed as an interrogation in the 1557 edition and in Ruddiman, but there is no mark of interrogation in the Aldine Euripides, and the line (addressed to Admetus) is clearly exclamatory.

142   *coniuge orbus* is an addition to the Greek (145).

143   The mark of interrogation is not in the 1557 edition, but it is in the Aldine Euripides and Ruddiman rightly prints it.

145   *funeri*   B. has rendered the general sense of the obscure text of the Aldine Euripides (148: ἐπ' αὐτοῖς).

147   *sciat* must mean 'He must realise that he is orphaned'; but Euripides (150) has written '*She* must know then, that she will die renowned. . .'

157   *decorum* rendering λευκόν ('white') in a general sense.

   *ex armario*   But κεδρίνων δόμων in the Greek is probably not a chest, but an inner chamber. It is possible that B. decided to render δοχῶν, 'receptacles', rather than δόμων.

165   *acerbo . . . funere*   Rhetorical elaboration of the Greek.
166   *Parca praecox*   The Greek merely has 'May they not die before their time' (168).
171–2   In the 1557 edition there is a colon after *comae* in 170. We have preferred to punctuate with a comma there and with a stronger stop after *doloris* at 172. *madida* must be feminine, agreeing with Alcestis, and accordingly it is better to take it with the preceding lines 168–70; this is the pattern of the sense in Euripides 170–3.
178   *me*   As Dähnhardt states, B. omits the troublesome sense of μονήν (180) in Euripides, which means either 'You have destroyed me and not Admetus' or 'You have destroyed me alone of all brides'.
181   *non castior*   This is a possible interpretation of σώφρων . . . μᾶλλον in the Greek, though it could also mean 'more prudent'.
185   *ex aedibus*   As at 140, B. has translated προνώπιος instead of προνωπής, 'stumbling'.
189   *hunc . . . illam*   B.'s emphasis on the sex of the children, not expressed by the Greek, adds pathos to the situation.
197   *sempiternum . . . arcessiit*   B. translates the Aldine reading οὔποτ' ἐκλελήσεται.
202   B. pads out the line prosaically.
203–4   *languidum . . . inertis*   Elmsley (like Murray in the O.C.T.) posits a lacuna in the Greek after 204; B. translates the Aldine text, which has no comma after παρειμένη δέ (203).
206–7   The equivalent lines in Euripides (207–8) are identical with *Hecuba* 411–12, except that προσόψεται replaces προσόψομαι in *Hecuba,* and Dale regards the repetition of ideas in 206 and 208 as intolerable. But the Aldine Euripides contains 206–208, and B. translates accordingly.
210   *rebus adsunt turbidis*   Cf. Cicero, *Phil.* 2.39, 'esse in turbidis rebus'.

212–286.   In B. we have first a short interchange between the Chorus and the maid-servant (212–49). This is the arrangement which B. found in the Aldine. All these lines are assigned to the Chorus by mss other than *L,* and in the O.C.T. Murray follows Hermann in assigning them to five different voices within the Chorus.
212   *O di*   The invocation in the Greek is to Zeus.
220   *O Apollo sancte*   B. here clarifies the invocation ὦναξ Παίαν for his audience.

## NOTES

224–7   The equivalent Greek lines (224–5) state: 'Be a deliverer from death; check the bloodthirsty Hades.'
230   There is a mark of interrogation at the end of the line in the 1557 edition and in Ruddiman, but the Aldine text of Euripides does not have it; the exclamation is more in keeping with the Greek.
234   There is a question-mark in the equivalent line of the Greek (230) in the O.C.T., but not in the Aldine nor in the 1557 edition of B.
   *tereti*   Dramatic elaboration by B.; the line is inspired by Ovid, *Met.* 10.113, 'pendebant tereti gemmata monilia collo'.
237   *videbis*   In the O.C.T. of the Greek ἰδού, ἰδού follows, but this does not appear in the Aldine, and B. likewise omits it.
238   *sed iam maritus*   Euripides (233) has 'She and her husband'; has B. misread ἥδ' as ἤδη?
242   *sub cava . . . viscera*   Rhetorical elaboration for κατὰ γᾶς (237).
249   *vitalem . . . vitam*   Admirably rendering the pattern of the Greek (242–3).
258   *flecte precibus*   But the Greek has 'Entreat . . . to take pity' (251).
259   *biscalmam*   Not in the *TLL*. *scalmus* is a thole-pin for an oar; δίσκαλμος exists in Greek, though δίκωπος (cf. Eur. 444) is commoner.
   *ratem*   The Aldine Euripides has deleted the words ἐν λίμνᾳ ('on the marsh', i.e. the Styx) which follow, and accordingly B. has omitted them.
260–1   *portitor . . . conto*   This passage is full of echoes of Virgil, *Aen.* 6 (298, 302, etc.).
263   *praesto cetera cuncta*   renders the Aldine reading τάδ' ἕτοιμα; B. has then to take ταχύνει as imperative, 'propera'.
269–70   *Pluto . . . celer*   B.'s rendering shows that the text of Euripides is perfectly comprehensible, though Murray obelises it. The following words μέθες με, excised by the Aldine (and the O.C.T.), are ignored by B.
271   The 1557 edition has a mark of interrogation at the end of the line; but the Aldine Euripides has a full-stop, and an exclamation-mark seems more appropriate.
275   B. has omitted the sentiment 'Death is near' which follows in Euripides.
283   *tolera*   In the Greek before the imperative there is a second adjuration in addition to 'By the gods', 'By the children whom you will leave motherless'. This does not appear in the Aldine text, which explains the absence of an equivalent Latin phrase here. Both the 1557 edition and Ruddiman insert no stop after *superos*, but this would distort the sense of the Greek.

287–408.

289  *salutem*  B. has not translated the difficult πρεσβεύουσα, 'putting you first'.

296  *aetate quamvis integra*  A baffling rendering until it is noted that the Aldine Euripides has ἠοῦς ἔχουσα δῶρ' ἐν οἷς ἐτερπόμην, 'when I had the gifts of morning' (i.e., youth) 'in which I took joy.'

298  The 1557 edition and Ruddiman punctuate with commas after *mater* and *linquere,* but the sense of the Greek encourages punctuation as in the text.

304–5  There is some rhetorical elaboration here; Euripides has: 'You would not grieve at deprivation of your wife, and leave your children motherless' (296–7).

315  *livor . . . ciet* renders the single word φθόνῳ (306).

318  *cruenta*  An additional touch to the Greek (310).

320  The equivalent line of the Greek (312) was rightly excised by Pierson as a repetition of 195; but B. translates it because it appears in the Aldine.

321–2  *quomodo . . . aetate*  The rendering of πῶς κορευθήσῃ is painstakingly full.

323  The comma after *dabit* faithfully follows the punctuation of the Aldine Euripides; contrast the O.C.T.

329  *timori* is not in the Greek.

331  *luce cassas*  A favourite phrase of B.; see e.g., *Medea* 1378n, 387 below.

336  *nil verebor*  In the Aldine Euripides οὐ χάζομαι (326) is printed for οὐχ ἅζομαι, but the difference in meaning is slight.

345  *luctus hic* translates the Aldine reading τόδε, not τὸ σόν ('Grief for you') at 336.

352  *dura . . . suspiria*  The line represents the single word στένειν (341).

354  *coronae floreae*  Perhaps inspired by Plautus, *Aul.* 385, 'hasce coronas floreas'.

355  *cantusve dulces*  Euripides: 'The music which possessed my house' (344).

356–7  *ad . . . sonos*  The Greek has 'I will not beguile my heart to sing to the Libyan pipe'.

359  *periti . . . artificis*  Plural in Euripides.

366  *lurida*  A picturesque addition to the Greek.

369–71  The Greek merely has: '. . .so as to rescue you from Hell by charming with songs the daughter or husband of Demeter'; the adjectives *blandum, furvae, duri,* all superimposed, add poetic intensity.

*furvae* here and *centiceps* (372) evoke Horace, *C*. 2.13.21, 34f.: 'furvae Proserpinae . . . belua centiceps'.
373 *silentes . . . manes* expands ψυχοπομπός in Euripides. *almum* is a further addition to the Greek (362).
378–9 *nam . . . collocari* In Euripides Admetus says that he will order the children (τούσδε) to do this, but the Aldine reads τάσδε . . . πλεύρας (366). Where B. has *uno sepulcro,* the Greek has 'In the same coffin of cedarwood'; B. obviously felt the improbability of the wood's surviving until the death of Admetus.
379–80 *et conseri . . . meum* 'And that my flank stretched out be joined to yours, close to you'—a clumsy but close rendering of the Greek.
386–7 The Greek contains the additional phrase ἐφ' ὑμῖν, 'over you', which gives point to the address to the children.
387 *luce cassam* Cf. 331n.
398 *sat superque cladis* The Greek has merely: 'It is enough that I die before you.' Cf. *Jeph*. 1253, 'patratur una caede sceleris plus satis'.
399 *sors saeva* A more spirited rendering of ὦ δαῖμον (384).

409–27. This monody, punctuated by two iambic lines from Admetus, is sung by the male child. "Children are usually kept anonymous in Greek tragedy" (Dale), so that Murray prints ΠΑΙΣ at 393, 406. But the name Eumelos appears in all the Euripides mss and early editions, which is why B. includes it.
409 *mater* For the colloquial μαῖα, 'mamma' of the Greek (393).
410–11 *neque . . . solis* In the Greek merely 'She is no longer beneath the sun'.
413 *languidulos* The pathetic adjective is not in the Greek.
420–22 *O me . . . eadem sors* renders well the traditional text of Euripides 409–11, where the lack of metrical correspondence with 396–8 suggests corruption.
423 *infrugiferos* has one reference (Ps. Ambrose) in *TLL;* it appears also in *Franciscanus* 102. The word is found also in Salmon Macrin's verses at about this date.

428–448.

432 *perculit* The Greek equivalent, προσέπτατ' (421), suggests rather the approach of a bird of prey.
440–1 In the Greek, the instruction is to yoke the four-horse chariot-teams and to draw up the single horses, and then crop all their manes;

B. does not appear to have grasped this. *superbam* is rhetorical elaboration.

443 *suaviloquae* Another of B.'s compound adjectives (cf. *Eleg.* 4.56); the Greek (430) mentions merely the 'sound' of the lyre.

446 *paribus officiis* The Greek has 'better' (433).

446–7 *neque . . . queam* Elaboration of Euripides' 'She is worthy of honour in my eyes'.

449–94.

449–50 *vale, quae . . . habitas* A slight misunderstanding of the Greek at 436–7, which has: 'May you dwell content in your sunless abode in the house of Hades.'

452 *nigricomans* Not found in Classical Latin; perhaps B.'s own coining to represent the similar compound in the Greek (438).

454–5 *vehit et subigit . . . ratem celerem* B.'s extra detail for Euripides' 'at the oar'.

458 *biscalma* See 259n.

460 *montigena* Another compound adjective not in *TLL;* it appears in Erasmus, *Hecuba* 1117.

466 *vere benigno* This is not in the Greek, but the Carneian month at Sparta heralded the beginning of the year, and B. wishes to make this clear.

468 *inque beatis* The Greek (452) clearly means 'amongst the rich blessings at Athens', i.e. amongst the rich olive-groves. B. translates literally, presumably because he is uncertain of the meaning.

474 *alno* A poetic rendering of κώπᾳ in the Greek. Cf. Sil. Ital. 3.458, 'Fluminea sonipes religatus ducitur alno'.

479 *terra levis . . . sit* The equivalent phrase in Euripides is the first known appearance of this expression, which became a motif familiar on epitaphs. *super ossa* is added by B.

483 *nec qui genuit* B. follows the sense of the Aldine Euripides, in which ὃν ἔτεκον is taken with what precedes. The sense of the O.C.T. is: 'Those hard-hearted parents who bore you did not preserve you . . . '

488–9 *iuventae iuvenis* The Aldine Euripides at 472 has νέᾳ νέου (the reading of *LP*) where the O.C.T. has νέᾳ only; B. reproduces the jingle.

489 *redimens . . . mariti* Not in the Greek.

491 *sponsam* renders ἀλόχου in the Aldine text, later excised by Wilamowitz.

492–3 *quae . . . mecum* A reversal of the order of the clauses in

Greek; this renders ἦ γάρ . . . ξυνείη (475), whilst *at . . . voluptas* renders τοῦτο . . . μέρος (474).

495–586.

497 *urbem*  B. translates the Aldine reading πόλιν, not χθόνα as in the O.C.T.
498 *Pheraeas . . . domos*  Plural because the Aldine has Φεραίων ἄστυ (*LP*) and not Φεραίου as in the O.C.T.
502 *hospes*  'host' or 'friend' here, as the Greek shows.
506 *caeso . . . rege*  The Greek implies rather than states that the king will be slain.
511 *an forte*  The formula is intended to deny the possibility, as in the Greek.
513 *ferarum*  'mountain-beasts' in the Greek (495).
515 *educator*  sc. *equorum*.
516 *frenat*  The sense of the Greek (498) is rather: 'He is the lord of the shield of golden Thrace.'
519–20 *manum non contulisse*  At first sight B. seems to have mistranslated here. But the Aldine Euripides has οὐ χρή, not εἰ χρή, at 501, with the meaning: 'I must not join battle with the offspring of Mars'. B. attempts to create sense from this by rendering 'It would have been best not to join battle. . .'. See Fries, 180 n.1.
521 *Cygno* translates the name Kuknos from the Greek (504).
524 *hostis*  Rendering πολεμίων (Aldine), not πολέμιαν (O.C.T.).
527–8 *clarum genus . . . rector inclite*  The laudatory adjectives are not in the Greek.
528–9 *salve . . . utinam*  In the Greek, Hercules' word χαῖρε (510) means 'rejoice' as well as 'greetings', and Admetus replies that he would like to rejoice if he could. B. tries to create a similar play with *salve*, 'be well'.
532 *fors*  'God' in Euripides (514).
534 B. has taken this line of Euripides (516) as a question; but the Aldine has no such mark of interrogation. The sense of the Greek is: 'Your father was indeed ripe for death, if he has gone.'
545–6 B. takes a couplet to render Euripides 527: 'The person doomed to die is dead, and he who has died lives no longer.'
546 *vivere*  Both the 1557 edition and Ruddiman read *iure*, but the Greek suggests that B. wrote *vivere*. It is true that this introduces an anapaest into the fourth foot, which Seneca avoids. But there are several examples of this in B.'s tragedies; see, e.g., 309, 552 in this play.

550  *mulier . . . modo*   The ambiguity in the Greek is beautifully rendered.

556  A rather prosaic rendering of Euripides 538 ('What action do you contemplate in patching together these words?').

557  *hospitis domum* translates the Aldine reading ξένου πρὸς ἄλλην (538).

558  *bona verba*   This phrase bears the sense of 'speak words of good omen', and is found in Terence, *Andria* 204 and often in Ovid (see *TLL*). It is used here to render οὐκ ἔστιν, 'no, no'.

560  *mortui sint*   In the Greek, 'they are dead' (541: τεθνᾶσι).

565  *posticum* 'backdoor', is familiar to B. from comedy (e.g. Plautus, *Stich.* 450, *Most.* 931). The Greek is slightly different in sense: 'Take him off and open the guest-chambers away from this hall' (the Aldine has τῶνδε).

568  *quod medium...*   B. tries to render the reading of the mss and Aldine, ἐν δὲ κλῄσατε (548), but this would have to be regarded as tmesis. Since the sense of ἐγκλείω ('shut in') is inappropriate, England's emendation εὖ δέ is accepted by Murray in the O.C.T.

569–70  *luctus ut . . . dolor*   Much more expressive than the Greek 549f. ('. . .that guests feasting hear lamentations or be grieved.').

571  *tanta*   The Aldine Euripides has τοσαύτης not τοιαύτης (O.C.T.).

575  A beautifully succinct rendering of Euripides 555–6.

579  *siticulosum*   Doubtless recalled from Horace, *Epodes* 3.16.

584  *ille*   B. wrongly takes τῷ μέν (565) as meaning Hercules, whereas the sense is 'to one individual'.

587–633.

587  *liberi*   In the Greek ἐλεύθερος goes with οἶκος. B. regards this as hypallage, and transfers the epithet to *viri*.

588  *qua*   The reading of all editions is *quae*, which has to be taken as object after *incola*, giving *incola* a strained participial sense. The easier reading *qua* follows *dignatus est* and limits *hospita*, which is in apposition to *atria*.

591–6  A noble rendering of Euripides 572–7.

592  *lanigeros*   This elaboration upon the Greek is taken over from Virgil, *Georg.* 3.287, 'lanigeros greges'.

593  *curvis . . . vallibus*   'Slanting hillsides' in the Greek.

594  *per prata virentia . . . blanda*   Neither of these touches is in the Greek.

## NOTES

602   *fulvicomantum*   Not in TLL; it may be another of B.'s compound creations. *flavicomans* appears in Prudentius, *Apoth.* 495.

605–6   *maculosus . . . hinnuleum chorus*   An expanded rendering of ποικιλόθριξ νεβρός (584–5); for *hinnuleum,* cf. Horace, *C.* 1.23.1.

608   *alticomum,* a compound which the Greek suggested to B., appears in Tertullian, *Jud. Dom.* 8.

609   *docto* for εὔφρονι, 'good-counselling'.

612   *limpidum*   The Greek has 'beautiful-flowing' (589); Catullus 4.24 is obviously in B.'s mind.

614ff.   The text at Euripides 590ff. is dubious, but B. has heroically struggled to make general sense of it.

618   *pertinet*   The subject must be *domus Admeti*.

624   *recipit*   The Aldine Euripides has the future δέξεται, not δέξατο.

627–30   *nam pudori . . . adest*   A fine rendering of Euripides 600–602. The Aldine does not have ἄγαμαι after these sentences; hence B. has not offered a translation.


634–786.

635   *rogum*   But πυράν (608) probably means *tumulus* here.

643   *sane* renders οὐδεὶς ἀντερεῖ (615).

644   *perpessu*   Cf. Cic. *Tusc.* 2.20, 'O multa dictu gravia, perpessu aspera'.

653–4   *manes . . . placidos bonosque*   An elaborated version of εὖ σοι γένοιτο (627).

655–6   The slight illogicality ('I think such a marriage is advantageous for men; otherwise *it is better* never to be acquainted with marriage-bonds' is the full sense) reflects the same construction in the Greek.

658   *amicum*   The contracted genitive plural *metri gratia*.

661   *fata . . . tollerent* clarifies the meaning of ὠλλύμην.

664–5   *nec . . . fuisti*   Though there is a mark of interrogation after the equivalent phrase in the O.C.T. of Euripides (636), the Aldine has a comma.

666–8   Likewise here B. has translated according to the Aldine punctuation, which has no question-marks (contrast the O.C.T. at 638, 639).

671   *aut*   The Aldine Euripides has ἦτ'ἆρα, which B. may have read as ἦ τ'ἆρα.

672–3   *supremo in limine, senecta languidus*   Two phrases much more vivid than the plain expressions of Euripides (643). Seneca, *Herc. Fur.* 1131–4 may have been in B.'s mind ('ite ad Stygios, umbrae, portus,/ite, innocuae, quas in primo/limine vitae scelus oppressit/patriusque furor');

cf. also Lucan 2.106, Prudentius *Cath.* 12.125f. (perhaps a reminiscence of Seneca).

682–4   *quod . . . luctibus*   The equivalent couplet in the Greek (651–2) is excised from modern texts because it repeats 295–6.

690   *a filio*   Implicit but not expressed in the Greek.

697   *quod ad te pertinet*   The sense of the Greek at 666 is rather 'quantum in tua potestate fuit' (Dale).

698   *iamdudum*   Rendering more emphatically the perfect tense τέθνηκα (666).

705   *nemo . . . queritur*   An addition to the Greek.

707   *bilem*   The Aldine Euripides has φρένα not φρένας.

708   *lacessis arrogans*   A rhetorical rendering of αὐχεῖς (675).

716   *non prior ut*   B.'s Aldine text has ὀφείλων, οὐχ ὑπερθνῄσκων. ('owing you this, but not dying on your behalf').

718   *morte*   'by dying' not 'from death'; cf. Euripides 684.

726   In the Aldine Euripides (691) there is a mark of interrogation after φῶς; the Latin suggests that B. reproduced this after *lucem est*. In the Greek there is a further question-mark after 691, but B. has introduced *puta* here instead.

727–9   A much more rhetorical version of Euripides 692–3. Hadrian's *animula vagula blandula* (*Carm. ap. Spart. Hadr.* 25) may have been in B.'s mind at *blandula tamen*.

735   *formose functa*   B.'s version loses the irony inherent in Euripides 698: 'She has died for you, a noble youth indeed!'

*periit*   the mark of interrogation at the equivalent point of the O.C.T. of Euripides is not in the Aldine.

*at enim*   For B.'s employment of this phrase in a sense other than 'But, you may say. . .', see *Medea* 241.

740   *amicos*   Again here there is no mark of interrogation in the Aldine Euripides.

747–8   B. found it too difficult to reproduce the rhetorical repetition of ἐξαμαρτάνειν (709–10) here.

754   *efferunt*   But the Greek has '*You* are carrying out. . .'.

760   *suave . . . suave*   Scanned trisyllabically, a late and rare practice.

762   *non funus effers*   The Greek βαστάζων (724) contains the sense of 'in place of yourself' which B. does not incorporate.

766   *haec, illa*   A curious contrast; in the Greek (728) ἥδε . . . τήνδε both refer to Alcestis.

769   *coniugis*   Clarifying σοῖσι (731).

774   *miseram*   Implicit in the Greek (736) but not expressed.

777   *nihil moratus*   An addition to the Greek.

780   *miserabilis* renders σχετλία (741), but the meaning of the Greek here is 'enduring'.
782–3   *bonus ac placidus Atlantiades*   The learned patronymic for Mercury is common in Ovid (*Met.* 1.682, 2.704, etc.). The two adjectives render πρόφρων.
785   *Persephone* specifying 'the bride of Hades' in the Greek.
786   *vitae . . . bene actae*   Not in the Greek.

787–908.

793   *fortuitos apparatus* would be cryptic if we did not have the Greek; it means 'hospitality as one finds it', 'pot luck'.
796   B. has not tried to render κίσσινον; ivy seems to have decorated large vessels.
801   *latrat* renders ὑλακτῶν (760), the howling characteristic of a wolf or dog.
808   *sicarium*   Much stronger than the Greek.
810   *nuda planxi pectora.*   B. seems to have misunderstood the Greek (768), which means: 'I did not stretch out my hand' (in farewell as the cortege passed).
816   *taetricum*   A stronger expression than πεφροντικός, 'preoccupied'.
828–9   *lubrica . . . vices*   The Greek (785) merely says: 'It is not clear in what direction the whim of fortune will proceed.' B. expresses this in a characteristically Roman idiom. For *lubrica fortuna,* see Curtius 7.8.24; Boethius, *Cons.* 1.5.28, 'cur tantas lubrica versat/fortuna vices?' Cf. B.'s *Miscell.* 1.1f. and below, 1239.
833   *nostrum*   The Greek says σόν, 'yours', rather than 'ours'. The translation evokes Horace, *C.* 1.9.14f., 'quem fors dierum cumque dabit, lucro/appone'.
838   *opinor*   In the Greek this is taken with the preceding line; '. . .if I seem to you to speak the truth—that is my opinion'.
841–2   *scyphus inversus*   A good rendering of the Greek: 'As the gurgle of the cup enters your throat' (798).
843   *effingat*   B. is too good a Latinist to have written *effinget.*
845–6   B.'s version is not so clear as the Greek. The sense here is: 'The life of the gloomy and melancholy is an ordeal rather than a life. . .'.
851   The second part of this line is in the interrogative in the O.C.T. of Euripides, but not in the Aldine, which B. has followed.
854   This line translates the Aldine reading οὔκουν· ὀθνείου γὰρ οὔνεκ'εὖ πάσχει νέκρου, which is quite different from the O.C.T. of Murray.

855 *familiare* renders the Aldine γ'οἰκεῖος (O.C.T. θυραῖος).
856 The line is punctuated as a question in our text as in the Aldine Euripides. The 1557 edition and Ruddiman have no mark of interrogation.
857 *tangant* We read the subjunctive as in the 1557 edition; R. hesitantly suggests *tangunt* to conform with the Greek.
858 *exterae* This is the 1557 reading, 'grief for a stranger'.
859 *adferam* The Greek indicates that this is subjunctive.
862–3 *rasile . . . lugubrem* This is the order in the Aldine Euripides 818f.; in the O.C.T. Murray has reversed the two expressions.
866 *recepit* Euripides actually wrote 'And *you* still gave me hospitality?' B. uses the third person for greater emphasis.
872 *credidi* The Greek has: 'He persuaded me by saying. . .'. B. alters this purposefully to represent the ambivalence of Admetus' words at 536ff. more faithfully.
873 *vi coactus* The Greek more exactly means 'doing violence to my feelings'.
876 *demens* Not in the Greek.
877 *sed culpa . . . tua est* A good rendering of the exclamatory infinitive in the Greek (832).
883 *O anime corque* renders καρδία ψυχή τ'ἐμή of the Aldine.
889–90 *nigrantis squalido . . . stolae* Perhaps a reminiscence of Ennius 339W, 'squalida saeptus stola'.
893 *e latebris . . . inruens* translates the reading of the mss and Aldine, λοχήσας (846).
897 *aucupantem* Picturesque elaboration of the hunting image.

908–989.

915 *almae* Conventional elaboration of the Greek.
917–18 B. appears to have misunderstood the Greek, which means: 'Death has handed *her* (the hostage) over to Hades.'
919ff. In the O.C.T. of Euripides Murray assigns the lines 872–6 separately to individual members of the Chorus, but the Aldine does not do this.
923–4 These lines seem to render Euripides 875, 'You do not avail her below'; the following lines in the Greek (876–7, 'Never to see the countenance of a dear wife face to face is grievous') are not rendered by B.
929 *ulli* A strange rendering, for Euripides has μετὰ τῆσδε, 'with her'.

930–31  *lectos . . . beatam* renders Euripides 883: 'I envy mortals unmarried and childless'.

932–3  *unam . . . luctus* translates the Aldine reading of Euripides 883–4: ψυχῇ δὲ μιᾷ τῆσδ' ὑπεραλγεῖν/μέτριον ἄχθος, 'It is a modest burden to lament the one life of Alcestis'. Murray rightly prints Stobaeus' μία γὰρ ψυχή, τῆς ὑπεραλγεῖν. . . , 'Such men have one life, and it is a modest burden to lament it'. B. seeks to make sense of the Aldine by omitting mention of Alcestis. The use of *sarcina,* an elaboration of the Greek, is a favourite Ovidian metaphor in this sense.

939ff.  B. follows the arrangement of the Aldine, which allots Euripides 889–94 to the Chorus as a whole.

949  *triste*  The Greek has merely κοίλην, 'hollow'.

950  *fida*  Euripides more emphatically says 'by far the best' (899).

958  *solam . . . spem*  Elaboration of μονόπαις (906). Cf. *Jephthes* 727: *sola . . . spes filia.*

959–61  *etsi . . . aevo*  Elegant, well-turned and more expressive than the Greek.

962  *O mutati . . . tecti*  An imaginative rendering of ὦ σχῆμα δόμων (912).

965–70  A splendid yet quite faithful rendering of Euripides 915ff.

987  *quae nova . . . imago*  More dramatic than Euripides' prosaic τί νέον τόδε; (931).

988–9  Again a higher-flown version than Euripides' 'Before now death has separated many from their wives'.


990–1019.

998  *domi*  The mss of Euripides and the Aldine have εἰσόδου at 943; ἐξόδου (O.C.T.) is Lenting's emendation.

1000  *maerore . . . conficit*  The Aldine (994) has ἐξολεῖ, apparently a misprint for the reading of *LP,* ἐξελεῖ; the correct form is ἐξελᾷ of *VB,* 'will drive me out'. B. translates as though from ἐξόλλυμι.

1008  *enecabunt*  The Greek at 950–51 suggests rather 'will drive me from outside in again'.

1010ff.  Fries 183 suggests that these lines (and 672ff., 681f.) were the inspiration for the theme of the *Jephthes,* which must accordingly have been composed later than the *Alcestis.* The suggestion was worth making, but is by no means certain.

1015  The sentence is posed as a question in the O.C.T. of Euripides, but not in the Aldine.

1016  *non ausus*  Euripides has 'not wishing' (958).

1019   A splendid rendering of Euripides 961, 'For I suffer ill-repute and ill-fortune'.

1020–76.

1020–22   B. incorporates the Horatian motif *profano . . . vulgo* (C. 3.1.1) into the theme of rising to poetic heights.
1025   *non raro*   The Aldine Euripides has πλεῖστον, not πλείστων.
1030   *manus*   The Greek (970) talks of 'the speech' of Orpheus, but B. changes to 'hand' to conform with the image of writing.
1035   *hanc . . . tulit*   This is not spelt out in the Greek.
1036   *solas . . . aras*   B. seems to have erred by taking μόνας (972) with βωμούς rather than with θεᾶς.
1045   *dextra facili*   The Aldine Euripides has the reading οὐ βίᾳ rather than σὺ βίᾳ; hence B.'s translation.
1048   *infrenem* is an attempt to render ἀποτόμου (981), 'sheer'; the notion is of 'a steep cliff-wall against which man dashes his head in vain' (Dale).
1049   *infragili*   'Inescapable' in the Greek; the Latin adjective is found in Pliny the Elder and Ovid.
1054   *notha*   This meaning for σκότιοι (989) is offered by B. following the explanation of the scholia of the mss *BV*. But the meaning of the Greek is probably 'in the darkness of death' (Dale).
1060–67   An excellent rendering with some rhetorical elaboration of Euripides 995–7.
1069–70   *haec . . . redemit*   In the Greek she merely 'predeceased her husband'.
1072   *sospita*   The imperative of the verb, rendering εὖ δοίης.
1073–5   *ita . . . colet*   Once again elaborating on the Greek, which means: 'Such are the words that will greet her' (1005).

1077–1246.

1086   *laetus* is not in the Greek; it accentuates Hercules' unseemly behaviour.
1090   The punctuation proposed here shows Hercules seeking to explain why he has come back again, not seeking to explain again why he has returned.
1095   *ancillam*   Rendering πρόσπολον from the Aldine, not προσπολεῖν.
1098   *sudore digna*   The Aldine reads ἄξιον πόνου (*LP*).

# NOTES

1103   *post haec*   B. does not make it sufficiently clear that the girl was an additional prize for boxing and wrestling.

1124   *caste*   Elaboration of the Greek (1049) necessary to clarify the sense.

1125   *an virum in commercio?*   The Greek clarifies this cryptic query: "Will she live, then, under the roof of men?"

1128   *tui* reproduces the Greek σοῦ literally. The sense is 'your interests'.

1135   *sponsamque vereor,* etc.   The sequence of thought is illogical here. 'I fear causing a double resentment, that of the citizens—lest someone charge me and say that I am betraying a wife who deserves the best from me, and that I enjoy the embrace of another girl—and I also reverence my dear wife. . .'. This anacoluthon is reproduced from the Greek, but B. omits 'I must take forethought for my wife' (1061). As a result of this, the phrase in 1137, 'me multa circumspicere par' stands by itself. In Murray's O.C.T. at 1060–61 the sense should run on from τῆς θανούσης to πολλήν, with the intervening ἀξία δέ μοι σέβειν in parenthesis; the punctuation is faulty.

1143   *horror obsidet*   In the Greek the girl is the subject of θολοῖ—'she perturbs my heart'.

1149   *divinitus*   A translation of ἐκ Διός in the Aldine Euripides, for which the O.C.T. has ὥστε σήν.

1152   *at cuinam* renders ἀλλὰ ποῦ, which the next line suggests means 'Where could this be?'.

1157   *dolendi . . . voluptas* clarifying ἔρως τις (1080). 'The pleasure in grief' theme is a feature of Petrarchan love-poetry which came into vogue in France in B.'s time.

1164   *taedae novae*   The Greek has '*longing for* a new marriage'.

1170   *stulte facis*   In the Greek 'You *incur the charge of* foolishness'.

1171   *ulla . . . femina*   B. seems here to be trying to improve the sense of a difficult passage; in the Greek Admetus says that *Hercules* will not call him a bridegroom.

1174   *nunc*   The Greek has νυν, not νῦν: 'Receive, then, . . .'; there is a splendid element of dramatic irony here, lost in B.'s incorrect translation.

1193   In the Greek (1116) Admetus addresses Hercules formally as 'lord', to register his resentment at the injunction.

1195   *sectum ad caput*   'to the trunkless head'. This is what the mss and Aldine edition of Euripides have (καρατόμῳ), but Lobeck's καρατομῶν ('as though to cut off the Gorgon's head') is rightly accepted by Murray.

1201   B. follows the punctuation of the Aldine Euripides.
1203   *lactans*   B. knows this word in the sense of 'beguile' from his favourite authors Plautus and Terence. The Aldine Euripides has ἐμπλήσσει, not ἐκπλήσσει, here.
1206   *cave esse credas*   Rendering the idiomatic ἐποιήσω of the Greek.
1213   This is framed as a question in the 1557 edition, and the reply of Hercules confirms this punctuation, which diverges from that of the Aldine Euripides.
1220   *tyranno* translates κοιράνῳ in the Aldine Euripides (1140).
1222   The Greek (1142) adds 'from ambush'.
1231   *dapes . . . sacras*   In the Greek merely 'lodge at our hearth' (1151).
1239ff.   Euripides' exodos is exactly the same as in *Andromache, Helen,* and *Bacchae,* and that of *Medea* differs only in the first line. B.'s rendering has echoes of his version of *Medea,* but is not unashamedly identical.

# SELECT BIBLIOGRAPHY

*Editions of the plays*

*Medea Euripidis poetae tragici Georgio Buchanano Scoto interprete* (Paris, Vascosan 1544)

*Jephthes sive Votum, Tragoedia, authore Georgio Buchanano Scoto* (Paris, Morel 1554; second edition, Paris, Vascosan 1557)

*Euripidis Alcestis, Georgio Buchanano interprete* (Paris, Vascosan 1556; second edition, 1557)

*Baptistes, sive Calumnia, Tragoedia, auctore Georgio Buchanano Scoto* (London, Vautrollier 1577; second edition 1578. Further editions in 1578 from Edinburgh, Charteris; Frankfurt, Wechel; Antwerp, Henricius). (For a full list of later editions, see McFarlane, *Buchanan, App. A*, and the forthcoming Buchanan Bibliography compiled by Dr. John Durkan.)

*Georgii Buchanani opera omnia curante T. Ruddimano,* (2 vols. Edinburgh, Freebairn, 1715; new edition, edd. Ruddiman–Burman, Leiden, Langerak 1725)

*Early Editions of Euripides*

*Medea, Hippolytus, Alcestis, Andromache* (Florence, Francesco de Alopa, ed. Lascaris 1495?)

*Euripidis tragoediae septendecim* (Venice, Aldus 1503)

*Euripidis tragoediae octodecim* (Basel, Hervagius 1537; later editions, 1544, 1551)

*Euripidis . . . tragoediae XVIII nunc primum . . . per D. Camillum* (pseud.) *et Latio donatae et in lucem editae* (Basel, Winter 1541)

*Erasmus' version of Euripides*

*Euripidis Hecuba et Iphigenia latine facte, Erasmo . . . interprete* (Paris, Bade, 1506; second edition, Venice, Aldus 1507). Modern edition by J. H. Waszink (Amsterdam 1969)

*General*

Aitken, James M., *The Trial of George Buchanan before the Lisbon Inquisition* (Edinburgh 1939)

Bradner, Leicester, 'Latin Drama of the Renaissance', *Studies in the Renaissance* 4 (1957), 31–70

Delcourt, Marie, *Etude sur les traductions des tragiques grecs et latins en France depuis la renaissance* (Brussels 1925)

Fries, C., 'Quellenstudien zu G. Buchanan', *Neue Jahrbücher für die klassische Altertum* II 4 (1900), 177–92, II 5 (1900), 241–61

Griffiths, Richard, *The Dramatic Technique of Antoine de Montchrestien: Rhetoric and Style in French Renaissance Tragedy* (Oxford 1970)

Hall, Kathleen M., ed., Jodelle, *Cleopatre captive* (Exeter 1979)

Jondorf, Gillian, *Robert Garnier and the Themes of Political Tragedy in the Sixteenth Century* (Cambridge 1969)

Lawton, H. W., *Handbook of French Renaissance Dramatic Theory* (Manchester 1949)

Lebègue, Raymond, *La tragédie religieuse en France 1514–73* (Paris 1929)

——*George Buchanan, sa vie, son oeuvre, son influence en France et au Portugal* (Coimbra 1931)

——*La tragédie française de la renaissance*² (Brussels 1954)

Lindsay, W. M., 'Buchanan as a Latin Scholar', in *George Buchanan: a Memorial 1506–1906* (ed. D. Millar, St. Andrews 1907)

McFarlane, I. D., *A Literary History of France. Renaissance France 1470–1589* (London 1974)

——*Buchanan* (London 1981)

——'George Buchanan and France' in *Studies in French Literature Presented to H.W. Lawton* (Manchester 1968)

——'George Buchanan and French Humanism', in *Humanism in France at the End of the Middle Ages and in the early Renaissance* (ed. A.H.T. Levi, Manchester 1970)

Mueller, Martin, *Children of Oedipus* (Toronto 1980), 156–71

Pertusi, Agostino, 'La scoperta di Euripide nel Primo Umanesimo', *Italia medioevale e umanistica* III (1960)

——'Il ritorno alle fonti del teatro greco classico: Euripide nel umanesimo e nel rinascimento', *Byzantion* 33 (1963)

Reiss, T. J., *Tragedy and Truth* (Yale 1980), 40–77

Rolland, Joachim, 'Le Jephthes sive Votum, tragédie sacrée de George Buchanan (1554)', *Revue des études littéraires* (1920)

Roston, Murray, *Biblical Drama in England* (Evanston 1968)

Stone, Donald, jr., *French Humanist Tragedy* (Manchester 1974)

Sypherd, W.O., *Jephthah and his Daughter* (Newark, Delaware 1948)

Ville de Mirmont, H. de la, 'Les tragédies religieuses de Buchanan', in *George Buchanan: a Memorial* (see Lindsay above)

Waszink, J.H., 'Erasmus and his Influence on Anglo–Dutch Philology', in *The Anglo–Dutch Contribution to the Civilisation of Modern Europe* (Oxford 1976), 60–72

# CONSPECTUS METRORUM

## IEPHTHES

| | |
|---|---|
| 1–102 | iambic senarius. |
| 103–122 | anapaestic dimeter. |
| 123–146 | iambic senarius. |
| 147–172 | lesser asclepiad. |
| 173–219 | lesser sapphic (with adonius at 176, 183, 194, 204, 219). |
| 220–340 | iambic senarius. |
| 341–360 | iambic dimeter. |
| 361–430 | glyconic. |
| 431–592 | iambic senarius. |
| 593–617 | pherecratean. |
| 618–745 | iambic senarius. |
| 746–748 | anapaestic dimeter. |
| 749–783 | iambic senarius. |
| 784–841 | anapaestic dimeter. |
| 842–1055 | iambic senarius. |
| 1056–1125 | anapaestic dimeter (with adonius at 1107). |
| 1126–1330 | iambic senarius. |
| 1331–1360 | anapaestic dimeter (with adonius at 1346). |
| 1361–1450 | iambic senarius. |

## BAPTISTES

| | |
|---|---|
| 1–280 | iambic senarius. |
| 281–344 | lesser sapphic (with adonius at 284, 288, 292, 296, 300, 304, 308, 312, 322, 333, 344). |
| 345–572 | iambic senarius. |
| 573–623 | anapaestic dimeter. |
| 624–832 | iambic senarius. |
| 833–862 | iambic dimeter. |

CONSPECTUS METRORUM

| | |
|---|---|
| 863–965 | iambic senarius. |
| 966–996 | glyconic. |
| 997–1109 | iambic senarius. |
| 1110–1165 | lesser asclepiad. |
| 1166–1263 | iambic senarius. |
| 1264–1315 | lesser sapphic (with adonius at 1286, 1315). |
| 1316–1360 | iambic senarius. |

Considerable uncertainty surrounds the metres of some lines of the Greek plays. B. often attempts to reproduce the metrical effects of Euripides, but in the early editions accessible to him the Greek lines are often divided arbitrarily.

## *MEDEA*

| | |
|---|---|
| 1–100 | iambic senarius. |
| 101–227 | anapaestic dimeter (with adonius at 106, 183, 190; anapaestic monometer at 149; anapaestic ternarius at 169). |
| 228–380 | iambic senarius. |
| 381–387 | anapaestic dimeter (with iambic monometer at 385). |
| 388–435 | iambic senarius. |
| 436–466 | anapaestic dimeter (with anapaestic ternarius at 449; glyconic at 465; adonius at 466). |
| 467–664 | iambic senarius. |
| 665–703 | iambic dimeter. |
| 704–801 | iambic senarius. |
| 802–804 | anapaestic dimeter. |
| 805–806 | anapaestic ternarius. |
| 807–870 | iambic senarius. |
| 871–907 | anapaestic dimeter (with anapaestic ternarius at 872, 878–9). |
| 908–1024 | iambic senarius. |
| 1025–1046 | anapaestic dimeter (with anapaestic ternarius at 1030, 1034, 1039; pherecratean at 1033). |
| 1047–1129 | iambic senarius. |
| 1130–1166 | anapaestic dimeter (with dactylic trimeter at 1130–31). |
| 1167–1311 | iambic senarius. |
| 1312–1316 | anacreontius (= iambic dimeter catalectic). |

1321–1359   anapaestic dimeter (with iambic dimeter catalectic at 1317, 1319; iambic dimeter at 1318; anapaestic monometer at 1320).
1360–1462   iambic senarius.
1463–1471   anapaestic dimeter.
1472–1473   iambic senarius.
1474–1490   anapaestic dimeter.


# ALCESTIS

1–79    iambic senarius (with anapaestic dimeter 30–39, anapaestic monometer 40).
80–132  mixed lyric metres: anapaestic dimeter 80–86, 90–98, 103–7, 109
          anacreontius (= iambic dimeter catalectic) 87
          iambic senarius 88–9
          iambic dimeter 99–102
          anapaestic monometer 108
          lesser sapphic 110–132 (adonius at 124, 128).
133–211  iambic senarius.
212–286  mixed lyric metres: anapaestic dimeter 212–15, 231–7, 240–9, 255–6, 259–64, 267–71, 274–8, 280–6
          iambic senarius 229–30, 238–9, 253–4, 257–8, 265–6, 272–3, 279
          trochaic dimeter 216, 218, 220, 222
          trochaic dimeter catalectic 217, 219, 221, 223–7, 235–7
          anapaestic ternarius 250–2.
287–408  iambic senarius.
409–427  anapaestic dimeter (iambic senarius at 417–18).
428–448  iambic senarius.
449–494  mixed lyric metres:
          dactylic trimeter hypercatalectic 449–57
          anapaestic monometer 458
          anapaestic dimeter 459–94.

## CONSPECTUS METRORUM

| | |
|---|---|
| 495–586 | iambic senarius. |
| 587–633 | mixed lyric metres: glyconic 587–8, 590–6, 598–600, 604, 606–10, 624–5, 629, 631–2<br>pherecratean 589, 597, 601–3, 605, 628<br>trochaic dimeter catalectic 611–23, 626-7<br>adonius 633. |
| 634–779 | iambic senarius. |
| 780–786 | anapaestic dimeter. |
| 787–907 | iambic senarius. |
| 908–989 | mixed lyric metres: anapaestic dimeter 908–9, 911–18, 925–38, 939–54, 955–70, 983–9<br>anapaestic ternarius 910<br>anacreontius 919–21<br>iambic dimeter 939–45<br>adonius 955<br>trochaic dimeter catalectic 922–4, 971–82. |
| 990–1019 | iambic senarius. |
| 1020–1075 | pherecratean 1020–3, 1033–4, 1036, 1038, 1046–7, 1051, 1053, 1059, 1068, 1070, 1073<br>glyconic 1024–32, 1035, 1037, 1039–45, 1048–50, 1052, 1055–8, 1060–2, 1064–7, 1071–2, 1074–5<br>dactylic trimeter 1054, 1063, 1069. |
| 1076–1238 | iambic senarius. |
| 1239–1245 | anapaestic trimeter. |

# INDICES

## A. Authors and Passages Cited

### 1. *Scripture*

**Genesis**
| | |
|---|---|
| 6.5ff. | 250 |
| 11.1ff. | 250 |
| 19.24ff. | 250 |

**Exodus**
| | |
|---|---|
| 14.6ff. | 250 |
| 14.15ff. | 280 |
| 14.21ff. | 250, 254 |
| 14.22 | 250 |
| 17.8f. | 254 |
| 34.15 | 293 |

**Leviticus**
| | |
|---|---|
| 18.16 | 278 |
| 20.21 | 278 |

**Numbers**
| | |
|---|---|
| 16.31ff. | 250 |

**Deuteronomy**
| | |
|---|---|
| 28.30 | 293 |

**Judges**
| | |
|---|---|
| 10.7ff | 247, 249 |
| 10.16 | 247 |
| 11 | 246 |
| 11.1 | 248 |
| 11.13 | 251 |
| 11.24 | 251 |
| 11.30f. | 248 |
| 11.31 | 254 |

**1 Kings**
| | |
|---|---|
| 15.22 | 261 |
| 16.7 | 256 |

**2 Kings**
| | |
|---|---|
| 14.7 | 254 |

**4 Kings**
| | |
|---|---|
| 6.8ff. | 281 |

**1 Par.**
| | |
|---|---|
| 15.16 | 253 |

**Nehemias**
| | |
|---|---|
| 9.17 | 288 |

**Job**
| | |
|---|---|
| 33.4 | 273 |

**Psalms**
| | |
|---|---|
| 1.2 | 261 |
| 27.9 | 283 |
| 32.12 | 283 |
| 50.18 | 260 |
| 67.6 | 283 |
| 67.10 | 283 |
| 90.13 | 276 |
| 93.21 | 292 |
| 118.105 | 261 |

**Isaias**
| | |
|---|---|
| 1.11ff. | 260 |
| 40.3 | 284 |
| 44 | 252 |
| 46 | 252 |
| 56.10 | 284 |
| 59.7 | 292 |
| 61.5 | 293 |
| 66.3 | 260 |

**Jeremias**
| | |
|---|---|
| 5.17 | 293 |
| 26.6 | 293 |
| 49.11 | 283 |

# INDICES

*Osee*
| | |
|---|---|
| 6.6 | 260 |

*Amos*
| | |
|---|---|
| 5.11 | 293 |

*Michaeas*
| | |
|---|---|
| 6.6 | 260 |

*Zacharias*
| | |
|---|---|
| 13.2 | 282 |

*1 Maccabees*
| | |
|---|---|
| 13.51 | 253 |

*2 Maccabees*
| | |
|---|---|
| 3.15 | 277 |

*Matthew*
| | |
|---|---|
| 3.1ff. | 282, 284 |
| 3.4 | 272 |
| 3.5 | 282 |
| 3.7 | 282 |
| 5.18 | 262 |
| 7.15 | 284 |
| 9.13 | 260 |
| 10.16 | 284 |
| 10.28 | 288 |
| 11.9 | 274 |
| 12.7 | 260 |
| 12.38 | 285 |
| 14.1ff. | 278, 290 |
| 14.3 | 282 |
| 14.5 | 291 |
| 14.8f. | 277 |
| 16.1 | 285 |
| 16.14 | 284 |
| 18.22 | 273 |
| 21.23ff. | 285 |
| 22.21 | 279 |
| 23.5 | 277 |
| 23.14 | 283 |
| 23.23 | 283 |
| 23.29ff. | 293 |
| 24.3 | 285 |
| 27.4 | 292 |
| 27.24 | 292 |

*Mark*
| | |
|---|---|
| 1.1 | 284 |
| 1.3 | 284 |
| 1.6 | 272 |
| 6.14ff. | 278, 290 |
| 10.51 | 282 |
| 12.40 | 283 |

*Luke*
| | |
|---|---|
| 1.5ff. | 271 |
| 1.15 | 271 |
| 1.39ff. | 271 |
| 1.76 | 274 |
| 3.1ff. | 284 |
| 3.4 | 284 |
| 3.14 | 278 |
| 3.19 | 279, 290 |
| 6.26 | 282 |
| 9.7ff. | 290 |
| 10.3 | 284 |
| 10.29 | 280 |
| 16.17 | 262 |
| 17.12 | 257 |
| 20.47 | 283 |
| 21.20ff. | 293 |
| 22.50 | 270 |
| 22.66 | 283 |

*John*
| | |
|---|---|
| 1.15ff. | 284 |
| 1.25 | 272 |
| 3.5 | 289 |
| 3.26 | 282 |
| 8.46 | 285 |
| 14.18 | 288 |
| 18.10 | 270 |
| 18.23 | 285 |

*Acts*
| | |
|---|---|
| 3.2 | 314 |
| 4.5ff. | 283 |
| 5.34ff. | 270 |
| 20.29 | 284 |
| 22.3 | 270 |

*Romans*
| | |
|---|---|
| 14.10 | 293 |

*1 Cor.*
| | |
|---|---|
| 1.25 | 262 |
| 3.19 | 262 |
| 6.18f. | 272 |
| 13.1 | 253 |

## INDICES

*2 Cor.*
   4.17       288
   5.10       293

*2 Thess.*
   2.13       288

*2 Tim.*
   4.7        289

*James*
   1.17       288

*1 John*
   1.5        288

## 2. *Other Authors*

Ambrose
  *Hymns*    252
  *In Lucam* 1.5.105    276

Ammianus
  22.5.3    308
  27.5.1    308

Apuleius    309
  *Apology* 34    290
  *Metamorphoses* 7.24    259

Arboreus, Joannes
  *Theosophia*    16, 254

Aristophanes
  *Birds* 959    315

Aristotle    8
  *Poetics* 1451b    269
              1453a    251

Ausonius
  *Ephemeris* 3.4ff.    252
  *Epigrams* 1.7f.    246
  *Epistles* 2.15    277

Bacon, Francis
  *Essays,* 23    276

Boethius
  *Consolatio* 1.5.28    326

Buchanan
  *Elegies*  4.56    321
               5.56    253
  *Epigrams*  1.40    269
                2.6    269

*Franciscanus*
  23    261
  102    320
  155    284
  328    269
  464    290

*Fratres fraterrimi*
  5.29ff.    276
  *Miscellanea* 1.1f.    326
                    3.11    289
                    8.17    271
  *Silvae*  1.14    253

Calvin
  *Institution de la religion chretienne*
    1.10f.    254

Cassiodorus    308
  *In Psalm.* 101.5    283

Catullus
  1.4    296
  4.24    324
  7    316
  101.10    289

Claudian
  18.266    259
  23.5    246
  26.551    275

Cicero    280, 302, 304, 311
  *Cat.* 1.14    261
  *Clu.* 105    291
  *Flacc.* 26    278
  *Leg. Agr.* 2.44    263

## INDICES

| | | | | |
|---|---|---|---|---|
| *Phil.* 2.39 | 317 | Euripides | 3, 5ff., 18f., 245, 247, 296 | |
| *Sest.* 101 | 286 | *Hecuba* 484ff. | 266 | |
| *Div.* 1.22 | 290 | 521 | 266 | |
| *Leg.* 3.35 | 291 | 562 | 267 | |
| *Off.* 1.23 | 276 | *Iphigenia at Aulis* | 248, 266 | |
| 1.97 | 291 | 16ff. | 256 | |
| 2.9 | 291 | 607ff. | 248 | |
| 2.19 | 255 | 631ff. | 253, 255 | |
| 3.95f. | 292 | 673ff. | 255 | |
| *Rep.* 2.47 | 277 | 819ff. | 264 | |
| *Tusc.* 1.51 | 279 | 1368ff. | 265 | |
| 2.20 | 324 | 1546 | 266 | |
| 2.21 | 257 | 1552 | 267 | |
| 2.32 | 260 | 1554 | 265 | |
| 2.36 | 266 | | | |
| 4.17 | 299 | Gellius 19.10.12 | 263 | |
| 5.6 | 281 | | | |
| | | Hadrian | 325 | |
| Curtius | | | | |
| 7.8.24 | 326 | Herodotus 2.39 | 260 | |
| | | 2.45 | 260, 315 | |
| Ennius | 167, 295 | | | |
| | | Horace | 8 | |
| *Epigrams* fr. 10W | 246 | *Odes* 1.4.4 | 283 | |
| *Annals* fr. 1W | 257 | 1.5.3 | 256 | |
| *Tragedies* fr. 247W | 263 | 1.7.27 | 280 | |
| 253ff. | 296 | 1.9.14f. | 326 | |
| 261 | 296 | 1.23.1 | 324 | |
| 269f. | 299 | 1.37.1f. | 253 | |
| 284 | 302 | 2.1.33f. | 277 | |
| 339 | 327 | 2.3.25ff. | 289 | |
| | | 2.13.13f. | 262f. | |
| Ennodius | | 2.13.21 | 320 | |
| *carm.* 43.23 | 277 | 2.13.34 | 320 | |
| | | 3.1.1 | 329 | |
| Erasmus | 4ff., 8, 18f., 167, 273 | 3.1.5f. | 279 | |
| *Adages* 2.4.60 | 276 | 3.2.20f. | 277 | |
| *De libero arbitrio* | 281 | 3.3.10 | 252 | |
| *Hecuba* 77f. | 249 | 3.4.31f. | 316 | |
| 99ff. | 249 | 3.5.29 | 277 | |
| 1117 | 321 | 3.17.12 | 293 | |
| *Iphigenia* 225 | 266 | 3.22.4 | 300 | |
| 708 | 247 | 3.27.67f. | 254 | |
| 838ff. | 253 | 3.30.6ff. | 289 | |
| 873f. | 255 | 4.2.3f. | 254 | |
| 916f. | 255 | 4.3.16 | 255 | |
| 926 | 266 | 4.4.57f. | 287 | |
| 1015f. | 250 | 4.5.18 | 290 | |
| 2000 | 265 | 4.11.22ff. | 258 | |

## INDICES

| | | |
|---|---|---|
| *Epodes* 2.1ff. | 256 | |
| 3.16 | 323 | |
| 7.13 | 275 | |
| 16.22 | 259 | |
| *Satires* 1.4.31 | 263 | |
| 2.3.14 | 290 | |
| 2.7.35 | 301 | |
| 2.8.72f. | 285 | |
| *Epistles* 1.1.28 | 270 | |
| 1.5.29 | 252 | |
| 1.14.19 | 289 | |
| 1.16.54 | 249 | |
| 1.18.23 | 293 | |
| 1.19.31 | 284 | |
| *Ars Poetica* | | |
| 119ff. | 269 | |

Hyginus 26.1    312

Jerome
*Ep.* 100.11    281

Josephus 15.75ff.    271

Juvenal 6.1ff.    275
7.145    277
8.1    272
9.126ff.    249
10    282
10.161    277
13.192ff.    286
14.19    290
14.37    284
14.298ff.    263

Lactantius
*Inst.* 3.1.3    275

Leo
*Sermones* 19.1    275

Licentius    269

Livy
*Praef.* 13    294
1.18.4    255
6.12.9    304
28.15.16    280
30.30.15    257
40.11.2    274

Lucan 2.106    325
2.145f.    277
7.810    289
9.701    276

Lucretius    19, 245, 252
1.96ff.    264
1.99    258f.
1.935ff.    285
2.1173f.    310
3.966    289f.
3.980f.    290
3.1011    290
4.546    290
4.1157    303
6.357f.    280

Luther    11
*De servo arbitrio*    281

Martial 4.11.1    275
6.80.1    251
10.64.2    285
10.72.11    288

Michel, Jean
*Mystère de la passion*    271

Montaigne    2, 4f., 19, 259
*Essais* 1.12    266
*Institution des enfants* 1.26    4

Ovid
*Amores* 1.2.15    248
2.13.8    250
3.9.28    289
3.9.64    274
3.11.22    302
*Ars Amatoria*
1.761f.    269
2.179f.    287
3.327    253
3.795    263
*Remedia* 680    283
*Fasti* 1.6    258
3.285    281
4.436    283
6.38    252

INDICES

| | | | | | |
|---|---|---|---|---|---|
| *Heroides* 11.82 | | 267 | Paulinus of Nola | | |
| *Metamorphoses* | | | *Ep.* 11.7 | | 260 |
| | 1.113 | 256 | 23.14 | | 283 |
| | 1.441 | 314 | 29.6 | | 265 |
| | 1.546 | 259 | *carm.* 22.149 | | 247 |
| | 1.682 | 326 | 25.162 | | 251 |
| | 2.325 | 316 | 32.34 | | 260 |
| | 2.704 | 326 | | | |
| | 2.848f. | 250, 314 | Paulus | | |
| | 3.348 | 281 | ex Fest. 173M | | 260 |
| | 3.528 | 256 | | | |
| | 4.450ff. | 290 | Petronius | | |
| | 4.667 | 260 | *Sat.* 88 | | 263 |
| | 6.265 | 314 | 116f. | | 263 |
| | 6.340 | 316 | | | |
| | 7.94 | 300 | Plautus | | 9, 247 |
| | 7.184 | 249 | *Amphitruo* | 186ff. | 251 |
| | 8.730ff. | 269 | | 232f. | 251 |
| | 9.59 | 252 | *Aulularia* | 147 | 307 |
| | 9.193 | 252 | | 385 | 319 |
| | 9.418 | 303 | | 796ff. | 309 |
| | 10.33f. | 289 | *Menaechmi* | 66 | 284 |
| | 10.113 | 318 | | 328 | 284 |
| | 10.288 | 263 | *Miles Gloriosus* | | |
| | 10.588f. | 252 | | 813 | 282 |
| | 12.29ff. | 259 | *Mostellaria* | 931 | *323* |
| | 12.157ff. | 253 | *Poenulus* | 410 | 288 |
| | 12.294f. | 266, 281 | *Pseudolus* | 231 | 288 |
| | 13.768 | 292 | *Stichus* | 450 | 323 |
| | 13.822 | 276 | *Truculentus* | 106 | 252 |
| | 14.291 | 304 | | 256 | 311 |
| | 14.416 | 266f. | | | |
| | 14.544 | 280 | Pliny, elder | | 329 |
| | 15.63f. | 246 | *H.N.* 8.105 | | 276 |
| | 15.127ff. | 261 | 19–22 | | 283 |
| | 15.180ff. | 251 | 29.66 | | 276 |
| | 15.371 | 276 | | | |
| | 15.410 | 276 | Pliny, younger | | 274 |
| | 15.626 | 258 | *Ep.* 1.20.12 | | 285 |
| | 15.871ff. | 289 | 6.16.13 | | 267 |
| | 15.875f. | 289 | 6.29.4 | | 285 |
| *Pont.* | 4.7.9f. | 266 | 7.1.6 | | 262 |
| | 4.8.47f. | 266 | | | |
| *Tristia* | 2.309 | 270 | Propertius 2.13.33 | | 263 |
| | 3.10.53f. | 266 | 2.26.5 | | 250 |
| | 3.12.29f. | 266 | 2.26.39 | | 312 |
| | 4.1.47 | 290 | 3.10.19 | | 265 |
| | 4.6 | 287 | | | |

343

## INDICES

Prudentius
  *Apotheosis* 171      247
               495      324
               885      254
  *Cathemerinon* 2.25      252
              12.125f.      325
  *Contra Symmachum*
              2.170      253
  *Epilogus* 1ff.      260
  *Peristephanon* 2.39      283
              5.30      283
              5.34      252, 254
              6.98      247
              10.1007      260
              13.55      254
  *Psychomachia* 640      247

Quintilian
                    257
         1.3.12      287

Rabelais      9, 17, 273
  *Gargantua* 14      261
                21      261
  *Tiers Livre* 48      264

Sallust      24
  *Catiline*      274
           1.1      256
           2.7      257
           2.8      270
           2.9      246
           16.3      290, 293
  *Jugurtha* 31.28      287
               85.9      268

Seneca, elder
  *Suasoriae* 6.22      270

Seneca, younger      7ff., 19, 256, 280,
                          295, 313, 325
  *Agamemnon* 358f.:      253
  *Apocolocyntosis*
                8      262
  *Hercules Furens*      247
              178ff.      250f.
              205      283
              414      252
              548      259
              592f.      252
              1131ff.      324
              1279ff.      248

  *Medea*      33f.      281
  *Oedipus*      303      266
  *Phaedra*      102      275
              177ff.      275
              1061      252
  *Thyestes*      353ff.      253
              584      250
  *Troades*      440ff.      248f.
              1099f.      266
              1144ff.      266

(Ps-Seneca)
  *Octavia*      168      248

Silius Italicus
              3.332      251
              3.458      321
              3.580      275
              4.430      252
              5.624      250
              15.226      283

Sophocles
  *Trachiniae*      257

Statius      247, 309
  *Silvae* 2.1.8f.      286
           3.2.102      250
           3.2.119      275
           3.3.80f.      247
           3.4.24ff.      315
           4.8.5      275
           5.3.72ff.      267
  *Thebaid* 3.63      249
             4.531      259
             5.743f.      265
             9.747f.      259
             10.703      285

Suetonius
  *Tiberius* 32      284
  *Domitian* 19      261

Tacitus      274
  *Germania* 39      253
  *Histories* 5.7      290
  *Annals* 3.4      275
           4.52      291
           14.2      255
           14.6      291

INDICES

| | | | | |
|---|---|---|---|---|
| Terence | | 8ff., 269, 331 | 3.537 | 284 |
| *Adelphi* 587 | | 310 | 4.70f. | 251 |
| *Andria* 204 | | 323 | 4.387ff. | 269 |
| *Eunuch* 552 | | 255 | 4.411 | 269 |
| *Hecyra* 621 | | 280 | 4.441f. | 269 |
| *Phormio* 287 | | 248 | *Aeneid* 1.94ff. | 264, 285 |
| | | | 1.306 | 289 |
| Tertullian | | | 2.54 | 298 |
| *Pall.* 3 | | 276 | 2.85 | 311 |
| *Jud. Dom.* 8 | | 324 | 3.75 | 314 |
| | | | 3.157 | 280 |
| Thomas Aquinas | | | 3.311 | 289 |
| *S.T.* 2a2ae 88.2 | | 16, 258 | 3.424 | 278 |
| | | | 4.366f. | 276 |
| Thomas of Celano | | | 4.440 | 274 |
| *Dies Irae* | | 254 | 5.124ff. | 288 |
| | | | 5.709 | 307 |
| Tibullus 1.4.13f. | | 266 | 6.270f. | 263 |
| 1.6.18 | | 283 | 6.298 | 318 |
| | | | 6.302 | 318 |
| Valerius Flaccus 4.507 | | 275 | 6.425 | 259 |
| | | | 6.548ff. | 290 |
| Varro Atacinus fr. 19M | | 276 | 6.882 | 248 |
| | | | 7.314f. | 294 |
| Velleius Paterculus 2.81 | | 257 | 7.646 | 265 |
| | | | 8.90 | 249 |
| Virgil | | | 8.334 | 258, 300 |
| *Eclogues* 1.16 | | 298 | 8.340 | 281 |
| 4.49 | | 305 | 8.524 | 251 |
| 8.39 | | 5 | 8.593 | 251 |
| *Georgics* 1.145f. | | 287 | 9.59 | 284 |
| 1.417 | | 289 | 9.504 | 251 |
| 1.508 | | 251 | 10.740 | 285 |
| 2.137 | | 263 | 11.104 | 311 |
| 2.151f. | | 276 | 11.202 | 280 |
| 2.458ff. | | 277 | 11.344f. | 288 |
| 2.461 | | 277 | 11.607 | 251 |
| 2.472f. | | 276 | 11.687f. | 265 |
| 2.502 | | 277 | 12.67ff. | 266 |
| 3.8f. | | 246 | 12.468 | 266 |
| 3.206ff. | | 248 | 12.662f. | 252 |
| 3.287 | | 323 | 12.666ff. | 275 |
| 3.361f. | | 266 | | |

# B. General

Abraham, 17, 32 (68), 50 (83), 259–61
Acastus, 232

Acheron, 216, 224, 229
Aegeus, 312

## INDICES

Aeschylus, 169
Aesculapius, 213
Aetna, 106 (140), 275
Agamemnon, 248, 253, 292
Aitken, J. M., 12, 14, 19f., 262
Alcestis, 265
Aldine, 6, 296–331 *passim*
Alexander Jannaeus, 271
Amalekites, 254
Ambrose, St., 17
Ammon (Jupiter), 215
Ammon, 16, 25, 27f. (64f.), 31–37 (67–73), 46 (79), 59 (91), 246f., 250, 252, 292
Amyot, Jacques, 7
Antipater (elder), 271
Antony, Mark, 100 (135), 271
Antwerp, 9
Apollo, *see* Phoebus
Arab (Arabia), 31 (67), 37 (72), 100 (135)
Aretas, 278
Argo, 169, 171, 183, 206, 296, 312
Argos, 227
Arnon, 25, 34 (69)
Artemis, 18, 175
Assyria, 49 (82), 110 (143), 260
Athens, 169, 224
Atlantiades, 232
Augustan poetry, 266, 283, 289
Augustine, St., 269, 274, 308
Aulis, 18
*Auvergne, Passion d'*, 271
Avernus, 42 (76)
Avranches, 18

Babel, 250
Bacchus, 169
Bade, Josse, 6
Baïf, Antoine de, 9
Baptist, John the, 4, 10–13, 17, 255, 258, 262, 268
Barclay, John, 263
Barthélemy de Loches, Nicolas, 8
Basel, 6, 247, 296
Berquin, Louis, 10, 11
Bèze, Théodore de, 9, 250, 261
Bible, 9f., 18, 245, 260, 269
Bistones, 225, 240
Bochetel, 7
Bologna, 6

Bordeaux, 1–5, 7, 10–12, 15, 208, 245, 253, 261, 268, 295, 313
Bossozel, Guillaume, 7
Bovelles, Charles de, 17, 281
Briçonnet, Guillaume, 272
Brissac, *see* Cossé
Bucer, Martin, 14–18, 245
Buchanan, G. Trial, 2–3, 5
– *Jephthes*, 2–5, 9f., 13–19, 269, 271, 292, 328
– *Baptistes*, 2–5, 10–13, 18–20, 245, 247, 255, 257f., 261f., 313
– *Medea*, 2–5, 245, 268, 313, 331
– *Alcestis*, 2–5, 265, 295, 297
– *Franciscanus*, 5
– *Fratres fraterrimi*, 5, 261, 271
– *Vita*, 2, 268, 295
Budé, G., 271

Caesar, 109 (143)
Calchas, 18
calumny, 99f. (134), 123 (155), 127 (158), 269f., 274, 278f., 287, 291
Carneian month, 224, 321
Castellio, S., 254
Castor, Grahame, 19
Catilinarian conspiracy, 274
Caucasus, 107 (140), 126 (158)
Caurus, 31 (67), 48 (81), 55 (87)
Cecropidae, 193
Ceneau, R., 18
Cephisus, 193
Cerberus, 127 (159), 290
Chamos, 34 (70)
Chaos, 32 (68)
characterisation: Gamaliel, 272–4; Herod, 268, 271, 275–80, 284, 291f.; Herodias, 268, 282, 284, 287; Iphis, 245, 248, 255, 264, 266; Jephtha, 245, 256, 258, 261, 264f.; John, 268; Malchus, 270–3, 280–7; sacerdos, 245, 259; Storge, 245, 249, 264; Symmachus, 245, 255–8
Charles I, 13
Charon, 219
Chimaera, 215, 315
Christ, 8, 16f., 118 (151), 248, 271f., 278–80, 282–5, 293
Christian Latin, language, 248, 254, 270, 277, 283, 308, 314

346

– literature, 247, 252, 260, 275, 279, 284, 290; *see also* Hymns
Cleopatra, 100 (135), 271, 275
Cocytus, 224
Coimbra, 1, 14f., 253
Colet, J., 273
Colines, Simon de, 16
Collège du Cardinal Lemoine, 8
– de Guyenne, 1, 4, 261
– de Marmontiers, 8
*Comedia Sancti Nicolai,* 8
comedy, *see* Roman comedy
composition of the plays, date, 4–5
– order, 1–4
compound words, 250
Constance, 24
Corinth, Corinthius, 169, 171, 176, 185, 189, 195
Cossé (Brissac), Charles de, 23, 245f.
– Philippe de, 24, 246
– Timoléon de, 246
Cranmer, T., 282
Crocus, Cornelius, 9
Croesus, 55 (87)
Cupid, 247
Cyaneae, 171, 296
Cyclops, Cyclopian, 31 (67), 213
Cycnos, 226
Cypris, 187f.

*Damon and Pythias,* 313
David, 102 (137), 131 (162)
Dead Sea, 271
*delatio,* 274
Delcourt, M., 19
Diana, 117 (149), 300
Dido, 272
Dione, 233
Dis, 203, 219, 223; *see also* Pluto
Domitian, 274
Donatus, 8
Dorat, J., 247, 313
dreams, 29f. (65f.), 248f.
Du Bellay, J., 247, 270, 313
Du Plessis-Mornay, Ph., 250

Edinburgh, 19
Edomites, 254, 271
Edwards, Richard, 313

Egypt, 31 (67f.), 49 (82), 110 (143), 250, 260, 271
Electryon, 235
Eliseus (Elisha), 280f.
Elizabeth, Queen, 276, 313
Elizabeth, St., 271
Emmanuel-Philibert, Duke of Savoy, 313
England, 5
England, Church of, 11
Ephesus, 270
Erectheus, 207
Erinyes, 206f., 290;
Espence, Claude d', 17
Estienne, Henri, 8
Eucharist, 14, 17f.
Eumenides, 127 (159)
Eurystheus, 214, 225
Euxine, 296

family, 40 (74), 49 (82), 255, 257
fate, 39 (73), 43f. (77), 47f. (80f.), 49 (82), 54f. (86f.), 56 (88), 59–62 (91–4), 99 (134), 124 (156), 249, 258, 262, 288, 298, 308
Fisher, John, 12
Fortune, *see* fate
France, 1, 5, 8f., 12, 15, 247, 269f.
François de Valois, 6
François I, 10f., 13, 313
free will, 281
French theatre, 1, 5–10, 19, 247, 261f.
French humanism, 1, 5–10, 268–70
Fries, C., 296f., 302, 309, 314

Gabinius, 100 (135), 271
Galilee, 271
Gamaliel, 270–4
Ganges, 107 (140)
Garamantes, 215
Garanderie, M. de la, 271
Garnier, R., 9f.
Geneva, 15
Gilead, 25, 246, 248
Girard, J., 15
*Golden Legend,* 270
Gorgon, 242
Greek tragedy, 6, 9, 247, 255
Gregory, St., 274
Grévin, Jacques, 10

347

Guarinus, T., 247
Guérente, G., 4

Hades, 300, 307
Hamilton, Patrick, 11
Hay, Archibald, 7
Hebrews, 37 (72), 114 (147)
Hecuba, 266
Helias, 118 (151)
Henri II, 211
Henry VIII, 11–13, 279
Hercules, 226, 241
Herod, 268, 271,
–Antipas, 10–13, 100 (135), 268, 271, 275–80, 284, 291f.
– Antipater, 271
– the Great, 271
Herodias, 11, 268, 282, 284, 287
Hermus, 55 (87)
Hervagius, 6, 296, 300
Higman, F., 20
Homer, 269
Hotman, F., 250
Hugh of St. Victor, 16
Hume Brown, P., 10f., 20
Hydra, 311
hymns, 252, 280

identification of characters, 10–13
idolatry, 131 (162), 254, 292
Idumaea, 38 (73), 100 (135), 271
India, 37 (72), 61f. (92f.)
innocence, 41 (75), 53 (85), 62 (93), 103 (138), 106 (140), 108 (141), 123f. (154f.), 127 (158), 131 (162)
Inquisition, 11, 19, 262, 282, 284, 287
Iolcos, 171, 184f., 219
Iphigenia, 18, 245, 255, 258f., 263–5, 267, 292
Iphis, 245, 248, 255, 264, 266
irony, 19, 249, 251–5, 257, 259, 265, 273f., 279, 282, 292, 302f.
Isaac 17, 27 (64), 247, 259f., 262
Isaac, daughters of, 54 (86), 114 (147)
Israelites, 33 (69), 250, 252, 254, 280
Ister (Danube), 61 (92), 266
Italy, 7, 9

Jabocus, 34 (69), 251
Jacob, 34 (70)

James V, 11, 13
James VI, 5, 268
Jephtha, 13–18, 245, 256, 258, 261, 264f.
Jerome, St., 16, 308
Jerusalem, 31 (67), 33 (69), 39 (73), 100 (135), 131 (162), 250, 271, 292f.
Jews, Jewish, 270–3, 277f., 280f., 284, 292
Jocelyn, H. D., 295
Jodelle, E., 1, 9f.
Joram, 254
Jordan, 30 (67), 34 (69), 250
Judaea, 59 (91), 100 (135), 271
Judas, 292
Julio-Claudian emperors, 274
Juno, 205, 272
Jupiter, 175f., 184, 191, 208, 216, 226, 231, 239, 242f., 247, 314

kingship (tyranny), 5, 10f., 13, 19, 31 (67), 44 (77), 52 (85), 103–5 (137–9), 107–8 (141–3), 110–4 (144–7), 121f. (153f.), 125 (156), 129f. (160f.), 250, 291f.

La Boétie, E. de, 250
Lanson, G., 8
La Péruse, J. de, 10
Larissa, 235
La Taille, Jean de, 10
Latin plays (Renaissance), 7–9
Latomus, Barthélemy (Masson), 14–17, 245
La Ville de Mirmont, 11, 20
Lebègue, R., 8f., 11, 13–15, 19f.
Lefèvre d'Etaples, J., 272
Lerna, 205, 311
Levites, 101 (135)
L'Hospital, M. de, 247
Libye, 107 (140)
Licentius, 269
Lisbon, 11, 19; *see also* Inquisition
London, 2
Low Countries, 245f.
Lucifer, 31 (67)
Luna, 300
Luxembourg, John of, 5, 167, 295
Lycophron, 248
Lydus, 230
Lynceus, 99 (134), 270

McFarlane, I. D., 12, 19f., 245–7, 268, 295, 313

## INDICES

MacMillan, D., 11
Maimonides, 272
Macrin, Salmon, 320
Malchus, 11, 270–3, 280–7
malice, 42 (76), 101f. (135f.), 256
Marchand, Ch., 246
Marguerite de France, 211, 313
Marot, Clément, 9
Mars, 24, 44 (77), 226, 246
Mary Queen of Scots, 12
Masson, see Latomus
Meaux, Bishop of, 272
Medus, 312
Mercury, 191, 247, 304
Michel, Jean, 271
Minerva, 24
Molossus, 228
More, Thomas, 11–13, 273, 279, 282, 294
Morel, Jean de, 247
– family, 247
Morel, G., 2
Moses, 101 (136), 102 (137)
Mucidan, 246
Muret, Marc-Antoine, 2, 4, 9
Mystery plays, 7

Nabataeans, 278
Nancel, Nicolas de, 7
Nebuchadnezzar, 254
Nicodemus, 271
Nilus, 33 (69), 61 (92), 107 (140)
Novesian, Melchior, 14

Olympus, 44 (78), 55 (87), 118 (150)
Ong, W. J., 7, 19
Orcus, 197, 213–6, 222, 224, 236, 238
O'Rourke, K. D., 20
Orpheus, 185, 222, 238
Othrys, 228
Ovid, 269, 323, 329

Palestine, 38 (73)
Pallas, 191
Pamiers, Bishop of, 295
Pan, 202
Pandion, 169, 188, 191, 207, 312
Parcae, 30 (67), 61 (92), 213–5
Paris, 1–4, 6f., 12, 14, 15–17, 25, 246
patriotism, 61 (92), 265, 267, 294
Paul, St., 275

Pelasgi, 171, 184f.
Peletier, J., 270
Pelias, 183f., 190, 206, 214, 224, 237
Pelion, 171, 228
Pelops, 189
Périgord, 246
Persephone, 232; see also Proserpina
Perseus, 226
Pertusi, A., 19
Peter, St., 270
Petrarchan love-poetry, 330
Pharaoh, 250
Pharia, Pharius, 31 (67f.), 107 (141), 114 (147)
Pharisees, 114f. (148), 273, 282f., 293
Pharus, 31, 250
Pheraeus, 225, 228, 241
Pherecydes, 169
Philip, half-brother of Herod, 278
Phoebus, 61f. (92f.), 117 (149), 180, 189, 204, 213, 227, 238
Phrygian, 230
Picardy, 246
Piedmont, 245
Placards, Affaire des, 10, 18
Pierides, 193, 224
Pilate, 292
Pirene, 172
Pittheus, 189
Pluto, 219, 232, 236
Portugal, 253
Proserpina, 222; see also Persephone
Proteus, 99 (134), 269
*pudor*, 276
Prynne, William, 13
Pythagoras, 246
Pythias, 313
Pythiodorus, 169

Quintianus Stoa, 8

Rahner, H., 290
Ramus, 7, 287
rashness, 46f. (79f.), 60 (91), 63 (94), 101f. (136f.), 104 (138), 106 (140), 111 (144), 116 (149), 131 (162), 257, 258
reason, (& unreason), 27 (64), 100 (134), 107 (140), 247, 272f., 286
Red Sea, 39 (73), 114 (147), 250

## INDICES

reformation, 10–19, 27 (64), 100–105 (135–9), 114 (147), 248, 250, 254, 259, 262, 268, 270, 272–4, 279, 281–4, 288, 291–4, 299
rhetoric, 1f.
riches & poverty, 44f. (78), 103 (137)
Rihel, Wendel, 14
Rogers, Daniel, 3, 295
Roman comedy, 297, 299, 309f., 315
Ronsard, P. de, 247, 270, 313
Roper, W., 279
Runnalls, G. A., 271

sacerdos, 245, 249
sacred & profane, 271
sacrifices, 16–8, 39 (73), 41 (75), 45–7 (78–80), 48–54 (81–6), 56f. (88f.), 59 (90), 63 (93–4), 248, 253, 259f., 262, 265–7, 272, 280
Sanhedrin, 268, 273f., 283f.
Sarmaticus, 61 (92)
Scaliger, 8, 306
Scotland, 1
Screech, M., 264
Scylla, 206f.
Scythicus, 36 (70), 176
Sebillet, T., 270
sententiae, 256f.
Septuagint, 254
Sibylla, 99 (134)
Sidonius Apollinaris, 308
Simonides, 169
Sinai, 250
Sion, 100 (135)
Siren, 128 (159), 290
Sisyphaeus, 182
Sodom & Gomorrha, 250
Sol, 182, 191, 206
Solomon, 131f. (162f.)
Sorbonne, 15f., 20, 314
Sosia, 251
Sparta, 224, 321
Staphylus, 169
Stephen, 271
Sthenelus, 243
Stoa, Quintianus, 8
Storge, 245, 249, 264
Strasbourg, 14
Styx, Stygian, 213, 216, 224, 236, 243
Symmachus, 245, 255–8

Syme, R., 271
Symplegadae, 171, 296, 310
Sypherd, W. O., 247, 251
Syrus, Syria, 31 (68), 38 (73), 271

Tagus, 37 (72), 252f., 263
Talmud (Babylonian), 272
Tantalus, 127 (159), 290
Tartarus, 39 (73), 45f. (79), 48 (81), 213
Tartessius, 62 (93)
Thanatos, 213
Themis, 175f.
Thessalus, 210, 221, 223, 230, 235, 238, 241
Thracian, 225, 240
Thompson, D. F. S., 12, 20, 262
Tilmann, Godfrey, 17
Tirynthius, 225
Tissard, François, 6
Titus, 293
tragedy, theory of, 8f.
Trajan, 274
Trinquet, Roger, 4, 15, 19, 245
Troezenius, 189
truth, 54 (86), 106 (140), 111 (144), 118–20 (150–2), 123f. (154–6)
Turks, 293
Turnèbe, A., 247
Turnus, 272, 275

Utenhove, C., 25, 246f., 313

Vahlen, 295
Vascosan, M., 2, 7, 313
Vautrollier, Thomas, 2
Venus, 193
Vesta, 217
Vesuvius (Vesevus), 106 (140), 275
virtue, 43 (77), 54 (86), 107 (141)
Volder, Guill.de, 9
vows, 14–7, 28 (65), 40 (75), 45–54 (78–86), 56 (88), 58 (89f.), 60 (91), 63 (94), 245, 247, 253f., 256–61, 265, 292
Vulgate, 253f., 270, 277, 282, 314

Walpole, 252
Waszink, J. H., 19
Wechel, C., 14
witchcraft, 282

Zachary, 271
Zoroastrianism, 260